COMMON
SCENTS

SUNY SERIES
LITERATURE...IN THEORY

DAVID E. JOHNSON, COMPARATIVE LITERATURE, UNIVERSITY AT BUFFALO
SCOTT MICHAELSEN, ENGLISH, MICHIGAN STATE UNIVERSITY

SERIES ADVISORY BOARD

Nahum D. Chandler, African American Studies, University of California, Irvine
Rebecca Comay, Philosophy and Comparative Literature, University of Toronto
Marc Crépon, Philosophy, École Normale Supérieure, Paris
Jonathan Culler, Comparative Literature, Cornell University
Johanna Drucker, Design Media Arts and Information Studies, University of California, Los Angeles
Christopher Fynsk, Modern Thought, Aberdeen University
Rodolphe Gasché, Comparative Literature, University at Buffalo
Martin Hägglund, Comparative Literature, Yale University
Carol Jacobs, German and Comparative Literature, Yale University
Peggy Kamuf, French and Comparative Literature, University of Southern California
David Marriott, History of Consciousness, University of California, Santa Cruz
Steven Miller, English, University at Buffalo
Alberto Moreiras, Hispanic Studies, Texas A&M University
Patrick O'Donnell, English, Michigan State University
Pablo Oyarzun, Teoría del Arte, Universidad de Chile
Scott Cutler Shershow, English, University of California, Davis
Henry Sussman, German and Comparative Literature, Yale University
Samuel Weber, Comparative Literature, Northwestern University
Ewa Ziarek, Comparative Literature, University at Buffalo

COMMON SCENTS

POETRY, MODERNITY, AND A REVOLUTION OF THE SENSES

JONAS ROSENBRÜCK

SUNY PRESS

Published by State University of New York Press, Albany
© 2024 State University of New York
All rights reserved

Printed in the United States of America

No part of this book may be used or reproduced in any manner whatsoever without written permission. No part of this book may be stored in a retrieval system or transmitted in any form or by any means including electronic, electrostatic, magnetic tape, mechanical, photocopying, recording, or otherwise without the prior permission in writing of the publisher.

Links to third-party websites are provided as a convenience and for informational purposes only. They do not constitute an endorsement or an approval of any of the products, services, or opinions of the organization, companies, or individuals. SUNY Press bears no responsibility for the accuracy, legality, or content of a URL, the external website, or for that of subsequent websites.
For information, contact State University of New York Press, Albany, NY
www.sunypress.edu

Library of Congress Cataloging-in-Publication Data

Names: Rosenbrück, Jonas, author.
Title: Common scents : poetry, modernity, and a revolution of the senses / Jonas Rosenbrück.
Description: Albany : State University of New York Press, 2024. | Series: SUNY series, literature . . . in theory | Includes bibliographical references and index. | Summary: "Attends to the much-neglected sense of smell in and around modern poetry to retrieve the possibility of a revolution of the senses"-- Provided by publisher.
Identifiers: LCCN 2024005584 | ISBN 9781438499710 (hardcover) | ISBN 9781438499727 (ebook)
Subjects: LCSH: Poetry, Modern--19th century--History and criticism. | Poetry, Modern--20th century--History and criticism. | Smell in literature. | Poetics. | Modernism (Literature)
Classification: LCC PN1260.5 R66 2024 | DDC 809.1/03--dc23/eng/20240520
LC record available at https://lccn.loc.gov/2024005584

Für meine Eltern

CONTENTS

ACKNOWLEDGMENTS IX

Introduction: Redistributing the Senses 1

Chapter 1: Hölderlin's Air 23

Chapter 2: Baudelaire's Perfumes 69

Chapter 3: Nietzsche's Chaos 95

Chapter 4: Brecht's Stench 125

Epilogue: Cleanup 153

NOTES 165

BIBLIOGRAPHY 211

INDEX 229

ACKNOWLEDGMENTS

I began work on this book at Northwestern University, where I had the good fortune of encountering a number of sharp, kind, and generous teachers and interlocutors, including Penelope Deutscher, Ryan Dohoney, Alessia Ricciardi, Nasrin Qader, Erica Weitzman, and Tristram Wolff. Susannah Young-ah Gottlieb has become a trusted mentor and friend; Jörg Kreienbrock and Samuel Weber were expert guides from the earliest stages of this project. Particular thanks are due to Peter Fenves, who continues to shape my work in innumerable ways. Conversations with friends and colleagues from various parts of my life have left an indelible imprint on my thinking, in particular those with Kyle Baasch, Kevin Barrett, Clay Cogswell, Priyanka Deshmukh, Gwenda-lin Grewal, Tobias Kühne, Katerine Niedinger, Helmut Puff, Benjamin Lewis Robinson, and Nica Siegel. I want to thank the Northwestern Prison Education Program, in particular the students at Stateville Correctional Center, and, more recently, students at Hampshire County Jail, for teaching me so much about learning. I am also grateful to Kristina Mendicino for her most useful support of this book, to Rebecca Colesworthy, editor at SUNY Press, for her skillful and competent help in bringing this book into the world, to Ryan Perks for his meticulous copyediting, and to Matthew John Phillips for preparing the index. I am equally grateful to my colleagues at Amherst College, in the Department of German and beyond, and am excited to continue working with Amherst's bright students.

This book is dedicated to my parents, Hanna and Andreas, who have always loved and supported me. The depths of my gratitude to them remain incalculable. I am similarly grateful to my brothers Simon and Ben. Lorenzo Conte, along with his family, has brought a type of joy and love into my life that continues to delight, surprise, awe, and sustain me—here's to many more years together.

Introduction

REDISTRIBUTING THE SENSES

It is remarkably easy to forget the things we are most familiar with. Whatever is most ordinary or most common is so deeply woven into the fabric of life that it often has trouble rising to the status of sensation, perception, or thought. Take the example of air: "This element," Luce Irigaray writes in her loving lament of the forgetting of the elements in Martin Heidegger's thought, "compels neither the faculty of perception nor that of knowledge to recognize it. Always there, it allows itself to be forgotten."[1] Always there: What could be more common to terrestrial life than existing in air? It is precisely this status of ordinariness that subtracts air from both sensation and thought, Irigaray argues, since it prevents air from manifesting or showing itself; since it precedes all place, air does not "take place" as a noticeable entry into presence. This non-phenomenality of air, in turn, is linked to its vast openness. By not asserting its presence, air allows for a boundlessness that lets everything else emerge. It is always there; "no other element is to this extent opening itself."[2] This openness of air is the opening of life and of dwelling, of presence and of absence, of speech and of silence. The element's openness finds correspondence, as Elias Canetti reminds us, in the fact that the human being incessantly opens itself to the air via the act of breathing: "to nothing is the human being so open as to air."[3] With each breath, human beings ineluctably exist in a mode of being-in-the-air that is marked by this doubled openness.[4]

Yet pace Irigaray, various recent phenomena have restored this double opening of the element of air and being-in-the-air to perception and thought, thus partially undoing its forgetting: airborne pandemics, environmental pollution, respiratory ailments, the racist violence contained in the gasping exclamation "I can't breathe," a pervasive sense of breathlessness—all of these phenomena force a confrontation with the fact that the "always there" of air is, in fact, differentially distributed among various populations, and, further, that the openness of air and being-in-the-air is markedly ambivalent: it opens to life, yes, but also to death; there is no definitive disentangling of life-promoting from life-threatening aerial exposure.[5] This ambivalent air—always there but sometimes painfully absent or fatally present—forces its way into appearance and undoes its forgetting.

The task then becomes to *make sense* of this appearance: How does the aerial medium register? How can its constitution be sensed, perceived, thought, theorized? How might one find orientation for and in being-in-the-air? In her recourse to the pre-Socratics, Irigaray provides a valuable clue, albeit one that she herself seems to immediately discard and forget: "But the element of air does not manifest itself. Except in the form of smoke? 'If all beings were to manifest themselves as smoke, noses would then be diagnostic experts.' . . . Air does not show itself. As such, it escapes appearing as (a) being. It allows itself to be forgotten even by the perceptual ability of the nose."[6] The task of *Common Scents* lies precisely in showing that, as well as how the nose makes sense of air by picking up on its *scented modulations*. The unforgetting of air can be helped along by an unforgetting of smell: air enters into *aisthesis*, into the realm of the senses and of sense, via its modifications found in smell.[7] As Aristotle puts it in a claim that will be developed throughout this book, "the human being, and all the land animals which breathe, cannot smell except when they are breathing,"[8] and it is the breath- and air-dependent sense of smell, and in particular the "common scents" of this book, that provide orientation in the vastness of the element and the openness of being-in-the-air. More precisely, *Common Scents* argues that olfactory sense-making lets appear the fact that all terrestrial life, human and nonhuman alike, shares an openness to the element that is common to all—a commonality that might turn out to be the great chance of life, or a catastrophic danger, or both.

World of Prose

Even in a time of the (partial) unforgetting of its aerial medium, smell itself still tends to be forgotten. This comes as no surprise. Remarks about smell, whether delivered in a scholarly or an everyday register, often amount to claims of marginality, loss, disparagement, revulsion, or irrelevance. Smell, after all, has long been located below the prized senses of vision and hearing and sometimes even at the very bottom of the hierarchy of the human senses. This denigration might be justified on philosophical grounds: for instance, in his thought experiment concerning a statue that is slowly endowed with one sense after another, the quintessential empiricist philosopher, Étienne Bonnot de Condillac, begins with smell, "because of all the senses it is the one which appears to contribute least to the cognitions of the human mind."[9] Along similar lines, Immanuel Kant calls smell the "most ungrateful" of the senses because olfactory phenomena are too ephemeral to become a steady object of sense perception, and, in any case, they produce more disgust than delight.[10] More importantly, according to Kant, olfaction's radically subjective character (in contrast to the "objective" senses of sight, hearing, and touch) subtracts it from the universal demand for communicability and agreement contained in the judgment of taste that defines the realms of beauty and aesthetics. The smell of a flower, for instance, can make "no demands [*keine Ansprüche*]. One person is delighted by the smell, whereas another's senses are clouded by it,"[11] paragraph 32 of the *Critique of the Power of Judgement* argues. Olfaction's subjective character and its strange resistance to aesthetic judgment even lead Kant to label it as "contrary to freedom [*der Freiheit zuwider*]."[12] Further examples could be multiplied almost at random: olfaction everywhere seems to be subject to a "philosophical abjection"[13] that refuses to engage odors as worthy of theorization, aesthetic attention, and conceptual elaboration.

Such a devaluation of smell can also take on a more historical bent when smell's marginality is attributed to its historical links to a deep, archaic past at odds with civilization or thinking. A claim of this sort is articulated in W. H. Auden's poem "Precious Five" (1950), a reflection on each of the five senses and their common function. Auden's poem argues that olfaction has been displaced from its ancient position at the "middle":

> Be patient, solemn nose,
> Serve in a world of prose
> The present moment well,
> Nor surlily contrast
> Its brash ill-mannered smell
> With grand scents of the past.
> That calm enchanted wood,
> That grave world where you stood
> So gravely at its middle,
> Its oracle and riddle,
> Has all been altered[14]

The nose used to be the organizing center of an "enchanted" world of grandeur. This world is now firmly a matter of a lost past—the repeated word "grave" even points to death and a burial—and the nose is exhorted to "be patient": disenchantment and loss of smell go hand in hand, but this doubled loss demands an orientation toward the "present moment" instead of a mournful or resentful turn toward the past.[15] This present, in turn, is described as a "world of prose," referencing the seminal phrase that appears throughout G. W. F. Hegel's *Lectures on Aesthetics*. The expression "world of prose," along with related turns of phrase such as the "prose of life" or "prosaic reality," designates a mundane "world of finitude and variability."[16] While a poetic state of the world, populated with gods and heroes, was structured by a mythology of unity and totality in which everything found its proper place, "contemporary prosaic conditions," according to Hegel, are subtracted from such a total and unified order. The difference between poetry and prose is thus not only one of genre—say, of speech as "oracle and riddle," in contrast to supposedly plain, propositional language—but also yields "two different spheres of consciousness: poetry and prose."[17] Auden's addendum to the Hegelian dictum can then be stated as follows: the sphere of consciousness governing the "present moment" has pushed smell to the margins. The movement away from a poetic state of the world toward a prosaic one parallels a movement away from smell's location at the "middle." Our present moment emerges, in short, as a doubled tendency away from both smell and poetry.

Yet in "Precious Five," nose and prose are inscribed in a relationship that is precisely *not* prosaic: they rhyme. The world of prose maintains a link to the nose poetically; or, put differently, locating a link between the "present moment" and olfaction falls precisely to that which goes counter to the former: poetry. This points to a first justification of this book's focus on poetry: odor and poetry are juxtaposed in their shared marginalization in the modern world of prose.[18] Of course, prose also speaks of scents and noses—but only as phenomena, Auden and Hegel suggest, that cannot be integral to its "sphere of consciousness." From a prosaic perspective, the smells of the present moment appear to be "brash" and "ill-mannered": they do not fit in with our times. In other words, the world of prose is at odds with smell's anachronism, and this anachronism becomes particularly legible in poetry since poetry itself is anachronistic.

This book, then, asks what place smell—and, by extension, poetry—might have in the world of prose. Rejecting the philosophical refusal to think odors, it argues that olfaction harbors rich conceptual resources, precisely *because* it is anachronistic and at odds with "the present moment." The potentialities of smell, however, are here not considered to lie in an ability to reactivate or bring back the deep history to which smell is tied: no restoration of "grand scents" or smell's enchantment is possible or desirable. This latter, in some ways, would be the line of thought traced by one of the best-known olfactory moments in European letters: the smell (and taste) of the madeleine in Marcel Proust's *In Search of Lost Time*. For Proust, smell lets emerge a past world, in this case the past world of childhood, in "form and solidity"[19] as the final words of the famous opening chapter state. Such a formed and stable reemergence of the past, "frailer but more enduring,"[20] as Proust puts it, appears neither possible nor desirable to the authors investigated here. Instead, *Common Scents* shifts attention "from memory to hope," to quote Auden once more. Unlike Proust, "Precious Five" assigns smell not the task of memory but a new task that emerges in one of the most radical ways imaginable—namely, by stripping the nose of its status as sense organ and reducing it to a spatial form: "now / In anxious times you serve / As bridge from mouth to brow / An asymmetric curve." In the quasi-geometric idiom of the poem, the nose's asymmetric curve is contrasted with "an apathetic sphere." A sphere constitutes a figure of perfect closure, and the descriptor "apathetic" names the deficiency of this perfection: closure does not admit of *pathein*, of the undergoing of passions. In contrast, the nose, by "thrust[ing] outwards," breaks this closure, and allows it to be "patient"—that is, to suffer and undergo. The breaking open of this perfect closure enables the nose to arrive at its new task:

> Point, then, for honor's sake
> Up the storm-beaten slope
> From memory to hope
> The way you cannot take.

In the world of prose, in anxious times, smell cannot move from the memory of a past world of "grand scents" to hope. The nose, then, assumes a double function. On the one hand, it remains as an index of a loss and an inability: the past is irretrievably gone; no path links it to the present moment and hence the path from memory to hope cannot be taken. On the other hand, smell points, precisely as this index of loss and inability, to a way beyond, even if it cannot take that way itself. Through its constitutive default, the sense of smell is opened to something beyond its default and beyond the present moment in which it fails.

The four main authors analyzed in this book—Friedrich Hölderlin, Charles Baudelaire, Friedrich Nietzsche, and Bertolt Brecht, all of them important interlocutors for Auden—will similarly seek a new function for smell in anxious times, and with it, for the poetic articulation of a world of prose. None of them will go so far as to strip the nose of its function in sense perception and reduce it to a mere slope, but all of them will think olfaction in relation to something akin to hope or its lack, if hope is understood as a relationship of the present to a future, a relationship that might turn out to be one of repetition, impossibility, or indeterminacy. For all of them, tracing smells "from memory to hope," these smells so ill-fitted for the present moment, means attending to the anachronistic, abjured olfactory element of the human sensorium and, via smell, thinking the opening of the world via that which thrusts out of it and cuts through its apathetic closure.

Distributing the Senses

The marginalization of the sense of smell in the modern world of prose constitutes what, drawing on the work of Jacques Rancière, can be called a specific "distribution of the senses." The senses are each assigned a differentially marked position within a general divvying up of the sensory apparatus and the field of the sensible. In Rancière, the notion of a "distribution" or "partition of the sensible" (*partage du sensible*) designates "the system of self-evident facts of sense perception that simultaneously discloses the existence of something in common and the delimitations that define the respective parts and positions within it."[21] The sensible is both that which is common to all and that which is carved up and ordered in divisive and exclusionary ways: the distribution of the sensible differentially assigns visibility and invisibility, audibility and inaudibility; it assigns positions, identities, and occupations, and orders these into hierarchies presented as "natural." In this sense, Rancière calls any hierarchical and fixed distribution of the sensible a *police* order: policing always implies a distribution of the sensible according to positions and subordinations (for instance, whose speech is considered "intelligible" and "rational," as distinguished from mere noise or unintelligible screams?). These hierarchies of inequality thus arise out of a specific "relation between sense and sense: between an 'x' that presents itself as given and the sense that one attributes to it, that is to say, the way in which one links it with another given, in which one attributes it a place, a signification."[22] In a distribution of the sensible, the full double meaning of the word "sense" comes to bear: sense crosses the boundaries that are supposed to separate the categories of sensible/intelligible and material/spiritual; it is across these conventional delimitations that a distribution of the sensible operates.

Politics, for Rancière, is thus what constitutes a rupture of the police order of the distribution of the sensible. Politics not only disturbs the hierarchical ordering of positions but effects two even more consequential operations: First, politics produces a "rupture in the idea that there are dispositions 'proper' to such classifications."[23] No distribution of the sensible can find a grounding in nature or alleged essences. And secondly, such a rupture is not merely a redistribution of hierarchical positions among those parts already included in the distribution of the sensible that makes up the police order, but lies, rather, in the voicing of the previously inaudible or the appearance of the previously invisible—in short, politics occurs when "the part that has no part" demands to partake or participate in the common from which it was previously excluded. Politics takes place when the places assigned within the distribution of the sensible are reordered and, further, the stability and legitimacy of preexisting "places" is disrupted.

Rancière's formulation of a distribution of the *sensible*, however, points to an oddity of his thought: within his work, a rather rigid hierarchical order of the *senses* reigns. While references to the visible and the auditory abound, the other senses rarely, if ever, enter Rancière's thought. Vision and hearing stand as the *arkhē* that subordinates the other senses; the common of the senses is unequally distributed. More precisely, Rancière's world is the "world of prose," which has cast out smell: the sense of smell—thoroughly elided from the "distribution of the sensible" in large part due to its traditional inability to enter "art"—occupies the non-position of "the part that has no part." Smell, it appears, does not count, and can make no claims on the shared commons of the sensible. Against this policing of smell, a politics of smell would effect a *redistribution of the senses*. Departing from the assumption of the equality of the senses, restoring smell to the sensible commons would not so much constitute an "olfactory turn" (as it could be modeled on recently proclaimed "auditory" or "tactile turns") that would seek to include olfaction within a new, reconfigured distribution of the senses. Instead, a politics of smell would dislodge any ordering of the senses. Smell, as the rest of this introduction and this book will show, is particularly well-positioned to rupture assignments of positions, places, and roles. It eludes a "proper count" by subtracting itself from the logic of properness and property, and it continually fails to stabilize into a consistent, policeable form. Smell, in short, elicits politics.

We Have Never Been Deodorized

Rancière's exclusion of olfaction, of course, comes as no surprise; it merely locates him firmly in our "present moment" governed by a logic of the elision of smell. This generalized atmosphere of erasing smell can be traced to the consequential hypothesis that the disappearance of smell's central role is part of the parallel progression of *deodorization* and *civilization*: the more human civilization moves away from the scents of "that calm enchanted wood," the more it becomes a civilization properly understood, and vice versa. The most influential version of this thesis was proposed by Sigmund Freud in his 1930 tract *Civilization and Its Discontents*. In a long footnote to the fourth section—thus situating this claim at the margin or threshold of the text—Freud proposes what he labels "a theoretical speculation."[24] The first claim of his speculation is this: prior to the "threshold of human civilization" lies a "devaluation of olfactory stimuli." Smell is devalued even before the threshold of human civilization and culture proper is reached. The civilizing process, and with it the negotiation of the nature-culture divide, as such contains as its presupposition an attenuation of olfaction.[25] In other words, one of the conditions of possibility for the emergence of culture lies precisely in a constitutive exclusion of smell from the distribution of the senses—culture emerges as deodorization. The obverse of this cultivating attenuation of olfaction is found in a new "preponderance of visual stimuli." Culture depends, so Freud argues, on the institution of sight as the dominant sense, and the civilizing process begins once seeing triumphs over smelling. Questioning the dominance of vision and attending to smells in their full force thus takes one out of the cultivating, socializing process—the danger of smell is the threat of a return of and to the prehistorical, the threat of a retreat beyond and before the threshold of the process of anthropogenesis.[26]

The crossing of the olfactory threshold of civilization is tied, for Freud, to two types of smells in particular. On the one hand, civilized deodorization derives from a turn away from the earth and toward the vertical dimension: "But the receding of olfactory stimuli itself appears to be a consequence of the human being's turning away from the earth, the decision to walk upright."[27] Any turning back toward the smells of the earth—as Hölderlin, Nietzsche, and Brecht in particular will perform it—thus throws off the human *Gang* (mode of locomotion or walking), the progression of humankind that holds itself in a state of uprightness and rectitude, stepping forward. Attending to the smells from below *inclines* the human and bends or inflects its vertical dimension, constituting what a contemporary scholar has termed a "critique of rectitude."[28] On the other hand, Freud argues that the assumption of an erect posture implies a change in sexual stimulation, more precisely, in the temporal structure of such stimuli: "Receding of olfactory stimuli through which the process of menstruation affected the male psyche. Their role was taken over by visual stimuli, which, in contrast to the intermittent olfactory stimuli, could maintain a permanent effect."[29] Like the smell of the earth, gendered, sexual smells (crucial to Baudelaire and Brecht) are at odds with the permanence and uprightness of civilization. Freud points here to a feature of smell that will regularly emerge in analyses of olfaction: whereas vision produces, at least potentially, a permanent stimulus, smells fluctuate, be it according to the rhythm of the menses or the biphasic structure of breathing that interrupts olfactory stimulation with each exhalation. In other words, the threshold to civilization is crossed precisely with the reaching of a permanence that triumphs over intermittence and rhythm: civilization *is* (supposed, intended, desired) permanence, and as such must exclude the rhythmic temporality of smell. Sensory stability—the precondition for any hierarchical ordering—is at odds with smell.

This Freudian "speculation" concerning the incompatibility of smells and civilization *tout court* has been modified repeatedly to mean that it is more accurately *modern*, bourgeois, European civilization that stands in a definitional relationship with deodorization.[30] The "world of prose," in which smells tend to be decentered and erased, is not the world of any civilization whatsoever, but more precisely the modern world of a few central European peoples and classes. Along these lines, Alain Corbin, the French historian of the *Annales* school, argues in *The Foul and the Fragrant*, a groundbreaking book in the emergence of sense studies over the past few decades, that a "new sensibility" with respect to odors and a veritable "perceptual revolution" mark modernity in France: "From about the middle of the eighteenth century, odors simply began to be more keenly smelled. It was as if thresholds of tolerance had been abruptly lowered; and that happened well before industrial pollution accumulated in urban space."[31] This was linked to new scientific developments (superseded by the later development of the germ theory of disease) in the 1770s and 1780s that were concerned with locating and eliminating "miasmas," odors that were thought to transmit illness, in particular odors of putrefaction and corruption. Corbin argues that these odors became regarded as "social emanations"—that is, as indicators of social status and a whole range of proclaimed virtues such as sexual purity. In the nineteenth century this link between odor, putrefaction, and disease eventually led to sanitary reformers using tactics "that created a clear distinction between the deodorized bourgeoisie and the foul-smelling masses."[32] Deodorization became a crucial tool of the "perceptual revolution's" aim to establish and guard class lines in and beyond the modern, European metropolis. In the form of newly emergent sewage, public health, and hygiene programs, a deployment of the "public nostril,"[33] as Zachary Samalin has recently called it, then also became "integral to the gradual consolidation of . . . state apparatuses and to major transformations in the way the social sphere was conceptualized and social space was regulated."[34] This project of olfactory differentiation and partial erasure or containment was further extended beyond questions of class and domestic state power to related ones of race and imperial power: "olfactory racialization" and olfaction's mobilization for colonial purposes came to constitute one particularly pernicious version of smell's implication in projects of sensory policing and hierarchizing.[35] In short, olfactory "failures" became regarded as indicators of the backwardness of the smelling person or place, betraying their exclusion from modernity or an alleged geographical, dominant center, which in turn often elicited exertions of state power or violence.

The flip side of modernity's tendency to deodorize, or rather to valorize deodorization and the control of odors, lies in the assertion, as Walter Benjamin puts it, that modernity stands under a "primacy of the optical."[36] The less the human sensory sphere is scented, the more heavily it becomes oriented toward and by visual stimuli. In recent years, thinkers such as Hans Blumenberg, Martin Jay, Jonathan Crary, and Caroline A. Jones have drawn attention to this "ocularcentrism" or "hegemony of vision" within modernity and have shown that such a dominance of sight among the senses is far from accidental or innocuous:[37] the vocabulary of truth, especially in the modern European tradition, but also reaching back much further, is constituted by terms such as "enlightenment," "illumination," "insight," "reflection," "idea" (as derived from *eidos*), *lumen rationis*, "clarity," or "the existentialist gaze." The very attempt of a *theory* of ocularcentrism and its others announces itself under a visual term: the word "theory" derives from *theōria* (meaning looking at, speculation, or contemplation). In short, we say "I see" when we mean "I understand"—and we build on this proclaimed homology between sight and insight a theory of the observer's position vis-à-vis truth as modeled on the paradigm of the sense of vision. Writing about the ocularcentrism of modernist art, Jones puts it succinctly: "To produce the I/Eye, to become modern, the narcissistic subject must subordinate nonocular senses and attend rapturously to that emergent self-reflective ego. As Lacan claimed, our cognitive awareness of ourselves as individuals is framed and produced most persuasively through the vision in the mirror; other senses become Other."[38] Becoming modern means seeing oneself as a seeing being and distributing the senses such that vision assumes an exalted and all-governing position. The self constitutes itself in this reflexive relation, and *only* in this reflexive relay. Put differently, the "immense deodorizing campaign" of modernity operates via a "transposition of everything into the idiom of images, of spectacle, of verbal discourse, and of writing and reading."[39]

This ocularcentrism of modernity, however, is restricted to being a matter of modernity's self-*image*—its own specular reflection, as it were. To use Freud's doubly visual phrase, sensory reality undercuts any such "theoretical speculation" of the modern I/eye on itself. Following and reconfiguring Corbin, historians have pointed out that modern deodorization campaigns concern "the removal of *particular* scents, notably fecal odors and the smells of human sweat, . . . [not] the removal of *all* smells."[40] And as the epilogue on Francis Ponge's soap poems below will show in detail, deodorization itself often produces new smells—namely, the smells *of* deodorization (such as the scents of soap, deodorant, or hygiene products). Beneath the self-image of modernity as deodorized, then, plenty of smells continue to give shape to modern sensory reality. More radically, modernity can even be understood as centrally concerned with smell's medium—that is, air—and thus as always at least latently maintaining a crucial relationship with olfaction: a recent explosion of scholarship in the environmental humanities and ecocriticism has argued for the centrality of *atmospheres*, with Peter Sloterdijk even defining modernity as a project of "air conditioning" that poses the critical task of making air conditions explicit and analyzing the structures of "atmotopes."[41] For such an analysis, an "olfactory aesthetics" (Hsuan L. Hsu) can be mobilized to detect, think about, and transform these atmospheres. The "spheres" of modernity are thus ineluctably intertwined with olfactory concerns, both in their tendency to be deodorized and in a movement of re-odorization or remainders of odors. In other words, smell as the excluded part continuously demands to be counted and registered: a politics of smell emerges to contravene modernity's policed, ocularcentric self-reflection.

Against modernity's self-image, it can thus be claimed that *we have never been deodorized*. Echoing Bruno Latour's famous dictum "we have never been modern,"[42] such a claim foregrounds the fact that deodorization, just like modernity, is a nodal point of contestation, not a place on one side of a dichotomy that is either attained or fallen short of. Modern concern with the distribution of the senses is thus found in both modernity's tendency toward deodorization *and* the forces that repeatedly counteract that tendency. Deodorization and re-odorization, like the modern and the premodern, are intimately intertwined: as the poets under investigation in *Common Scents* show, modernity's relationship to smell is one of an often unnoticed but nevertheless forceful and consequential agonistic struggle over how the positions of the senses are ordered and reordered and over where, in particular, smell falls in this distribution of the senses.

Emancipation, a Revolution of the Senses

The broader question raised by these considerations concerns the relationship between the senses and history. If the sense of smell changes its position within the human sensorium over the course of history, then the senses must be, as Walter Benjamin puts it in his canonical essay "The Artwork in the Age of Its Technological Reproducibility," "not only naturally but also historically conditioned" (*GS* 1:478). Benjamin adapts this claim from the young Marx, in particular from the 1844 *Economic and Philosophical Manuscripts*, which he studied in the 1930s shortly after their discovery and publication.[43] For Marx, it is a given that "the *entire so-called world history* is nothing but the generation of the human being through human work, nothing but the becoming of nature for the human being."[44] This applies to the senses too. In a crucial passage concerning the senses, Marx writes, "The *formation* [*Bildung*] of the 5 senses is the work of the entire preceding world history" (*MEW* 40:541–542; emphasis in the original). The formation of the "precious five" thus lies in the "work" of world history. Work, in turn, is first and foremost a process of externalization (*Entäußerung*) and appropriation (*Aneignung*). Marx combines here, as so often in the *Manuscripts*, a Feuerbachian materialism, in particular its strong emphasis on the senses and their epistemic value, with a formally Hegelian notion of the process of history and the formation of the subject through work: the formation of the senses occurs in and as a process of transformation between self and other, subject and object, inside and outside. The malleability of the senses lies in their implication in the work of history that proceeds through this dialectic of externalization and appropriation. This also means, conversely, that the unfolding of history can (partially) be traced in the unfolding of the formation of the senses.

Our task with respect to the senses, according to the young Marx, then becomes taking charge of this process of sense formation and the work that produces this formation. No longer blindly governed by the march of world history, the human being is supposed to form and educate the senses in a manner that is appropriate to its very humanity. Thus far, the senses have been restrained and subjected to alien forces, therefore languishing in an atrophied state—against all this, Marx demands "the complete *emancipation* of all human senses." Of this emancipation, Marx states, "But it is this emancipation precisely because these senses and properties [*Eigenschaften*] have become *human*, subjectively as well as objectively. The eye has become a *human* eye. . . . Need or enjoyment have therefore lost their *egoistic* nature, and nature has lost its mere *utility* since use has become *human* use" (*MEW* 40:540). The young Marx here advances a double claim. On the one hand, the emancipation of the senses leads them beyond a mere egoistic status that reduces nature to utility. In an echo of Hölderlin's account of the relationship between need and smell that will be developed below, Marx returns to this point throughout the *Manuscripts*: emancipating the senses means freeing them from their subservience to mere need. Only once a state has been reached where basic needs are met can the senses become free to develop without the yoke of necessity. On the other hand, this emancipation of the senses, for Marx, would constitute new social relations by bringing the human being into its full humanity: Reconfiguring the human sensorium's constitution—that is, redistributing the senses—not only produces new relations between human being and nature but also between human being and human being, precisely by making such relations human. As becomes clear in the further exposition of Marx's argument, these new social relations derive from a shift where what belongs to the *other* becomes *my own*—and vice versa. An emancipation of the senses lies in the reduction of alterity in a newfound sociality in which alienating distance and difference have disappeared: the "human," emancipated senses allow for a thorough appropriation of the sensory realm that issues into "the sensory appropriation of the human essence [die sinnliche Aneignung des menschlichen Wesens]" (*MEW* 40:539) for and by the human. In an argument that will be criticized below, Marx insists here that the emancipation of the senses consists of an ineluctably linked and mutually conditioning constellation of the terms "self-production," "appropriation," and "humanity."

This emancipation of the senses further constitutes a crucial aspect of a term that is sparsely present in the *Manuscripts* but is nonetheless central to contemporaneous writings by Marx and his thought as a whole as it pursues the program of emancipation: revolution. Walter Benjamin emphasizes this connection when, in his notes for the *Arcades Project*, he quotes the key passage from the 1844 *Manuscripts* concerning the emancipation of the senses—and adds the remark "concerning the doctrine [*Lehre*] of revolutions" (*GS* 5:801).[45]

The emancipation of the senses that the young Marx envisioned, so Benjamin's note suggests, would constitute a *revolution of the senses*. Paying attention to the sensorium's distribution teaches us that revolutions are not just matters of violent action, proclamations of rights, or mass mobilizations, but are also embodied, sensual, and sensory affairs. Rendering the senses free from their subjection to egoism and utility would overturn and abolish the present state of the world. Such an overturning would also undo the distribution of the senses that keeps them in their hierarchized and policed state: emancipating the senses, in other words, would consist in redistributing them and disrupting the police order imposed on them. Redistribution and revolution stand in a relationship of mutual definition: redistributing revolutionizes, and revolutionizing redistributes. This should be understood in the exacting sense that Rancière attributes to distribution:[46] a revolution of the senses would not only reorder the hierarchized positions of the senses; instead, the genuinely political moment of redistribution lies in destabilizing the very existence of hierarchical positions. A revolution of the senses would count the "part that has no part" and undo the carving up of the common of the senses.

For Benjamin, such a revolution of the senses implies a shift away from one sense toward another. The task of a revolution of the senses cannot be fulfilled by just any sense: "*The tasks that are posed to the human sensorium during times of historic turning [geschichtlichen Wendezeiten] are not at all solvable via the path of mere optics, that is, via contemplation. They are mastered gradually according to the guidance of tactile reception, through habituation*" (*GS* 1:505; *GS* 7:381; emphasis in the original). In times of historic turning (*Wendezeiten*)—which is to say, in revolutionary times—the tasks posed to the human sensorium cannot be solved by vision, but rather require a different sense—for Benjamin, touch—that functions not via contemplation (one translation of which would be *theōria*, visual beholding) but habituation. The *phenomenality of revolution* is subtracted from vision: the "primacy of the optical" or the ocularcentrism of modernity must be replaced by a different sensory mode. The potential contained in the revolution of the senses, or rather the potential *of* a revolution of the senses, is thus intertwined with the proclaimed hegemony of vision as its impediment or *katechon*. Benjamin's suggestion that touch could replace vision can be supplemented by the thesis that smell, too, is suited, perhaps even better suited, to the task of a revolution of the senses:[47] as *Common Scents* will show in detail, olfaction is a sense of habituation as opposed to contemplation, and it is also a sense often found at the moment of a *Wendezeit*—when memory of the past, to return to the idiom of "Precious Five," turns to or attempts to turn to a different future. Conversely, the erasure of smell constitutes an erasure of the potential to solve the tasks posed by revolutionary times. An insistence on the spectacular, the theoretical, or the contemplative marks a refusal of revolution.

At this point, a grammatical ambiguity of the syntagma "revolution of the senses" takes center stage: Does the "of" constitute an objective genitive (the human sensorium is being revolutionized, overturned—that is, reconfigured) or a subjective genitive (the senses effect, stage, or bring about a revolution)? It is this latter reading that became a strong temptation in a certain strand of Western Marxism, especially for thinkers who considered the 1844 *Manuscripts* not only a legitimate and alive part of the Marxian oeuvre but rather its fulcrum. With respect to the senses, the main proponent of this strand is Herbert Marcuse, one of the very first to write about the *Manuscripts* when they were discovered in the 1920s.[48] For Marcuse, it is the combination of Feuerbach's sensuousness and the Hegelian concept of work that yields Marxian revolutionary praxis, and the emphasis needs to be continuously placed on both aspects. In this sense it is true that "for Marcuse undiminished sensuousness, as presented by the Feuerbach-Marx conception, is not only the result of realized communism but—even more so—the indispensable precondition for communism coming about at all, for it becoming *historically efficacious [geschichtsmächtig]*."[49] According to Marcuse, the senses can become *geschichtsmächtig*: they can become a *revolutionary agent*, as catalyst or even acting subject.

Marcuse's *Counterrevolution and Revolt*, one of his responses to the student movements of the 1960s, thus argues for the "subversive potential of sensibility"[50] by drawing on all three points—emancipating the senses from need, building new social relations, and regaining humanity for humankind—that were crucial to the Marxian passage quoted by Benjamin. Marcuse, however, claims much more directly that a new "radical sensibility" plays a crucial part in attempts at political overturning: "Conditioned and 'contained' by the rationality of the established system, sense experience tends to 'immunize' man against the very unfamiliar experience of the possibilities of human freedom. The development of a radical, nonconformist sensibility assumes vital political importance in view of the unprecedented extent of social control perfected by advanced capitalism: a control which reaches down into the instinctual and physiological level of existence. Conversely, resistance and rebellion, too, tend to activate and operate on this level."[51] In the terms of Auden's "Precious Five," Marcuse seeks to draw on the "ill-mannered" nature of sensibility: faced with containment and constriction, the "brash" nature of, for instance, smell opposes itself to the control exerted by the capitalist system. The foreclosure of the "possibilities of human freedom" would be undone by a sensibility that becomes "radical," or goes to the root; a suggestion that unmistakably bears traces of the attempt of a *return* (to a presumably more "instinctual" past) and an appeal to humanity's essence.

This train of thought issues, for Marcuse, into a reworking of Kantian-Schillerian aesthetics as a potentiality of revolutionary praxis—but the fundamental question of the viability of this agential view of the senses overrides any detailed questions concerning its proposed mechanisms. "To be transformed into a new ethics [*Sittlichkeit*]," Seyla Benhabib argues in her critique of Marcuse, "the subversive potential of this new sensuality [*Sinnlichkeit*] must be reimmersed in the tissues of history."[52] It is precisely over this path from the senses to history and action that we encounter a sign that designates this path as "the way you cannot take." Marcuse's appeal to a radical sensibility fails to recognize that in a world of prose, sensibility no longer stands in the "middle," and that any return to it underneath capitalism's anesthetic of conformity is blocked precisely by the problem it is supposed to help solve. In other words, the new radical sensibility as Marcuse envisions it presupposes an already completed revolution—and thus cannot bring it about. Any direct appeal to the revolutionary potential of the senses as agent fails to follow the dictum that opened "Precious Five": *be patient*. This appeal to patience, it must be emphasized, is far from a fatalist or quietist exhortation to stay within an "apathetic sphere" (here reencountered in the shape of capitalism's anesthetic of conformity). Instead, the question becomes how smell might point the way beyond this sphere of closure and, in its act of "asymmetric" pointing, open this very apathy—without presuming direct agential powers. Smell's revolution of the senses has only, to adapt another of Benjamin's expressions, a "weak force." It is a patient and indexical revolution: smell both indicates the direction in which revolution would lie and enables a sensory experience—an undergoing—of what such a revolution would be. In short, smell makes a revolution of the senses *sensible*.

Smell and the Expropriation of the "Sense of Having"

Revolutions, sensible or otherwise, redistribute. They redistribute power, hierarchical positions, visibility, social relations, and, perhaps above all, property relations. The question of who owns what constitutes the core of many an attempted and successful revolutionary overturning of the status quo. It is therefore not surprising that the nexus *revolution-property* also lies at the heart of the question of the senses in Marx and the shape of a potential revolution of the senses. Marx introduces the passage concerning the emancipation of the senses quoted above with the following, crucial claim: "The abolition [*Aufhebung*] of private property is therefore the complete *emancipation* of all human senses" (*MEW* 40:540). The emancipation of the senses is tied to the abolition (or sublation) of private property—that is, to a change in property relations and a change in what is considered *eigen* (proper, one's own, self-). Private property, conversely, produces an "absolute poverty" of the senses that has reduced the multifaceted—Marx repeatedly bases his critique on lateral terms such as "one-sided [*einseitig*]," "many-sided [*vielseitig*]," or "all-around [*allseitig*]"—sensory condition of the human being to a single sense, the "sense of having [*Sinn des Habens*]." The reign of the sense of having has made us "stupid and one-sided"; it precludes any relationship to objects that is not one of possession. This sense of having thus impoverishes triply, according to the trifold meaning of "sense": under a regime of private property, the world only has *meaning* for us through having and accumulation; we only *perceive* things through the optic of whether they are ours or not, whether they can be acquired or not, whether we can act such that we will be able to acquire them or not; and lastly, having provides *orientation* in the world for our actions, desires, and thoughts.

Within the multifaceted sensory field that Marx seeks to mobilize against the one-sided sense of having, olfaction stands out for directly undoing the principal characteristics of this sense: first and foremost, smell tends toward dissolving the egological subject that constitutes the root of the sense of having. Only a subject conceived of as self-thetic and self-appropriating can be singularly oriented by the sense of having. By contrast, as the chapters of *Common Scents* will show in detail, the provocation of smell lies precisely in the fact that a smell cannot be had and cannot be grasped in an act of taking into the proper. Smell, instead, threatens with dissolution and dispersal; it blurs the line of demarcation between subject and other, letting the other inside of the subject and thus destabilizing both of these terms. The delimiting qualities of the terms "subject" and "other" evaporate in the sensory mode of existence that is found in smelling. Its atmospheric and ephemeral character overrides any "one-sided," or, for that matter, two-sided, demarcations and instead situates being-in-the-air as "all-around [*allseitig*]," so to speak, as surrounded and surrounding. As Theodor W. Adorno and Max Horkheimer put it in their *Dialectic of Enlightenment*, "While seeing, one remains who one is; in smelling, one comes undone [*im Riechen geht man auf*]."[53] The choice of the German verb *aufgehen* is exacting in its proliferating meanings: in smelling, one opens up; rises upward; finds fulfillment; has a dawning realization; expands outward. All of these possibilities of transformation are predicated on the coming undone of smell that derives from olfaction's tendency to lose what is mine and what is proper (*eigen*) to me: "Of all the senses, the act of smelling, which is attracted without reifying [*vergegenständlichen*], testifies most sensuously to the urge to lose oneself to the other [*ans andere sich zu verlieren*]."[54] The sense of smell disallows a return to oneself, a being-at-home-in-the-other—and instead constitutes the temptation, chance, and danger of losing oneself. With smell, an *expropriating* mode of sensory existence emerges: whatever was considered mine, at home, or within my purview tends toward loss in a movement into otherness.[55]

This provocative claim can be further motivated by reflecting on smell's medium, air. For human beings, smelling is impossible without air. In fact, as Aristotle—who, like many other ancient Greeks, was rather interested in olfaction[56]—puts it in the closing sentence of book 2 of *De Anima*, "The act of smelling is an act of perception, whereas the air, being only temporarily affected, merely becomes perceptible [αἰσθητός]."[57] In other words, smell can be understood—as will be developed in greater detail with respect to Hölderlin's olfactory poetics in chapter 1—as a modulation of the aerial medium. Air, in turn, might constitute, as Elias Canetti has argued, "the last common property. It belongs to all people collectively."[58] This consideration of air as a common property has a long and distinguished pedigree. The *Institutes* of Marcianus (second century CE), quoted in Justinian's *Digest* and widely considered a standard work of Roman law that is still cited in contemporary legal papers and court opinions,[59] state that "The following things belong in common, by natural law, to all: air, flowing water, and the sea."[60] The air is considered a *res communis omnium*, a thing that belongs to all in common. No one can accumulate it privately, divide it up for individual purposes, or remove it from the commons. Air subtracts itself from and circumvents the privatizing "sense of having"—it moves sense from the *sphere of egoism* to the *atmosphere of the commons*.

Lest this appeal to the commons appear hopelessly naive, an objection should be addressed: How does this common character of the air relate to what one scholar has recently called the intensifying contemporary phenomenon of a "monetization of the air"?[61] What to make of the commodification of smells, for instance in perfumes (so important to Baudelaire)? More broadly, how does the "atmospheric differentiation," diagnosed by Hsuan L. Hsu and others, which "generates and maintains comfortable, breathable spaces for some while unevenly exposing the bodies of the poor and vulnerable to risky inhalations,"[62] relate to air's claim to be a *res communis omnium*? The argument of *Common Scents* in all its chapters will be that the common status of the air is never a stable given—rather, it is a question of air's *commoning tendency*, which is repeatedly interrupted or temporarily stultified. What the poets under investigation in this book (re)discover and seek to strengthen is not a common *state* of the air or the world, but rather a tendency toward the common in which the sense of having "comes undone."

One way of strengthening air's commoning tendency is to make it perceptible and draw attention to it—otherwise it will, as Irigaray's *The Forgetting of Air* emphasized, continuously allow itself to be forgotten. This is where smell reenters: the sense of smell can be understood as the—or, more modestly, a—sense of the commons; in other words, smell, according to the argument of this book, is a *sensus communis*. The "common scents" of this book's title make sensible the commons and hence seek to strengthen the tendency that counteracts the sense of having's claims even to the air. The phrase "commoning tendency" thus also seeks to do justice to the characteristics of smell developed thus far: any claim to a definitive and closed status of the common would run counter to smell's ephemeral and elusive nature. Hence it is always a question of a tendency and of a verbal form, of a movement and an inclination instead of a state: the authors investigated in *Common Scents* articulate the olfactory counter*forces* that resist the subordination of smell to the sense of having. In other words, drawing attention to the forgotten sense of smell functions as an incitement to "unlearn" the world of private property.[63]

The possibility of understanding the status of air through the concept of a possession by *all*—of common possession—as Canetti had claimed it for air following Roman law, however, is threatened by a different, radical possibility: that of a possession by *none*. Put differently: Might air and smell be subtracted from the order of possession *tout court*, even a common possession by "all people"? Roman law knows the concept of a *res nullius*, an object not possessed by anyone. In a first instance, this simply means, as Daniel Heller-Roazen has summarized, that the *res nullius* is an object that is "still to be acquired by a private individual"[64] and can be acquired temporarily; a wild animal would be an example of such a *res nullius*. However, a specter looms large in the conception of the *res nullius*: the specter of the possibility that such a thing might *remain* without an owner in perpetuity, precisely because an acquisition of it is impossible. This worry motivates one of the most rigorous philosophical reflections on possession, Immanuel Kant's *Doctrine of Right*—Kant being a philosopher who, in his old age, became severely concerned that a "revolution in the air" was impeding his ability to think. In the *Doctrine of Right*, Kant leaves aside such aerial concerns or, perhaps, erects the doctrine of right over and against such a revolution.[65] He bases his doctrine on a "postulate" of practical reason that stipulates the possessability of all outer things: "It is possible for me to have any external object [*jeden äußern Gegenstand*] of my choice as mine, that is, a maxim by which, if it were to become a law, an object of choice would *in itself* (objectively) have to *belong to no one* [*herrenlos*] (*res nullius*) is contrary to rights."[66] Yet the air might precisely be such a *res nullius* that eludes appropriation "an sich," in itself and objectively. The argument supporting this far-reaching claim would be this: the point of departure for Kant's considerations of possession in the *Doctrine of Right* is the supposedly straightforward case of what he calls physical possession or simply "holding [*Inhabung*]"—namely, the holding of an object in one's hand. This is hard to imagine for the case of air: I cannot hold or grasp it; neither can I stand on it, occupy it, or "sit" on it, as the German term *Be-sitz* indicates. This distinguishes the air from the earth or "Boden" that constitutes Kant's primary object of investigation for the question of originary possession. None of the relations to air available to us resemble what Kant imagines under the rubric of "holding."

The faltering of this first instance of possession, then, also affects the extension of property relations into an "intelligible" possession that does not depend (or no longer does) on holding: this extension is supposed to be guaranteed precisely by the postulate of practical reason cited above—but this postulate relies on a definition of an "external object" that is at odds with the character of air. The air (and by extension smell) eludes the status of "res": the air cannot be divided into discrete units ("airspace" can, but the air "itself" cannot).[67] Its continual movement, its ephemerality—what for Nietzsche will emerge as air's *chaotic* tendency against which ocularcentrism issues a call to order—evades all grasp; it is always only medial and shared.[68] A comparison to the other complex case of possession that Marcianus mentions and that is troubling to Kant expands this argument: the sea. In the case of the earth, *Be-sitz* eventually goes back to a possible relationship of grounding: the owner becomes "fundiert," which is to say he becomes grounded or "bases" himself.[69] The sea complicates this because no one can stay on it or "occupy" it long enough in order to gain a firm footing.[70] Nevertheless, there exists a substitute that supplies a type of fleeting grounding: ships. The existence of ships underscores, in a final consequence, the similarity of earth and sea in the context of Kant's theory of possession: both supply a *surface* of the globe "onto which every first possessor can set foot [*auf den sich jeder erste Besitzer fußen kann*]."[71] While precarious and unsettled, the sea is nevertheless similar enough to the earth to allow for a relationship of quasi-grounding. Air is structured differently: while airborne "ships" (say, airplanes or helicopters) do exist, our primary relationship to the air is not one of surface and ground but rather one of a constant but fluctuating atmospheric surrounding, submerging, and interpenetration. Air is in and around, not underneath us. An index of how this constitutes a vast problem for possessability can be found in the Kantian use of the term "external" to define the range of things that are possessable—more precisely, his definition of "an object *distinct* from me [*einen von mir unterschiedenen Gegenstand*]."[72] Such an *Unterschied* is severely weakened in the air: in contrast to the earth or the sea, air is never just outer and distinct; it enters and exits, thus ceaselessly intermingling with me and undoing its distinctness from "me." (Kant's remarks on smell in his *Anthropology* seem to intuit this undoing of externality when they emphasize the "innig [inward, intimate]" character of smelling, its "innermost taking in [*innigste Einnehmung*]."[73]) To recall Canetti once more, "To nothing is the human being so open as to air."[74] This indistinct openness, in turn, leads to the two components of the word *Gegen-stand* (object) coming undone: for air, any *gegen* (against) of *Gegenstand* never stabilizes into a firm opposition, which would let a surface emerge that allows for grounding and hence possession. Similarly, air never "stands" across from or underneath us: it moves around and through us. Air is neither *gegen* nor *stand*, but, to use a term developed extensively in chapter 1, *durchgängig*: it goes into and through the subject. All of this, then, suggests that air is subtracted from the order of possessability.

Smell, in turn, makes air as an unpossessable medium *sensible*: it allows perception of it and lets it enter into *aisthesis*. In a scent, an abolishing of separations, of boundary stones, and the delimiting of any *gegen* becomes sensible. In other words, smell provides sense in the absence of the sense-making of the sense of having: it does not bestow meaning on the world by relating it to what is "mine" (or "yours") but rather lets us perceive things that are constitutively subtracted from what is possessable. Smell orients us—if this is still an orientation—away from possession and toward unbounded mediality. The sense-making of smell thus establishes a nonproprietary relation, which can further be understood as an *improper* relation: it is subtracted from the reign of the *Eigen* as that which is my own and proper to me.

This radical subtraction from all logic of the proper also extends to the concept of an emancipation of the senses and the attendant concept of revolution. One of the key features of the Marxian account consisted of a reduction of the tension between alterity and properness, or rather a subsumption of everything "other" under that which can now be considered mine: "The senses and the enjoyment of the other human beings have likewise become my *own* appropriation" (*MEW* 40:540; emphasis in the original). This conversion of the appropriation of "the other human beings" into "my own appropriation" functions through the mediating term "human." Indeed, the reconciliation of the human being in the concept of humanity constitutes the primary goal of the *Manuscripts*: "actual appropriation of the human essence through and for the human being; therefore as a complete and conscious return, which arises within the whole wealth of the prior development, of the human being for itself as a *social* [*gesellschaftlichen*], that is, human human being [*menschlichen Menschen*]" (*MEW* 40:536; emphasis in the original). The crucial word here is "return": a homecoming and a turning backward.[75] While Marx certainly is explicit throughout his work that a literal return to archaic times—say, to primitive communism—is neither possible nor desirable, he nevertheless conceives of the emancipation of the senses as a return to that which is proper to humankind after its long erring in the desert of alienation. This return constitutes the young Marx's avowed "humanism": emancipation (as part of the arrival of "positive communism") is humanism as a retrieval of humanity's proper, its *Eigen-tum*—and it is this movement that the formation of the senses is then supposed to trace and follow. All strife, scission, or irreducible difference in the sensory realm would be reconciled in this homecoming; the senses would enter a state where their exercise precludes any loss of the human being in a world that would be alien to humanity. In short, "emancipation and retrieval [*Wiedergewinnung*]" (*MEW* 40:546) go hand in hand:[76] the *new* human being, central to much of Marx's work and to much of Marxism, as well as its brutal aberrations, is still a new *human* being and always accompanied by the claim that it is constituted by a homecoming into the true essence of humanity.

At the core of such humanism thus lies a program of self-appropriation and self-possession, even if it is of the species: humanity wants to finally, eventually have itself. Humanism, in other words, is beholden to the sense of having. Despite Marx's repeated disavowals of an abstract essence of the human, his operative terms, as Derrida and others have argued,[77] remain essentializing in an anthropocentric manner: labor and praxis, in particular, are considered to be exclusively human. Qua beings that exist in the air, however, human beings have no access to a "home" that would be essentially human: other beings breathe too—the air is the medium precisely between us and all kinds of other beings, not only animals but also plants. Hence in air, by virtue of it being subtracted from the order of possessability, there can be no return, no homecoming to a human home that would be that which is mine and mine alone. Smell, in short, makes sensible the nonhuman(ist) character of being-in-the-air: "common scents" are common to *all* terrestrial life, human and nonhuman alike.

A corollary of this non-anthropocentric notion of the commonality of air and smell can then be designated as follows: the "revolution of the senses" that can be sensed in smell must be other than a Hegelian-Marxian turn from impotence to power or a mere redistribution of property. This revolution would not reconfigure who owns what but would, rather, via a turn through the common of "common scents," subtract from property relations *tout court*. Tracing smell thus amounts to an attempt to "sketch out a non-metaphysical 'concept' of revolution that does not begin with self-production and self-appropriation," as Werner Hamacher writes in his seminal study of the late Hölderlin whose poetry will be central to the first chapter of *Common Scents*.[78] This would be a *patient* "concept" of revolution: one that undergoes and exposes itself. It would also be a concept of revolution better suited to the twinned nature of a world of prose that has never been deodorized: faced with the "way you cannot take," the nose moves away from the discourse of a "radical sensibility" oriented toward return and appropriation to a sensibility marked by "break, limitation, transgression, infertility, interlude [*Zwischen*], postponement or deferral; only where spirit and history accept their impotence as the uncertain and unknowable condition for their efficacy, can there take place that which could only still provisionally be called a revolution."[79]

Smell points the way.

Tracking Down the Argument—In Medias Res

One of the delightful oddities of studying the appearance of odors in literature lies in the fact that, once the dictum "we have never been deodorized" has been accepted, olfaction surfaces in the reading of all kinds of authors and texts. Yet this ubiquity constitutes only the other face of these moments' often ephemeral or even fugitive character: a persistent stench or overpowering fragrance appears occasionally, but more common are scents that are a mere *whiff*, easily ignored and lost track of. In this sense, the theme of this book resembles the elusive vernacular that Dante tried to track down in *De vulgari eloqentia*, where he compares the object of his hunt with a panther who "has left its scent in every city but made its home in none."[80] Yet while smell is nowhere at home—that is, while it has no single, *proper location*—it is nevertheless marked by perceptible differences: "Its scent may still be stronger in one city than another."[81] Dante indicates here a geopoetics *in nuce*: language is distributed differentially across the earth. Reading smell, similarly, consists of detecting, cataloging, and analyzing these geopoetic differentials of scent that mark and articulate olfaction's fluctuating intensities—its dissemination—across different topoi: reading smell tracks the frequency of smell asserting itself, disappearing in deodorization, or reemerging in unexpected fashions.

A corollary of smell's differential distribution across a range of places that all fail to become its proper home can be designated as follows: the "theme" of this book is not thematic in a strong sense. It cannot be posited in front of the reader as a stable object, nor can it be offered up for theoretical contemplation. Rather, common scents are often read off—as a fleeting whiff of indeterminate phenomenality—of other related objects, constellations, or topics: a garden, a woman's hair, the earth, a city, soap, the morning air. Reading smell thus always finds itself in medias res, in the middle of things: not being able to articulate itself through a thematic, direct address, reading smell departs not from some kind of imagined origin or a fixed, removed vantage point of theoretical investigation, but rather begins and stays among the ordinary facts of ongoing living, facts that tend to escape theorization or scholarly reflection. In a sense, reading and writing smells must therefore attempt what one commentary on Dante calls "writing what has never been read and reading what has never been written"[82]: by turning the elusiveness of smells into an asset for thought, *Common Scents* introduces into the sphere of reading and writing what has, like the common vernacular of Dante's time in the face of hegemonic Latin, been overlooked, unheard of, never touched upon, and excluded from (literary) taste.

Common Scents finds itself in medias res in yet another, more important sense: in addition to smell's geopoetically differential distribution and dissemination, it is precisely the *middle* that emerges throughout the book as a second governing spatial term. For instance, as chapter 3 will show, the extreme point of Nietzsche's olfactory thought is found in a collapse of boundary markers and borders that leaves only the earth as an orienting middle. Similarly, chapter 1 will show that Benjamin's important phrase of "the middle of all relations," found in his Hölderlin essay, finds sensory concretion and articulation in the late Hölderlin's use of olfactory tropes. This link between smell and a thought of the middle is far from accidental. It is already contained in olfaction's ineluctable tie to the air: air constitutes one of the *media* of human life, where a "medium" is that which is in between, an interval, in the middle. Smelling thus locates the smelling entity not just in the middle of things but also in the medium of things, or perhaps, as one scholar has recently put it, in the *"medium of life."*[83] Life is always mediated and media-bound—this fact becomes perceptible in smell. Put differently, smell maintains a crucial relation to the mediality of living: while we see limits and borders, we smell the medium and the middle. A scent's ability to insistently locate beings in the "atmosphere of the commons" brings out the fact of life's in-betweenness and the shared character of this in-between. The medium of air, modulated and made sensible in smell, is what is common to all. In it and in the common scents that accompany it, all terrestrial life, human and nonhuman alike, *shares exposure*, a sharing and an exposure that are simultaneously the great danger and the great chance of living.

The principle of selection of the five authors making up the investigation of this shared exposure of *Common Scents* can be articulated as follows: The four main chapters (on Hölderlin, Baudelaire, Nietzsche, and Brecht) are arranged into two pairs in complementary ways. In the first ordering, Hölderlin and Brecht frame the book as two of the most eminent poets of revolution in the Germanophone tradition. While Hölderlin's poetry responds to the French Revolution of 1789, Brecht's responds to the Russian Revolution of 1917 (and its failed, weak echo in Germany in 1918–1919). Hölderlin develops, through smell as a modulation of the *air*, a poetry of futurity that opens the present to a "coming revolution" that will supersede the French Revolution. Brecht, correspondingly but divergently, develops smell as an excretion of *bodies* (whereas bodies are almost entirely absent from Hölderlin's olfactory poetics). This corporeal, Brechtian

Introduction | 21

smell turns stinking human beings into "virtual revolutionaries" (Benjamin) that carry the potential of revolution even under the conditions of consumer capitalism's order of deodorization, which he experienced with special intensity while in exile from fascism in Los Angeles. According to Hölderlin and Brecht, "revolution's chances"[84] thus might lie precisely in smell's ability to figure revolution as an olfactory whiff that in its ephemerality disrespects all boundaries and borders, and cannot be subordinated to notions of property, force, or power. Between these two foremost poets of revolution, the book turns to the constellation "Baudelaire contra Nietzsche," as, respectively, an acutely smell-sensitive poet and a philosopher who took pride in his ability to smell what others ignore. Baudelaire's great interest in odors, in particular in the gendered question of perfumes, here constitutes the counterpart to Nietzsche's claim, in *Ecce Homo*, that his "genius" resides in his "nostrils"; a claim that points to (olfactory) corporeality as the touchstone of the value of life. Nietzsche's inclusion in a constellation of writers more readily identified as "poets" is justified in this context by the fact that his olfactory genius—implicitly positioned as rivalling Baudelaire's, as the third chapter will show—appears most forcefully in *Thus Spoke Zarathustra*, a work Nietzsche himself (rightly) called "a poetic work."[85]

In a second ordering, the construction of the book is made up of two different pairs. First, Hölderlin's and Baudelaire's treatments of odors constitute competing ways to delineate two beginnings of self-consciously modern poetry in the European tradition: tracing their respective use of olfactory tropes amounts to an investigation of poetry's relationship to the senses and hence to sense-making in the modern age. Nietzsche and Brecht then stand for two divergent and often opposed conceptions of revolution. Nietzsche's thinking of smell unfolds along the lines of his disturbing thought of the "eternal recurrence of the same," which echoes the old, astronomical meaning of "revolution" as a cyclical return. An avid reader of Nietzsche, especially of *Thus Spoke Zarathustra*, Brecht, by contrast, mobilizes smell for an explicitly Marxian revolution that would bring about a postcapitalist world, in which common scents index the commonality of communism. And finally, the epilogue directly confronts the desire for deodorization that inevitably eradicates undesirable odors (and, by extension, undesirable bodies). Francis Ponge's *Soap*, begun in 1942 at the same time as Brecht wrote his exquisitely fragrant *Hollywood Elegies*, addresses this question in the context of the *cleansing* effected by National Socialism and the possibility of resistance to it—the latter of which Ponge finds in the smell of mundane, everyday *cleaning*. The book's epilogic "cleanup" then ends with a term from Ponge that needs to be inscribed over all reflections contained in this book: the "object" of smell, if it is one, must be read through the "objoy" it imparts—a joy that, hopefully, opens up the shared, common space between writer and reader.

1

Hölderlin's Air

In the 1790s, revolution was in the air in Swabia, Friedrich Hölderlin's home. In the *Tübinger Stift*, where the poet studied with his classmates Schelling and Hegel from 1788 to 1793, "democratic and anarchic orientations [*Gesinnungen*]" (*KA* 3:612)[1] had taken hold after the French Revolution, leading Carl Eugen, Duke of Württemberg, to anxious interventions aimed at tamping down any sentiment of uprising or rebellion. Going to the source of this revolutionary fervor, however, could easily lead to devastating disappointment. One need only witness Johann Gottfried Ebel, an early translator of Emmanuel-Joseph Sieyès who had arranged for Hölderlin to find work in Frankfurt. Out of enthusiasm for the Revolution, Ebel had gone to Paris in September 1796, but, in a letter to Hölderlin written soon after his arrival in France, he speaks bitterly of his deep disillusionment concerning the state of politics in France.[2] Revolution might have been in the air in those years, but this air no longer seemed fresh and invigorating as much as stale and used up, at times even poisoned, suffocating, and depressing.

Of greater significance than Ebel's disappointment, however, is his friend's response. Hölderlin acknowledges that he shares the deeply felt sense of pain his friend experienced: "I know that taking leave of a place where one had seen, with great hopes, all fruits and flowers of humanity blossom once more is infinitely painful" (*KA* 3:251). These flowers of humanity—and flowers will be a central concern of this chapter—had blossomed briefly in a moment of hope. But like all flowers, they wilt, and one must take leave from their decay in a movement of infinite—that is, uncontained and uncontainable—pain. Yet beyond this shared commiseration, Hölderlin offers an incisive "consolation": "I believe in a coming revolution of all orientations and manners of imagination [*an eine künftige Revolution der Gesinnungen und Vorstellungsarten*] that will make everything prior blush with shame" (*KA* 3:252).[3] Despite all disappointment, the poet believes in yet another revolution that will put to shame everything that came before it— including all other revolutions that so quickly gave and give rise to disillusionment. Anticipating but not aligning with later discourses of repeated or "permanent" revolutions, Hölderlin is oriented here not toward a revolution that has already happened or that might occur in the present but toward a revolution that, for now, can only be designated as "coming." Put differently, today's wilted flowers of humanity orient us toward a coming moment of renewed and greater blossoming, and it is in floral decay that this renewal can be sensed.

Hölderlin's exacting phrase indicates what makes this coming revolution different from everything that preceded it: it will concern "Gesinnungen," which could be translated as orientations, dispositions, convictions, or attitudes. It is not a revolution of violent overthrow or seizing power, of positing rights or terroristic purges. It is rather an overturning of orientations or, more precisely, as the word *Gesinnung* indicates, an overturning of how *Sinn* is produced and functions. The coming revolution concerns sense: sense as meaning, orientation, and, as this chapter will argue, the senses of sense perception or *aisthesis*. All prior revolutions will be superseded by a revolution of sense, which, as was developed in the introduction, would be an eminently political revolution. Against certain notions that Hölderlin's interest in *Gesinnungen* constitutes a "merely" aesthetic conception of revolution, this chapter insists that weaving the question of sense into the question of revolution, as Hölderlin does, produces an expansion and intensification of the political question of revolution—and only in such a coming revolution of *Gesinnungen* can the embarrassing failure of prior overturning be overcome. The "belief" in this kind of revolution is not without a grounding in the present, Hölderlin goes on to argue: in the disappointment of his time, in the "fermentation and dissolution" that surround him, he detects certain "harbingers [*Vorbote*]" that announce what is to come. In processes of decay—in wilted flowers, for instance—one might discern signs of the future. The task of reading such harbingers in Hölderlin's own poetry is the task of this chapter: reading the announcements of a coming revolution, especially of how the making of *Sinn*, of *Gesinnungen* in the most copious sense, might be overturned. To read these indications of a coming revolution, one needs to take seriously, according to the argument developed here, the idea that revolution was in the air for Hölderlin, and more precisely, one needs to turn to the air that Hölderlin breathed and in which he wrote: what comes lies in the air, and relating to the air both prepares and detects this arrival.

Anthology: Reading, Hölderlin

Yet an obstacle to reading these revolutionary harbingers in Hölderlin immediately presents itself: few poets in the German and indeed European tradition are said to be as difficult, at times even impossible, to read as this poet who would come to be elevated to the status of "poet of poets." Not only the polished complexity of his middle or "mature" (*reif*) phase but, even more incisively, the unique eruption of an unheard-of poetic voice in his so-called late work and the rupture of the "latest," mad poet—both key concerns of this chapter—have raised the question of how this poet can be read and whether he can be read at all. As if anticipating the myriad challenges his readers would face, Hölderlin himself gives, at various points, indications of how one should read, and, indeed, how one should read him. One of the most forceful articulations of such advice to the reader can be found in the prologue to *Hyperion*, Hölderlin's only novel, the last version of which was written between 1796 and 1798, around the time he composed his consolatory letter to Ebel. Much of the novel consists in unfolding in ever greater complexity the dissonances that make up Hyperion's world, such as joy/suffering, man/woman, German/Greek, nature/art, evolution/revolution. Proper reading, according to the prologue, concerns just these dissonances and would aim at their "dissolution in a certain character [*Auflösung . . . in einem gewissen Charakter*]." To achieve this, two modes of reading must be avoided: "The one who merely smells my plant does not know it, and the one who picks it merely to learn from it, also does not know it" (*KA* 2:13). The parallel structure of the repeated "merely [*bloß*]" indicates that reading should neither be just like smelling a plant, which would produce "empty pleasure [*leere Lust*]," nor just like gathering it, which would be in the service of "mere thinking [*bloßes Nachdenken*]." Reading Hölderlin requires both thinking and pleasure, understanding as well as aesthetic enjoyment—a novel mode of reading that arises out of thinking through the plucking and smelling of a plant.

The success of such a reading faces a double threat. On the one hand, the "mere" picking or plucking of the plant stands as a metaphor for a reading that gathers up and appropriates. Reading on this model assembles, draws together, and establishes unifying relations; it establishes a certain commonality in the sense of bringing into a common, shared relation. Initially on a literal level: out of the multiplicity of letters, reading constitutes a (single) word, which then is related to a sense, out of the multiplicity of potentially infinite senses. Such gathering further occurs between reader and text: the reader is drawn into the sphere of the text, and the text is drawn into the sphere of the reader. And lastly, reading gathers the multiplicity of texts into a single "oeuvre" signed for and governed by the name of an author. The mere existence of a text is related back to an *auctor* who is considered the origin of these texts. Martin Heidegger, one of Hölderlin's most insistent readers, summarizes this model of reading as gathering in "What Is Called Reading?": "That which carries and directs in reading is the gathering [*die Sammlung*]. Onto what does it gather? Onto the written, onto that which is said in the writing."[4] Reading (*Lesen*), as the etymology of the German word already indicates, would then be nothing but an act of gathering or collecting (*die Lese*).

Yet the prologue to *Hyperion* indicates the danger of such an approach. Reading, as an operation that resembles picking a plant and gathering it, would be a reading that deracinates. The reader takes the text from the original context in which it grew organically, and violently inserts it into a new context, seeking to grasp and keep it. Cut off from its root, the text is subjected to the whims of a power that appropriates mere parts of it (leaving behind the roots, for instance) for its own purposes—purposes alien to the text itself. Appropriating a text in this way produces an emptiness, a gap: the alliteration of *Pflanze* (plant) and *pflücken* (pluck) in Hölderlin's text draws attention to their difference—the *Lücke* (gap) left after the plant has been plucked. This emptied-out place indicates that the fatal flaw of plucking-reading lies in a misunderstanding of the proper kind of dissolution: instead of resolving the "dissonance" between plant and human being, between text and reader, between object and subject, the second term in this constellation completely dissolves the first into its own sphere and leaves a *Lücke* where the object sought out for understanding used to be. This is the problem of mere reflection, of "bloßes Nachdenken." Mere thinking, according to Hölderlin's objection that already foreshadows his disagreement with some of the philosophers of his time (in particular J. G. Fichte), discovers only its own activity since for it the object qua independent object does not exist.

The counterpart to such failed reading qua gathering is figured as smelling a plant. In contradistinction to the gesture of plucking that takes into possession, smelling leaves the plant intact: it does not touch the plant itself but only engages with one of its emanations, its scent. The object is not dissolved into the subject by an act of seizing possession, of understanding as grasping (*be-greifen*), but is left whole, and wholly in its place, creating no gap or hole. Here, no gathering up, no keeping takes place but instead a letting be that substitutes the *dissipation* of smell for the grasping of possession. The (textual) object is allowed to disperse, and only via an entry into the sphere of this dispersal does the subject attempt to relate to it.

According to the prologue of *Hyperion*, however, reading cannot be only like smelling either: some unifying gathering, some deracination and appropriation always take place. The task of reading is rather to dissolve the dissonance between plucking and smelling. In other words, one should not only smell and not only pluck; rather, one should smell and pluck in conjunction; that is, to continue the figure, one should assemble a bouquet of plants that dispenses a joint scent—not in order to extract something from them that could be kept but to smell what is grasped and to grasp what is smelled. *Hyperion*'s prologue thus proposes an *anthological* activity in the literal sense, a gathering (λέγω) of flowers (ἄνθος), a "Blütenlese" or florilegium—but one that would be a joining and assembling not governed by the desire to unify but rather a gathering intimately related to the dissipation figured by smell. Reading qua olfactory anthology would draw together text and reader, subject and object, in a transformative relation that joins the two without dissolving one into the other. It would gather dispersal and disperse gathering, in a movement that could be named the movement of "common scents," where the dissipation of scent is located or brought into what is communal, shared, gathered up, led together, common.

Yet the very difficulty of Hölderlin derives from the fact that he himself throws into question the possibility of successfully following his advice to the reader. Both the ability to gather and the ability to smell—as well as their relation—are continuously reconfigured and, eventually, cast into severe doubt. This chapter traces the twists and turns of such a development in detail, but the grand arc of its trajectory can already be indicated by referring to the last Hölderlin, who from 1838 to his death signs his poems by a name other than his patronym: Scardanelli. Both Scardanelli and Hyperion, as Roman Jakobson and others have shown, should be understood as anagrammatic rearrangements of the poet's name:[5] these two names thus register the question of the unity of "Hölderlin," as well as the question of reading as gathering on a literal level—that is, gathering (and anagrammatically dispersing) by the letter. This act of dissolving and rearranging names, preserving and guarding their memory in a different form, in other words, of transposing a (seemingly, allegedly, hopefully, dreadfully) *proper* name into dispersal, occupies a decisive place in Hölderlin's work—exposing reading to the threat of expropriation and hence to the threat (or promise) of its failure.

Hölderlin-Scardanelli points to these limits of readability and anthology through the very act of an anthological plucking of flowers that has lost all reference to smell but stands in close relationship to *Hyperion*. This underdoing of olfactory anthology—this unsettling limit of reading—can be found only in the contested margins of Hölderlin's oeuvre: it can only be found in the reports about his life, in the third-party accounts of who Hölderlin became in the second "half of life," accounts whose veracity is always under threat. Those accounts confirm that Hölderlin's love for flowers endured even into the last years of his period of "madness," as, for instance, the writer Emma Niendorf attests: "Uhland sent him in the last few weeks another vase with flowers. Hölderlin lifted them with joy and admiration, looked at them and exclaimed: 'These are splendid-Asiatic [*prachtasiatische*] flowers'" (*FHA* 9:424).[6] Relatedly, it is precisely *Hyperion* that endures as the only work of his that Hölderlin accepts and that, in fact, continuously brings him great pleasure: "It is his *Hyperion* that can occupy him for days" (*FHA* 9:308). However, this love for flowers combined with the repeated confrontation with *Hyperion* leads to a disturbing perversion of the anthological activity found in the prologue to the epistolary novel. The author of the *Hyperion*-emulating novel *Phaëton*, Wilhelm Waiblinger, who spent a significant amount of time with the "mad" poet in the 1820s, describes the following, frequently recurring scene from Hölderlin's time at the household of the carpenter Zimmer, where Hölderlin was housed after being released from a psychiatric clinic: "He then entertained himself with picking flowers and when he had gathered a sizable bouquet, he tore it apart and put it in his pocket" (*FHA* 9:307). Concerning Hölderlin's life more than a decade later, another contemporary repeats these details in similar form: "His favorite place is open nature, but the latter is restricted for him to a small garden by the Neckar. Here, he often stays for days and nights and—tears out grass or picks flowers and hurls them into the Neckar" (*FHA* 9:329).[7] Throughout the years of his madness, Hölderlin-Scardanelli seems to do two things: reading Hölderlin-Hyperion—but how does a "mad" poet read?—and performing the very mode of anthology advised by that novel in a literalized and violently perverted form. It is as if, upon reading the delicate, complex instruction for anthological activity found in the novel, Hölderlin-Scardanelli goes out to enact this anthology in a manner that vacillates between gently mocking parody, violent rejection, and "mad," meaningless repetition. Is there meaning to be found in Hölderlin-Scardanelli gathering up a bouquet of flowers and throwing it into the Neckar? Or is it the eruption of nonsense, of a reality or a madness that eludes the framework of meaning, the blossoming of some threatening "flowers of evil"? Might a different reading, beyond meaning, be possible that lies in establishing a relation to whatever the phenomenon of the flower-throwing Hölderlin might be? And what happened to the activity of smell that has so thoroughly disappeared not only from Hölderlin-Scardanelli's perverse anthologizing but also, as this chapter will show, from his poems?

The Aerial Sphere, Modulated

The path to Hölderlin-Scardanelli's "mad" relationship with anthology and reading is long and complex. The world of *Hyperion*, that other anagram of Hölderlin's name, seems infinitely far from it. Yet it is in those earlier years of the writing of the epistolary novel that a more systematic inquiry into Hölderlin's task of a "dissolution of the dissonances," of what could be called his onto-poetological task, must begin. This task, alongside the concern with unity and gathering, finds elaboration and specification in contemporaneous letters and theoretical fragments. These reflections, in dialogue with the philosophical systems of Hölderlin's time, also constitute the principal foil for his poetic deployment of smell, of smelling flowers in particular: the trajectory of his poetic development indicates how scents constitute, in ever-intensifying fashion, one of Hölderlin's responses—as a poet—to the tasks of philosophy as he encountered them. In smell, Hölderlin stages a revolutionary overturning of the language in which thinking can occur, away from the "iron concepts" of philosophy and toward an ephemeral, olfactory language of poetic anthology and dispersal.

Just a few months before the publication of the first volume of *Hyperion*, Hölderlin writes a text, dated to winter 1796–1797 by his editor, D. E. Sattler, that addresses the "dissonance" found in the novel as the "strife [*Widerstreit*] between subject and object" (*FHA* 19:249). The *Fragment of Philosophical Letters*, the nucleus of a rewriting of Friedrich Schiller's *Letters on the Aesthetic Education of the Human Being*, argues that the conflict between subject and object cannot be resolved merely from the position of the subject, nor from the object alone. Instead, it is in the relation between the subject and that which surrounds it that the "strife" can be made to disappear and give rise to a different experience—namely, the experience of a spirit or god: "Neither out of himself alone nor solely out of the objects [*Gegenständen*] that surround him can the human being experience that there is more than a mechanical development [*Maschinengang*], that there is a spirit, a god in the world; but he can experience this in a livelier relation that is lifted above necessity [*in einer lebendigeren, über die Nothdurft erhabnen Beziehung*] and that relates him to all that surrounds him" (*FHA* 14:45). The relation through which an experience beyond "strife" takes place is livelier, more vivid than either of its relata. Echoing Kant's *Critique of the Power of Judgment*, which excludes all "interest" from aesthetics proper, and anticipating the young Marx's demand that the senses be freed from necessity, such an intensification of life goes hand in hand with, in fact appears equivalent to, a rising above need or necessity ("Nothdurft"): the crucial relation between subject and object cannot be one that occurs in a context of need.

One way to rise above necessity, according to Hölderlin, is to feel one's relation with one's element in a "durchgängiger" fashion. By the end of the eighteenth century, "durchgängig" had primarily come to designate something that is generally or universally the case. The older meaning, indicated by *Grimm's Dictionary*, giving the Latin equivalents of *pervius, penetrabilis*, however, can still be heard in Hölderlin's use of the word when he defines this relation as a "more manifold and more intimate relation [*mannigfaltigern und innigeren Beziehung*]" (*FHA* 14:46): "durchgängig" refers not to a thorough, all-covering relation of a fixed center point to a surrounding manifold, but rather to a relation in which the element goes through (*Durchgang*) the subject into its "innermost" being. The "through" of this relation affects the relata by thoroughly penetrating them and preventing their closure as mere poles of the relation. It designates a relation that is dynamic and whose intimate character derives from a movement (*Gang*) not between but into and out of the relata.[8] Achieving a "dissolution of the dissonances" between world and self, subject and object occurs in this interpenetrative, "more intimate" relation.

As the *Fragment* describes it, a relation that rises above necessity can only emerge in a "sphere" that is individuated and determined. What Hölderlin terms "sphere" could also be designated as *medium*: it is that which constitutes the middle, the in-between, that which englobes and opens the space of relation. In Hölderlin's poetry one of the major manifestations of such a determinate and individuated "sphere" is found in air, a contested but important term of his poetics.[9] In medial terms, the human subject always finds itself in the element of air, is surrounded by it, and relates to the world through it. Hölderlin's intense attention to the air thus anticipates in some ways the "atmospheric turn" in recent ecocritical and environmental humanities discourses indicated in the introduction: his poetic articulation of the air constitutes, as it were, an ecocritical intervention *avant la lettre* by thoroughly locating the question of the subject-object relation in the atmospheric medium that is the air.

Attending to the air, one can easily designate a relation in this sphere that is determined by "necessity": breathing. The base term of the comparative term "livelier" that marks Hölderlin's *durchgängigere Beziehung* is the "lively" of the merely physical need to breathe to maintain life. Breathing, in this sense, is simply a necessity-based relation to one's sphere; a "higher connection [*Zusammenhang*]" (*FHA* 14:46) will have to modify the relation to air beyond the necessity of breathing. Any such connection, in turn, must be felt or sensed: "so that he *senses* [*empfindet*] more thoroughly his more thorough connection with the element in which he stirs" (*FHA* 14:46; emphasis added). With respect to necessity, however, the aerial sphere is hardly perceptible. In fact, it altogether escapes perception when breathing as the necessary, need-based relation between the subject and its sphere constitutes the only relation to air; absent any respiratory troubles, the extreme habitual character of breathing prevents air from entering perception and instead constitutes only the baseline of the subject's continued existence. The medium in its pure, undisturbed, and need-responsive form, then, is not perceptible; only a modification that disturbs its purity can make it so. One such disturbing modification of air, in turn, can be found in smell. "The act of smelling," as is already argued by Aristotle in the closing sentence of book 2 of *De Anima*, "is an act of perception, whereas the air, being only temporarily affected, merely becomes perceptible [αἰσθητός]."[10] A disruption, in this case smell, enables the medium of air to enter *aisthesis*, from which, in its pure, unmodified form, it would otherwise be subtracted. In short, the olfactory modification of the aerial sphere allows it to enter aesthetics in the strict sense and rise above mere need to constitute a "higher connection."

In Hölderlin's work, smell is one of three main modifications of the sphere of air, which in the context of his poetry are more accurately described as "modulations" of air. The tripartite division of aerial modulations first becomes legible in Hölderlin's early poetry. While the latter is largely characterized by a striking conventionality, bordering on the epigonal (especially with respect to Schiller and Klopstock), it nevertheless provides a reliable overview of his poetic treatment of air: these three modulations will be a constant through line in Hölderlin's aerial-olfactory vocabulary, even if their differentiation and functionalization change and intensify continuously, especially in the "late" Hölderlin. Exemplarily for the early poems stand the following verses from a 1792 hymn, written while Hölderlin was still in the *Stift*, titled "Hymn to Love":

> Love brings to young roses
> Morning dew from high air,
> Teaches the warm airs to caress
> In the scent of the mayflower

> Liebe bringt zu jungen Rosen
> Morgenthau von hoher Luft,
> Lehrt die warmen Lüfte kosen
> In der Maienblume Duft (*FHA* 2:40, vv. 17–20)

The modulations are threefold: air can be warm—that is, receive a thermal modification; it can move, often as wind, here as a tender caressing; it can be scented.[11] These three modulations produce different spheres and correspondingly different relations between a subject and its surrounding element; all three, however, respond to the demand of a "dissolution of the dissonances."

With respect to poetry, each aerial modulation—warmth, movement, smell—constitutes a sphere whose relationship to poetry differs, with smell emerging as the privileged modulation since it figures the proper state needed to produce poetry. In the third maxim of a text edited as "Seven Maxims" or "Reflections," probably from 1799, Hölderlin develops *in nuce* a theory of poetic enthusiasm or inspiration, *Begeisterung*, a key poetological term of his time that Klopstock had reintroduced from the ancient poets. For Hölderlin, the poet's enthusiasm, his being in a state of spirit or *Geist* (*Begeist-erung*), depends on his soberness or sobriety (*Nüchternheit*). This soberness can also be understood as the keeping or gathering of one's senses, a "sober recollecting [*Besinnen*]" (*KA* 2:519). The "best" soberness or *Besinnen*, in turn, lies in a feeling that consists of two aspects: on the one hand, warmth, as that which spurs on spirit and produces its agility. On the other hand, a "tenderness" that "prescribes the limit to it [spirit]" (*FHA* 14:69). Tenderness limits spirit; warmth drives it onward—jointly they allow for sober enthusiasm. The lines from "Hymn to Love" offer an exacting image of this sober enthusiasm: "teaches the warm airs to caress / In the scent of the mayflower." In the scent of the flower, both warmth and tenderness are present and joined; they find what is common to them both. Smells move warmly and tenderly, thus spurring on and simultaneously limiting themselves just the right amount to produce "those more tender and more infinite relations" (*FHA* 14:48) of which the *Fragment* speaks. Smell consequently figures the state appropriate to producing poetry: *Duft* (scent), as the olfactory modulation of *Luft* (air) marked in the minute change of a single letter, joins *Begeisterung* and *Besinnung*; it modulates the sphere of air in such a way that the subject is enthused and sober, finds both *Geist* and *Sinn*, both spirit and sense.

Smell, carrying the characteristics of sober and enthused feeling, is thus a privileged modulation of air in the Hölderlinian poetic vocabulary for a reason that can be specified further by going back to the text of the *Fragment*. Air's warmth as well as its tender movement are felt by the "sisters, brothers" (v. 9) of the poem when the air comes into *contact* with them; in other words, with respect to these modulations, the subject's relation to air is superficial. Both thermal and tactile engagement with air leave the relata whole; air surrounds the subject but leaves it as a closed pole of the relation. By contrast, smell is "sensed" when scented air *enters* the subject via breathing; it penetrates the subject rather than merely making contact with it. This feature of smell had already been stressed in a negative vein by Kant, who emphasizes the "innig [inward, intimate]" character of smelling in his *Anthropology*: for him, the so-called mechanical senses (vision, hearing) are "senses of *perception* (superficial)" while the chemical senses (taste, smell) are senses "of *enjoyment* (innermost taking in) [*des* Genusses (*innigste Einnehmung*)],"[12] with smell, in fact, being "even more intimate [*noch inniglicher*]" than taste.[13] Smell thus constitutes the extreme case of a sensory intimacy or innermostness, which consequently enables an entering into an inward and intimate relation with the aerial medium that is not possible for the other senses. Only smell makes the medium of air as a thoroughly penetrative and non-superficial—that is, "innig"—medium perceptible as Hölderlin's *Fragment* demands it in order for the dissonances between subject and object to disappear. Olfaction, in short, figures a state of being in which the strife of "separations" disappears in intimacy without erasing division *tout court*. For the young Hölderlin, scents are the privileged modulation of the aerial element that enables poetry to address its onto-poetological task of lifting the shared, common sphere that relates subject and object into a state beyond necessity and beyond the strife of the subject-object division.

From Philosophy to Poetry, from *Anschauung* to Smell

The function of smell as one of three main modulations of the medium of air in the early Hölderlin is superseded by a novel olfactory poetics as the poet develops it in his middle period. The ode "Heidelberg," written in asclepiadic meter, stands for this new engagement with smell as it begins in Hölderlin's work around 1800, a date generally recognized as a major turning point in his trajectory. (This new engagement could similarly be traced in "Der Gang aufs Land" and other poems from that period.) In contrast to the earlier "Hymn to Love," fragrance appears in "Heidelberg" in isolation from the other two modulations of air—namely, warmth and movement: smell gains an independent specificity and is no longer understood as the coming together of tender movement and warmth—and it is this new articulation that also allows Hölderlin to sharpen his poetic divergence from the philosophers of his time, developing olfaction into the site of his objection to the "iron concepts" of philosophy and thus showing how poetry's relationship to *sense* constitutes the crucial point of its divergence from philosophy.

The decisive olfactory image occurs in the last of the eight stanzas of "Heidelberg":

> Shrubs came blossoming down to where in the bright valley,
>   Leaning against the hill or fond of the riverbank,
>   Your joyous alleys
>   Under fragrant gardens rest.

> Sträuche blühten herab, bis wo im heitern Tal,
>   An den Hügel gelehnt, oder dem Ufer hold,
>   Deine fröhlichen Gassen
>   Unter duftenden Gärten ruhn. (*FHA* 5:468)

The progression of the poem as it leads to these fragrant gardens can be schematized as a successive search for an image of the reconciliation of passing time and fixity, of human agency and nature, in short, an image of the "dissolution of all dissonances." At first, Heidelberg's bridge over the always flowing river figures a constellation of both movement and stillness. This image is superseded by the lasting transience of the natural river and the always returning "eternal sun" as they contrast with the ruin of Heidelberg's historic castle, which has been destroyed by the elements. The bridge as an image of a human-made reconciliation of transience and stability is thus overwhelmed by the moving river and the elements' power to destroy the castle, both standing for nature's triumph over human construction. The eighth and final stanza just quoted, however, reintroduces human agency and ability to construct lastingly in the image of the alleyways and gardens. The alleyways and gardens can resist the fate of bridge and castle, and instead lead to the final word of the poem, "ruhn," rest or calm. This singular reconciliatory force of the gardens can not only be attributed to a long-standing literary and cultural tradition that identifies gardens as the supreme reconciliation of nature and civilization, but also to these gardens in particular: Heidelberg's gardens of Hölderlin's time, as Dieter Henrich has pointed out,[14] were built on the ruins of the old, destroyed city, thus emerging out of the historical destruction of the civic.

The crucial difference between the fragrant gardens and the bridge can be further explicated with the conceptual tools of the *Fragment of Philosophical Letters*: as explicated above, whether a human being lives a "humanly higher life" depends on the question of necessity or need. As the second stanza of "Heidelberg" indicates, the bridge "resounds" from the "wagons" passing over it, an activity tied to remedying a lack or want. Building a bridge is a human activity that relates to the world as determined by necessity: the flowing river (an abyss, an *Abgrund* of sorts, to anticipate a term of great importance in the late poems read below) restricts the human being. Consequently, a human interaction with the river that lies in building a bridge does not rise above the demand to remedy this restrictive lack. By contrast, no such restriction can be found in the scented garden: it corresponds neither to a determinate need nor a physical obstacle; neither its origin nor its function is tied to necessity. In emphasizing the potency of smell's independence from lack and necessity, Hölderlin draws on a long tradition that goes back to Plato's *Philebus*, a text that in all likelihood would have been known to him given his extensive knowledge of ancient Greek texts in general and of Plato in particular. In the *Philebus*, Socrates and his interlocutor, Protarchus, discuss whether the good life is one of pleasure or intelligence (which could here perhaps be rendered as understanding, thus harkening back to the opposition posited in *Hyperion*'s prologue). In the course of the discussion that seeks to determine the right mixture of pleasure and intelligence, Socrates introduces a distinction between "pure" and "impure" pleasures. The impurity of pleasures such as eating when hungry or scratching an itch derives from the pleasure being inextricably mixed with pain; namely, the very hunger or itchiness they come to replace. By contrast, there are pleasures that are "felt by the senses, pleasant, and unmixed with pain" and "the want [ἐνδείας] of which is unfelt [ἀναισθήτους] and painless."[15] In a passage referenced by many modern artists and architects, Socrates then names three as falling into this category: "those arising from what are called beautiful colors, or from forms, most of those that arise from odors and sounds."[16] Smells, so the argument goes, "have no necessary pains mixed with them."[17] No previously felt pain or lack, no *Nothdurft*, determines olfactory pleasure since the lack of olfactory satisfaction is ἀναισθήτους, unfelt and imperceptible, and thus does not enter *aisthesis*, hence enabling olfactory satisfaction to enter *aisthesis* pure and unaffected by pain or want. The pleasure of the fragrant gardens is thus "higher" in accordance with the *Fragment*: because no pain is mixed into it, it enables an aesthetic experience that "lifts itself" over lack and thus constitutes a "livelier" relation. In short, in Heidelberg's fragrant gardens, *Durft* (need) becomes transformed, through the minute change of a single letter, into *Duft* (scent).

Of even greater importance is that the final image of "Heidelberg," beyond figuring a rising above necessity, constitutes Hölderlin's response to the philosophy of his peers and friends, what came to be called German Idealism;[18] Hölderlin develops, through smell, his response to the "ancient quarrel" between philosophy and poetry as it took place in his time. More specifically, the fragrance of Heidelberg's gardens constitutes a poetic transformation of a central term of post-Kantian philosophy: "intellectual intuition." This latter had been introduced into philosophical discourse by Immanuel Kant as a negative, limiting term: intellectual intuition refers to an intuition (*Anschauung*) that is non-sensible—that is, an intuition that is not receptive but rather spontaneous, in other words, productive out of itself. Kant hence names it an "intuitus originarius," or an "original intuition [*ursprüngliche Anschauung*]" that would be available to "the primordial being alone but never to a dependent being."[19] In such an intuition "possibility (thinking) and actuality (being) [would] coincide":[20] anything intellectually intuited must *be* by virtue of that very intuition.[21] Intellectual intuition consequently goes against the very bedrock of what Kant had established as the basic structure of the *human* faculties. According to his critical enterprise, anything we, as human beings, intuit must come from the outside and be given to us: there cannot be such a thing as a productive intuition.

This very term "intellectual intuition" becomes one of the key terms through which objections to the Kantian project are formulated, eventually leading to the development of the Idealist philosophies of Fichte (who gives the term its first full post-Kantian articulation in his *Aenesidemus Review*), and of Hölderlin's two friends and classmates, Schelling and Hegel. In dialogue with these thinkers, Hölderlin takes up *intellectuale Anschauung* at two decisive moments of his development. In the years of the completion of *Hyperion*, Hölderlin uses the term for the first time, in a text edited as "Judgment and Being" (Beißner) or "Being Judgment Possibility" (Sattler). Here, following his friend Schelling to a significant degree, Hölderlin radically reconfigures the Fichtean notion of intellectual intuition, which had tied it to the I: "Where subject and object are unified as such, not just partly, and are therefore unified such that no division whatsoever can be carried out without damaging the essence [*Wesen*] of that which is to be separated, there and nowhere else can one speak of a *being as such* [*Seyn schlechthin*], as it is the case with intellectual intuition" (*FHA* 17:156). Intellectual intuition concerns a state in which object and subject are joined "most intimately" (*innigst*), this intimate relation being such that it cannot be disjoined lest it is subjected to a violent act of "damaging." The name Hölderlin gives to this unification is "being as such [*Seyn schlechthin*]," without any reference to an I. The passage quoted above continues: "But this being should not be confused with identity. When I say: I am I, then the subject (I) and the object (I) are not unified in such a way that no separation whatsoever can be carried out without damaging the essence of that which is to be separated; to the contrary, the I is possible only through this separation of the I from the I" (*FHA* 17:156). The I, according to Hölderlin, is only possible through an opposition (*Entgegensetzen*) in self-consciousness; but such an opposition, like all acts of consciousness, requires the constitution of an object, a *Gegen-stand*. Intellectual intuition, in line with Hölderlin's anti-Fichtean impetus, cannot be the intuition of an I and is not a matter of "identity"; rather—and this will be decisive for olfaction's relationship with intellectual intuition—it is the intuition of an *inner, inward*, indeed, *intimate intertwinement of subject and object*, whose separation, even in an "analytic" operation, would be violent.

Intellectual intuition occurs for the last time in Hölderlin's extant writings in a text that begins "The lyric, in appearance ideal poem," dated to 1798–1799 by Schmidt and Beißner, to summer 1800 by Sattler, thus potentially written alongside "Heidelberg." In keeping with "Being Judgment Possibility," intellectual intuition is here said to be of "a unicity [*Einigkeit*] of everything living" (*FHA* 14:370).[22] Yet in contrast to the text from 1795, this "unicity" is *dynamized* and through this dynamic conception comes to include the very "separation" that "Being Judgment Possibility" designated as a violent injury of unity: the unicity of intellectual intuition "speaks itself the easiest" when one says that both "actual separation . . . and connection . . . are only a state of the originally one [*Ursprünglich einigen*] in which it finds itself *because it must step out of itself* [*weil es aus sich herausgehen müsse*]" (*FHA* 14:370; emphasis added). The unicity of intellectual intuition, far from resisting all division, instead requires a stepping out of unity into temporary states of division and (re)joining. The reason for this lies in the impossibility of unicity ever coming to a "standstill" that, Hölderlin writes, "cannot occur in it since the manner of unification must not always remain the same" (*FHA* 14:370). There is no unification that could become static: any standing still in unification calls for a stepping out of it and a reentering into new unicity, an ever-repeating process induced by the fact that unicity is always *too much* or *too little*: the "separation of the parts" takes place "because they feel themselves as too unified . . . or not unified enough" (*FHA* 14:371). For Hölderlin, in short, the unification of intellectual intuition is always hyperbolic, always stepping out and overshooting.

The final verse of "Heidelberg," the fragrance of the gardens, rather exactly figures intellectual intuition in all the complexity that accrues to it in Hölderlin's poetic transformation of his theoretical reflections. This can, in a first step, be shown through poetological considerations: In "The lyric" intellectual intuition is explicated as part of a larger development of a tripartite division of poetic tones, Hölderlin's famed *Wechsel der Töne* (variation or alternation of tones). According to this intricate poetics,[23] each tone is a "metaphor": the "naive" tone corresponds to "a feeling"; the "heroic" tone to "great striving [*Bestrebungen*]"; and, decisively, the "ideal" tone to an "intellectual intuition" (*FHA* 14:369). As a number of scholars have shown, "Heidelberg" ends, as most poems from that period of Hölderlin's work, in the ideal tone. By implication, this instance of the ideal poetic tone, as linked to intellectual intuition, is thus also correlated with the olfactory modulation of air—in other words, in the final moment of "Heidelberg," smell, intellectual intuition, and the ideal tone correspond to each other. Similarly, the naive and heroic tones can be linked to the other two modulations of air developed above: warmth and movement. Warm air figures the naive tone: the thermal modulation constitutes a metaphor of "a feeling," corresponding to the near equivalence of warmth and feeling developed in "Seven Maxims." Air modulated as movement or wind, in turn, corresponds to the heroic tone: while warm air harmoniously surrounds the subject, moving air opposes itself to the subject by exerting force on it and forming a resistance to it. It is thus the metaphor of an oppositional "striving." The correspondence of the fragrant gardens and intellectual intuition can similarly be shown on the level of the poetic image: in the garden, the human being qua (cultivating) subject and nature qua (cultivated) object are intimately "unified." Neither one can be separated from the other and both appear as moments of the intertwined "originally one [*Ursprünglich Einigen*]"; a separation of the two would "damage" the phenomenon of the garden. Furthermore, the existence of the subject as an "I" has been completely attenuated or even effaced: nowhere does the final stanza mention the "ich" that appeared in the first stanza. In the scented garden, in accordance with the early Hölderlin's conception of intellectual intuition, "being as such" beyond any violent separations of subject and object can be intuited.

But in accordance with the hyperbolic demand of unicity that Hölderlin's later reflections emphasize, the final image of a vivid unification figured in the gardens' fragrance cannot be one of self-containment or sufficiency. The descriptor "fragrant" figures this, too, with precision: the smell *emanates* from the gardens. While the last word, "rest," might at first suggest finality and closure, the smell evoked concerns rising up and dissipating outward. The peace of the fragrant gardens, the intellectual intuition that they figure more successfully than the bridge or the castle reclaimed by nature, is dynamic: the poem closes with an image of opening, performing precisely the demand "it must step out of itself" (*FHA* 14:370), as "The lyric" phrased it. "Heidelberg" thus produces the "stepping out" characteristic of Hölderlin's last word on intellectual intuition, disallowing any standstill. The poem's final image of the garden goes out of itself; it transcends itself in the scent that arises from it—the poem transcen*ts* itself.

This transcenting articulates a suspicion that was only barely legible in Hölderlin's "theoretical" writings on intellectual intuition but that now emerges more clearly: the suspicion that the German word translated as "intuition," *An-schauung*, is, in fact, a misnomer for the process that occurs in the beholding or rather sensing of the complex movement of unicity stepping out of itself. The visuality of *An-schauung* as a "looking at" always implies a distance and thus a "separation" between the one looking and what is looked at. It implies an object as Gegen-*stand*, a setting opposite (*Entgegensetzen*) as "Being Judgment Possibility" emphasized, and thus already precludes the higher unicity Hölderlin seeks to articulate—by drawing on a visual term, the "iron concepts" of philosophy restrict thinking to a structure that is at odds with what they seek to think. As it emerges in Hölderlin's poetry, olfaction, by contrast, is more fitting: its literally *durchgängig* (that is, "thorough" in the sense of *going through*) character, with smell emanating from the object, entering the subject, and being returned out of the subject into its surroundings, dilutes the "Gegen" (counter, against, ob-) character of intuition so far that it approaches more closely the movement of intellectual intuition as thought by Hölderlin. This is registered clearly by the stanza progression of "Heidelberg": scent emerges at the end of a series of substitutions in the visual-auditory register, indicating that only a shift out of these aesthetic registers into the olfactory register suffices to address the task posed to poetry. (Some of Hölderlin's late poems, as will be shown below, perform a similar sequence of substitution.) The progression of the poem indicates that "being as such" is not locatable as a conditioned, determinate *Gegenstand*, but rather, like scent, is always simultaneously "most intimate" and elsewhere in its "stepping out," at the same time intimately going through and beyond itself—and it is for this reason that poetry carries the day in its ancient quarrel with philosophy: poetry articulates, beyond the strictures of the "iron concept" of *Anschauung*, being's unicity in a movement of transcenting.

Sinnlicher Lateness

Barely half a year after the completion of "Heidelberg," probably in the winter 1800–1801, Hölderlin provisionally finishes an elegy titled "Bread and Wine." This elegy opens with an image of "gardens" that are, like Heidelberg's gardens, marked as fragrant: "and the fountains / Always welling and freshly flowing next to fragrant beds [*an duftendem Beet*]" (KA 1:286). Part of a calm, resting city ("Round us the city rests" reads the first verse), these fragrant gardens are the setting for the arrival of "night." This night is the temporal condition marked by an absence of, or ignorance on the part of, the gods: "But friend! we come too late. Though the gods are living / They live above our heads, up in another world" (KA 1:289). Our condition is that we come "too late [*zu spät*]." Whatever other relationship to the gods used to obtain, we arrive after it, in a time that no longer allows for such a relation. In this time of being "too late," our condition is marked by disunion, parting, and severance. Consequently, the image of the opening stanza, the peaceful fragrance of the gardens that constituted a last echo of "Heidelberg," appears in a new light: whatever accomplishment of reconciliation and unicity scent might have figured just a few months before is now cast into doubt by the articulation of a radical division and abandonment. This condition of lateness thus reconfigures smell's privileged position as figuring the unicity of being as such: olfaction no longer unfolds in a context where final reconciliation and unification appear possible, but rather must be rethought and rearticulated in the temporal condition of a "lateness" marked by scission and dissensus.

Hölderlin's own description as "late" has been echoed in literary studies in the development of the category of his *late poetry*, generally said to begin around the time of "Bread and Wine." This category seeks to contribute to a periodization of Hölderlin's stunningly rapid poetic trajectory as an attempt to account for the unheard-of voice erupting in the years after 1801; it is likewise part of a more general attempt by figures such as Theodor W. Adorno and Edward Said to develop an account of "lateness" as an ordering term for literary and cultural production.[24] With respect to Hölderlin, however, lateness is rarely linked to his own understanding of having come "too late."[25] In fact, most accounts of the starting point of his lateness and the reason for this marked shift instead seek recourse to one of two options: eros or politics. The first option refers to Hölderlin's spurned love, his failed relationship to the already married Susette Gontard, who for Hölderlin was his "Diotima" and "a being in this world with whom my spirit can and will linger for millennia." The second option detects a growing disillusionment with the aftermath of the French Revolution and with the republican aspirations in the German states in the years right before and after the turn of the century, and attributes to them a radicalizing and intensifying effect on Hölderlin's poetic praxis, thus explicitly tracing a poetic revolution in relationship to political revolution.[26] Without questioning the validity and, in certain cases, even the necessity of these approaches, lateness will here be read without direct reference to the erotic and political events occurring in Hölderlin's life. Instead, as the rest of the chapter will argue, the lateness of Hölderlin's late poetry can be understood through the reconfiguration of the role of olfaction in his corpus: after "Heidelberg" and its poetic transformation of the "iron concepts" of philosophy, the late poetry moves even further in developing smell's relationship to unicity, and it is precisely this transformed relation between olfactory sensibility and unicity that contributes to a definition of Hölderlin's lateness. In other words, Hölderlin's engagement with both the question of poetry's relationship to philosophy—its ability to address the ontopoetological task of a "dissolution of dissonances" that philosophy fails to live up to[27]—and the structure, function, and *Sinn* of *Sinnlichkeit* are altered in a way that leads to and constitutes his late poetry. Hölderlin's lateness can be found, not exclusively but decisively, in a rethinking of the function of the senses—and this reconfigured sensibility also reconfigures what "too late" might mean when it turns, in the last of the late poems read below, from a thinking of the night described in "Bread and Wine" to a thinking of the air of the morning or tomorrow (*Morgenluft*).

Increased attention to the senses and the sensory in the late Hölderlin has been diagnosed by several scholars, both as the prevalence of "concrete" sensuousness and in the form of synesthesia.[28] Hölderlin's olfactory lateness more specifically departs from two verses that appear in the *Homburger Folioheft*, in a marginal note to the draft of a hymn that will be crucial below: our condition can be understood as a state of being "in doubt and irritation / For more sensuous are humans" [in Zweifel und aergerniß, / Denn sinnlicher sind Menschen]. In the late Hölderlin, in which the calm and peace of the final image of "Heidelberg" and the opening image of "Bread and Wine" are abandoned—they will return, transformed as a "generic" calm or peace, in the "latest" Hölderlin—they are abandoned in the face of "doubt" and "irritation," both deriving from the *intensification* of sensuousness marked by the comparative "sinnlicher." No longer is the problem addressed in *Sinnlichkeit* posed in a context where the finality of calming could be reached, even if it is a finality of "stepping out of." Instead, human beings have become doubtful of any calm and are cast into an irritation that is marked by intensified sensuousness—and thus also by a *more of sense*, even if this more is shot through by the bifurcation of doubt.

The late intensification of the sense of smell, then, is related to the question of unicity, not unlike synesthesia, which is generally understood as a quest for a unity of the senses. This link between smell and unicity lies in two tendencies at odds with each other. First, the late poems intensify the importance of air and smell as the element most conducive to addressing the onto-poetological task of poetry, especially with respect to the question of unity. Air and smell allow in privileged form for the emergence of what Walter Benjamin, in his reflections on the late Hölderlin, calls—with a paradoxical turn of phrase—the "monarchy [*Alleinherrschaft*] of relation" (*GS* 2:124). Benjamin argues that, in the late poem he interprets ("Blödigkeit," often translated as "Timidness"), "all units of the poem already appear in an *intensive interpenetration* [*intensiven Durchdringung*]; the elements are never graspable in a pure state but only the joining of relations [*das Gefüge der Beziehungen*] in which the identity of a single being is a function of an infinite chain of concatenations through which the poetized unfolds itself" (*GS* 2:112; emphasis added). Benjamin names this "intensive" spatiotemporal penetration or permeation characteristic of the late Hölderlin the "plasticity of shape [*Plastik der Gestalt*]" or the "plasticity of being [*Plastik des Daseins*]" (*GS* 2:119). Yet this interpenetration finds even more intense—it is still a question of comparatives here—expression in the "Durchgang," the going through of smell, replacing the visual-tactile connotations of "plasticity." In other words, what Benjamin discovered in the late Hölderlin is further sharpened when what he calls the "*intuitable* elements [*anschaulichen* Elemente]" (*GS* 2:108; emphasis added) are removed from the sphere of vision and touch and placed in the aerial-olfactory sphere that is more conducive to the articulation of Benjamin's key insight: air as medium is, in fact, the "middle of all relations" (*GS* 2:124). The "anschaulich" of Benjamin's analysis might be read as the remainder of a terminology that resists the very establishment of the supreme reign of relationality that Benjamin discerns as key to Hölderlin's lateness: the *sinnlicher* olfaction of the late Hölderlin, by contrast, is more conducive to the emergence of the "monarchy of relation."

Secondly, and seemingly pulling in the opposite direction of the reign of the all-pervasive relationality just described, the late poems tend in their *sinnlicher* character toward subtracting themselves from this quest for unity in a *disarticulation of unity*:[29] if smell both figures and transforms the unity of intellectual intuition in the middle period of Hölderlin's work, then its function with respect to unity in the late Hölderlin is intensified as the suspension or falling apart of this very unity. By subtracting itself from the quest for unicity, late olfactory sense-making constitutes a "revolt against synthesis," as Adorno formulated it in his well-known essay on parataxis in the late style of Hölderlin. Adorno, however, limits the extent of this revolt by referring to what he sees as the inherently synthetic nature of all language: "The paratactic revolt against synthesis attains its limit in the synthetic function of language as such. What is envisioned is a synthesis of a different kind, language's critical self-reflection, while language retains synthesis."[30] The *sinnlicher* disarticulation at stake here, by contrast, does not recognize such a "synthesis of a different kind." Rather, the task or, more exactly, the *Aufgabe* (that is, the task *and* the failure) of poetry is now to disarticulate this very unity: it traces the lines of fissures, of breakage, and of opening that come to disrupt the calm, polished, and ordered unicity that "Heidelberg" displayed in paradigmatic fashion.

Adorno's phrasing of a "synthesis of a different kind, language's critical *self-reflection*," points to the crucial moment at which Hölderlin's olfactory lateness diverges from the recuperation of unity as the philosopher imagines it. This can be seen in a double sense. First, olfaction undoes both "self" and "reflection." Reflection functions on the model of speculation—that is, of the seeing of (oneself as) an other. In other words, it belongs to the field of *Anschauung* that Hölderlin's poetry aims beyond with its olfactory tropes. Similarly, the term "self" no longer holds up in the face of the disarticulation taking place in lateness; instead, its dispersal or dissemination, as will be shown in greater detail below, replaces it. Secondly, and even more urgently, when Adorno envisions a self-reflection *of* language, then poetic language's use of olfactory tropes resists such a self-relation in peculiar fashion: while language is (at least partially) visual (in writing) and auditory (in speech), thus allowing language to reflect itself and reflect on itself in the poetic treatment of certain visual or auditory tropes (say, an echo or a mirror) and articulate its visuality (in the spatial, optical arrangement of verse) and audibility (in particular in rhyme and rhythm), this does not hold for olfaction: language does not smell. An olfactory trope, then, does not allow poetic language to turn toward itself in the same way as a visual or auditory trope might—instead, it opens language to a different mode of sense-making, beyond or to the side of any model of "language's critical self-reflection."

Taken together, these two tendencies of the late Hölderlin—a tending toward the monarchy of relation, on the one hand, and toward a disarticulation of unity, on the other—suggest that his late poetry aims to develop an *all-pervasive relationality that does not constitute a unity*—and, harkening back to reflections developed above, one name of such a relationality might be "common": the common names all that which stands in relation without becoming unified. In sum, the decisive import of Hölderlin's intensified olfactory sensuousness lies in its ability to articulate relationality as precisely emerging out of the fissures, breaks, gaps, dispersals, and dissipations that open up any unity. It is the task of reading these late poems to demonstrate just how late scents achieve such an endeavor.

A Geopoetics of Smell

The complex disarticulation of the unifying tendency of smell leading to the monarchy of relations that occurs in the late, *sinnlicher* Hölderlin finds one of its most forceful formulations in two verses from "Patmos," a late poem that marks the climax of his olfactory poetics: "here and there [*da und dort*] / Infinitely God disperses the living" ("Patmos," v. 121–122). For Hölderlin, smell is, like "the living [*das Lebende*]," always "da und dort": when present, it opens a place (*da*), but as this opening it is not "here" but only elsewhere (*dort*). It can neither be grasped (it is "hard to grasp" as a different line from "Patmos" reads) nor definitively localized. It is therefore everywhere and nowhere: its atmospheric, ephemeral character constitutes a unique type of place that is disseminated and dispersed but nevertheless takes place.

These disseminated places, as both "Patmos" and Hölderlin's other late poems make clear, must be thought in relationship to the earth (once more anticipating ecocriticism's recent interest in "earth" as an ordering term for critical inquiry). The "disarticulation of unity" of the late poetry occurs through a proliferation of olfactory locales that dot the earth, being dispersed all over it but in this very dispersal being brought into relation. Hölderlin's olfactory poetics is thus a "geopoetics of smell" in the strict sense: it is the earth on which smell, in a literal sense, *takes place* both by occurring in relation to it and by constituting earthly places.[31] His poems, in a way, constitute an "olfactory travel report," an account of the journey of poetic spirit through differently scented places. This journey produces poetic experience (*Erfahrung*) in a strict sense: poetry is a "fahren" through, going through poetic space; the undergoing of a transformative movement that takes, in the case developed here, from one fragrant place to another. The principle underlying such poetic *Erfahrung* and Hölderlin's geopoetics can be called, with a precise phrase coined by Luigi Reitani, "a principle of *topographical difference*."[32] Accordingly, each element of Hölderlin's geopoetics of smell attains its defining features only as a part of the larger economy of which it is but one part; its distinctive characteristics emerge from it being other than the places, structures, and movements it stands in relation to and is contrasted with. A differential determination of olfactory places thus eventually aims at what Heidegger calls an *Erörterung*: it "asks about the placeness of place [*Ortschaft des Ortes*]."[33] In other words, a geopoetics of smell asks, via the question of how smell takes place on the earth, what "place" in Hölderlin's late poetry means and how it relates to the dispersal and dissemination of both places and scents.

The terrestrial dispersal articulated by this geopoetics cannot be thought apart from its temporal dimension. The temporal reach of Hölderlin's olfactory geopoetics is spanned open by two locales whose designations are thoroughly temporal: on the one hand, a place designated as an olfactory origin; on the other, a journey into the Far East of the poet's own time that opens onto an undetermined future. Both are located, significantly, in Asia and indicate the frame in which all other olfactory moments of Hölderlin's poetry find their differential localization. First, origin. An incomplete *Gesang* ("song," as Hölderlin calls his late poems) titled "The Eagle" traces the east–west movement of civilization from its Asian origins through Greece and Italy to Germany. The origin of the eagle's flight—that is, of the *translatio* of civilization—lies precisely in a place marked by a strong fragrance out of which the westward movement's trajectory begins: "But in the beginning / Out of the forests of the Indus / The strongly fragrant one / My parents came" (*StA* 2:229, vv. 9–12). The notion of a strongly fragrant ("Starkduftenden") origin of civilization is in line with the philosophy of history dominating Hölderlin's time, especially Herder's work. This philosophy of history is bound up with an imaginary of human difference that is, while not coterminous with, nevertheless intimately connected to the intensifying colonial and imperial projects of that time:[34] *Sinn*, in this racializing imaginary, is differentially distributed across different groups of humans, where "sense" is alternatively understood as sensuality (attributed predominantly to non-European and southern European peoples) or as reason (as opposed to nonsense, then attributed to the Germans). With respect to the alleged fragrant origin of human history, Herder thus argues in his *Ideas for a Philosophy of the History of Humanity* (1784–1791) that Asia stands at the origin of human civilization and is deeply suffused with odors: "The Indian," he writes, has the most refined sense of smell among all the peoples and he "breathes desire: he swims in a sea of sweet dreams and enlivening smells."[35] Hölderlin, who was intimately familiar with Herder's work, takes up this thought of the Indus as fragrant origin and places all further olfactory locales of his geopoetics *after* an emergence out of this "strongly fragrant" place.[36] This, then, can be recovered from "The Eagle" beyond the racializing imaginary of human difference: geopoetic movement is predicated on an emergence out of a strongly fragrant origin. All olfactory locales on the earth are, on the one hand, comparatively weaker scented than the origin and hence marked by a diminution of *Sinnlichkeit*; conversely, intensifying sensuousness reestablishes a relation to the origin. On the other hand, olfactory locales owe their movement and dissipation, their mobility and dispersal precisely to this leaving behind of strong fragrance; their comparative weakness indexes their distance from the origin and with it their ability to move and transform.

The second pole of the late Hölderlin's olfactory geopoetics is equally found in Asia, but as a contemporary movement toward, not out of, this fragrant place. The journey is found in the fragmentary song "The Titans," which is located in the *Homburger Folioheft* right next to "Patmos." The pertinent verses from "The Titans" read as follows:

> But I am alone.
>> and sailing into the ocean
>> The fragrant islands ask
>> Where they have gone (*FHA* 8:675)

The poetic I is "alone" since "Many have died" and the remaining men have sailed off toward fragrant islands—that is, toward the "Spice Islands," as the East Indies were known.[37] These verses echo a well-known line from the song "Remembrance": "But now to Indians / The men have gone" (vv. 49–50).[38] The adventurous, heroic seeking of fragrance (spice) leaves the poetic I behind. Yet, in contrast to the movement of emergence out of origin that the eagle traced, the movement of these seafaring heroes is not unidirectional, at least it is not intended as such. The men set sail to retrieve fragrance and then bring it back to their home. This is a commercial movement, where commerce designates an exchange that always returns, that must return for it to be a *commercium*. While the *translatio* of "The Eagle," spurred on by the strong fragrance of the origin, was a singular, albeit complex, movement of unidirectional transfer, the spice trade constitutes a continuous, reciprocal cultural exchange that binds together foreign cultures, through the possibility of a commercial, seafaring crossing over and returning. The relation it would constitute, if it were to succeed, would be a two-way movement; it is the possibility of a going toward the foreign origin and then returning from it that is at stake in this poetic articulation of the spice trade. And the possibility of such a return is of the highest importance since the state of aloneness deeply troubles the poetic I: "It is good to hold / To others. For no one bears life on his own" (*KA* 1:391), as the continuation of the poem states. With the departure of the men toward the "fragrant islands," the very possibility of bearing life is thrown into doubt: the dissemination at stake in Hölderlin's geopoetics cuts to the core of the ability to live. Only a successful return of those seeking out fragrance would enable living.

Yet it is precisely this return that "The Titans" describes as having faltered: the seafaring heroes are missing. Their main function in the poem is to throw up the question "where they have gone." The syntax of the verses suggests that the question could be ascribed to the fragrant islands as the questioning subject: the seafaring men might then be thought to have begun their return journey from the islands, loaded with fragrance. But the men cannot be located with precision: they have set off into the ocean, and whether they will bring back the fragrance of Asia to the poetic I's homeland remains undetermined. In other words, fragrance is caught in an in-between stage where the utter failure of a return that would complete the two-way movement is possible but not confirmed. In this in-between state, the establishment of a new, unheard-of relation to the origin of culture can still succeed, but all that the poetic I is left with, for now, is a question. "Not yet, however, / Is it time" read the opening lines of "The Titans": in the last instance, the question of the Spice Islands points to a future that has not yet arrived and whose arrival is all but certain. These two olfactory instances—the emergence out of a strongly fragrant origin and the uncertain, doubtful question posed by the attempt of a reciprocal, two-way exchange relation that opens onto a future—measure out the span of the late Hölderlin's geopoetics of smell.[39]

The Smell of Lemons

The dispersal of geopoetic movement and the uncertain, in-between moment of the poet are unfolded in paradigmatic fashion in a late fragmentary *Gesang* that begins with the words "Namely from the un-ground" ("Vom Abgrund nemlich"); that is, in a poem that begins with a departing not from an origin but from an abyss—and that will move toward the city, the civic of civilization, as the geopoetic place where smell attains a new function and effect. This movement, as a tracing of the poem's trajectory will show, is both *ecstatic* and *eccentric*:[40] it moves through and out of the center (in this case the city of Frankfurt), out of any central point that would hold together, and it spurs out of any standing, out of all *stasis*. Of great import for Hölderlin's poetics is the insight that this eccentric and ecstatic condition is tied to the possibility of voice ("Stimme") and song ("Gesang")—and that both of these *ek-* qualifications are linked, in "Namely from the un-ground," to smell: smell introduces a diremption, in the form of *olfactory pains*, into any standing, and this painful smell is found elsewhere, outside of the center, precluding the gathering into one central point. Hölderlin thus develops an intensified and more complex version of the Freudian thesis, outlined in the introduction, that smell stands in a disruptive relationship to the civic and to civilization and hence is pushed to civilization's margins—that is, out of the civilized and civic center. Analyzing Hölderlin's poetic articulation of this thought thus also enables a better understanding of smell's revolutionary force: its ability to overturn established states and lead out of fixed, stable hierarchies—all of which occurs here in relationship to a reflection on poetry and poetic voice.

The fragment in question is found on a well-known page from the *Homburger Folioheft*, numbered 75 in the *Frankfurter Hölderlin-Ausgabe*, at the top of which stand the words "Die apriorität des Individuellen über das Ganze" (The apriority of the individual over the whole) and that also contains the verses concerning the "doubt" and "irritation" produced by the "more sensuous" condition of human beings that were quoted above. The sketch of the poem, edited differently by each editor, begins with the following lines:

> Namely from the un-ground we have
> Begun and walked
> Like the lion
> Who peers out
> In the fire
> Of the desert

44 | Hölderlin's Air

> Vom Abgrund nemlich haben
> Wir angefangen und gegangen
> Dem Leuen gleich,
> Der luget
> In dem Brand
> Der Wüste (*FHA* 8:851)

The poem begins by simultaneously designating "our" mode of beginning and, since these are its first words, its own mode of beginning: "vom Abgrund," from the abyss or the un-ground. In the perfect tense, it presents the paradox concerning the ground of the beginning of the poem's *Gang*: an *Abgrund* is precisely that which does not enable a beginning "from," *vom*. The poem's ground from which it pushes off is an un-ground. There is no starting point, no (thetic) position that grounds the poem's movement; there is only a doubled setting in motion through prepositions that designate a movement away from: *vom ab-*. A locomotion without an originating locus—hence the perfect tense, only ever designating that the beginning of the motion must have taken place since now, in the time of the poem, it moves.

Moving, the poem names, and names first and foremost its ungrounded beginning: "Vom Abgrund *nemlich*," "*Namely*, from the un-ground."[41] The first operation of naming in this poem, so the "namely" highlights, names the un-ground from which the poem sets off. Names are here not a *mis en abyme*, a setting into an abyssal relation of self-referential or non-referential play, but more precisely a setting *off* from such an abyss. The poem includes "its" un-ground by naming it as that which precedes it and is excluded from it. If in the beginning was the word ("we have / begun"), then this word only names what is excluded from naming. The words "Namely from the un-ground" break the word's status as *archē*, as origin and governing principle, and substitute for it the ungrounded, unfounded beginning of a named *vom ab-* movement.

Having set off, the movement of the poem finds itself in the desert. From the un-ground emerges a desolate and inhospitable, uncultivated and wild place. The danger posed by this wildness, however, is quickly domesticated by an apotropaic replacement of the lion by a dog, and of the desert by gardens: "But soon, like a dog, my voice will walk / In the heat of the gardens' alleys." Recalling the gardens of "Heidelberg" and, more faintly, of "Bread and Wine," these gardens are structured by passageways ("Gassen") that guide the movement through them. Only now, once the process of domestication has reached the state of gardens, with all their implications for the relationship between nature and civilization that were unfolded above, can "my voice" be introduced. The first explicit pointing to the linguistic act of poetry, previously only implied in the "namely" of the opening line, this voice is inscribed into the difference between two place names that both begin with the word "Frank."

> But soon, like a dog, my voice will walk
> In the heat of the gardens' alleys

Where human beings live
In France
But Frankfurt, according to the shape that
Is the imprint of nature
Namely of the human being, is the navel
Of this earth.

Bald aber wird, wie ein Hund, umgehn
In der Hizze meine Stimme auf den Gassen der Garten
In den wohnen Menschen
In Frankreich
Frankfurt aber, nach der Gestalt, die
Abdruk ist der Natur
Des Menschen nemlich, ist der Nabel
Dieser Erde. (*FHA* 7:350)

The emergence and movement of poetic voice are ascribed to the "human beings" who "dwell" in France. This latter, as *Frankreich*, is contrasted ("but") with *Frankfurt*, meaning that poetic voice belongs to France but not to Frankfurt.[42] This contrast is further articulated by the poem along two dimensions that must be understood as two different versions of civilization:[43] first, the German city, in which Hölderlin lived for a time alongside his philosopher friend Hegel, is associated with "Gestalt" or shape; this is civilization, qua the civic, as formed and figured. Instead of the wandering, turning movement associated with the voice found in France, Frankfurt combines in this "Gestalt" a single "imprint" of nature and humanity: "according to the shape that / Is the imprint of nature / Namely of the human being." Given the complexity of the relationship between nature and human being in Hölderlin's work elsewhere, the smooth transition from "of nature" to "namely of the human being" is striking: Frankfurt stands for the accomplished and calm attainment of a gestalt that captures, on the model of an imprint, the joining of human being and nature. This gestalt makes Frankfurt into the "navel" of "this earth." It designates Frankfurt's geopoetic position as center and origin.

Yet the poem does not dwell in formed, central Frankfurt, but rather moves back to France, back to where "voice" was possible. In other words, "Namely from the un-ground" develops a movement out of gestalt and articulates what kind of poetic movement emerges when the center and its formative power are abandoned, and the poem's movement enters its "Ausland," the foreign lands.[44] In France, poetic voice is transformed into song, in a transformation that completes the domestication of movement in the fortification of a city: "but now to hold forth, fortified song / of flowers as a new formation from the city" ("nun aber zu gestehen, bevestigter Gesang / von Blumen als neue Bildung aus der Stadt").[45] From the naming of the abyssal un-ground through the semidomesticated voice, the poem arrives now ("nun") at fortified song as a "new formation from the city." All wildness is domesticated and civilized, in a city that echoes Frankfurt but cannot be identified with it since the center has been left behind: it is formed (*Bildung*) and as a formation it can stand—"gestehen" not only designating "to confess" or "to hold forth" but also, in an older linguistic layer, meaning a "strengthened," or fortified, standing.[46] The firmness and stability of song result from the erecting of a stand that brings to a standstill the *gegangen* and the *umgehn* of the previous verses: the city ("Stadt" also deriving from standing) marks the opposite pole of the excluded un-ground from which the poem initially set off as the point of standstill of the movement away from the unground. Yet this fortification contains within itself the traces of the movement that brought the poem to this point: the gardens through which the voice wandered return in the form of flowers, so crucial to Hölderlin's work and his intensifying trajectory. Through this paradoxical linkage of the fragile flowers and their fortification, poetry seems to narrate the process of reaching a state of reconciled civilization. Put differently, this song of civilized flowers seems to finally solve the onto-poetological task that Hölderlin's work continually faced: it proposes a harmonious "dissolution of the dissonances," in this case dissolving the dissonances of firmness and fragility, of lastingness and ephemerality—the song of *Bildung* leads together, in a quasi-anthological, gathering operation, the delicateness of flowers and the rigidity of civilization.

These flowers implicitly conjure up scents, and the progression of this song precisely moves toward a smell. Yet this smell turns out to be painful and threatens to subvert all fortification and every firm stand and hence any reconciliation:

> but now to hold forth, fortified song
> of flowers as a new formation from the city, but where
> to the point of pains a smell of lemons rises
> up to the nose, from Provence

> nun aber zu gestehen, bevestigter Gesang
> von Blumen als neue Bildung aus der Stadt, wo
> Bis zu Schmerzen aber der Nase steigt
> Citronengeruch auf, aus der Provence (*FHA* 7:350)

At the very moment when the novel formation of fortified song is reached, a sharp dissonance splits apart this standing: from the "Provence," another movement indicating, *prepositional* name, disruptive, dangerous sensuousness returns in this smell of lemons, a smell so sensuous that it produces pains. The city, which had still partly resembled Frankfurt's unifying gestalt function, is now disrupted by a pain that repels: the latter's principal effect is a reaction of flight, avoidance, or setting off. Civilization qua the civic is disrupted and a split within *Sinnlichkeit* is introduced: while the implied smell of flowers existed in harmony with fortified song, the smell of lemons—set off from and indeed in opposition to the preceding phrase by yet another "but"—pushes away from song. Here, too, Hölderlin's poetry is engaged in a project of adapting and reordering the terms of Kantian philosophy. In his *Anthropology from a Pragmatic Point of View*, Kant develops a theory of pain that precisely hinges on its motive and its splitting force: pain is that which "immediately (through the senses) drives me to leave the state I am in [*meinen Zustand*] (to step out of it)."[47] Pain effects a movement of going out of a state understood as a *Zu-stand*; it produces a veritable emergence out of a standing still or a stasis. Pain, in other words, disrupts any *verweilen*, any "lingering" that, as will be shown in greater detail below, is crucial to Kantian aesthetics: it is in this sense that the pain of the smell of lemons produces a stepping out of song that would be a fortified, closed *Zu-stand* of civilization that enables Kantian beauty. Song can neither stand nor linger: it must move.

The ecstatic character of this non-fortified, intensified smell, its "more sensuous" character and the pain it produces, thus destabilizes the very firmness of "fortified song." This disruption has far-reaching consequences: the late Hölderlin's poetry repeatedly raises the demand for firmness as a key poetic imperative, most insistently in the closing verses of the first, completed version of "Patmos" that will be analyzed in detail below. "Patmos" demands, in one of its best-known verses, "that the solid letter / be taken care of" ("daß gepfleget werde / Der feste Buchstab") (*StA* 2:172). If taking care (*pflegen*, one version of culture) of the solidity or firmness of the letter constitutes the poetic vocation, then the threat posed by smell is grave: the painful, ecstatic quality of the "more sensuous" disruption is not some minor inconvenience but rather goes to the heart of the task of song. The unsettling of "fortified song" by olfactory pains registers a major disturbance in the functioning of poetry: faced with intensified *Sinnlichkeit* in the form of the smell of lemons, song falters and loses its firming and forming, civilizing and cultivating function.

The curious designation "smell of lemons," *Citronengeruch*—a hapax legomenon[48] in Hölderlin's work—illuminates the transformation of *Sinnlichkeit* effected by the late Hölderlin that underlies this vexing tension between song and smell, between *Bildung* and olfaction. The best-known literary occurrence of lemons in Hölderlin's time, and arguably still in German letters today, can be found in Goethe's *Wilhelm Meister's Apprenticeship*, published in 1795–1796, less than a decade before Hölderlin wrote "Namely from the un-ground." The first line of the poem known as "Mignon's Song," which opens the third book, reads, "Do you know the lands where the lemons blossom" ("Kennst du das Land, wo die Zitronen blühn").[49] Lemons here are endowed, in their blossoming, with an attractive force: the words "Dahin! Dahin!" close out each of the three stanzas. Goethe's lemons are part of the alluring and beckoning path of the bildungsroman; the foreign country that they are associated with harbors no threat or disruption but instead contains the promise of formation, education, and enriched civilization. In "Namely from the un-ground," then, Hölderlin seems to remember and address Goethe's criticism that his poetry was too abstract and that he knows nature "only via tradition [*nur durch Überlieferung*]" (Goethe to Schiller, June 28, 1797): it is as if Hölderlin deliberately takes up one of Goethe's most accomplished moments of concrete sensuousness—but only to show the literary giant and his readers that such a moment does not lend itself to calm contemplation as part of the southbound journey of a bildungsroman.[50] Indeed, it is precisely *Bildung* that Hölderlin's lemons disrupt: undoing the Goethean reduction of the lemon to a blossoming, Hölderlin foregrounds their painful smell and opposes it to the "Bildung" of fortified song.[51] This smell of lemons, however, should not be misunderstood as a "wild" or thoroughly uncivilized phenomenon since it also derives from cultivation: the lemons of Provence are part of the large, time-honored agricultural production of that region. The tension that the smell of lemons articulates is consequently the tension between two dueling conceptions of civilization and cultivation: the firm, static song of *Bildung* and gestalt, on the one hand; an ecstatic, *pro-* movement that disarticulates form, stasis, and stand, but nevertheless maintains a relationship to cultivation, on the other.

The force of the disruption of Goethean, *Bildung* sensuousness is captured in the "pains" triggered by the smell of lemons. These pains might express, as Martin Heidegger argues in his 1942 lectures on Hölderlin's "The Ister," a knowledge of difference: "But pain is the proper knowledge of being different [*des Unterschiedenseins*]."[52] On this reading, the pain accompanying the smell of lemons would be the indication of the difference between the fragrant object and the smelling subject: the two never converge completely, but an ineluctable difference between them remains; the "dissolution of the dissonances" aimed at in the onto-poetological task fails. For Heidegger, however, this separation of pain merely appears as the precondition for the ultimate belonging together of that which is separated, as he goes on to argue in the passage just quoted, here with respect to the painful difference between humans and the gods: "But pain is the proper knowledge of being different in which the belonging to each other of humans and gods first has the separation of distance [*Geschiedenheit der Ferne*] and hence of the possibility of closeness and thus the good fortune of appearing. Pain belongs to being-able-to-show [*Zeigen-können*]; it belongs to the poet as the knowledge of his own being."[53] Aside from the question of whether pain can indeed become "knowledge" and might not instead always resist knowing, several aspects of the Hölderlinian lines indicate the inadequacy of Heidegger's approach to pain for the question of the painful nature of the smell of lemons. Instead of belonging to the poet as the "knowledge of his own essence," pain is set off from song by a "but": it disturbs the fortified song reached just then and sets the stand of fortification back into motion through its rising up. Similarly, the pain does not accompany the poet's *ability* to show ("Zeigen-können") but rather happens to an indirect object ("der Nase" is dative): the nose is *exposed* to this pain, where this exposing, to echo a famous dictum by Paul Celan, might very well be the condition of poetry. This exposure does not turn into an ability but is instead given, arriving from elsewhere. Heidegger seeks to re-domesticate the "schmerzlicher Riß," the rip of pain, as Hölderlin terms it in one of his Pindar translations, by inscribing it into a "belonging to each other": the verses quoted, by contrast, give no indication that the smell of lemons belongs to anyone or anything, neither to the nose nor to the city; its movement is rather one of mere exposition. This exposition, resisting a gathering, can be read most insistently in the plural form "pains [*Schmerzen*]" as it contrasts with Heidegger's "the pain [*der Schmerz*]": that which produces the scission within song is not itself a singular phenomenon that could be named by a definite article. The splitting brought about by these olfactory pains is not a sundering into a duality that could be reassembled into a synthetic unity but rather produces a multiplied *splintering* whose multiplicity cannot be precisely counted or determined.

These olfactory pains, then, indicate something rather different from Heidegger's conception of Hölderlin's pain: they name a double disarticulation of unity. First, they produce an unworking of the unity of the sensory subject: not only does the nose (which constitutes an extremely rare reference to the body in Hölderlin's treatment of smell and his poetry, which generally contrasts sharply with that of Baudelaire, Nietzsche, and Brecht, whose olfactory poetics is primarily linked to bodies), not only does this nose appear here in isolation from a more fully formed human being, but the dative case "to the nose" further indicates that the sensory subject is a subject qua being *subjected* to this experience; its sensory experience is nothing but subjection and exposure to smell. Secondly, this disarticulation repeats itself on the level of song: a gap between song and *Sinnlichkeit* is introduced just when their final convergence appears to have been reached in the fortified, civic song about flowers. The smell of lemons pushes away, back from song, as the opposition between city and smell of lemons contained in the "but" indicates. This smell thus also pushes back from the song that names and sings *it*; it pushes back from the very poem that contains it, or rather that contains its site of exposure. The aesthetic-poetic principles of representation and articulation that would guide formed and forming song are thrown into a state of severe doubt and unworking. At this point of a radical destabilization of poetry caused by and articulated through smell, the question poses itself: What different kind of poetry might emerge from this exposure and this disruption? How might song respond to the exigencies of such a smell?

Breathing the Future

The beginning of a response to these questions can be found in the song "Patmos," a poem that not only constitutes the culmination of Hölderlin's geopoetics of smell but also one of his most intense articulations of the "coming revolution" with which this chapter opened: in "Patmos," smell—through the disruptive force that the lemons introduced—opens up the future and, by that very token, makes sensible a coming revolution. Hölderlin began writing "Patmos" in 1802, in the context of an intra-Christian polemics concerning the status of scripture, more precisely, concerning the question of the firm, formed, fortified, and unchanging nature of scripture: the pietistic Landgrave von Homburg, a minor nobleman in the ever-shifting landscape of German states, had asked Friedrich Gottlieb Klopstock for a poem countering the Enlightenment-inspired, historical-critical approach to interpreting the Bible that was gaining prominence at the turn of the century. Klopstock declined due to his deteriorating health and because he thought he had nothing more to add to his already numerous publications on religion, including the *Messiade*, a poem of considerable import to Hölderlin. The latter, having heard of the landgrave's wishes through his friend Isaac von Sinclair, produced a poem in lieu of Klopstock, and dedicated the completed version to the landgrave. Yet, crucially, the poem's polished version that responded to this specific occasion does not subsist: Hölderlin continuously reworks and unworks his text, and it is in those revisions that the decisive progression of the poem is located; Hölderlin's late poetry and its sense gain specificity and force precisely in their re- and unworking.[54]

"Patmos" opens with a stanza that joins and transforms the two key versions of poetic movement found in the sections above—namely, the setting off from an abyss, on the one hand, and a movement across water, more precisely, a movement between insular, "most separate [*getrenntesten*]," positions, on the other. While "Namely from the un-ground" sought a poetic movement that departs from the un-ground and gains its motion through a prepositional structure, "Patmos," in its first stanza, seeks a different relation to the un-ground: "and fearlessly over / the abyss walk the sons of the Alps / On bridges lightly built" (*StA* 2:165, vv. 6–8). It is here a question of going across the *Abgrund*, or, more precisely, as the prepositions "über ... weg" indicate, of finding a *Weg*, a path over the abyss: in the center of the stanza stand bridges, and these bridges thus not only cross over the un-ground but also bridge the two halves of the stanza itself. In the second half of the stanza, the possibility of a movement across the un-ground becomes the object of an invocatory poetic prayer of sorts that closes out the first stanza: "So give us innocent water / O wings give us, with sense most loyal / To cross over and to return" (vv. 14–15). In contrast to the bridges of the "sons of the Alps," whose identity must be left suspended here, the first-person subject of this stanza asks for a different mode of crossing an abyss: the prayer for water indicates that one possibility for a movement across an *Ab-grund*, a movement between "mountains most separate," is to turn these "peaks" into islands in a sea of water. While such a seafaring movement would be volatile, insecure, and *ungrounded* in a precise sense, it would nevertheless enable a crossing-over that creates a path (*Weg*). "Patmos," then, opens with the poetic subject asking for the possibility of a movement that acknowledges the impossibility of a firm and secure movement but can still guarantee safe passage and return: not only a going over to what is most separated, "on mountains most separate," but also a turning back, a *trope* that enables the turning of the path (ὁδός, *Gang*) of the poem to cross the "un-ground" and to return (to itself). Remarkable for not being reworked in any version of this heavily worked-over poem, the last line of the first stanza—"To cross over and to return"—thus explicates both the thematic desire of the poetic I and the formal task of the poem itself as a tropic, turning endeavor. All of this is tied, in the first stanza already, to the question of *sense*: the movements of the I and the poem are guided by the "most loyal sense [*treuesten Sinns*]." Unfolding the exact shape of this sense and the movement it elicits then becomes the task of the rest of the poem.

The following three stanzas explicate this turning endeavor and the attendant development of sense as a tripartite, geopoetic movement: first, the second stanza describes the "abduction" of the poetic I away from its "home" (v. 24); this abduction leads to "Asia" (v. 31) in the third stanza; and finally, in the fourth stanza, from Asia westward, a return that pauses halfway on the titular island. As a number of commentators have pointed out, the sensory vocabularies describing Asia, on the one hand, and Patmos, on the other, are marked by a stark, albeit by no means entirely consistent, contrast.[55] The aesthetic regime governing Asia is predominantly visual: "in fresh splendor [*in frischem Glanze*]" (v. 25), "blinded" (v. 31), "gold-adorned" (v. 35), "in the light" (v. 38), to name just the most striking ones. Patmos, by contrast, is both introduced via hearing ("And when I heard / That of the near islands one / Was Patmos [*Sei Patmos*]," vv. 51–53) and is marked in its most powerful descriptions as auditory: "Lamenting / for home" (vv. 64–65), "she gladly hears" (v. 68), "her children / The voices" (vv. 68–69), "the sounds / They hear him and lovingly / It resounds" (vv. 71–72). Further analysis, however, shows that this visual/auditory dichotomy is shot through, not unlike the movement found in the last stanza of "Heidelberg," by an urgent concern with an altogether different, third aesthetic regime: an aesthetics of air and smell. While already present in the first, "completed" version of "Patmos," the presence of aerial-olfactory concerns increases considerably as Hölderlin revises the poem again and again: the emphasis on sight and hearing gradually dissolves and is replaced by a subdued but insistent thought of air and olfaction. In this shift toward air and smell, poetic language also crosses the limit of Adorno's understanding of the late Hölderlin: neither "self-reflexivity" (a specular, visual model) nor an echoing is available to the reworked language of "Patmos." Poetic language is opened to an aesthetic regime radically severed from itself, foreclosing a turn of the poem to itself. In the ever-intensifying revisions of "Patmos," the language of the late Hölderlin cannot relate to "itself" but is opened beyond itself—a replacement that is symptomatic of the "unfinished," open structure of the later rewritings of this song.

In terms of this aerial-olfactory aesthetic, the first pertinent moment occurs in a formal position that could hardly be endowed with more significance: the triadic structure of the stanza divisions of this poem, of great importance to any analysis of this highly regular (in its first version) poem, situates "to return [*wiederzukehren*]" (the last word of the first stanza) in relation to two other terms, the words closing out stanzas two and three: "fragrant" and "palaces." The geopoetic move toward Asia goes through several visual images to culminate in an olfactory peak, as it were:

> But soon, in fresh splendor,
> Full of secrets
> In golden smoke
> Quickly grown up
> With strides of the sun
> With a thousand peaks fragrant
> Asia blossoms for me . . .
>
> Doch bald, in frischem Glanze,
> Geheimnisvoll
> Im goldenen Rauche, blühte
> Schnellaufgewachsen,
> Mit Schritten der Sonne,
> Mit tausend Gipfeln duftend,
> Mir Asia auf . . . (vv. 25–31)

Standing in the structural position of "to return," "fragrant" modifies the second occurrence of the "peaks" of mountains in "Patmos," suggesting that these fragrant mountaintops maintain a decisive relationship with the "mountains most separate" from which the poetic I seeks safe return in the first stanza. Asia, as was shown above with respect to "The Eagle" and Hölderlin's transformation of Herder's philosophy of history, is said to be the fragrant origin of civilization, and it is this origin of civilization toward which the poetic I of "Patmos" is "abducted" or "led away" from its "house" and "home [*Heimath*]." This movement toward the fragrant origin, then, transforms the *Heim* of *Heimath* into the secret of *Geheimnis* ("geheimnisvoll"): origin offers no home, but—*secretus*—is that which is set apart and separated.[56] The fragrance surrounding the origin indicates this ambiguous inaccessibility: the "peaks" of Asia remain "most separate" but nevertheless allow the poetic I to enter an (aesthetic) relation with them precisely via their smell. Origin provides no place in which one could dwell but instead exerts a force that produces a movement toward and away from it, mediated by its smell.

The third stanza, adding the word "palaces" to the series made up of "to return" and "fragrant," intensifies this inaccessibility: the fragrance emanates from "witness to life immortal / On inaccessible [*unzugangbaren*] walls / Age-old the ivy grows" (vv. 40–41). *Unzugangbar*: the fragrant origin to which the poetic I has been abducted after its invocatory plea for safe passage turns out to be inaccessible and secret, and thus turns into a veritable point of stoppage blocking the poem's *Gang* or movement. These inaccessible walls, containing *in nuce* the outlines of "another teichology,"[57] belong to an architectonic construction that in Kant's third *Critique* appears as one of his first examples of beauty: palaces. Set on yet another mountaintop, these palaces bear olfactory traces: the "festive / divinely built palaces" are "held up / by living pillars, cedars and laurels." The cedar tree has been known since antiquity primarily for two qualities: on the one hand, its wood is lauded for its incomparable resilience stemming from its hardness or firmness, its *Festigkeit*; on the other, it is said to have unsurpassable olfactory qualities.[58] The cedar palaces thus mark the hope for a *synthesis of firmness and fragrance*: in contrast to the formation-disturbing smell of lemons, the smell of cedars is not opposed to fortification but conversely emanates precisely from such firm resilience and durability. But "Patmos" immediately puts such a remarkable synthesis beyond human grasp: these cedar palaces are "divinely built" (v. 45).[59] Producing a synthesis of firmness and fragrance is the prerogative of the divine: capturing fragrance and stabilizing its ecstatic as well as its eccentric character (one could read a palace as marking the center) is impossible for mortals.

This inaccessibility thus forces the poetic I to redirect its path away from the divinely built, firm, and secure palaces. In other words, having run up against *Unzugangbarkeit*, "Patmos" goes elsewhere. It leaves Asia behind and, at the beginning of the second triad of stanzas, turns to islands, the islands between Asia and the poetic I's home, as the beginning of the fourth stanza elaborates:

> But around Asia's gates there murmur,
> Pulling this way and that
> In the uncertain plain of the sea
> Shadowless straits enough,
> Yet the skipper knows the islands.

> Es rauschen aber um Asias Tore
> Hinziehend da und dort
> In ungewisser Meeresebene
> Der schattenlosen Straßen genug,
> Doch kennt die Inseln der Schiffer. (vv. 46–50)

Among those islands, one in particular attracts forcefully, named here in the central verse of the first stanza of the second triad with a peculiar turn of phrase: "Was Patmos [*Sei Patmos*]." The subjunctive, here employed to render indirect speech, already indicates the ontological diminution of this island. Patmos is characterized by poverty, a lack of light ("dark grotto") that contrasts it with the blinding light of Asia, and an almost desert-like lack of "springs [*Quellen*]" that indicates its distance from the (Asian, fragrant) origin.[60] On such an island, no "thousand peaks fragrant" can exist; palaces built from fragrant and firm trees give way to a "poorer house." In short, the desert-like character of Patmos stands in an inverse relationship to the olfactory riches of palaces and gardens. This reduced, subdued *Sinnlichkeit* accords with the island's *exilic* character:

> And when, shipwrecked or lamenting
> For home or
> The departed friend,
> One of the foreigners
> Draws near to her, she gladly hears it

> Und wenn vom Schiffbruch oder klagend
> Um die Heimath oder
> Den abgeschiedenen Freund
> Ihr nahet einer
> Der Fremden, hört sie es gern (vv. 64–68)

Patmos belongs to the foreigners. Since both *Heimath* (home) and the *Geheimnis* (secret) of origin are closed off in their inaccessibility, all that is left is an exilic, foreign, insular, poor, and ontologically diminished place. In particular, Patmos welcomes and is hospitable ("gastfreundlich") to all those whose plea for safe passage ("to return") was confounded in lamentation and shipwreck, in a moment that echoes the fragmentary poem "Die Titanen" analyzed above: some seafaring heroes do suffer defeat and fail to return and cross over the abyss of the un-ground; they are *abgeschieden*, deceased and separated.

The central stanza triad of "Patmos" articulates this condition of *Abgeschiedenheit*, with all the multivalences this word harbors, as the world-historical condition after the event that constitutes the core of this poem: the disappearance of Christ.[61] Among the many complex aspects of these stanzas, the key event for the questions posed here is the *apostolic dispersal* after the death of Christ and the various ways in which his memory may be guarded in such dispersal—because the guarding of this memory precisely concerns not only the possibility of a regathering or a unity of dispersal but also the question of the appropriate aesthetic register (visual, auditory, or, perhaps, aerial-olfactory), or, in other words, the exact shape of "most loyal sense." A first such attempt would be to forge an image, as the eleventh stanza indicates:

> Even though the mine shaft holds iron
> And glowing resins the Etna,
> And so I would have the riches
> To form an image, and, in his likeness,
> See how he was, the Christ

> Zwar Eisen träget der Schacht,
> Und glühende Harze der Aetna,
> So hätt' ich Reichtum,
> Ein Bild zu bilden, und ähnlich
> Zu schaun, wie er gewesen, den Christ (vv. 162–166)

The *figura etymologica* "Ein Bild zu bilden" draws attention to the fact that this would be a visual memorialization of the vanished Christ. The very material needed for such an image (iron) indicates that this image would be marked by firmness and durability. It also points to such an image's incompatibility with the locus of the poem, Patmos, since the island was introduced as the "poorer house" (v. 62), thus lacking the "riches" required.[62] Instead of such a rich remembrance of Christ, then, the closing lines of "Patmos" turn away from iron-clad images to a remembrance in and through language, more precisely in and through the "care" and "interpretation" of the "firm letter": "that the solid letter / be taken care of and the existing [*bestehendes*] be well / Interpreted" (vv. 224–226). The firmness of the cedar palaces (inaccessible and set apart from human beings due to their "divinely built" origin) and of the iron-made image of Christ (it, too, rejected) returns one last time in transformed fashion: it is the letter alone that can receive the attribute "firm" and still remain in the human realm. The task of poetry is to care for the firmness of the letter qua "Buch-stab": the second part of this word originally meaning "that which supports, renders stiff." The remembrance of Christ in the dark night of his absence is made firm in the letter that stands, *Be-stehen-des*. In the first, completed version of the poem, then, the visual-auditory dichotomy between Asia and Patmos is dissolved into the letter of language that must be thought of as both visual (as an inscription) and auditory (as at least potentially spoken), joining in standing firmness.[63]

Some scholars have suggested that this hardness is, in fact, the defining feature of Hölderlin's understanding of poetry: poems "must be superlatively hardened, dense [*dicht*], denser, the densest, so dense that nothing denser can be thought beyond it. And this was what Hölderlin understood poetry to be: a joining of language with the highest possible density in the smallest space possible."[64] Yet the fate of "Patmos" itself, very much like the fate of "fortified song" that becomes disrupted by the smell of lemons, undermines any such claim: all firmness is undone by a difficult-to-determine succession of repeated alterations, deletions, and rewritings; in this poem, the stand of the *Bestehendes* of the letter is continuously destabilized and fails to achieve any new mode of enduring—a failure that is also marked by a shift away from the visual-auditory synthesis achieved at the end of the "completed" version of "Patmos." In the last consequence, these revisions propose an altogether different poetry than the one envisioned in the closing lines of the version gifted to the landgrave. This other poetry would be "richer" and "more wondrous" or "more miraculous" than before:

> John. Christ. Him I wish
> To sing, like Hercules, or
> The island which was held firm and saved. . . .
> But that
> Does not work. Differently it is a fate. More wondrous.
> Richer, to be sung.
>
> Johannes. Christus. Diesen möcht'
> Ich singen, gleich dem Herkules, oder
> Der Insel, welche vestgehalten und gerettet. . . .
> Das geht aber
> Nicht. Anders ists ein Schiksaal. Wundervoller.
> Reicher, zu singen. (*StA* 2:181, vv. 151–157)

Again, the poem faces an inability to go somewhere: "Das geht aber nicht" ("But that / Does not work") designating an impasse. A singing of Christ that would be like a singing of an island "held firm and saved" is impossible. No singing of Christ can hold firmly or steadily; it is never in a state of salvation where the saving has already occurred. The fate of song is different: more wondrous and miraculous, since to speak of something one cannot grasp and hold steady goes beyond com*prehension* and is strictly incomprehensible. It is this incomprehensibility that marks the turning of the poverty of Patmos into a greater wealth: singing Christ must achieve the incomprehensible by making more out of less, by turning diminution into riches.

This "differently" poetry has a precondition that goes to the heart not only of Hölderlin's olfactory poetics but also of the status and function of his late poetry more broadly. This precondition, in fact, must be grasped and comprehended:

This we must
Grasp first. Like air of the morrow are namely the names
Since Christ.

Begreiffen müssen
Diß wir zuvor. Wie Morgenluft sind nemlich die Nahmen
Seit Christus. (*StA* 2:182, vv. 162–164)

The three modulations of air developed above—warmth, wind, smell—are replaced by an altogether different modulation, one that also alters the notion of a medial modulation: *Morgen-*. This "Morgenluft" is marked by an irreducible ambiguity, an ambiguity that takes up the multiplicity of meanings contained in the "coming revolution" so dear to Hölderlin. On the one hand, "Morgenluft" is the air of the morning and the dawn, of the beginning of something new that has already begun; the night of "Bread and Wine," for instance, would be superseded by such an arrival of morning. But on the other hand, it is also the air of *morgen*, of the indexical tomorrow—and as such, always still to come. In this sense, the word "Morgenluft" marks and announces an altogether different air, whose only determination is that its determinations are still outstanding. All prior modulations of the medium, along with their ontological or poetological functions, are superseded by this modulation that remains to come.[65]

The lines just quoted develop this to-come with exacting specificity: in this different and "more wondrous" poetry, all *names* open onto a radically undetermined future. It is names that are like "Morgenluft"—that is, their determinations remain to come.[66] All names only announce the coming of something new, something not yet determined—they name only that their naming is still to come. The tropological structure of these verses, however, complicates this correspondence between "Morgenluft" and names: "*Like* Morgenluft are *namely* the names." The "namely" of the departure from the abyss of "Namely from the un-ground" returns in this *figura etymologica*, which by repeating the etymon of "namely" and "names," replaces the previously used figure of this type, "ein

Bild zu bilden" (to form an image). It highlights that the simile concerning the character of names is constituted by an operation of naming—but this very naming, too, remains to come and undetermined. To the demand of a song that would hold steady and grasp (*vesthalten*), that would determine names through its poetic means, "Patmos" responds, "But that / Does not work." What must be grasped first and foremost, a priori ("This we must / Grasp *first* [zuvor]"), is precisely the withdrawal of names from all grasping. Any poetic determination of names—and here even the word *Morgenluft* must be seen as falling under the purview of this transformation of names—must show the to-come character of just this determination: whence the irreducible ambiguity in the meaning of "Morgenluft" as morning and tomorrow. Poetry names that its own naming, too, remains to come.

Morgenluft thus rigorously marks an opening onto the future of all determination. In this way, it returns in reconfigured form to the diremptive function of the smell of lemons. The ecstatic and eccentric disarticulation of unity, which had introduced a painful fissure into both the subject and the poem, opens the very fissures of futurity. Only through this fissuring can an opening occur; only through the disarticulation of unity can an indeterminate, not-yet-determined future arise. This opening function is also indicated by the only other use of "Morgenluft" in the extant writings of the late Hölderlin; the overall orientation of this earlier passage from "Germania," however, strongly contrasts with the revised "Patmos":

> O drink the airs of the morning
> Until you are opened up
> And name what lies before your eyes;
> No longer may the unspoken
> Remain secret
> After it was veiled for long

> O trinke Morgenlüfte,
> Bis daß du offen bist,
> Und nenne, was vor Augen dir ist,
> Nicht länger darf Geheimnis mehr
> Das Ungesprochene bleiben,
> Nachdem es lange verhüllt ist (*KA* 1:336–337)

In these verses of "Germania" (the rest of the stanza seems to weaken and even take back the demand voiced here),[67] the opening of *Morgenlüfte* appears to be preparatory for the exhortation to name the "secret" that is no longer allowed to remain "unspoken." By contrast, the "Morgenluft" (in the singular) of "Patmos" does not indicate that any unspoken secret would finally be spoken; it is not an opening onto a final naming of truth or Parousia. Rather, it opens precisely onto that which is *not* "before your *eyes*": it opens onto that which cannot be seen and cannot, at least in a visual sense, appear or be presented to the eyes—the phenomenality of the future is subtracted from the visual realm.

The enjambed addition "Since Christ" unfolds this fate of names on Patmos with greater precision: "Like *Morgenluft* are namely the names / *Since Christ.*" As Wolfgang Binder has argued with respect to this passage, "Since Christ history [*Geschichte*] no longer narrates closed stories [*Geschichten*], examples of which are the myths of Heracles and Peleus, but rather unforeseeably open events that are 'richer, to be sung.' Within the horizon of salvation history, which brings everything temporal into the light of the eternal future, historic figures, deeds, and names become symbols of a futurity, which wafts within them like the air of the morning."[68] Binder combines in this passage two ramifications of the appearance and disappearance of Christ in world history. On the one hand, all events and deeds *after* Christ obtain only preliminary validity. They do not establish fixed or firm (*vest*) historical markers but merely point to the return of Christ and the final but still outstanding Parousia. On the other hand, all events and deeds *before* Christ also change status: while these had constituted the steady and continuously existing narrative that enabled the intelligibility of the world and of life (this, to be sure, is one of the main functions of myth), their ability to stand firm is *evaporated* by the appearance of Christ. Previously, the structure of time and space, human relations and relations between the mortals and the divine were governed in strict and firm accordance with these myths, even if they, internally, might have been dynamic. Christ, by contrast, stands for—perhaps is nothing other than—the supersession of any and all mythic fixities and their opening onto an "uncertain" future.

It is crucial that this Christic disruption of myth is articulated via the phenomenon of "Morgenluft" since the impetus to move away from mythological names to an aerial or elemental phenomenon is part of a larger strategy in the late Hölderlin: "mythology," as Brigitte Duvillard among others has argued, "is made transparent onto appearances in nature. The renunciation of mythological personifications leads to a consistent naming of the gods in accordance with the sky, which underscores their atmospheric lack of shape and boundaries."[69] The late Hölderlin, in keeping with the intensified *Sinnlichkeit* developed above as one of the criteria of his lateness, turns to meteorological, atmospheric, and sensible phenomena to articulate what in myth receives determinate names: it is this "atmospheric lack of shape and boundaries" that allows the late Hölderlin to effect his reconfiguration of the shape of the gods and of determination more generally.[70]

Yet the verses "Like *Morgenluft* are namely the names / Since Christ" do not limit their scope to only mythological (Greek) names or historical names, or even both; they concern all names, even and especially, the name—if it is one—of "Christ."[71] The determination of this name, too, stands under the doubled "Morgen" of a morning and a to-come. Consequently, "Christ" cannot be subsumed under the demand of a "care" for a "firm letter" and the interpretation of the "existing [*Bestehendes*]" that the complete, first version of "Patmos"

Hölderlin's Air | 59

delineated. Instead, Christic firmness is replaced by lingering and transience, as another late revision of Patmos suggests: "I stay for a while [*Weile*], he said" (*StA* 2.1:181, v. 139). Christ stays and lingers for a bit—he said.[72] Christ speaks himself for, as a while. This, too, is part of Hölderlin's transformation of Kantian philosophy: whereas in Kant's *Critique of the Power of Judgment* the maintaining and conserving character of *weilen* is foregrounded, and indeed established as one of the criteria of beauty, the *Weile* of Christ is introduced only so that it can pass. As transitory and transient, this *Weile* thus borders on *Eile* (hurry or haste): lingering is almost entirely subsumed by vanishing. This is one of the most provocative of the many provocations found in the revised version of "Patmos": the disappearing lingering of Christ seems to replace the lingering of beauty. Or, perhaps, all lingering is inscribed into the Christic context. Lingering and disappearing, the name of Christ thus differs doubly from other types of Christic signs found in Hölderlin's poetry. Earlier poems knew signs that exist independently of the Christic name such as bread and wine, as the elegy of that title emphasizes: "As a sign that once they had been here and once more would / Come, the heavenly choir left a few gifts" (*KA* 1:290, vv. 131–132). The transience of the Christic name removes the Christic sign from this realm of gifts that have been left behind and instead locates it in the realm of *Weile* and ephemerality; the name "Christ" preserves (itself) only as transient: "Thus, Christ is the word that passes away, and the trace of a word in which the passing word is held fast [*festgehalten*]."[73]

The ephemerality of the Christic name and of all names demands an altered notion of phenomenality and the regime of *aisthesis* that governs it: it can no longer be a question of a "firm letter" that joins the visual and the auditory. The future of *Morgenluft*, as the description of the "more wondrous" poetry insists, thus precisely effects a shift away from the visual register: "Unforeseeable [*Unabsehlich*] / Since him the tale." Since Christ, saying is not only subtracted from prediction but is unforeseeable in the strict sense. The withdrawal from images and a weakening of visuality that was already present in the first version of "Patmos," replacing the "ein Bild zu bilden" of Christic remembrance with the "firm letter," intensifies even more in the revised versions. The aerial regime of *Morgenluft* requires a different relation to Christ, superseding both vision and hearing. This different relation has, in fact, already been inscribed at the heart of both the title and the topos of this poem: P*atmos*, *Atem*, *atmen*—breathing, breath. Instead of the presumed stability of the *Bildung* of a *Bild*, breathing replaces seeing. Only in the "breathing breath / Of song [*atmen Othem / Der Gesänge*]," to quote from "Whatever Is Next [*Das Nächste Beste*]," does the ephemeral futurity of "Morgen" become perceptible.

The aesthetic mode that lets breathing enter *aisthesis*, in turn, is olfaction: as developed above, air becomes sensible in its olfactory modulation, and all olfaction depends on air. "Morgenluft," in the oscillation of its meaning between morning and to-come, maintains a correspondingly ambiguous relationship to smell: the air of a fresh morning, to be sure, is characterized by a particular fragrance. The to-come of futurity, however, cannot be said to have a scent of its own, at least not in the literal sense of the word "scent." Nevertheless, a faint trace of just such a scent of futurity can be found in "Patmos": it is the name "Christ" itself that bears an olfactory trace. The Greek *christos*, like the Hebrew *messiah* (from *mashiach*), means "the anointed one."[74] From the viewpoint of *Sinnlichkeit*, the operation of anointing is primarily an olfactory one, as the Old Testament/Hebrew Bible insists.[75] Christ's humanity becomes evident, indeed perceptible, in the fact that he admits of olfactory modifications and, conversely, his divinity is marked by the specific smell of anointing.

Christus and *Morgenluft* thus stand in exact correspondence to each other. The transience of the name "Christ," its (self-)preservation as a mere vanishing trace, finds in "Morgenluft" its properly messianic articulation: only as "passing away," as non-firm, as a while passing into *morgen* can it be open to the future.[76] In order to be *the messiah*, the messiah must not *be* (himself)—but disappear, into a tomorrow. The aerial paradigm of transient, ephemeral, messianic names thus seeks to answer the question of "what language is after the fleetingness of the *logos* and the frailness of form was revealed in Christ."[77] In other words, "Christ did not found something within time but rather opened time."[78] And it is this opening of time that can be read in the olfactory trace of the name "Christ"; a name that preserves this trace not as a "firm letter," but precisely, and only, as disappearing and transient. The destabilization of "fortified song" brought about by the smell of lemons that disrupts all lingering leads here to a new, "more wondrous" poetry that, in its turn toward air and scent, articulates a breathing and thus smelling of the future. In the ephemeral aerial-olfactory sense of this futural breathing at the heart of "Patmos," the space and rhythm of what is to come, including, perhaps, of a "coming revolution," open up.

Latestness: Tending toward Deodorization

With the *Morgenluft* of the reworked "Patmos," Hölderlin's geopoetics of smell and his poetic trajectory more broadly reach an extreme point. Despite (or perhaps because of) its radical openness, this extremity appears to many readers of Hölderlin as an *end* point beyond which no real poetic movement is possible. Norbert von Hellingrath, Hölderlin's first systematic editor, already proposed such an interpretation in his lecture "Hölderlin's Madness [*Wahnsinn*]," delivered in 1916 while he was on leave from his deployment in World War I. In this lecture, Hellingrath traces Hölderlin's alleged madness in the form of an *aberration of sense*, as the German word *Wahn-sinn* indicates. In his tracing of the erring of sense (perhaps a loss of its previous "loyalty"?), Hellingrath quotes precisely the "Morgenluft" passage and labels the phase of the revisions of "Patmos" out of which this passage emerged as "baroque": "One thing applies to the Baroque just as much as to this stage of Hölderlin: it is something extreme, something last [*ein Äußerstes, Letztes*]; there is no onward [*es gibt kein Weiter*], yes, it is almost no longer something last, already a 'beyond'; it is comparable to the peculiar smell of cut [*abgeschnittener*] flowers."[79] In a remarkable image, Hellingrath links the "there is no onward" of the revised "Patmos" to the fragrance of cut flowers: the late Hölderlin's poetry, so the comparison suggests, emerges from a cut that severs off the life source, but it is precisely due to this being "beyond" (*darüberhinaus*) that its peculiar characteristics can emerge. Posthumous smells, emerging once more from anthological activity, mark the poetics of *Morgenluft* as the point beyond which nothing is possible—except for, of course, the decay of these flowers; the turning of the smell into the sweetly stink of putrefaction (of great interest to the poet of the next chapter, Charles Baudelaire), and, eventually, the complete disintegration of the bouquet and its return to the earth.[80]

When Hellingrath claims repeatedly "but there is no onward," then the argument developed here will show that there is, in fact, an "onward" of Hölderlin's poetry, even if it reconfigures radically what poetry, and in particular poetic movement and a poetic treatment of smell, come to mean. In the century since Hellingrath's lecture on "Hölderlin's Madness," most scholarship on the so-called latest (*spätester*, the superlative of *spät*, late) Hölderlin and the question of a possibility of an "onward" *after lateness* can be roughly assigned to one of two major methodological approaches. On the one hand, the question of "madness" is foregrounded and, indeed, made the deciding criterion for how Hölderlin's poetry can or cannot be read, and should or should not be included in his corpus. A tripartite division governs this approach: first, the latest Hölderlin's poetry is ignored or degraded in its importance precisely because it was written by a "mad" poet; here, madness and poetry are assumed to be, often a priori, incompatible. Consequently, and since Hölderlin's madness is taken as a given, his latest poetry is dismissed. Secondly, and conversely, Hölderlin's madness is considered proof of his prophetic mission or quasi-divine status. According to this interpretation, especially popular with certain Romantics and the George circle, Hölderlin's madness is accounted for in one of two ways: either it is said to derive from his having been overwhelmed by the gods due to his superior closeness to them; or, alternatively, what appears as madness to his fellow human beings is more accurately described as Hölderlin having taken leave from the world to dwell with the gods.[81] Despite holding Hölderlin's madness in a certain high regard, adherents of this interpretation tend to—somewhat paradoxically, to be sure—ignore the latest poems and instead focus on the shining through of the approach of divine closeness in the late poems. The third interpretative option undercuts both positions by questioning whether Hölderlin was really mad at all. This thesis of a "noble simulant," first prominently proposed by Pierre Bertaux, does not always seek to deny any validity of a clinical diagnosis of mental illness, but is instead directed against establishing "normal"—that is, in this context, average bourgeois—consciousness as the measure of "health" and "sickness."[82]

The second major methodological approach proposes to set the (clinical, pathographic) question of Hölderlin's madness aside and instead turns to the texts produced after 1806 to evaluate them without (or with only passing) reference to the poet's alleged or real mental state. Such text-based approaches either denigrate the literary quality of the latest poems, such as in Jochen Schmidt's claims that these poems are "oddly without any tension" and a mere "game of building blocks" (*KA* 1:512), or they ascribe a valuable, perhaps even crucial, position within the Hölderlinian corpus to them. The most productive and provocative version of this latter position can be found in D. E. Sattler's writings about the latest Hölderlin. In a text titled "al rovescio," Sattler argues that the two halves of Hölderlin's work "belong to each other necessarily and on equal footing."[83] Their mode of belonging together lies in the second half *taking back* what the first half developed: "his present poetic practice runs through the phases of the prior one (equally backwards, as it turns out) and adds what the latter had lacked in tones and moods."[84] In fact, this complementary reversal must be understood, according to Sattler, who here echoes in some ways Hellingrath's claim regarding an "Umschwung," an about-turn, as the enacting of the thought of reversal that can be found so prominently in the late Hölderlin before 1806: "In truth the real figure of what had previously only been an ideal thought breaks in here: 'complete reversal' [*gänzliche Umkehr*] as a categorically other alteration. . . . Like in life, this cathartic movement is, according to its tendency, antititanic: a turn toward meekness, toward pure receptivity."[85] A turning—no longer intentional because it is precisely the ability to intend that is being undermined here—toward receptivity and passivity.

Partly confirming Sattler's thesis and in keeping with the definition of "lateness" developed above, Hölderlin's "latestness" will here be defined through the role of *Sinnlichkeit* in these latest poems. The thesis can be indicated as follows: After 1806, Hölderlin's poetry *tends toward a state of deodorization*. In the pre-Scardanelli phase, merely two instances of an olfactory trope can be found in his extant poems; after 1838, however, the extant poems do not contain a single instance of olfaction. The aerial medium itself does not disappear from the poems (and also is not *actively* deodorized, as in the soap poems by Francis Ponge that the epilogue to this book studies) but is in fact named frequently: that its olfactory modulation is lacking, then, is even more significant.[86] In this deodorized *Sinnlichkeit*, vision is instituted as the all-dominant sense. And under the sign of vision's reinstituted hegemony, the tendencies of olfactory lateness are taken back. Both the intensified interpenetration that came to replace the unifying function of *Anschauung* and the disarticulation of unity are attenuated and weakened to the very point of being effaced. The "inviolable uniformity and wholeness" that Roman Jakobson diagnoses in the latest poems lie in a unity conceived of as *Einfalt*: a simplicity that cannot tolerate the complex folding of lines of tension, fissure, and opening articulated by smell, but that instead seeks refuge in monovalent vision. In other words, the breathing of the future, the making sensible in its *Morgenluft* character of a "coming revolution," is progressively effaced.

The trajectory of Hölderlin's poetry thus points, to modulate a formulation by Roland Barthes, toward an *olfactory degree zero*. This degree zero takes the double form of a temporal and a sensory (ocular) version that Hölderlin's very last extant poem, "The Outlook" ("Die Aussicht"), presents in exemplary form. The opening line of "The Outlook" reads, "When into the distance human life goes in dwelling [Wenn in die Ferne geht der Menschen wohnend Leben]" (*FHA* 9:226). The opening words of this verse reference the opening line of an earlier poem from the latest period—a poem that is in fact one of the only two poems that contains an olfactory trope:[87] "When from a distance, since we have parted" (*FHA* 9:62), which Sattler edits as parts of the "Hyperion Fragments" and consequently dates to the first years Hölderlin spends at the Zimmer household.[88] In those years, Hölderlin still harbored plans to write a third part of *Hyperion*, as Sinclair reported (see *FHA* 9:37). The deodorized end point of Hölderlin's poetic practice, his very last poem, thus stands in a tight constellation with the olfactory poetics developed above. First, it reworks what is conceivably the last olfactory moment in the Hölderlinian corpus. This moment, in turn, is inscribed in the last version of an attempt to continue *Hyperion*, which provided an opening moment of Hölderlin's olfactory poetics through its reflections on anthology while also pointing already to the perversion, destruction, or repetition of such anthological gestures in the life of the "mad" poet who gathers flowers and throws them into the Neckar.

Spoken from the position of Diotima, "When from a distance," then, positions this last smell moment in opposition to the *Ferne*, the far and the distant with which it opens:

> When from a distance, since we have parted,
> I am recognizable to you still; the past,
> O you sharer of my sufferings!
> Still can mark something good for you
>
> Wenn aus der Ferne, da wir geschieden sind,
> Ich dir noch kennbar bin, die Vergangenheit
> O du Theilhaber meiner Leiden!
> Einiges Gute bezeichnen dir kann (*FHA* 9:62, vv. 1–4)

The opening "When [*Wenn*]," so characteristic of the latest Hölderlin, introduces a distance or farness marked by difference and separation, by the *Scheiden* (cut) of *Unterschied* (difference) and *geschieden* (parted), perhaps also echoing the "abgeschieden" (departed) so crucial in "Patmos." By contrast, it is precisely as a negation of such "Ferne" that the olfactory moment in the poem is articulated. The sixth stanza, the first to shift into the mode of remembering directly, thus reads:

> Was it spring? Was it summer? The nightingale,
> Singing sweetly, lived with birds that were
> Not far away in the bushes,
> And trees surrounded us with smells.
>
> Wars Frühling? war es Sommer? die Nachtigall
> Mit süßem Liede lebte mit Vögeln, die
> Nicht ferne waren im Gebüsche
> Und mit Gerüchen umgaben Bäum' uns. (vv. 21–24)

The memory of "something good" that the first stanza had hoped for emerges as and through a feature of olfaction that will be central to Nietzsche's olfactory poetics: the suppression of farness ("not far") in the nearness required to smell. The verb describing the smells of this closeness of the remembered togetherness further articulates this absence of farness: "umgaben," here translated as "surrounded," indicates not only that the two lovers were immersed in a fragrant, harmonious atmosphere, but that this being surrounded appears as a *Gabe*, a gift received from elsewhere—but from a close, nearby elsewhere that can be named ("trees").

In this fragrant surrounding, determinacy and distinction become attenuated and seem to approach disappearance: the *Schied* or cut of the opening stanza is dissolved into an indeterminate "Was it spring [*Frühling*]? Was it summer?" In great contrast to the late Hölderlin, where a word such as "Frühling" could be endowed with the full weight of a thought of futurity and renewal, in this latest poem both the rigorous determination of time and its opening have been suspended. Whether it is spring or summer, "mornings, evenings" (v. 31) as a line from stanza eight reads, matters little: *Morgenluft*, it can be inferred, would be just like *Abendluft*—no tomorrow or morning is in the air. (This ever-sameness, coincidentally, constitutes the core of Brecht's olfactory indictment of the air in Los Angeles, as chapter 4 will show: it is always the same, no matter what time or season.) Similarly, art seems to dwell in (almost) unarticulated closeness with nature: "The nightingale, / Singing sweetly, lived with birds." The nightingale, not only in literary history but also in Hölderlin's own poem associated with poetry, the bird whose song stands for a natural outpouring of a "sweet song," lives indiscriminately with the other birds who do not sing. Song and non-song are "with" each other, in sweetness.

The word that functions as the transition out of this sweet, olfactory memory will become the titular word of the very last poem: "outlook" or "view." Reflecting on her beloved, Diotima introduces a scission into "everything beautiful" that the poetic I had held on to:

> And he had retained everything beautiful that,
> On blessed shores, most precious also to me,
> Blossoms in the lands of our home
> Or hidden, from an outlook high up,

Where one can also look at the sea,
But where no one wants to be.

Und alles Schöne hatt' er behalten, das
An seeligen Gestaden, auch mir sehr werth
Im heimatlichen Lande blühet,
Oder verborgen, aus hoher Aussicht,

Allwo das Meer auch einer beschauen kann,
Doch keiner seyn will. (vv. 37–42)

The sweet and harmonious dwelling of the "surrounded" of the past smell finds here its counter-term in the "outlook high up" where "no one wants to be." Once the spell of the past is broken by the introduction of a high-up point from which one can behold beauty but where one does not want to dwell, the poem ineluctably moves out of (olfactory) memory into (visual) mourning: "Those were beautiful days. But / Then followed mournful dusk" (vv. 47–48).

In the second half of the latest poems, in those signed with the name "Scardanelli," this sadness and this mourning disappear, at least on the surface. Instead, the word "Vollkommenheit," perfection or fulfillment, asserts itself more and more insistently, in a significant turn of phrase that has become a sort of watchword for scholarship on the latest Hölderlin,[89] as a "perfection without lament." With the disappearance of a "mournful dusk" turning into the assertion of *Vollkommenheit*, olfaction, too, disappears. Instead, vision and with it the "outlook" gain the upper hand. Reworking the first verse of "When from a distance," the opening lines of the last extant poem of Hölderlin, titled "The Outlook," and in all likelihood written only days before his death, thus read,

When into the distance human life goes in dwelling
Where into the distance the time of the vines glistens up

Wenn in die Ferne geht der Menschen wohnend Leben,
Wo in die Ferne sich erglänzt die Zeit der Reben (*FHA* 9:226; vv. 1–2)

The direction of the opening line has been reversed: no longer a hope for a memory to emerge *out of* distance or farness but life now goes "*into* the distance." Phonetically, "Ferne geht" inscribes both the poet's position at the very end of his life and the changed notion of temporality in these poems: *Fer . . . geht, vergeht* (passes, passes away). Time passes, in an ever-same rhythm of the seasons:

That nature completes the image of the times
That she lingers while they glide past quickly
This occurs out of perfection, and then the sky's height glistens
For human beings, like trees are crowned by blossoms.

> Daß die Natur ergänzt das Bild der Zeiten,
> Daß die verweilt, sie schnell vorübergleiten,
> Ist aus Vollkommenheit, des Himmels Höhe glänzet
> Den Menschen dann, wie Bäume Blüth umkränzet. (vv. 5–8)

This "gliding past," the smooth and quick passing out of existence of the times while nature "lingers" (*verweilt*)—an utterly different "while" than the Christic *Weile* of "Patmos"—derives from perfection and fullness (*Vollkommenheit*). All intimation of a (messianic, revolutionary) temporality that might announce something new—all *Morgenluft*—has been lost:[90] the loss of smell goes hand in hand with the institution of an "empty" (v. 3) and perfect or fulfilled temporality, where emptiness and perfection are but two sides of the same phenomenon.[91] The Scardanelli poems know only the present tense, to a degree that all tensing seems to disappear and a kind of eternal present asserts itself—futurity vanishes into the present.

The changed temporality finds its *sinnlich* counterpart in the triumph of vision in "The Outlook." In the final word of the poem, blossoms—previously so crucially tied to smell—appear one last time: "like trees are crowned by blossoms." But the "crowned [*umkränzet*]," like all crowns of great import to Hölderlin, stands merely as a rhyme echoing the visual "glistens [*glänzet*]" of the previous verse, suppressing any olfactory modulation of the blossom. This deodorized perfection reflects the position of the poem, no longer a geopoetic locality but rather a mere stance or position freed from all "topographical differentiation." It is the "position at the window," so often occupied in the latest Hölderlin's poems, that marks the "enframing showing," as Bart Philipsen has termed it, of "The Outlook." The subject is present only in this framing, and perspective—as a purely visual construct, crucial to Nietzsche as will be argued below—asserts itself: "The subject has removed itself from the field of vision. . . . The perspective is purely optical, and the horizon is that border where the lines of the landscape approach each other."[92] From this position, no closeness is admitted: smell would disrupt the carefully constructed ocular distance that allows for the claim of perfection to emerge; only via this reduction to vision can the effacement of the tendency of lateness occur and make room for a different *Sinnlichkeit* that calms the intensification and the danger of the late songs. Deodorization erases both air's and poetry's ability to articulate the opening of an indeterminate future—in these latest poems that have moved beyond the fragrance of cut flowers, the possibility of a "coming revolution" is subtracted from sense. What remains is the task, taken up by some of the poets who follow Hölderlin, to re-odorize poetry and, via this re-odorization, to open up once more the possibility of a coming revolution of the senses.

2

Baudelaire's Perfumes

Poetry's words arise "like flowers," as Hölderlin once put it, and these words adorn in delicacy and fragility. Readers might gather the choicest poems in a florilegium, or anthology. They might marvel at the arbitrary, asemantic connection that links flowering (*floraison*) to reason (*raison*) and suggests a logic of poetry intertwined with organic growth and decay.[1] Yet while the association between flowers and poetry is at least as old as Sappho (fragment 55) and Plato (who compares poets to bees flitting from flower to flower in the *Ion*), the exact status of this link is far from clear. For Hölderlin, as the previous chapter showed, poetry's putative floral character oscillates between two poles: On the one hand, an endorsement of this analogy grounded in poetry's complex delicacy requiring sophisticated care. On the other, an enigmatic and disquieting conception deriving from the "mad" Hölderlin tearing out flowers and throwing them into the Neckar, a conception echoed faintly in Hellingrath's comparison of Hölderlin's late poetry to cut flowers on the verge of the sweetly odor of wilting and putrefaction. This juxtaposition of exquisiteness and decay, of sophistication and darkness, Georges Bataille argues, is in fact part and parcel of both the life cycle of flowers and what he calls "the language of flowers": "Risen from the stench of the manure pile—even though it seemed for a moment to have escaped it in a flight of angelic and lyrical purity—the flower seems to relapse abruptly into its original squalor: the most ideal is rapidly reduced to a wisp of aerial manure."[2] The opposition and ineluctable intertwining of these two poles—of the most ideal and the most base, where neither one can be had without the other—is articulated in intense fashion in a book of poems whose title joins them in a single phrase: Charles Baudelaire's *The Flowers of Evil*. These poems, as the introduction briefly indicated, will be read here as constituting the second of two competing beginnings—Baudelaire joining Hölderlin—of self-consciously modern poetry in the Franco-German and perhaps more broadly European tradition. Baudelaire, according to the argument of this chapter, renews the theme of poetry's floral character in a sinister key and thus reopens the question of odor (largely through a poetics of perfumes)[3] that the latest, "mad" Hölderlin had so insistently closed. This resurgence of olfaction in Baudelaire, then, poses a number of questions: What do flowers of evil smell like? How does their exquisite complexity relate to the threatening underside of disorder, chaos, dissipation, and nonsense?

And what does it say about modernity—its distribution of the senses and its sensory poetics—that one of its supreme poetic articulations arrives under this title?

Revolt, Baudelaire's Dream

Few books of poetry can claim a status as unique in the European tradition of letters as *The Flowers of Evil*. As Jean-Paul Sartre writes in his study of Baudelaire published in 1947, this quintessential poet of modernity is marked by a "profound peculiarity [*singularité*]." This singular peculiarity can be traced to the "original choice that Baudelaire made of himself . . . this absolute commitment [*engagement*] through which everyone of us decides in a particular situation what he will be and what he is."[4] True to his existentialist orientation, Sartre locates this original choice in Baudelaire's attitude toward the world as it is in its facticity and the corresponding freedom of creation that moves from being to existence. According to Sartre, Baudelaire's peculiar, even unique choice finds expression in two aspects of his poetry in particular: on the one hand, a stance of *revolt*; on the other, an insistent, almost obsessive interest in *smells*. What is the relationship between these two? Do revolt and smell mutually articulate each other, or do they dislodge and reconfigure what constitutes the "Baudelairean poetic fact"? Sartre shies away from addressing these questions directly—for good reason, as will be shown below—but understanding Baudelaire's "profound peculiarity" will require just such a response.

The olfactory pole of Baudelaire's original choice, his fascination with olfaction, is well-known, and his poetry has even occasionally been labeled the most scented in the European tradition.[5] Yet Sartre's specific designation of the reason for the ubiquitous presence of odors is significant: to Baudelaire, smells constitute precisely those "objects in the world that seem . . . to be the most eloquent symbols of that reality in which existence and being would merge."[6] Smells' "metaphysical lightness" allows them to float above being, as it were, while nevertheless being present; they display a certain "discretion" that suspends them between being and nothingness, or, put differently, that makes them hover between facticity and the standing out of existence. In this sense, smells are intimately related to secrets: a secret's mode of being is equally dubious, and it is for this very reason that Baudelaire is fascinated by secrets just as much as by smells. In smells and secrets, the poet can disengage facticity without betraying it; he moves toward a freedom beyond that which is.

This (attempted) movement also characterizes the other pole of the poet's original choice, his attitude of *revolt*.[7] Revolt seeks to detach itself from the facticity of the world and deny the weight of being. Sartre, rather conventionally, distinguishes such a revolt from "a revolutionary act": "the revolutionary wants to change the world; he exceeds it toward the future [*il le dépasse vers l'avenir*], toward an order of values that he invents. The rebel [*révolté*] takes care to preserve the abuses from which he suffers in order to be able to revolt against them ... he wants to neither destroy nor exceed but simply rise up against order [*se dresser contre l'ordre*]."[8] Baudelaire's revolt must be seen in the specific historical context of his time: at the midpoint of the nineteenth century, after three main revolutions in France and multiple additional insurrections—and his own initial enthusiasm for the 1848 revolution and his participation in street fighting[9]—Baudelaire stands as the poet of revolt who no longer aims for a revolutionary act that could establish a new order, but rather remains in the stance of mere oppositional revolt. The original choice the poet makes in his situation and hence the locus of his peculiarity, according to Sartre, is one of rebellion and uprising, cut off from a further orientation toward a future—a morning or a tomorrow, as Hölderlin's *Morgenluft* indicated it—that would come after that which he rebels against.[10] But whence Baudelaire's confinement, in an age of revolution, to mere rebellion? And is there, perhaps, a secret lodged at the heart of this revolt that reconfigures its alleged opposition to revolution?

Baudelaire himself uses the word "revolt" as the title of the penultimate section of *The Flowers of Evil*. Located between the sections "Flowers of Evil" and "Death," "Revolt" encompasses three poems, all of which belong to Baudelaire's earlier period. The closing quatrain of the first poem, "The Denial of Saint Peter [Le Reniement de Saint Pierre]" (written toward the end of 1851, just around the Bonapartist coup in December of that year), delineates in intense form the poet's revolt and its sources:

—Certainly, as for me, I will leave with satisfaction
A world where action is not the sister of the dream;
I'd use the sword and perish by the sword!
Saint Peter denied Jesus ... he did right!

—Certes, je sortirai, quant à moi, satisfait
D'un monde où l'action n'est pas la sœur du rêve;
Puissé-je user du glaive et périr par le glaive!
Saint Pierre a renié Jésus ... il a bien fait! (*OC* 1:122)

These dense lines, a reconfiguration of several passages from the Gospels,[11] unfold an argument that demonstrates the necessity and nature of revolt. The poetic I rebukes the refusal to take (violent) action to defend the Christ, even at the price of perishing oneself: "revolt" embraces the sword, or, more precisely, revolt consists in a rebellion against the interdiction on acting even if such acting leads to the perishing of the actor. In a world where such an interdiction on action reigns, renouncing—an action only in a privative sense—this very world is the only action possible. Revolt, then, would be a taking leave from a world where action is not taken, where a dream remains alone.

Baudelaire's Perfumes | 71

As always in Baudelaire, the Christic-satanic vocabulary of "Revolt" is interwoven with or functions as an overlay of a different, related concern: the question of tyranny, violence, and action in the political realm. As scholars have shown extensively,[12] in nineteenth-century France, especially in the imagination surrounding 1848, Christ stood in for the Second Republic, and the engagement of Christic themes allowed for a covert, yet clearly legible, engagement with the political developments of the time. The last stanza just quoted thus repudiates, as Richard D. Burton has argued, "the Christ-Republic in its present humbled, non-violent, and essentially powerless incarnation."[13] The attitude or stance of revolt is necessitated by a world, a "situation" as Sartre would put it, in which political dream and political action fall apart: they are not related; no family resemblance or affinity can be established. The requisite action to save the dream did not arrive. And out of the chasm between the two emerges a mere disavowal or a cursing ("reniement" carries both of those connotations)—a negating that finds nothing beyond that very negating itself. A first glimpse of the secret at the heart of Baudelaire's allegedly nonrevolutionary revolt thus becomes possible: the poet, whose second given name was Pierre (Peter), does not so much, as Sartre argued, *refuse* the "revolutionary act" but rather *laments* precisely that this action had not been taken. The taking leave from the world upholds the demand for a different world precisely by serving as an index of the failure for such a world to arrive. Baudelaire's revolt, in short, inscribes the desire for action and remains—in its dream quality—oriented toward it.

The failed siblinghood of dream and action and what it reveals about the relationship between revolt and revolution constitutes a key aspect of Walter Benjamin's lengthy study *The Paris of the Second Empire in Baudelaire*. The latter closes with an evocation of the verse in question and goes on to affirm and recover the siblinghood of dream and action: "In a famous line Baudelaire lightheartedly takes leave from a world 'where action is not the sister of dream.' His dream was not as abandoned as it seemed to him. Blanqui's action was the sister of Baudelaire's dream. They are entwined into each other [*ineinander verschlungen*]" (*GS* 1:604). It is Auguste Blanqui, to whose proletarian-revolutionary society of conspirators Baudelaire might have briefly belonged,[14] whose action complements the Baudelairean dream. The intimacy of poet and revolutionary far exceeds their divergences: "But deeper than their differences reaches what was common to them both, reaches the defiance and the impatience, the force of indignation and of hatred—and also the impotence [*Ohnmacht*] that was both of their lot" (*GS* 1:604). This, then, is the secret of Baudelaire's revolt: pace Sartre's claim that the poet wants to "neither destroy nor exceed [*dépasser*]" the world against which he rebels, Baudelaire's renouncing of the world cannot be understood apart from its intertwinement with the quintessential revolutionary action that seeks to both destroy and exceed. The meaning of Baudelaire's poetic dream is contained first and foremost in its inextricable link with political action—even if, perhaps especially if, this siblinghood of dream and action consists in shared impotence.

This intertwinement of dream and action, of rebellion and revolution, of taking leave and exceeding is figured with exactitude by Baudelaire's odors. The core of Sartre's indictment—and the linchpin of his distinction between revolt and revolution—consisted in the charge that Baudelaire wanted to maintain and preserve the abuse of the world so that he could revolt against it. He merely wanted to "rise up against the order [*se dresser contre l'ordre*]."[15] In this line of thought, there is a certain melancholic side to Baudelaire: he is said to hold on to what he rails against. He *takes a stance* against the world, but this stance depends on that very world. Yet as Sartre himself shows in manifold ways—and as this chapter will develop in detail—Baudelaire is precisely *not* a man who takes firms stances: the uprightness required for such a stance, as indicated in the etymology of "se dresser" that points toward directness and rectitude, is incompatible with Baudelaire's original choice. His mode of existence is not one of heroic, binary opposition, but rather modeled on the atmospheric, floating, evaporating, surrounding character of scents. Sartre is thus correct, albeit in an exacting way he does not grasp, that Baudelaire "positions himself in the face of them [the idols] in an attitude of resentment [*ressentiment*], not of critique."[16] Ressentiment, as Eve Sedgwick has pointed out, must be heard through the French "sentir" as meaning not just to feel but to smell. Ressentiment is a "re-sniffing."[17] What Sedgwick writes of Nietzsche can be said with equal justification of Baudelaire—namely, that he is "the psychologist who put the scent back into sentimentality. And he did it by the same gesture with which he put the rank and the rancid back into rancor."[18] Baudelaire's method, as it were, consists in getting a second sniff of the world. He moves beyond that which is by smelling it, and in smell enacts an attitude toward the world that is not one of opposition but closely follows the character of scent: smells as precisely those "objects" that blur the line between being and nothing, between facticity and existence, and that enable Baudelaire's unusual attitude of ressentiment. If smells float above and around the world, then they are just that in the world which moves beyond it while not completely abandoning it. Smells figure a taking leave from the world that arises out of it without standing in opposition to it. In this sense, odors are also what enables Baudelaire's dream to intertwine with Blanqui's deed, where the latter is the acting on and moving beyond the world. In smell, as the rest of this chapter will show, revolution and poetry meet: for Baudelaire, they intertwine in shared ressentiment as much as in shared impotence; they neither accept what is nor merely refuse it. Instead, Baudelaire's poetry and revolution re-sniff and transform or, more precisely, transcent the world.

Perfumes: Poetry like Lazarus

This singular and far-reaching potential of scent in *The Flowers of Evil* can be found not so much in the odors of the titular flowers or related organic, natural occurrences but rather in made, created *perfumes*. Perfumes, whose industrial production and increasingly democratic consumption exploded during Baudelaire's lifetime,[19] are paradigmatic instances of the pair nature/artifice: a perfume is made, but from substances that are recognizably natural. Perfume-making constitutes a quasi-existentialist choice to create out of and beyond facticity. The artifice of a perfume, as Richard Stamelman argues in a cultural history of the craft, leads nature into a type of *artificial afterlife*: "Perfume is the transformation of mortal and material substances—destined for decomposition and 'garish withering,' as Bataille says—into a liquid and a vapor that preserve the floral aroma beyond the natural span of the flower's life."[20] Perfumes live on: their existence extends beyond what was naturally allocated to them; not quite through a process of "drawing the eternal from the transitory," as Baudelaire's well-known description of the task of modernity goes, but as a drawing of a living on from the transitory. Being made, living on: perfume's resemblance to poetry comes into view. They meet in *poiein*, in the freedom of making that transforms the given into its afterlife.[21]

A second and arguably even more important reason for Baudelaire's pronounced preference for smells in the form of perfumes can be derived from the opening line of *My Heart Laid Bare*, one of his "intimate journals." Here, Baudelaire lays claim to having found a principle that could account for "everything": "Of the vaporization and centralization of the *I*. Everything is there" (*OC* 1:676). Baudelaire draws this claim from Ralph Waldo Emerson's *The Conduct of Life*. In the preceding journal titled "Hygiène,"[22] Baudelaire quotes a line from Emerson's essay "Power," of which his own line in *My Heart Laid Bare* functions as a translation: "The one prudence in life is concentration; the one evil is dissipation" (*OC* 1:674). Within Baudelaire's poetic universe, this doubled nature of concentration and dissipation finds paradigmatic instantiation in perfumes: as a liquid, they are highly concentrated, both in the sense of being contained or "centralized" into a single, strictly delimited space (the flacon to which Baudelaire dedicates a whole poem analyzed below) and in the sense of being an extract whose olfactory qualities have been heightened by concentration. Conversely, a perfume comes into its own only when this concentration is vaporized, again in a literal sense: it is sprayed out of its concentration into a vapor. This dissipation is arguably the dominant side of Baudelaire's work. The supremacy of dissipation comes into focus through the Emersonian passage that links dissipation to *evil*: the *Flowers of Evil*—certainly rather far from being called *The Flowers of Prudence*—are concerned with dissipation precisely because they are concerned with evil, and vice versa.

The deep saturation with Anglophone sources (that is, a certain decentering and perhaps vaporization of Frenchness) found in Baudelaire's thought of dissipation goes even further. On the same page where Baudelaire cites Emerson on dissipation and concentration, he also quotes the following: "The hero is he who is immovably centered" (*OC* 1:674). If heroicness and concentration go hand in hand for Emerson, and concentration sides with prudence, then the Baudelairean hero—so crucial to most interpretations of this poet's work and his relationship to modernity (Benjamin, for instance, claims, "The hero is the true subject of modernité" [*GS* 1:577])—must inversely be "movably dissipated" if he is to be a hero in a world of evil: with respect to evil, the hero cannot but give up on concentration and give himself over to vaporization. Perhaps his body is a "censer," as a recurring image in *The Flowers of Evil* suggests, or perhaps dissipation occurs as a pipe that smokes up the smoker "through a type of transposition" (*OC* 1:42), as *Artificial Paradises* puts it.[23] What is clear is that the Baudelairean hero does not "erect himself" against the world, as Sartre's description of the "rebel" argued, but rather suffuses the world with "his" vaporization. In fact, the dedicatory poem "To the Reader" already explicitly develops vaporization as the fundamental condition of the world of *The Flowers of Evil*: "and the rich metal of our will / Is all vaporized by this skillful alchemist" (*OC* 1:5). The knowing alchemist, Satan, vaporizes our will: without a hard, metallic, ironclad will, a "hero" cannot oppose himself to anything at all. Baudelaire's heroes instead seep into the world and through this seepage move in, through, and against it—"Everything is there," including an elucidation of Baudelaire's choice of the title *My Heart Laid Bare*. The latter is drawn from a very short text titled "The Unwritable Book" that Edgar Allan Poe published, significantly, in 1848: "If any ambitious man have a fancy to *revolutionize*, at one effort, the universal world of human thought, human opinion, and human sentiment, the opportunity is his own—the road to immortal renown lies straight, open, and unencumbered before him. All that he has to do is to write and publish a very little book. Its title should be simple—a few plain words—'My Heart Laid Bare.'"[24] This is the quasi-syllogism presented by Baudelaire's journal entry and its Anglophone intertexts: writing to lay bare one's heart would revolutionize the world; laying bare one's heart finds "everything" in dissipation and concentration; writing dissipation and concentration would—if it were possible—revolutionize the world.[25]

This writing of dissipation in Baudelaire's poetry, the poet's articulation of perfume's essential vaporization, occurs primarily in an interplay with materiality both as what provides the ground for vaporization and as what seeks to constrain and contain it. This can be seen in exemplary form in the opening verses of the poem "The Perfume Flask [Le Flacon]." Composed of seven quatrains, the poem begins with a verse that transforms a line from Baudelaire's most famous poem, "Correspondences." The first tercet of the latter begins, "There are perfumes fresh as the flesh of children [*Il est des parfums frais comme des chairs d'enfants*]" (*OC*

1:11). The freshness of these perfumes is replaced, in "The Perfume Flask," by strength and force:

> Strong perfumes exist for which all matter
> Is porous. One would say they penetrate glass.

> Il est de forts parfums pour qui toute matière
> Est poreuse. On dirait qu'ils pénètrent le verre. (OC 1:47)

Perfumes, some strong perfumes at least, can penetrate all matter. This strength epitomizes their nature as indicated in their name: *per*fumes are what moves through, comes forth, and expands. Olfactory strength lies in the ability to pierce all matter. Such a penetrating force has a specific name in Baudelaire: spirit. Perfumes are characterized by a certain "high spirituality [*haute spiritualité*]" (OC 2:716) insofar as they escape, transcend, and penetrate spirit's opposing term, matter. This is, within the economy of Baudelaire's thought, a corollary of perfume's status as the artifice that freely creates as a transformation of base nature: spirit is to matter what artifice is to nature. Perfumes straddle the divide of each pair of this analogy, and it is from this capacity to produce an intermediary movement that their privileged place in Baudelaire's oeuvre derives.

The penetrating character of perfume, as the subsequent stanzas show via an elaborate description of the "old flask" and its olfactory expansion, issues into the main function of such fragrant force: it triggers an involuntary memory. The central stanza of the poem articulates the mechanism of such a memory most forcefully:

> Here is the intoxicating memory that flutters
> In the troubled air; the eyes close; Vertigo
> Seizes the vanquished soul and pushes it with both hands
> Toward an abyss obscured by human miasmas

> Voilà le souvenir enivrant qui voltige
> Dans l'air troublé; les yeux se ferment; le Vertige
> Saisit l'âme vaincue et la pousse à deux mains
> Vers un gouffre obscurci de miasmes humains (OC 1:48)

The fragrance has taken hold of the soul, to the degree that the eyes close and only smell and memory are left. The nearly violent, and hence involuntary, character of the memory's imposition in smell is legible throughout this stanza ("troubled," "vanquished"). The true "force" of this memory-smell is further emphasized by the direct transformation of the preceding poem "Evening Harmony" effected by this central stanza: in the former, the "air of the evening" was filled with a "melancholic and languishing vertigo!" Smells fill the evening air in a way that establishes harmony, a harmony that might be vertiginous but in a mellow, gentle manner. By contrast, at the exact point where the first half of

"The Perfume Flask" turns into the second, this "Vertigo" is taken up—but now as a violent agent (its agential status emphasized by the capitalization of the first letter) that seizes the soul and pushes it toward an abyss. The sonic qualities of the word "verse" reverberate in these lines: both the word "Vertigo [*vertige*]" and its position at the central turning point—*versus*—of the poem draw attention to poetry's vertigo inducing quality. The turn of the verse seizes the reader's soul and pushes—turning and spinning with each new line—toward an "abyss obscured by human miasmas."

This abyss, in the first place, is the empty space of the stanza break that immediately follows the invocation of "abyss [*gouffre*]." Yet, when this abyss is crossed, it reemerges right away and leads to the crucial—it is precisely a question of the *crux* of the matter here—articulation of the functioning of memory and its intertwinement with odors:

> Vertigo knocks down the soul at the edge of an age-old abyss
> Where, like odorous Lazarus ripping his shroud,
> The spectral cadaver of a rancid, charming, and sepulchral love,
> Moves in its awakening.

> Il la terrasse au bord d'un gouffre séculaire,
> Où, Lazare odorant déchirant son suaire,
> Se meut dans son réveil le cadavre spectral
> D'un vieil amour ranci, charmant et sépulcral. (*OC* 1:48)

This is how memory works: a smell seizes your soul and leads you to a miasmic abyss, out of which a "spectral cadaver" emerges. The "old love" that has been reawakened by the "force" of the perfume remains, even in its charming movement, sepulchral. The decisiveness of this conception of memory becomes clearer in contrast with an earlier poem from *The Flowers of Evil* that is equally concerned with perfumes and their power to evoke memories. In "The Perfume," the second section of the spectral, four-part poem "A Phantom," the very charm of the past is described in starkly divergent terms: "Profound, magical charm with which the restored past [*le passé restauré*] / Intoxicates us in the present." In the present, we are intoxicated by the profound charm evoked by an exquisite perfume—the charm of the *restored* past. In the French context, one could hardly imagine a more charged term to describe the relation of present to past than "restaurer," pointing toward the restoration of the (past) monarchy over the (present) republic. The logic underlying this movement can thus be easily indicated: it is a return to a prior state that occurs within a restricted economy of (political) forms that excludes innovation, newness, excess, and irretrievable loss. "Le passé restauré" stands for a recovery—in fullness, in life—of what had temporarily, but only temporarily, passed out of fullness and life. It is precisely such a recovery of the past that the "strong perfumes" of "The Perfume Flask," in contrast to "The Perfume," deny. What returns in these smells is nothing but a cadaverous specter. What has fallen—as the word "cadaver" indicates—can, in fact, start to move again but only in spectral form, where spectrality is precisely the name for "something" whose ontological status is dubious and ambiguous: specters haunt indeterminately between being and nonbeing; they are, as Jacques Derrida writes apropos of Marx's specters, "sensible insensible."[26] Here the full family resemblance, as it were, of a specter and an odor becomes legible: each in its own way constitutes "a paradoxical incorporation, a becoming-body, a certain phenomenal and carnal form of spirit."[27] And this is Baudelaire's account of the functioning of memory and its relation to the past: the past can only return in spectral form, as the paradoxical incorporation of the incorporeal—as an odor, a specter.

The recourse to spectrality—over and against restauration—plays out via Baudelaire's transformation of one of the most scented episodes in the Gospels: the story of Lazarus. This episode, as narrated in the Gospel of John (11:1–44), turns on a triumph of life over the stench of death and the "human miasmas" that accompany it.[28] After Lazarus has died, Jesus comes to visit the deceased's sisters. When he witnesses the great grief of those devastated by death, he speaks to Martha, one of the sisters: "'I am the resurrection and the life'" (11:25). What follows is often considered the crowning miracle of Jesus's "Seven Signs" recounted by John: the only other resurrection (other than Jesus's own) known in scripture. But first Martha formulates, in explicitly olfactory terms, the objection to such a resurrection: "Jesus said, 'Take away the stone.' Martha, the sister of the dead man, said to him, 'Lord, by this time there will be an odor [ἤδη ὄζει], for he has been dead four days'" (11:39). What stands in the way of life and resurrection is the smell of death—only to be overcome by the greater force of the son of God who resurrects Lazarus and, in fact, *restores* him to life. Baudelaire's poem shifts the terms of this scene slightly but decisively: the position of Christ who utters the words "Lazare, veni foras" is occupied here by the perfume—the poem effecting an olfactory substitution for Christ. Pursuant to this substitution, "odorous Lazarus" is not restored to life but rather returns in the form of a spectral cadaver, still "rancid." The stench of death is not effaced but rather persists; death's rancidness is reinscribed and perpetuated by its solicitation via a "strong perfume."[29] No restoration of the past but a mobilization of that which has passed, *as passed*, in smell. In other words, Baudelaire rereads resurrection as ressentiment: resurrecting equals re-smelling. The stench of death attached to "odorous Lazarus" cannot be erased (this would be the promise of Jesus's "I am the resurrection and the life"), but also does not figure death as absolute negativity, end point, eternal sleep, or immobilization: it moves, "in its awakening." Death is doubled and mobilized in smell.

In a final turn, the last two stanzas of the poem then establish a troubling but incisive link between this notion of memory as spectral resurrection, on the one hand, and poetry, on the other.[30] This was already hinted at in the opening two verses since their phonic qualities extend the force of strong perfume even further: in "One would say they penetrate glass [*le verre*]" the homophony of "verre" (glass) and "vers" (verse) indicates that this poem, too, is thoroughly suffused by smell. The penultimate stanza, then, opens with the word "ainsi," setting up the following chain of equivalences: the poem or the poet (only designated by a "je") stands in the position of the flask containing the perfume that conquers the soul. What then escapes from the poem-flask and seizes the soul? What "penetrates" the verse and is equivalent to the perfume of the preceding stanzas? The poem at first only names it thus: "lovable pestilence [*aimable pestilence*]." This oxymoronic construction continues with "beloved poison" and reaches its climax in the final verse: "liquor / that wears me down, o the life and death of my heart!" The equivalent to the perfume—what is contained in the poem—is the conjunction of life and death. Life-death is that which penetrates all; it constitutes the vertigo-inducing "troubled air" in which spectral cadavers become resurrected. This, then, is the conception of poetry as it emerges from this dense Baudelairean reflection: poetry is the making of a flacon-coffin for life-death, from which the latter emerges to expand and pour forth (*per-*). Poetry makes the containers of spectral cadavers that move like odors, inducing vertigo and seizing souls. In it, no restoration of the past is possible, but instead a living-on rises up again and becomes lovable.

A Woman's Hemisphere

While the resurrection of Lazarus appears at first glance to play out between the two male figures, Jesus and Lazarus, alone, a third, triangulating figure emerges as significant, a figure that is itself doubled: Lazarus's sisters Mary and Martha. These women are above all the ones who are concerned with smell. Martha had pointed out Lazarus's stench of death as an obstacle to resurrection, and it is Mary who in the following episode (John 12:1–11) initiates one of the most complex accounts of fragrance contained in the Bible, an account further intertwined with reflections on life and death. In this episode, commonly known as the "Anointing of Bethany," Jesus dines, "six days before the Passover" (12:1), with Lazarus, Mary, and Martha. In the presence of Lazarus—that is, in the full presence of death restored to life—Mary then "took a pound of costly ointment of pure nard and anointed the feet of Jesus and wiped his feet with her hair; and the house was filled [ἐπληρώθη] with the fragrance of the ointment" (12:3). Once more, fragrance is characterized through its ability to pour forth, but here the Greek is maximally saturated with meaning: ἐπληρώθη is the aorist form of πληρόω (to make full), the word that gives us the term *pleroma*, indicating a totality or fullness of divine presence. The house (*oikos*) was made full (Luther's German translation reads "erfüllte," completed or fulfilled) by smell. The meaning of Mary's action is thus intensely overdetermined. First, while the verb generally translated as "anointed" (ἤλειψεν) in this passage differs from the verb that gives the title "Christ" (χρίω), meaning the Anointed One, Mary's act nevertheless appears as a repetition of the material instituting act of anointing that makes Jesus into the Christ. Secondly, such fragrant fulfillment functions proleptically: it anticipates the fulfillment of Jesus's fate and the fate of all in the House of the Lord. Jesus himself hints at this when he says, "Let her keep it for the day of my burial." Once more, biblical fragrance—this time the fragrance applied by a woman—marks the triumph of life over death.

Mary's act of a fragrant making-full, as Anne Carson points out in her reading of this scene (which is titled "Economy, Its Fragrance"[31]), is inscribed into several questions of economy: "But Judas Iscariot, one of his disciples (he who was to betray him), said, 'Why was this ointment not sold for three hundred denarii and given to the poor?'" (John 12:4–5). Judas voices the demand for an ethics of calculation, for an *ethics of economy* in the multiple valences of that word. The position of Mary, by contrast, is the position of excess, waste, luxury, and gratuitousness. Jesus sides with the feminine, non-calculating, and luxurious position, with a devastating justification: "The poor you always have with you, but you do not always have me" (12:8). Calculation and economy, and indeed an ethics of taking care of the poor, stand on the side of that which is "always"; fragrance, woman, and Christ are subtracted from such perpetuity. The latter trio thus not only exceeds all economizing imperatives but also exceeds a calculus of time based on homogeneity. In economy, everything returns in sameness; in fragrance, a rupture of difference announces itself. Since rupture is a temporal term and that which is ruptured is time as continuity, the onset of Christic—that is, of anointed or messianic—time is subject to an impossibility of determination: from within the economy of time, it cannot be calculated when the aneconomic will emerge. Whence the function of fragrance: in its excessive and wasteful character, fragrance makes sensible—but not calculable—this beyond of calculation and this onset of a different time.

In several poems, Baudelaire takes up these considerations and intensifies one of the structuring devices of the anointing scene: the logic of sexual difference that assigns the aneconomic to woman and the calculus to man, leaving the Christic figure in the third position of an arbitration that sides with the woman. Throughout Baudelaire's poems, women figures recur who appear to refer to Mary of Bethany as their archetypal instantiation. Not only are women associated with luxury, gratuitousness, and waste, but they are often reduced, *pars pro toto*, to the female body part (if it can be called that) most poignantly present in the account of Mary of Bethany: she uses her *hair* to dry Jesus's feet; a woman's "head of hair," her "chevelure," similarly structures many of Baudelaire's poems about women. Mary's hair enables her to make contact with Christ in a gesture of remarkable intimacy and tenderness. The very top of her body touches the very bottom of his, bringing high and low in contact. For Baudelaire, it is this question of the possibility of contact between man and woman that permeates all his reflections on sexual difference. More precisely, sexual difference poses itself as the question of the possibility or impossibility of a relation between the male, poetic I and the female other, and in his work, it is precisely a woman's fragrant "head of hair" that functions as the nodal point that enables (or fails to enable) such a relation. The fragrant hair of woman articulates the form Baudelaire attempts to give to sexual difference and the relation across that difference—in short, for Baudelaire, gendered relations are fragrant relations, and fragrant relations are gendered relations.[32]

The problem of such a relation, for Baudelaire, is easily designated. In his collection of notes titled *Fusées*, he writes, "Love wants to exit from itself, merge [*se confondre*] with its victim, like the victor with the vanquished, and all the while preserve the privileges of the conqueror" (*OC* 1:650). Love seeks an exit out of the self-referential closure of the I: as Sartre puts it, "the original attitude of Baudelaire is that of a man bent over [*d'un homme penché*]. Bent onto himself, like Narcissus."[33] Baudelaire inclines: toward himself, closing himself into self-reference. Any exit out of this bending back onto oneself must, for the poet, guard the "privileges" of domination—that is, of an assertion of the will. Domination, of course, merely seeks to extend the sphere of the self onto the other and thus reduce all alterity. A full "exit from himself," however, would also only lead to a merging and a resulting homogenization: "se confondre," like the English "confuse oneself," indicates a mode of fusion. Between these two modes of merging—under the domination of the male I or in the female other—can there be a third mode that would guard difference? Underneath Baudelaire's ostentatious misogyny, which has been studied so intensely by feminist scholars,[34] and which has rightly been seen as "operat[ing] like a structural necessity and a theoretical axiom that undergirds the very poetic principles of *Les Fleurs du mal*,"[35] can a more profound—or at least a different—desire to establish a relation that is non-fusional be found? Can sexual difference be thought beyond domination and beyond dissolution? And regarding the link between fragrance and sexuality, is there in Baudelaire something that goes beyond the bigotry of the "male sniff," as one scholar has termed it in analogy to the male gaze?[36]

The tension between a desire to "merge with its victim" and to uphold difference and foreclose the loss of self in the other structures exactaxly a pair of poems titled "Head of Hair [*La Chevelure*]" and, for the corresponding prose poem version, "A Hemisphere in a Head of Hair [*Un hémisphère dans une chevelure*]," and both of these poems turn to smell to figure this tension. The former opens with a chain of ecstatic evocations of the scent of the titular hair that culminates, at the end of the second stanza, in the following claim: "As other spirits sail on the waves of music / Mine, oh my love! swims on your perfume" (*OC* 1:26). Spirit floats on the smell of this hair. This state is achieved by a plunging movement, a movement that Émile Benveniste, in his posthumously published, extensive notes on Baudelaire, points out as a general principle of Baudelaire's body of work: "It is characterized by *the total immersion in the imaginary repre-*

sentation. This must be understood in the physical sense, immersion in the head of hair, an inverse plunge into the upper air."[37] This general principle undergoes an exacting specification in two crucial lines from "Head of Hair":

> I will plunge my head enamored with intoxication
> Into this black ocean where the other is enclosed

> Je plongerai ma tête amoureuse d'ivresse
> Dans ce noir océan où l'autre est enfermé (*OC* 1:26)

The fragrant hair, where the other is enclosed: it is into this space that the I will plunge. Note the shift to the future tense for the first and only time in this poem. The decisive action—taking the leap into alterity—is announced and by that very token postponed. Yet fragrance opens the possibility that the plunge might be taken; it makes sensible the space into which the plunge would leap. Sartre, once more, puts his finger on the importance of this olfactory relationality: "The smell in me is the fusion of the other's body with my body. But it is a disembodied body, vaporized, yet certainly staying entirely itself."[38] It is the *vaporization* of body into odor that enables a fusion of one body with another, letting each stay "entirely itself." To breathe the other's fragrance: an ecstasy without loss; a "merging with" that nevertheless preserves the privileges of the I; a relation across sexual difference that fuses *and* safeguards difference—this, at least, is the promise contained in the fragrance of the "head of hair."

Yet the expression "amoureuse d'ivresse" (enamored with intoxication), which describes the lyric subject, "reverses the expected order of priorities, making not of love but of intoxication the ultimate end."[39] Part of the operation that seems to enable love is a displacement of its object: love is not oriented toward "the other" but toward intoxication. The other becomes the mediating term through which intoxication is reached; woman appears as a mere occasion and slips away by being elided underneath her function. This is already legible in the reduction of the woman figure to a detached "head of hair." As Elissa Marder argues, this hair should not too easily be read as a synecdoche, but instead is more accurately described as a fetish: "Hair epitomizes the fetish because it incarnates a fundamental confusion about the limits between life and death and hence it negates the difference between presence and absence."[40] The price of a relation across sexual difference based on the olfactory vaporization of bodies is this: smells teeter on the boundary between being and nothingness; they erase the demarcating line between that which is firmly present and that which is definitively absent—and it is this fetishistic, phantomatic quality that, for Baudelaire, endows smells with their specific significance for sexual difference. In other words, the sexual relation of "breathing the other," Baudelaire's seeming escape route between the absence of all sexual relation, on the one hand, and sexual difference as the fusion of domination or ecstatic loss, on the other, is rigorously spectral: dissipating the *pleroma*, the fulfilled presence of the Christic scent poured forth by Mary of

Bethany's gratuitous excess, the smell of "la chevelure" is nothing but a dubious, phantomatic trace of a relation.

Could it be any other way? Could fragrant hair figure a non-spectral sexual relation that is not based on the tacit or explicit elision of woman? At this point, one of the perennial questions of Baudelaire scholarship—how to interpret the differences and convergences of *Les Fleurs du mal* and *Le Spleen de Paris*, the "little poems in prose"—poses itself once more. "A Head of Hair" finds its counterpart in and is transformed by a prose poem titled "A Hemisphere in a Head of Hair." Much is shared by the two texts: while the former consists of seven stanzas, the latter is made up of seven paragraphs; most of the imagery and a fair number of phrases are found in both; and the title of the prose poem was initially identical to the title of the lyric poem. Yet the eventual change of the prose poem's title—particularly charged with meaning in a poem concerned with the head—marks a sharpening of the constellation of fragrance, sexual difference, and relation to alterity. The addition of "hemisphere" indicates that at stake in the smell of the woman's hair is the question of whether, and if so, how, the two distinct halves of sexual difference can be made whole or, more cautiously, moved out of their "hemi," "half" character.[41]

Such a movement does indeed occur in the smell of the hair-hemisphere. At first, the latter conjures up a state of hallucination or imagination: "Your hair contains a whole dream [*tout un rêve*]" (*OC* 1:300). This dream then transports toward and issues into a term closely related to the titular hemisphere: the dreams transport to a place "where the atmosphere is perfumed." The dream contained in the fragrant *hemisphere* of woman is that it transports into a fragrant *atmosphere*: no longer split into halves, an atmosphere is properly spherical; it is unified without the mark of a binary structuration. Yet far from an indeterminate mixing—the fusional threat of "se confondre" still looms large—the continuation of the sentence emphasizes individuation and a certain *infrastructure* within this atmosphere: "where the atmosphere is perfumed by [*parfumée par*] the fruits, by foliage, and by human skin." The "par-" of perfume, as the repetition of "par" emphasizes, arises from that which constitutes the outer container of the human body: the skin. This is the dream: a dissolution of the bipolar hemispheric structure into a submerging subtracted from all "hemi" modifications but safeguarding individuation and the outer delimitation of bodies. Baudelaire's poetry is defined by *a desire for the atmospheric* that is simultaneously a *desire for corporeal integrity*. In fact, the atmospheric and the integral condition each other in this poem, crucially overcoming the double threat of spectrality and fusion, and it is precisely their interplay that produces the overcoming of all splits—this is what perfume promises.

The poem offers a precise account of why such high hopes would be vested specifically in perfume's atmospheric potential. The plunging into the hemisphere transports—as so often in Baudelaire, fragrance moves elsewhere—into specific regions: "it contains the open sea where the monsoons carry me toward

Baudelaire's Perfumes | 83

charming climates [*vers de charmant climats*]."⁴² Two things are laid one over the other: sexual difference and geography, with a geography of sexual difference emerging. Woman is associated with warmth and charm. But beyond this somewhat stale and conventional poetic imaginary, the greater significance lies in the word "climate" itself, as it derives from *clima*, κλίμα, incline, slope, or inclination: what matters is not so much which region the poet is transported to but rather *that* he is moved, via inclination, into a climate. Through smell, the poet inclines—feminine fragrance transports out of a stance of erect uprightness. This is the Baudelairean rejoinder to the Gospel's account of Mary of Bethany and Jesus Christ: it is not so much the excessive, aneconomic character of the feminine that matters in fragrance. Rather, fragrance embodies the desire for the atmospheric as it leads to inclination, which forfeits erectness, and instead converts the hemispheric into the atmospheric.

This desire for the atmospheric and the climate of inclination also constitutes *a desire for the common*: on the one hand, the atmosphere of fragrance allows for an abandonment of sexual difference as binary scission or heroic, oppositional struggle; on the other, it allows for an avoiding of fusional (and thus homogenized) or merely phantomatic relationality. This is Baudelaire's exacting and beautiful suggestion of what the common could be: through fragrance, we incline toward each other, moved out of our hemispheres into a shared climate. This inclination is thus very much distinct from the narcissistic inclining that Sartre ascribed to Baudelaire: the poet does not incline onto himself but rather tilts into the charm of that which he shares with others. The hope for sexual difference, as it is contained in fragrance, lies precisely in this inclinatory desire.

"Star without Atmosphere"

As the shift from hemispheres to atmosphere indicates, smell, in Baudelaire, moves, opens, and expands. Semantically, this also always entails an expansion of the poetic vocabulary called forth by the olfactory "primary lived experience [*vécu primaire*]," as Benveniste called it. Such an expansion is poignantly contained in the word "hemisphere," as it can refer to "the half of the terrestrial *or* celestial globe," as defined by the *Littré*. Dotting the celestial hemisphere, one would find stars. Stars as signposts that would enable a deciphering of the spatial and temporal coordinates of the cosmos, however, have disappeared from Baudelaire's poetry: this, in fact, is one of the defining characteristics of modernity, its inability to look up to the heavens for orientation.⁴³ The celestial hemisphere lacks a legible order that would constitute a coherent totality out of all that is. At this point the question of Baudelaire's women figures reasserts itself in a new light: "the stars do not simply fall, fade, or disappear in Baudelaire's poetry. The place left vacant by their absence is almost always . . . inscribed on the female body."⁴⁴ The woman's hair, in particular, emerges as "an intoxicating replacement for the missing firmament itself."[45] Baudelaire's insistent interest in establishing, through the hemisphere of woman's fragrance, an atmosphere thus receives a deeper significance: atmosphere remedies the lack of astral orientation. It quiets the feeling of cosmic loss and through its gentle inclining locates the subject in a world adrift.

Yet in its attempt to replace the guiding stars, Baudelaire's poetry must grapple with a peculiarly strained relationship between astral orientation and the atmosphere. This was first observed by Benjamin, perhaps because his interest in Baudelaire's siblinghood with Auguste Blanqui—who, late in his life and while incarcerated, wrote his strangest work, titled *Eternity by the Stars*, which seeks to plunge the depths of cosmic order and its relation to human (revolutionary) action—directed his attention to the question of Baudelaire's relationship to the stars. Benjamin's observation is contained in the enigmatic final sentence of his seminal essay, "On Some Motifs in Baudelaire." Having developed his well-known account of modernity as marked by a "demolition of the aura in the lived experience of shock [*Chockerlebnis*]," which reshapes what experience can(not) be, Benjamin concludes his essay with the following claim: Baudelaire's poetry is located "up in the sky of the Second Empire as 'a star without atmosphere' ['*ein Gestirn ohne Atmosphäre*']" (*GS* 1:653). According to Benjamin, Baudelaire's poetry, while providing an astral substitute, precisely lacks what many of the poems seek to establish: an atmosphere. Benjamin draws this formulation of a star lacking an atmosphere from Nietzsche's early essay *On the Use and Disadvantage of History for Life* (1874), published just two years after Blanqui's *Eternity by the Stars*. Nietzsche argues that "Everything living needs around itself an atmosphere, an enveloping layer of vapor full of secrets. If one takes away this casing, if a religion, an art, or a genius is condemned to orbit as a star without atmosphere [*Gestirn ohne Atmosphäre*], then one should not be surprised by a quick withering and becoming hard and barren" (*KSA* 1:298). Life needs an atmosphere—without the latter, impotence, decay, and decadence reign. This is, of course, the condition of *The Flowers of Evil*, with the only qualification that it is precisely out of such a lack of fertility that something new sprouts. The more troubling insight stems from the first part of Nietzsche's essay, which establishes just what this life-giving atmosphere consists of: "Thus we will deem the ability to partially sense unhistorically as the more important and more originary one, insofar as it contains the foundation on which something right, healthy, and great, something truly human, can first and only grow. The unhistorical is similar to an enveloping atmosphere in which alone life generates itself, only to disappear again with the annihilation of that atmosphere" (*KSA* 1:252). Being unhistorical, being able to forget enables life. It constitutes the protective envelope of an atmosphere that allows life to live. Any erasure of atmosphere, an erasure that Nietzsche implicitly but crucially identifies with being historical, would lead to life's decay. Benjamin's claim that Baudelaire's poetry lacks an atmosphere would then mean that this poetry is *thoroughly historical* and because of its historical, unforgetting character struggles to live, always teetering on the edge between life and death, decay and flowering, cadaver and resurrection.

Baudelaire's passion for perfumes and fragrant atmospheres, his desire for the atmospheric then slightly modifies Benjamin's suggestion: Baudelaire's poetry is engaged in a continual attempt to establish or restore atmosphere—an atmosphere that would allow life to emerge by forgetting, without letting life be immediately split into two hemispheric halves. This poetry oscillates between acknowledging and even celebrating its status as a "star without atmosphere," on the one hand, and seeking precisely to remedy this lack, on the other. In its treatment of atmospheres, Baudelaire's poetry negotiates its complicated relationship to history and forgetting. Put differently, the poetic gigantomachy between atmospheres and their absence plays out as a battle of two competing conceptions of relating to time and time's relationship to the atmospheric, a battle that this chapter now turns to.

Addictive Time, Adorable Eternity

The threat of a disappearance or erasure of atmospheres goes to the heart of Baudelaire's poetry. An olfactory version of a lack of the atmospheric can be designated easily: a loss of smell, the *threat of deodorization*. (The epilogue on Francis Ponge below will take up this "threat" once more and think more explicitly about the potentialities contained within it.) Deodorization, for Baudelaire, threatens the poet's orientation, his desire for the atmospheric, and his thought of relationality. The surprising centrality of deodorization in a work otherwise filled with odors is thus what Benjamin remarked upon in "On Some Motifs," as always infallibly guided to the one detail or line that casts everything else in a different light, when he refers to "The Taste for Nothingness [*Le Goût du néant*]" as the fulcrum of the splenic failures that permeate *The Flowers of Evil*. The decisive, well-known line reads, "Adorable spring has lost its scent" (*OC* 1:76; *GS* 1:641). Spring, the time of flowering—that is, the time of the emergence of flowers, flowers of evil included—no longer smells. But how could spring be spring if its flowering does not bring forth one of the most distinctive effects of such blossoms—namely, their odorous suffusion into the atmosphere of the time of renewal? This deodorization brings about resignation, the dominant affect of the poem: the entire constellation of perfumes—spectrality, life-death, merging, resurrection, aneconomic excess, a relation across sexual difference—everything that made smell troubling but also pregnant with potential is erased in this line. While smell teetered on the edge between being and nothingness, deodorization collapses this tension and leaves only a "taste of nothingness," as the title of the poem puts it. As Benjamin points out, Baudelaire says "something utmost," something extreme in this verse: deodorization constitutes the limit of Baudelaire's poetry, the point at which it loses itself and further loses the possibility of experience. Deodorization—the sensory mode of what Benjamin elsewhere describes as the loss of "aura," a deeply atmospheric and aerial term[46]—partially subtracts the world from *aisthesis*: the world no longer appears to the sense of smell and thus subtracts itself from experiential sense-making. Such a loss is inconsolable: it can be neither compensated for nor quieted.

To this inconsolable deodorization corresponds the ineluctable reign of time, the truncated "temps" (time) of the "prin-temps" (spring), stripped of its first, new character that the prefix "prin" indicates. The crucial verses in this respect read, "And Time engulfs me minute by minute, / Like immense snow engulfs a stiffened body." Instead of the tender embrace of a fragrant atmosphere that guards and conjoins bodies in their integrity, it is now Time that envelops in an ever-proliferating splitting: "minute par minute," small division upon small division falls on the I of the poem. This perpetual division renders stiff and subtracts from life (the stiffness of the body signifying rigor mortis). A moment of sphericality returns but only in the mode of unattainability: "From up high I contemplate the globe in its roundness / And I no longer seek there the shelter of a hut." Without atmosphere, the designation of roundness moves from the enveloping of scented air to the globe seen from afar: the only thing that is left is the distance of visual contemplation. The position of a "from up high," reminiscent of the position of the latest Hölderlin, forecloses the possibility of finding shelter. Cast out from fragrance/atmosphere, the lyric subject is thrown into the ever-proliferating cutting up of time that renders homeless.

The reign of Time and its relationship to the loss of a certain scenting find renewed articulation in a prose poem found in *Le Spleen de Paris*: "Double Bedroom [*La Chambre Double*]" (*OC* 1:280).[47] The setting is explicitly one of "the shelter of a hut": the account of this doubled room, whose autobiographical resonances with Baudelaire's life continuously in search of accommodations have been pointed out by scholars, foregrounds the question of the possibility of being sheltered. "Double Bedroom" articulates this possibility through a doubled description of the scented atmosphere of the room, the second half of which entertains a close but transformative relationship with deodorization as "The Taste for Nothingness" presents it. This doubleness is, in the first place, an expression of the ineluctable ambiguity, perhaps even duplicity, of place, in particular, of all places that offer themselves as "shelter." In "Double Bedroom," the twofold character of two hemispheres that join into one atmosphere is collapsed into a single room that oscillates between two atmospheric characterizations extended through time. If, as Francoise Meltzer has argued, Baudelaire's poetics crystalizes into a "seeing double," then "Double Bedroom" establishes a "smelling double" as the operative relation of Baudelairean sensing.

The first iteration of the room is marked precisely by what the poem concerned with a woman's head of hair tried to establish so insistently: an atmosphere. In the bedroom, a "stagnant atmosphere" calms all movement and, once again emphasizing smell's affinity with spirit, envelops the subject's existence in a "room truly *spiritual.*" The fifth paragraph, which constitutes the center of the first half of the poem, explicates this atmosphere in explicitly olfactory terms: "A most exquisitely chosen infinitesimal scent mingled with a very light humidity swims in this atmosphere, where slumbering spirit is rocked by hothouse sensations." The designation "infinitesimal" as it is applied to this most "exquisite" odor points to the climax of the first room's description: "there are no longer minutes, no longer seconds! Time has disappeared; it is Eternity that reigns." In the infinitesimal—that is, the infinitely small (but not nonexistent, not deodorized)—character of the lightest smell, the non-infinitesimal division that is time understood as the succession of minutes and seconds disappears. In other words, pushing division to its limit lets something other than division appear and in turn makes divisive time disappear. Such disappearance of time, of course, is paradoxical: How could one think disappearance if not in temporal terms? Yet this is precisely the character of this atmosphere: once in it, any notion of its emergence falls away, and what is left is only—eternity. And in eternity, a different kind of life emerges: "what we ordinarily call life, even in its happiest expansion, has nothing in common with this supreme life that I now know." It is not a question of a quantitative expansion of "happy life." Instead, in this atmosphere beyond divided time, a life of a different kind asserts itself.

This insight from the first half of "Double Bedroom" corresponds to an insight derived from "The Taste for Nothingness." In the latter, the reign of time emerged out of the disappearance of smell and "adorable spring"; in the former, the overcoming of the reign of time lies precisely in a finest smell and an atmospheric reign of eternity. This, then, is Baudelaire's suggestion: certain exquisite smells make time disappear and instead let eternity emerge; inversely, the disappearance of such smells spells the reign of time. These smells, as the adjective modifying spring in "The Taste for Nothingness" indicates, are *adorable*. Adoration, as Jean-Luc Nancy has argued in recent reflections on the "deconstruction of Christianity," is "a relation to a presence with respect to which it is not a question of making it manifest itself 'here' but, on the contrary, of knowing and affirming it as essentially 'elsewhere,' as opening the 'here.'"[48] The small, confined "doubled room" is opened—via its exquisitely scented atmosphere—to an elsewhere, the elsewhere of, as Baudelaire puts it, "an eternity of delight." Whereas Time "engulfs" or swallows up, the scent of eternity transports and throws wide open the confines of ever-same division. This adorable opening, however, is "nothing but an open body. Through all their openings, bodies dwell in adoration."[49] Sensing the smell of springtime or a lulling atmosphere, the body is opened onto itself and onto the world, an opening that occurs above all in "respiration."[50] Deodorization, by contrast, shuts the body in, closes it up, and forbids the opening of *sense*. Adoration, which Nancy opposes to "addiction," a term that will become relevant in the second half of the prose poem, is the name of "a praise of infinite sense"[51]: adorable smells allow for the opening of sense-making to occur, and it is this opening that turns the merely happy life into the "supreme life" of a different kind.[52]

The central paragraph of the prose poem, its hinge as it were, bursts this atmospheric bubble of eternity and the adoration that accompanies it: "But a terrible, dreadful knock [*un coup terrible, lourd*] rings out at the door." The room is not, after all, opened only through its adorable atmosphere that transports to an eternity of delights: it also has a more mundane opening—namely, a door—a door that receives a knock, a knock that appears to be so frightful that the word "coup," repeated twice more in the rest of the text, immediately refers to a different semantic field: its echo solicits a coup d'état. The state (of the room) is disrupted, usurped, and taken over.

This coup, like so many coups not only of Baudelaire's time but more generally, consists of the return of a specter: "And then a Specter entered."[53] The identity of this haunting revenant, true to the "essence" of spectrality, is indeterminate. The poem proposes three possible interpretations: it is "a bailiff come to torture me in the name of the law"; or a concubine who multiplies misery; or a journal editor who demands "the continuation of a manuscript." All three are figures of an *economy of debt*: the law, femininity, and (paid) writing are equally presented as entering violently and demanding what is their due.[54] The opening of the room (through its door) strikes open the adorable, "stagnant atmosphere," and insists on reigniting circulation. The anti-atmospheric character of the demand for payment recalls distinctly the figure of Judas: the latter, it will be recalled, chastised Mary for her fragrance that suffused (and made full, *pleroma*) the entire house and instead demanded its sale. The bailiff, the lover, and the editor reintroduce, just like Judas, the specter of poverty: the calculus of money and debt destroys the atmosphere of eternity (eternity being certainly the "perspective" from which Mary and Jesus view the waste and luxury of the precious nard) in favor of a scarcity that needs to be calculated with. Inversely, atmosphere-fragrance can now be seen as the opposite, more precisely, as the suspension (an *Ausschaltung* or *epochē* of sorts) of any and all calculating impulses. The calculation of debt and money divvies up the undividable enveloping of smell—a betrayal, the poem emphasizes, of "infernal" proportions.

And money, as always, is time. The reignited circulation—of money, of words that have been paid for—emerges as equivalent to the return of time: "Oh! yes! Time has reappeared; Time reigns sovereignly now." The *arrest* of time that turned into the reign of eternity is liquified, mobilized, and consequently flows into a reign of time. This triumph of time receives an olfactory articulation explicitly positioned as the symmetrical replacement of the fragrant atmosphere of the first room: "And this other-worldly perfume, which intoxicated me with a perfectioned sensibility, alas! is replaced by a fetid odor of tobacco mingled with I don't know which nauseating mildew. Now one breathes here the rancidness of desolation." This is what an economy of debt smells like: a fetid odor of tobacco mixed with mold. Both of these references are highly significant: mold or mildew,

Baudelaire's Perfumes | 89

deriving from an overwhelming intensification of the very light humidity of the first room, stands at the intersection of putrefaction and growth; more precisely, it is the life-form that emerges from the decay of something else. Its "nauseating" quality is the visceral, sickening cousin of the "Vertigo" of the smell of resurrection as the "rancid" smell recalls the "old rancid love" that was resurrected in "The Perfume Flask": another spectral cadaver of sorts, worthy of ressentiment and the rancor of the rancid, as Sedgwick put it. The smell of economy is the smell of a perverting, decadent overgrowth emerging from the disintegration and putrefaction of the "supreme life" of fragrance-atmosphere. Economy grows out of and as the expansion of decay and degeneration.

The fetid odor of tobacco, in turn, opens a field of olfactory associations that is highly significant for modernity: the relationship between smoking and time. Smoking segments time, or, rather, it articulates the passing of time as a movement of repeated division. Each drag of, say, a cigarette cuts time into homogenous pieces and lets it move as a regularized flow that washes away the "stagnant atmosphere." The smell of tobacco thus corresponds to the emphasis on *seconds* in the second half of "Double Bedroom": "I assure you that the seconds are now strongly and solemnly accentuated." The reign of time in the prose poem echoes and reprises the reign of time in "The Taste for Nothingness": the latter's "minutes" correspond to the former's "seconds," and the deodorization of spring is reconfigured in the stink of smoking, which overpowers adorable fragrance. In this sense, the smell of tobacco makes sensible a type of *bad infinity*: it is a "taste for the infinite," as one of Baudelaire's favorite phrases has it, but this infinite tastes bad, literally.[55] It is the infinity of mere formal division and endless repetition, a far cry from the "praise of infinite sense" characteristic of atmosphere and fragrance. In this context, smoking, as a bad olfactory infinity, can be seen to come to replace a prior historical instantiation of scented burning: it replaces incense burning, the ritual that establishes a relationship to transcendence and thus, perhaps, an adorable opening. Smoking, in short, is the (perverted, bad) incense burning of modernity.[56]

After the coup and through the double warping of eternity found in smoking and moldy decay, time reestablishes "its brutal dictatorship." The coercion of time's dictatorship is congruent with one of smoking's most important features: its *addictive* nature. Ad-diction (the counter-term to adoration in Nancy's idiom) and dict-atorship, both going back to the Latin word *dīcere* (to say), stand in an exacting correspondence: they both compel with force and suture shut. The world, as "Double Bedroom" puts it, has become "narrow." Time is dictatorial in its addictive quality: no escape is possible, but without escape there is only decay and desolation. Each of the seconds thus speaks: "I am Life, insupportable, implacable Life!" Life under dictatorship cannot be borne and yet it is inescapable. The poem thus can only end in damnation: "Live, damned one!" Without exquisite, infinitesimal fragrance-atmosphere, without adoration and eternity, life is nothing but a damning to the economy of debt and exchange, dictating compulsion and addictive repetition, a repetition compulsion compelling life.

Yet smoking—its olfactory, atmospheric emanations and its relationship to time—also points to a breach in the dictatorial, addictive hold that the time of seconds imposes.[57] Is there not an excessive, gratuitous quality to smoking? Is not tobacco strictly a luxury item, letting precious money go up in smoke—money that could be spent, say, on the poor that Judas claimed to be concerned with? In his reading of a different Baudelairean prose poem, Derrida has developed the nucleus of a "poetics of tobacco" that consists of two contradictory aspects. The first aspect draws precisely on the excessive character of smoking: "using itself up in pure loss, for pure, auto-affective pleasure, so close to the voice, this singular natural product that is tobacco."[58] Smoking, via the requisite act of breathing so close to speech and *diction*, would be the pure pleasure arising from the body affecting itself: praising, as it were, its mere openness to being affected and its susceptibility to pleasure. Smoking's second aspect derives from "the reinscription of tobacco into the economic cycle of exchange—contract, gift/return of the gift, alliance—[which] follows necessarily the incessant movement of a *reappropriation of an excess.*"[59] Qua modern product, tobacco is inevitably structured by the commodity form, the latter having already been present in smell's commodified form as perfume (and reemerging once again in Brecht's reflections on the political economy of smell in chapter 4 below). Any excessive quality smoking and its smell might have becomes recuperated into the terrible economizing imperative embodied by the "coup" of the bailiff or the editor.

Baudelaire's poem from its title—that is, from its head, *caput*—onwards emphasizes that these two sides of the poetics of tobacco (and by extension, of smell) are inextricable: the room is *double*. The temptation to read "Double Bedroom" as a chronological progression where the first atmosphere is irretrievably dispersed by the second—and, indeed, the seconds—relies on a methodological principle of reading that is only tenable if the reign of Time has already been accepted: succession as supersession is an effect only of chronological time. Against such unidirectional, rectilinear reading, the poem asserts the ineluctable doubleness not only of tobacco, thus insisting on holding both principles of Derrida's poetics of tobacco in relation, but also of time: the penultimate paragraph introduces a disorienting qualification of the seeming ever-sameness of seconds and their dictatorial reign. Repeating its crucial terms twice, the paragraph reads, "There is only one Second in human life that has the mission of announcing good news [*une bonne nouvelle*], the *good news* [la bonne nouvelle] that causes for each of us an inexplicable fear." A single second—different from all others—might emerge out of the flood of seconds and announce glad tidings: glad tidings that, in their clear Christic reference, announce rupture, "newness" (*nouvelle*), and, perhaps, a *Second* Coming.[60] Certainly, this news, perhaps like all genuine news, causes fear, fear in the face of the unknown that would break up addictive or dictatorial compulsion, which is, after all, all too familiar.[61] Yet this fear also indexes an opening through which the first room, with its fragrant atmosphere, maintains, despite everything, a link to this time of seconds. It is this opening that Baudelaire adores above all.

Revolutionary Anesthetic

The adorable atmosphere of fragrance would at first glance appear to be an "artificial paradise," as Baudelaire's prose texts on hashish and opium develop it. His description of the "taste for the infinite" closely resembles the analysis of olfactory sense-making developed thus far. For instance, the onset of such a paradisal state is unforeseeable and spectral: "this marvelous state, I say, comes with no early warning signs. It is as unforeseen as the phantom" (*OC* 1:402); similarly, this "type of haunting" (*OC* 1:402) is described as "intermittent," not unlike the rhythmic breathing in of smells. Lastly, the reader finds conspicuous references to both Lazarus and an economizing "coup" in the opening pages of *Artificial Paradises*: it is a question of, "as the author of *Lazarus* says, 'sweeping up paradise with a single stroke' [*d'emporter le paradis d'un seul coup*]" (*OC* 1:402). Drugs, with one fell swoop, bring about a paradisal state. Given these similarities, it might be surprising to read that Baudelaire explicitly excludes perfumes, along with alcohol, from his inquiry into artificial paradise: "leaving aside . . . perfumes whose excessive usage, while rendering man's imagination more subtle, gradually exhausts his physical forces" (*OC* 1:403). Fragrance is exhausting: like Hölderlin's "Patmos," Baudelaire's text worries about the anesthetic qualities of fragrance that derive from exhaustion. Smell might stimulate the imagination and its transporting qualities, but excessive use of its force will use up the force of the smeller and issue into an inability to perceive anything further.

Yet this exhaustion in and through perfumes is, in fact, a deep desire traceable throughout *The Flowers of Evil*; its exclusion from *Artificial Paradises* seems to be an apotropaic gesture. Recall the "slumbering spirit" of "Double Bedroom": the primary effect of the "most exquisitely chosen infinitesimal scent" was precisely a lulling of spirit. An intensification and clarification of this soporific function of fragrance is developed in "Lethe," one of the "condemned" poems that was included in the 1857 collection but removed from subsequent editions (see *OC* 1:813). The poetic subject wants to

> Bury my pained head
> In your skirts filled with your perfume
> And breathe, like a withered flower,
> The sweet afterscent of my defunct love.

> Dans tes jupons remplis de ton parfum
> Ensevelir ma tête endolorie,

> Et respirer, comme une fleur flétrie,
> Le doux relent de mon amour défunt. (*OC* 1:155)

This desire to bury oneself in perfume culminates, in the next verse, in a proclaimed turn away from life: "I want to sleep! To sleep rather than live!" (*OC* 1:156). Olfactory desire consists here of a desire to slide out of life: a paradoxical desire, to be sure, since to sleep one needs to be alive. This paradoxical desire is enabled by the exhausting effects of perfume: in it, perfume rhymes with the "défunt," dead but also the defunct—that is, out of order, deactivated, suspended—character of love, and it is this being put out of order of love that Baudelaire desires to breathe in. Behind Baudelaire's "solution" to the conundrum of sexual difference—namely, his attempt to "breathe" woman—lies a deeper desire: "In *Les Fleurs du mal*, the male speaker almost never wants to sleep with the woman—he wants the woman to put him to sleep."[62] Fragrance, of woman and otherwise, ultimately aims at the temporary cessation of life's activity that is found in sleep.[63]

Sleep had already figured in peculiar fashion in Baudelaire's delineation of what "revolt," this crucial stance of his according to Sartre, looks like. The poem concerning the disavowal of Saint Peter opens with a question: "What does God do with the stream of curses / That every day rises up toward his dear Seraphines?" (*OC* 1:121). The (highly blasphemous) answer: "He falls asleep to the sweet noise of our dreadful blasphemies." God is lulled to sleep by the white noise of constant blasphemy directed at Him; indeed, it is godly to be able to fall asleep in the face of perpetual rebellion. Along these lines the poetic subject of "Lethe" neither joins the slanderous chorus of blasphemy, nor does it proclaim the necessity of rebellious action or take leave from a world where "dream" and "action" are unrelated. Instead, it seeks to approach the godly falling asleep: the stance of revolt is displaced into a gradual falling asleep—that is, a temporary passing out of sensation.[64] Baudelaire's dream, in the end, is a dream of that which enables dreaming: sleep.

This desire to fall asleep constitutes a subspecies of what Benjamin designates as Baudelaire's "deepest will": "To interrupt the course of the world—that was Baudelaire's deepest will" (*GS* 1:667).[65] Falling asleep, or rather making (oneself) fall asleep, is an interruption of the course of the world and with it also an interruption of the perpetually recurring revolts that, impotently, try to redirect the world's course: Baudelaire's interruptive desire issues into his attempts "to thrust the world into its heart *or to sing it to sleep*" (*GS* 1:667; emphasis added). This soporific interruption, however, should not be understood as something that strikes abruptly. It is not quite the "emergency brake" of Benjamin's well-known aperçu regarding two diverging understandings of revolution: "Marx says that revolutions are the locomotives of world history. But perhaps it is wholly otherwise. Perhaps revolutions are the seizing of the emergency brake by the human race that is traveling on this train" (*GS* 1:1232).[66] In a slight displacement of Benjamin's proposal, the truly "revolutionary act" for Baudelaire would be neither an acting in opposition to the world (revolt) nor the sudden arrest of the course of the world *tout court* (revolution as emergency brake, strike). Instead, Baudelaire proposes a type of *revolutionary anesthetic*: a tender and gradual exhaustion of forces that leads to a temporary standstill, preceding, perhaps, an awakening to come. It is in perfumes—and their exquisite suspension of the course of the world—that Baudelaire catches a whiff of such a revolutionary lull.

3

Nietzsche's Chaos

Why I Have Such Flair (and Socrates Does Not)

Friedrich Nietzsche's so-called autobiographical book from 1888, *Ecce Homo*, in a section titled "Why I Am So Clever," contains a brief but incisive remark that indicates his relationship to Charles Baudelaire, that most fragrant poet of the European tradition. "Who was the very first *intelligent* follower of Wagner?" Nietzsche asks, before responding: "Charles Baudelaire . . . that typical decadent . . . he was perhaps also the last one" (*KSA* 6:289).[1] A first few mentions of Baudelaire can be found in Nietzsche's unpublished notes in the mid-1880s, but it is only in 1887 and 1888, when Nietzsche had access to Baudelaire's posthumous oeuvre—including the passages from *My Heart Laid Bare* that were analyzed as central to Baudelaire's olfactory poetics in the previous chapter—that he develops a pronounced stance vis-à-vis the poet.[2] And this position could hardly be more significant. Richard Wagner was Nietzsche's "first free breath [*Aufathmen*] in my life" and "a revolutionary" who would enable him to free himself from the suffocating "swamp air" of Germany (*KSA* 6:288). He was his "antipode" and perhaps his only worthy adversary. If Baudelaire, in turn, was Wagner's first and perhaps last "intelligent" follower, then the question arises whether the constellation *Nietzsche contra Wagner*, so important for Nietzsche and his reception, might not find an intensification in the constellation *Nietzsche contra Baudelaire*. Who Nietzsche is can be discerned in its "intelligent" form in the contrast between the philosopher, if he is one, and the poet—a contrast that has everything to do with being able to breathe freely, overcoming decadence, and finding the right stance with respect to a "revolutionary."

The prologue to *Ecce Homo* had opened with a plea for proper recognition that sets up the urgency of understanding who Nietzsche is and how he relates to those juxtaposed with him: "*I am such and such. Above all, do not mistake me* [ich bin der und der. Verwechselt mich vor Allem nicht]" (*KSA* 6:257). Beware, reader: in reading the self-narration of Nietzsche's life, you shall, above all, avoid falling into the trap of substitution or (ex)change (*verwechseln*); the danger of misunderstanding what Nietzsche has *in common*, or rather what he does not have in common, with those around him is of the greatest concern.[3] One of the most idiosyncratic—and hence potentially most revelatory—characteristics Nietzsche ascribes to himself in *Ecce Homo*, seeking to set himself apart, relates precisely to the struggle *Nietzsche contra Baudelaire* and the questions of air, breath, and smell. In the opening paragraph of "Why I Am a Fate," having advanced his famous claim that "I am not a human being, I am dynamite" (*KSA* 6:365), Nietzsche goes on to unfold his explosive, nonhuman, "such and such" quality: "I was the first one to *discover* truth because I first sensed—*smelled*—the lie to be a lie. . . . My genius is in my nostrils" (*KSA* 6:366).[4] In order not to mistake Nietzsche, we need to recognize the true locus of his explosive genius: his nostrils.[5] If Baudelaire's poetry and his "existential choice" are characterized by an unprecedented emphasis on olfaction, then Nietzsche's discovery of truth, in turn, functions through smell in an unprecedented manner. Nietzsche's nostrils will outdo Baudelaire's "intelligent" nose, and his explosive character derives from a superior, genial way of smelling—a perceptual operation intended to distinguish him from both the first intelligent follower of his great antipode and the common, ordinary lives surrounding him.

Through this self-description, Nietzsche further proposes that the history of philosophy can be reconfigured and indeed exploded—"I am dynamite"—by a nostril-centric genius: the "discovery" of truth and lie, the explosion of previous misunderstandings of the nature of truth occurs for the first time once a philosopher smells. Philosophy—in one of the many, often parodic, variants of the Nietzschean retelling of its history—becomes an olfactory affair. To *Ecce Homo*'s chapter headings "Why I Am a Fate" and "Why I Am So Wise" thus tacitly corresponds the claim "Why I Have Such Flair," with "flair" taken in a double sense: Nietzsche has style as well as a peculiar ability to sniff out something (as the French *flairer* indicates); in relation to philosophy, Nietzsche's peculiar wisdom will emerge out of the interplay of style and sniffing. And indeed, in *Twilight of the Idols*, written the same year as *Ecce Homo*, Nietzsche explicitly establishes a direct link between wisdom (the σοφία of philosophy) and smell. Developing "the problem of Socrates," he writes, "Might wisdom perhaps appear on earth as a raven inspired [*begeistert*] by a little smell of carrion?" (*KSA* 6:67). Wisdom, more precisely, *Socratic* wisdom, appears on earth—the very site of Nietzsche's polemical contestation, a site that will eventually be the source of one of his two "new smells" that will be analyzed extensively below—as being inspired or enthused by a "little smell." This smell, when inspected "from up close," reeks of decay and carrion. It is not a wisdom of life but rather a wisdom of the decay of dead life. Socratic wisdom and its smell are thus above all a "problem": they indicate a doubting of the worth and value of life and draw inspiration from death and decay.

Nietzsche's characteristic flair thus stands not just in competition with Baudelaire's fragrant, intelligent poetry but also in a direct struggle with Socratism. It responds to the intertwined tasks of attempting to overcome the "problem of Socrates" (the doubting of the value of life) and of sniffing out a smell that is other than the "little smell" that enthuses this problematic Socratic wisdom.[6] With respect to the latter, Nietzsche's nostrils thus inscribe themselves into a long tradition that knows of Socrates's snub nose as a crucial feature of his appearance. In Xenophon's *Symposium*, for example, Socrates had proclaimed to be particularly adept at picking up scents in contrast to the beautiful Critobulus: "For your nostrils look down toward the ground, but mine are wide open and turned outward so that I can catch scents from all about."[7] While his nose might not be considered as beautiful as Critobulus's straight nose, Socrates's is more functional: not merely turned downward but into multiple dimensions, exposed to his surroundings in a manner that allows him to pick up on something the merely beautiful (Critobulus) misses. When Nietzsche claims to be an olfactory genius he consequently performs a double gesture: on the one hand, he positions himself in the very arena that Xenophon's Socrates claimed for himself, the realm of being particularly discerning when it comes to olfaction; on the other, he claims to outdo Socrates and smell something Socrates did not detect—namely, the very smell of Socrates himself and the putrefaction inherent in Socratism.

The image of the carrion-smelling raven of wisdom used in *Twilight of the Idols* adds further nuance to Nietzsche's claim that his flair reconfigures the tradition of philosophy and its conceptions of truth and lie. Flying at the beginning of a book concerned with twilight, this raven, one of only two references to this animal in Nietzsche's writings, constitutes the ornithological counterimage to the owl of Minerva, as it has long been associated with the wisdom and perspicuity of philosophy, in particular in Hegel's *Philosophy of Right*.[8] Philosophy, according to Hegel, only appears as the thought of the world once the world has been formed: the appearance of wisdom in the world derives from (a stage of) the world having completed itself and having become fully actualized; it appears "late." The Socratic raven, like the owl, appears at dusk—but not because the world has actualized a certain stage but because it is decaying. Here, no futural phenomenon such as the air of the morning or of tomorrow, crucial to Hölderlin's aerial-olfactory poetics, attracts the bird; rather, it is the opposite: Socrates and Plato, *Twilight of the Idols* insists, are "symptoms of decay" (*KSA* 6:68).[9] Philosophy feasts on putrefaction and is lured into appearing on earth by the smell of carrion. And its inspiration, its spirit (*begeistert*) derives precisely from the stench of this decadence that spurs on a bird's flight.

A closer look at this raven (*Rabe*), at the very name of this bird, reveals an inscription of Nietzsche's opposition to the understanding of philosophy as the august and serene appearance of wisdom that the owl had embodied: anagrammatically rearranged—exploded by nonhuman dynamite, as it were—this raven spells *but* (*Rabe, aber*). Like Socrates, Nietzsche will smell: *but* his smelling will detect putrefaction at the core of proclaimed wisdom. This localized and partially playful inscription of objection finds a more exacting articulation in the *Ecce Homo* passage proclaiming Nietzsche's olfactory genius: "I was the first one to *discover* truth because I first sensed—*smelled*—the lie to be a lie. . . . My genius is in my nostrils. . . . I contradict [*widerspreche*] in an unprecedented manner and am nevertheless the opposite [*Gegensatz*] of a naysaying spirit" (*KSA* 6:366). As olfactory genius, Nietzsche is the opposite, the *Gegensatz* that counters all naysayers. The logic of this unusual *Widerspruch* is precisely predicated on his olfactory genius: Nietzsche's flair contradicts or objects without becoming a naysayer, and, as this chapter will demonstrate in detail, only a shift toward olfaction enables such non-naysaying objecting.

This *Widerspruch* of Nietzschean flair is most incisively, and perhaps in a sense always, directed against his contemporaries. It situates Nietzsche as out of his element: it sets him apart and distances him from those around him. The best-known mode of this distancing objection is temporal: Nietzsche's *Widerspruch* instantiates and produces his being "untimely" (*unzeitgemäß*), his being out of joint with his time in the mode of a not yet. Recognizing this untimeliness is part and parcel of not mistaking Nietzsche. This temporal mode of Nietzsche not belonging to "his" time finds a *sensory* equivalent in his claims about olfaction. His olfactory genius, so *Ecce Homo* claims, lies in the fact that he made the discovery of the truth about lies "first"; no one else before him, none of his contemporaries could smell what he smelled. The sensory logic of olfaction accounts for such pervasive non-perception, such rampant ignorance of a smell by appealing to habit: we do not smell (anymore) what we are used to.[10] Something as familiar to me as, for instance, my own body odor cannot appear to me in olfactory perception; my habituation precludes my sensory access to the most familiar. The sensory equivalent to Nietzsche's untimeliness, then, lies in his being out of step with the sensory habits of his time. Nietzsche's flair locates him at a distance from those around him; it breaks up calcified habits and discovers a mode of objecting that promises a different type of wisdom. Qua olfactory genius, his sensory constitution is "aussergewöhnlich," a word he uses repeatedly in the 1870s: he is extraordinary in the literal sense of the German word as out of habit and outside of the common—Nietzsche's scents are supposed to (but, as we will see, in the last consequence fail to) be other than the "common scents" of his milieu.

Nietzsche contra Theory

One of the habits that Nietzsche opposes, indeed one of the most formidable opponents any philosopher could have chosen to attack, is the habit of according vision an epistemological privilege over all the other senses. Tied up with the Socratic type, the "victorious" history of the eye—with its attendant vocabulary of seeing or beholding in clarity the truth, of a visual *eidos*, and phenomenality understood through luminosity and visibility—might indeed be considered of a rare continuity and dominance in the history of philosophy. Nietzsche's grand claim of an olfactory genius, his distinctive flair, must be understood as a strategy in his duel with ocularcentrism, as a decisive charge that is supposed to express his "entire force, agility, and weapon mastery" (*KSA* 6:274). Put differently, Nietzsche's struggle concerns the *distribution of the senses embodied in theory* and the question of its possible rupture and redistribution. As such, this redistributive struggle is part of an analysis of the interplay between philosophy and a philosopher's bodily and sensory constitution that Nietzsche develops, expands, and refines throughout his writing from the 1870s onward (and, one might add, long before "sense studies" with its "auditory" or "tactile turns" became an established and named field of study). The statement in *Ecce Homo* concerning Nietzsche's "such and such" quality of being an olfactory genius constitutes the culmination of a long reflection on the intertwined nature of thinking and the constitution of the sensory apparatus of the thinker—Nietzsche's very being, in short, could be understood as the locus of an *agon* among the senses, especially vision, hearing, and smell, with the balance of powers in this triangulation constantly changing.

The first sustained iteration of a reflection on this *agon* or struggle can be found in Nietzsche's first published book, *The Birth of Tragedy*. Disputing Socrates's own claims that he is particularly attuned to odors, Nietzsche argues that Socrates in fact marks the emergence of a type of human being who is governed by one sense alone: vision. The perceptual apparatus of the new type of human being that emerges at the beginning of philosophy is governed by "the one large cyclops eye of Socrates" (*KSA* 1:92). Nietzsche further names this new type of human being the "type of the *theoretical human being*" (*KSA* 1:98). Socrates is the "archetype [*Urbild*] and progenitor" (*KSA* 1:116) of a new human being who is theoretical in the etymological sense of *theōria*: a human being of spectating vision, oriented toward a gaining of knowledge conceived of on the model of beholding an idea or a form. It is against the backdrop of this dominance of theory—at first primarily thought to lie in a triumph of vision over hearing, and thus of visual form over music, but later as a triumph of vision over all other senses and the body more broadly—that the late Nietzsche will assert the importance of his olfactory genius. Seeking to claim olfactory genius for himself alone, Nietzsche relegates Socrates to the ocularcentric realm of a misguided history of philosophy as *theōria*.

The other side of the coin of Socrates's—that is, the theoretical human's—visual fixation lies in his decadence: that he is a phenomenon of decay derives from the atrophy of his other senses in service of the eye alone. Within the economy of *The Birth of Tragedy*, the process of decadence and decay is articulated as the end of tragedy at the hands of the theoretical human being. This decay begins with Euripides and amounts to a strengthening of the dominance of *form* and *figure*, producing an ocular hegemony that "purifies" tragedy of the Dionysian countertendencies of chaos and deformation, terms that will emerge as crucial to Nietzsche's thinking of odors. This Euripidean tendency culminates in Socrates, who continues the tendency toward form and figure. Socrates embodies and brings into the Greek world an "optimism" that constitutes the boundless, limitless triumph of the Apollinian in a new form of life: "The theoretical human being.... New form of life [*Neue Daseinsform*]. Boundless Apollinism" (NF 1870, 6[13]). Under this ocular hegemony, the Greek tragic age ends: "The antique world runs aground [*geht ... zu Grunde*] on the ἄνθρωπος

Nietzsche's Chaos | 99

θεωρητικός. The Apollinian element again splits off from the Dionysian and now both become perverted [*entarten beide*]" (NF 1870, 7[7]). The theoretical human being is a symptom of decay in a double sense: on the one hand, the state in which the tendency toward vision and form was being counterbalanced by a Dionysian counterforce ends. But on the other hand, the Apollinian reign of form, too, decays: as the very state of form—that is, of figuration and delimitation—its "boundless [*grenzenloser*]" reign is paradoxical and undoes itself without its own boundary. With the triumph of *theōria*, a whole world, a whole mode of world making and sense-making, deteriorates and decays. Form and figure eventually run aground on the theoretical human being.

This usurpation by the eye must be understood as a revaluation of its function: neither was the eye originally made for contemplative seeing nor was the perceptual apparatus as a whole subordinated to this one sense alone. This double movement constitutes, in the framework of Nietzsche's thinking, an act of *active forgetting* that serves an organism's increasing of power. In the well-known twelfth section of the second essay of *Toward the Genealogy of Morals* Nietzsche thus writes, "with each essential growth of the whole, the 'sense' of the individual organs also shifts—under certain conditions can their partial perishing [*Zu-Grunde-Gehen*] . . . be a sign of growing strength [*Kraft*] and perfection" (*KSA* 5:315). The triumph of one sense organ, the eye, and the loss of purpose, the "becoming useless," of the other senses go hand in hand—and both are part of a reconfiguration of the forces of a particular being and the "sense" that accrues to each sense; the plurality of the senses is continuously open to reinterpretation and redistribution. The ocularcentric constitution of the perceptual apparatus of theoretical man is thus far from a necessary structure: by contrast, it is contingent and perpetually open to reconfiguration. If a different type of being emerged for which an atrophy (a running aground) of sight and a strengthening of the other senses—of smell perhaps—would mean an increase in force, then such a restructuring could occur. Nietzsche's emphasis on his ability to smell consequently indicates that he is a being engaged in just such a redistribution of the senses—in other words, via his olfactory genius, Nietzsche pursues a very specific goal: to overcome the dominance of the ἄνθρωπος θεωρητικός and, with it, to distance himself from Socrates and the whole "problem of Socrates" concerning the question of the value of life. Through the strengthening of olfaction in the *agon* of the senses, Nietzsche will become a new, different type of being that not only steps out of the sensory habits of his time but also objects to the "little smell" of decay and carrion that brought Socratic wisdom to the earth. His wisdom, in other words, is directed against the monolithic distribution of the senses embodied by (theoretical) ocularcentrism and points toward a rupture of this order that would bring about new bodies, new sense, and, in the last consequence, a new politics of sensing bodies.

Compromising Smell

In his battle against the theoretical human being, Nietzsche's distinctive flair is thus part and parcel of his strategy to mark out his distinctive position, his "such and such" quality. Recognition of his peculiarity requires, as a note from the time of *Ecce Homo* indicates, "to not mistake oneself for the others, to feel the distance" (NF 1888, 15[98]). In other words, Nietzsche's struggle to not be mistaken for someone he is not amounts to a struggle to *put distance* between himself and those he might be mistaken for. The writings after *Thus Spoke Zarathustra* turn such distance into a key Nietzschean term, especially in the syntagma "pathos of distance." *Beyond Good and Evil*, the first book written after the completion of the last part of *Zarathustra*, makes this pathos the cornerstone of Nietzsche's theory of "nobility"; *Toward the Genealogy of Morals* ties it to the creation of values and the so-called slave revolt. More generally, distance constitutes a condition of possibility for any *ordering*: there must be distance between two (distinct) instincts, beings, or states for one to rise above—to be more noble than—the other or even just to be separate and set apart from it.

Yet Nietzschean distance, in the secondary literature virtually exclusively discussed for its moral and political implications,[11] maintains an uneasy relationship with Nietzsche's thought of a struggle of the senses and its implications for the conception of truth. If it is smell that is supposed to set Nietzsche apart as a genius and, among other things, mark the distance from Socrates and those detected to be decadent, then this distance's conditions of possibility inevitably hinge on smell's relationship with distance and its correlate terms perspective, order, and differentiation. The first step of analyzing distance's relationship to smell is deceptively simple: to smell, Nietzsche's writings emphasize, one has to be *near* the odorous object. In contradistinction to vision (and to a certain degree, hearing), the "insight" of smell is always one of closeness but not contact (as in touch).[12] In this vein, the astrophysicist Johann Karl Friedrich Zöllner argues in *On the Nature of Comets* (1872), a book Nietzsche cherished immensely and read repeatedly throughout his life, that smell is positioned rather exactly as the middle term of the five senses if one orders them according to the spatial (and temporal) scale on which they operate: "one cannot miss a gradual widening of the spatial and temporal realm from the general sense of touch through the sensing of taste, smell, hearing, and sight."[13] If ordered according to their spatial and temporal reach, smell is located precisely in the middle, making it the sense of a *medium* reach. In Nietzsche's own work, the link between proximity and smell is stated most clearly in *Thus Spoke Zarathustra*. In a section titled "On Immaculate Insight [*Erkenntnis*]," elaborating the impossibility of cognizing something in an immaculate manner, Zarathustra states how this nearness needed for smelling undoes any notion of "pure" insight: "I once thought I could see a god's soul play in your games, you purely cognizing ones! No better art than your arts did I once thought possible! Farness [*Ferne*] concealed from me the filth of snakes and a dreadful smell: and that the cunning of a lizard was sneaking around lustfully. But I came *close* to you" (*KSA* 4:158). Nietzsche underlines "close": only by giving up "farness" can one detect the "dreadful smell" that indicates the absence of a "god's soul" and reveals instead the deception underlying the notion of pure cognition or insight. Zarathustra's "But [*Aber*]," introducing the key term "close" and echoing the yes-saying objection of the raven (*Rabe*), is directed against this concealing and camouflaging effect of distance; it dissolves the "once" of the seeing distance into the new insight of a proximate "here." Without distance, the appearance of both godliness and the best art disappear, and instead, foreshadowing an important olfactory moment analyzed below, animality (a snake, a lizard) appears. In smell, the pretense of godliness that characterizes a distant mode of "insight" is replaced by nearness, impurity, and animality.

This destruction of the illusion of purity, however, is just as much directed against Zarathustra himself, as the one who discovers this illusion, as it is against those who seek to uphold it. The nearness of smelling is *compromising*: the smelling subject needs to forgo distance and approach its object, thus entering the same sphere and exposing itself to contagion.[14] Being distant, not only could the "purely cognizing ones" guard their purity, but anyone seeking to know them could as well. Zarathustra's coming close to smell them compromises his purity just as much as theirs since his cognizing of the "purely cognizing ones" is not a pure cognition itself; he, too, must give up any pretense to a godly soul and find himself (in the narration of the book often literally) surrounded by animals. This compromising quality of smell, in turn, amounts to a severe weakening of any pathos of distance. The proximity of smell closes the gulf that is supposed to separate. The reciprocity of exposure—I enter your olfactory realm to detect your flaws, leaving me exposed to contagion and detection by you in turn—undoes any nobility and even threatens differentiation as such: olfactory genius always tends toward ending up in the commonality of shared—that is, *common*—scents. "The danger lay in proximity" (*KSA* 6:157), Nietzsche emphasizes in *Ecce Homo*: proximity renders possible all kinds of mixing, confusing, and mistaking, and consequently draws out the facts of common, proximate, and shared existence. The "nearest nearness" (NF 1888, 22[29]) required by smelling threatens the ability "to be different [*verschieden*]"; the *Scheiden* of difference and separation is attenuated and endangered when one comes close. Distance acts as the guardian of differentiation beyond and out of commonality—a guardian easily overwhelmed by smell's proximity. What Nietzsche's nostrils detect, in short, is this: in smell, any pathos of distance—and consequently the related terms of nobility, value creation, and ordering—threatens to fall into a stinking, common bathos of nearness.

Distance, Perspective, Chaos

Yet the compromising *reduction* of distance found in smell constitutes only half the story, the easier half no less. In a passage concerned with "a last trait of my nature," from *Ecce Homo*'s last section, titled "Why I Am So Wise," Nietzsche replaces nearness as the crucial term of olfaction: "I am characterized by a completely uncanny irritability of the instinct for cleanliness [*Mir eignet eine vollkommen unheimliche Reizbarkeit des Reinlichkeits-Instinkts*] so that I perceive the nearness or—what am I saying?—the innermost [*das Innerlichste*], the 'innards' of every soul physiologically—I *smell* it" (*KSA* 6:275). Faintly echoing Hölderlin's reflections on *Innigkeit* and in exact correspondence to the invasive character of olfactory perception that already troubled Kant, the term "nearness" is undone in the inwardness, in the "innards," of Nietzsche's deployment of his genial nostrils.[15] While proximity could still be seen to be an oppositional term to distance, and consequently to stand in a privative relation to it, smell, in its radicality, undoes the near/far opposition when it becomes "innermost": another being's inside becomes perceptible; what one would conventionally call the perceiving "subject" is thus not only "near," not in contact, but is located, beyond such designations, at the extreme point of the inside turning out and the outside turning inward, unsettling the very foundation of oppositionality.[16] Such an intensification of smelling's relation to distance is daring and dangerous, as the passage just quoted indicates: Nietzsche hesitates with an incredulous "what am I saying?" right before moving from "nearness" to "the innermost." This feature of his "nature," presented as a "*last* character trait," is not only uncanny but "*completely* uncanny"; the diminished hold of the distance/proximity schema on the ordering of perception is an extreme point of uncanniness, in particular because Nietzsche presents it as something that is his own and proper to him (*mir eignet*). As the thinker of distance par excellence, Nietzsche is expelled from his home (*un-heimlich*) when he smells—and yet this expulsion (a type of expropriation moving beyond a logic of the proper, as it were) is very much part of his nature and, in fact, concludes his entire discussion of *his* wisdom. The "last" point of this wisdom is reached precisely in uncanniness, when the "innermost" nature of smelling threatens both that which is his own and the notion of distance as such while simultaneously constituting, in this expropriating movement, that which is proper to Nietzsche.

Nietzsche's move away from "nearness" thus indicates the extreme point of the incompatibility of the pathos of distance (and hence nobility, aristocracy, rank ordering, etc.) and olfaction. Yet the reference to "the innermost" points to a deeper and perhaps even more consequential problem inherent in smell, which can be stated as follows: without the notion of distance, there cannot be a robust conception of perspective. Smell—and this is the crucial threat Nietzsche's nostrils pick up on—threatens to *dissolve perspective*. More precisely, it dissolves the "spect" part of perspective while reconfiguring the "per" as the invasion of "the innards": olfaction concerning "the innermost" of the perceived object means that it occurs at a point of indistinction and mingling where the inside is the outside, the outside the inside. Bereft of both the inner/outer and the far/proximate distinction, a smelling subject fails to construct anything resembling a stable and determinate perspective. Olfaction threatens—and this language of threat and danger is important here—to overturn perspectivism.

The argument for this far-reaching conclusion can be reconstructed as follows. Perspective is a visual or optical term. Both the term itself and any number of passages from Nietzsche's work could demonstrate this; the famous passage concerning "perspectival seeing" from the third essay of *Toward the Genealogy of Morals* illustrates it perhaps most succinctly. Once more opposing any notions of a "pure" cognition, Nietzsche writes, "there is always the demand here to think an eye that cannot be thought at all, an eye that is thoroughly supposed to have no direction [*Richtung*].... There is *only* perspectival seeing, *only* perspectival 'cognition'" (*KSA* 5:365). Cognition appears equivalent to seeing; the eye dominates this theory of insight. It is out of this perspectival seeing that one cannot escape.[17] Nietzsche insists on the eye having a *direction*: perspectival seeing is always directed—that is, oriented in a particular way. This is the first feature of perspective significantly weakened in smell: while some tracking and tracing of odors is possible, in particular for beings such as dogs, olfaction does not have a "direction" in the manner of a line of sight that Nietzsche designates as crucial to his concept of perspective. Odors, by contrast, waft about. Their diffuse nature makes determinately directed perception faltering and dubious. Instead, olfactory perception is atmospheric: no single orientation guides it; it instead englobes without a determinate "direction."

The line of sight structuring a perspective allows for a determination of *depth*, the distance of the seen object from the seeing subject. The world, when accessed through the mode of visual sense-making, is structured by a degree ordering in terms of proximity and farness; vision thus prepares the ground for a "pathos of distance." The possibility of precise depth perception, in turn, depends on *binocular* vision. (This also attributes a new connotation to Nietzsche's description of Socrates's cyclops eye in *The Birth of Tragedy*: that Socrates only has a *single* eye already indicates that the world-historical development he initiates is one of equalization and vulgarization, a tending toward decadent commonality, which derive from a misjudging of distance.) Binocular vision produces so-called binocular disparity or parallax that enables stereopsis, or properly three-dimensional depth perception.[18] Only the difference between the perception of each of the two eyes constitutes a perception of how far away—how distant—any given object within a perspective is. (A similar phenomenon obtains in hearing, where distance is discerned via echolocation, which is based on the difference between the two ears.) Nothing equivalent, however, occurs in olfaction: the twoness of the nostrils appears to be no more than nature's practical joke since they do not in any way produce an equivalent depth perception and do not contribute to the detection of the distance of an odorous object. Determining such distance requires that the perceiving subject move; in other words, one must alter one's position in space, and only from the difference in perception in the two positions can such a thing as "olfactory location" arise. Consequently, merely atmospheric perception can hardly be considered perspectival in Nietzsche's sense: it allows neither for a determinate "direction" of perception nor a definitive degree ordering into far and near, background and figure. All these crucial features of perspective, according to the great provocation of Nietzsche's notion of smell, become severely weakened in olfaction—the world, when accessed through the mode of olfactory sense-making, tends toward being subtracted from perspectives as ordering.

The term "perspective," in Nietzsche's thought, is twinned with "horizon," as Martin Heidegger emphasizes in the Nietzsche lectures he gave in Freiburg between 1936 and 1940. According to Heidegger's influential analysis, perspectival thinking is marked by the interplay of perspective and horizon: "The horizon always stands within a perspective, within a seeing-through [*Durchblick*] into what is possible."[19] A horizon *delimits*, according to its Greek root, while a perspective draws a line through and beyond such delimitation. Given the troubled relationship of perspective and smell, what, then, would be the relationship between horizon and smell? Just like the "through" character of perspective, the delimitation by a horizon is lacking in olfaction: while sight's limits can be seen, there is nothing in smell that delimits it from within and would be detectable via smell. Smell's reach is either determined by the diminishing of its ability to perceive (it continuously decreases until it approaches zero, the "olfactory degree zero" so important to the latest Hölderlin and again to Ponge) or by an externally imposed limit, such as a container. (One such container would be a cave, a decisive locale in *Thus Spoke Zarathustra* that will be analyzed below.) The indeterminate, wafting-about nature of a smell subtracts it from the determinate delimitation of a horizon. In a note written in 1881, as part of his preparations for *The Gay Science*, Nietzsche delineates the far-reaching consequences of such an absence of horizons and perspectives: "What kind of sponge was it with which we erased the entire horizon around us? How did we accomplish wiping away this eternal, firm line that all lines and measures until now referred back to, according to which all master builders of life built until now, without which there seemed to be no perspective, no order, no art of building at all?" (NF 1881, 14[25]). We find ourselves, Nietzsche argues, in a world where horizons, "firm lines," have been wiped out and perspective has dissolved. This is the world as smell detects it: in olfaction, measured and ordered organizations of the world have become unsettled, vaporized. Such an attenuating of delimiting lines hampers life: "And this is a general law: everything living can become healthy, strong, and fertile only within a horizon" (*KSA* 1:251).

One name for such an absence of order, Nietzsche emphasizes at various points, is "chaos." That term occupies a crucial place in his thought, as it reprises the Dionysian tendency toward deformation that the theoretical, ocularcentric human being suppressed. *The Gay Science* puts it succinctly in aphorism 109: "The character of the world as a whole, by contrast, is in all eternity chaos, not in the sense of a lacking necessity but of a lacking order, arrangement, form" (*KSA* 3:468). In other words, there are no hierarchies and hence no "pathos of distance" in the world, when considered "in all eternity": even the very existence of *form* is doubtful from the non-perspective of eternity. Heidegger subsequently establishes the term "chaos" as the counter-term to the twin pair of perspective and horizon. Olfaction's troubled relation to both perspective and horizon consequently suggests that smell stands in a significant relationship to chaos. Following Heidegger's analysis, two core meanings of chaos can be distinguished: on the one hand, "χάος means initially the yawning [*das Aufgähnende*] and points in the direction of the immeasurable, unsupported, groundless, gaping openness."[20] Chaos names the ungrounded opening of becoming that is "immeasurable." On the other hand, Heidegger argues that a different understanding of chaos emerges in modernity: "For us, the chaotic designates that which is jumbled, confused."[21] Both of these meanings can be detected in the analysis of olfaction's dissolution of perspective and horizon: the absence of a "delimiting" horizon makes it "immeasurable, unsupported," a middle and medium of opening; the impossibility of establishing a rank ordering leads to it being "jumbled, confused." In short, the weakening of the hold that the terms "perspective" and "horizon" assert over the world moves smell into the vicinity of anarchic chaos, severely casting doubt on any understanding of Nietzsche as the arch proponent of aristocratic hierarchies.

Put differently, olfaction is chaotic because it consists in a disintegration, deformation, or, to use Nietzsche's own term, in an *explosion*. In a note roughly contemporaneous with the aphorism on chaos from *The Gay Science* cited above, he argues exactly this: "Noses would be thinkable whose olfactory nerves would be tickled only by the ejections of a volcano. The surfaces of all fragrant things indeed seem to be in a state of perpetual explosion; the force with which they send out small masses must be enormous [*ungeheuer*]" (NF 1881, 11[277]).[22] Odors are cast out from the surfaces of all fragrant things. More precisely, what might to the eye appear as a smooth and flat surface (*Oberfläche*) is in fact in a constant state of explosion. The force that produces such a movement cannot be detected by vision's attention to surface but rather becomes perceptible only in smell. Seeing is subject to "the lie of unity, the lie of thingness, substance, duration" (*KSA* 6:75): the testimony of the eye is that in seeing, the seen object persists as unified, substantial, and enduring. Smell's entering the innards of a being, by contrast, displaces and, in fact, explodes the schema of surface and depth that guides the ocularcentric notion of truth. An odorous thing qua odorous appears to the senses as far from being a self-contained, unified, and persisting substance. It must instead be understood as a process: "things present themselves to smell only to the degree in which they are constituted themselves by a process, in which they dissolve into the air with practical effects."[23] Insofar as a thing is fragrant, it is dissolving and thus is becoming other than what it is. This self-alteration in olfaction is precisely the instantiation of smell's chaotic nature: the smell of a thing results from the phase change that leads particles out of the organized, solid or liquid, state into a gaseous state, where the particle has a greater degree of freedom and a higher capacity to move around—hence tending toward a disordered, disintegrated—that is, more chaotic—state. If something smells, it is involved in a process of disintegration, becoming more chaotic as it continues to emit scent. This is the key, dangerous "insight" Nietzsche's olfactory genius discovered: in odors, one can detect that the world continuously tends toward disorganization and chaos.

In this explosive character of smells Nietzsche's claim of a nostril-centric genius meets his self-description, in the same section of *Ecce Homo*, as dynamite: attention to olfaction functions like dynamite in that it explodes the "lies" upon which a philosophy of substance or unity might be built. Such a philosophy functions by setting up ideals against that which is perceived as "the inconstant, deceptive, changing, 'stinking' etc." (NF 1884, 26[203]). The *eidos*, the unchanging form, the seen shape is supposed to protect against change and inconstancy, against stink and chaos. A rediscovery of the "stinking" unsettles all ideals: its explosive character renders smell anti-idealistic. This was already implied in the incompatibility of distance and perspective, on the one hand, and smell, on the other: ideals, by necessity, are set up at a distance. They are seen from far away; they provide "direction" and have meaning only within a certain perspective, delimited by a horizon. The invasive and explosive nearness of smell, by contrast, explodes all ideals, leaving in its wake chaos, overturning, and change.

This chaotic nature of air, detected in a-perspectival smell, is in the last analysis also responsible for the compromising nature of smell. Threatening the possibility of a definitive pathos of distance and the possibility of any (rank) ordering, smell thus also threatens the possibility of valuation *tout court*. For Nietzsche, all values are perspectival: they exist only as delimited by a horizon, relative to a context in which they weigh and matter. The very condition of possibility for values lies in the existence of a "direction" (*Richtung*), of lines of limitation, and of the guardian of difference constituted by distance—all countered by the nonvisual structures of smell. This is also the reason for smell's association with the herd in many of Nietzsche's writings. The herd is marked by unformed mediocrity, interchangeable proximity, by the "common scent" of its constituent elements. It does not allow for anything to stand out; it is marked by what Nietzsche in a different context calls "*compromising* mediocrity" (NF 1887, 10[67]), a tendency toward *Gleichgültigkeit*—an absence of ordering and subordinating judgments—that eliminates any individuality, constantly leading to the very "mistaking" that the prologue to *Ecce Homo* sought to prevent. Living in the herd means compromising and being compromised in ordinariness and the mediocrity of the middle. As a corollary, the extreme point of compromise reached in smell threatens greatness. In air, be it "bad" or not, greatness (*Größe*) does not exist. Greatness would be a perspectival phenomenon that finds no equivalent in the olfactory realm. No optics, no greatness—all that is left are the common scents of the middling space of chaotic compromise and confusion.

When Nietzsche, in *Ecce Homo*, describes his "proprium" as possessing a unique "olfactory genius," then this claim is indeed "completely uncanny": if his work is primarily directed toward a "transvaluation of all values," if he is to be the philosopher of a non-decadent future marked by a pathos of distance, then these claims as articulated through olfaction constantly threaten to undermine him. The conventional image of Friedrich Nietzsche as a philosopher of distance, nobility, and force is compromised in the smell that he himself celebrates and ascribes to himself. The allegedly proto-fascist philosopher who is said to celebrate his uniqueness as part of a generalized celebration of aristocracy and hierarchy in fact celebrates his uniqueness precisely in an idiom that does not allow for the characteristics it is supposed to produce and secure. When one gets up close, "near" to Nietzsche's self-description—up close with the peculiar Nietzschean flair—it appears much less as a laudatory, ennobling designation than the name of a deeply troubling, compromising, and confounding problem: Nietzsche's olfactory genius and chaotic smells tend toward dissolving much of what he is thought to hold dear.

New Smells

Faced with this compromising character of smell, what is an olfactory genius to do? If the problem at first appeared to lie in the "little smell" of carrion and decay that inspired (*begeistert*) Socratic wisdom as it appeared on earth, closer inspection—getting up close to smell—revealed that it is rather the logic of olfactory sense-making itself that constitutes the main problem. Two paths, a crossroads of sorts, present themselves at this point. On the one hand, one could abandon smell by seeking distance from it. A passage in book 3 of *Thus Spoke Zarathustra* indicates such a line of flight: "Finally my nose is redeemed from the smell of all humanity [*vom Geruch alles Menschenwesens*]!" (KSA 4:234). Such a redemption—a *deodorization*, to use a term that points to the epilogue on Francis Ponge's cleaning poems—promises a redemption from compromising, and the temptation to seek out such redemption is strong: smelling, sniffing out the innards of one's contemporaries is a "perpetual self-overcoming" that sickens the one who smells in this fashion. Convalescence, restitution of the self and of the home are needed after a while, as the passage from *Ecce Homo* proclaiming Nietzschean flair declares: "But I need *loneliness*, that is, convalescence, return to myself, the breath of a free, light, playful air" (KSA 6:276). A deodorizing "return to myself" would mean a return to a "free air," away from the compromising features of smell. Yet a corollary of such a turn away from olfaction would lie in the ceding of the *agon* of the senses to the already dominant one: giving up on smell, seeking salvation from it, would let the ἄνθρωπος θεωρητικός triumph; it would entail a loss in the battle for a different being that overcomes the "problem of Socrates" and the dominance of the single cyclops eye of theory.

A second path, admittedly more difficult to delineate, runs through an altercation with smell, with its compromising character, its attenuating of the pathos of distance, and its affinity with chaos. Instead of seeking redemption from smell, one would seek to *smell otherwise*. Such an attempt would, in a first step, entail a giving of oneself over to smell and *not resenting* olfaction and the contagion it produces. In the term "ressentiment," in fact, such a "smelling otherwise" becomes legible: Nietzschean ressentiment, as Eve Sedgwick has pointed out, can be thought literally, by drawing on the root of *sentir*, as a sort of "re-sniffing."[24] The Nietzschean intervention of his peculiar flair, as the rest of this chapter will show, consists in the affirmation of the compromising nature of smell, an affirmation combined with subsequent reconfigurations, overcoming transformations, and transvaluations. In the words of *Ecce Homo*: Nietzsche's flair lies in an objection (*Widerspruch*) to smell that does not say no to it. Olfaction is not resented but re-smelled.

Such re-sniffing will find and produce (*erfinden*, invent) *new smells*. One of the 1882 preparatory notes for *Thus Spoke Zarathustra* thus states, "Have I not invented a new smell . . . —Thus spoke Zarathustra" (NF 1882, 4[186]). As the book richest in olfactory tropes within Nietzsche's corpus, *Thus Spoke Zarathustra* must be inscribed in this context of novelty:[25] Zarathustra's smells come to replace old smells in an operation of re-sniffing. Part of the unusual, extraordinary character of this protagonist and this work lies in an olfactory and aesthetic renewal and overturning—a renewal that pitches itself against the putrefying decadence Nietzsche's nostrils have detected and that Nietzschean flair transvalues.

The new smells invented by Zarathustra, two of which will be developed in detail here, directly respond to the compromising nature of smell: both are integrally part of Zarathustra's efforts to reconfigure in ever-changing ways the roles of distance, separation, and differentiation; they attempt to compensate for the loss of horizon and perspective without falling into the trap of an illusory, reactionarily reinstated pathos of distance. Continuing a thought developed prominently in the Hölderlin chapter, they are also part of a "geopoetics of smell" in an exacting, double sense: on the one hand, they are tied to specific geographic locations. Zarathustra encounters these smells in his wandering about: they must be read as situated and sited. This necessitates, in the structure of *Thus Spoke Zarathustra*, particular attention to their location in the architecture of the book: while the first of the two "new smells" developed here (the "smell of the earth") is found in the first three books of *Thus Spoke Zarathustra*, the second (the "smell of eternity") occurs in book 4, which has a very different status than the first three, both editorially and within the logic of the text. On the other hand, these smells are also part of a *geopoetics* in a strict sense: they are tied to the earth as their site of contestation. In *Twilight of the Idols*, Nietzsche had described Socratic wisdom as arriving *on earth*, inspired by a "little smell." It is this sensory configuration of the earth that is re-sniffed. From these new smells, a novel *eco-logy* or, perhaps more exactingly, a novel *eco-graphy* emerges.[26]

Smell of the Earth

The first instance of a "new smell" occurs at the very end of book 1 of *Thus Spoke Zarathustra*. Zarathustra refers here to a smell of convalescence—that is, to a sensory and aesthetic modulation of the element of air that would be conducive to healing: "Truthfully, the earth shall one day become a site of convalescence! And already a new smell surrounds it, a smell that brings salvation—and a new hope!" (*KSA* 4:101). This new, salvation-bringing smell is at its core the smell of a promise. Its futural dimension culminates in a dictum toward the end of book 3, where Zarathustra addresses his soul thus: "your breath already smells [*duftet*] of futural songs [*zukünftigen Gesängen*]" (*KSA* 4:280). What is intimated, what becomes perceptible in Zarathustra's new smell is the futural dimension of existence that manifests itself "already" in smell. Fragrance announces the *Zukunft*—where this "zukünftig" echoes distinctly Hölderlin's coming ("künftig") revolution—and the future and overturning that it announces concern the transformation of the earth into a "site of convalescence."

Yet the logic of this smell of the earth, in particular its origins, structure, and precise function, remain unclear at the end of book 1. It is as if Zarathustra placed these words at the end point of one of his speeches—as a gift that has not yet fully arrived, perhaps not unlike Nietzsche himself—to mark that this pronouncement itself still awaits a future in which it is developed more fully and its promise to bring "salvation" can be understood. Such a further development indeed occurs in the next part, in a section titled "On the Sublime Ones," which speaks of a smell of the earth once more and links it to a pale, sickly man who needs a "last self-overcoming" to heal from his predicament. This smell of the earth constitutes a major reordering of the Kantian-Schillerian aesthetic schema of sublimity and beauty.[27] In this, Nietzsche re-sniffs the tradition of philosophical aesthetics that has excluded olfaction from its realm: criticizing the sublime one and presenting an aesthetic counter-term to him constitute the main task of this section's smell.

The key characteristic of the sublime one, from which the section departs, is his will, more precisely his "heroic will" (*Helden-Willen*), which marks him as having emerged from a fight or struggle: "The hunter returned grimly from the forest of knowledge. He came home from the fight with wild animals." The hard-won "knowledge" of the sublime one, in the aesthetic tradition stemming from Kant, lies in the insight that the human being is, partially, *supersensible*: in the encounter with the overwhelming sublime object such as a mountain or the sea, against which any kind of physical resistance would be futile, the beholding subject discovers that he or she exists, to a degree, apart from and above sensibility.[28] Robert Gooding-Williams, following this line of inquiry, thus helpfully reads "On the Sublime Ones" as "Zarathustra's rejection of Kant's and Schiller's belief that the sublime is a *disclosive* mode of experience. For Kant and Schiller, the sublime heralds human transcendence by *revealing* the fact that human beings are supersensible subjects existing apart from nature and appearances. For Zarathustra, the sublime reveals no such fact, but rather prompts human beings *mistakenly* to believe that they are supersensible subjects."[29] In Zarathustra's speech, the sensibility against which sublimity sets itself up, however, receives a double specification that not just objects to but rather displaces the Kantian-Schillerian paradigm.[30] On the one hand, the sublime one encountered by Zarathustra specifically believes himself to be *above the earth*; he is marked by a "contempt for the earth" (*KSA* 4:151). In other words, the sublime one believes his sublimity to lie in a certain "pathos of distance" that sets him apart from and above the earth, through his fighting struggle. His heroic will is supposed to lift him up (as the root of the German word for "sublime," *erheben*, indicates) above the earth. On the other hand, the sublime one seems to gain his knowledge not, as sublimity in Kant, from a confrontation with inanimate nature but with animality. The object of Zarathustra's laughter is a man who believes he gains elevated insights by hunting down animality, by asserting dominance over uncivilized wildness. Yet such a fight with "wild animals" does not in the least detach or separate him from them—quite to the contrary, it inscribes the hunter into a kind of mimetic relationship to his prey, where he becomes what he attempts to prey upon: "He came home from the fight with wild animals: but a wild animal still looks out of his seriousness—one that has not been overcome!" The sublime one struggles with wild animality, with his own wild animality, but such struggle fails and, in the end, is futile.

Both aspects, animality and the earth, come together in the counterimage to the earth-despising hunter—the epitome of sublimity according to this section—that Zarathustra presents: a bull ploughing the earth. The ploughing bull engages both terms from which the sublime one sought to distance himself (earth, animality) and thus undoes the possibility of a "contemptuous" distancing. The sublime one, so Zarathustra's exhortation goes, "should act like the bull; and his happiness [*Glück*] should smell of the earth and not of contempt for the earth. I want to see him as a white bull, as he strides in front of the plough, snorting and roaring: and his roaring should even praise everything earthly!" (*KSA* 4:151).[31] Agriculture replaces (sublime) hunting. The wildness of animals is domesticated and tamed in a bull that submits to the weight of a human-made tool. The "contempt of the earth," a contempt (*Verachtung*) that does not heed, respect, or take care of (*achten*) the earth, is replaced by a taking care of the earth that tills or cultivates it. Sublimity is displaced by cultivation.

The image of the bull pulling a plough articulates that such a cultivating relationship transforms the separating desire underlying any pathos of distance. Sidestepping images that might suggest a subservient submission, immediate union, or unarticulated unity with the earth, the plough splits open the earth and thus inscribes difference into it.[32] If Zarathustra states that "his *Glück* should smell of the earth," then this smell arises from the earth having been opened up and turned over: cultivated and made newly fertile, no growth arises yet but instead a smell is set free from what was previously the inside of the earth. Olfaction, again, presents itself as an opening of surfaces, an explosion of sorts:[33]

what in vision and from an elevated, sublime distance might appear as the flat and closed surface of the earth is for olfaction the rising up from and out of such a surface, thus denying the earth the status of having a closed and smooth surface—a denial, crucially, of "the lie of unity, the lie of thingness, substance, duration" (*KSA* 6:75). The earth, too, is not "one." The distance of height above the earth that the sublime one imagined possessing is thus replaced by a separation that consists of an internal articulation, an incision into wholeness that introduces lack via an operation that presupposes a *getting close* to the earth. Cultivation can only take place in the proximity of what it seeks to cultivate. Put differently, culture—here merely a different term for the process of cultivation—consists in approaching the earth and opening what first appears as self-sufficient and whole (the earth) by introducing an articulating lack (furrows) that results in an uplifting (smell).

The smell of the freshly tilled earth articulates Zarathustra's conception of *Glück*, a term oscillating between happiness, luck, and good fortune. (It will also be crucial to Brecht's olfactory poetics read in the next chapter). The emergence of *Glück* depends on the fulfillment of Zarathustra's demand that the sublime one "unlearn" his "heroic will." Only through this unlearning can his sublimity become beauty and, eventually, give rise to the *Glück* that smells of the earth: "But the *beautiful* is the heaviest thing precisely for the hero. It cannot be seized by a forceful will. . . . To stand with relaxed muscles and an unharnessed will [*mit abgeschirrtem Willen*]: this is the most difficult thing for you all, you sublime ones" (*KSA* 4:152). The will has to be "abgeschirrt": unharnessed, unyoked, put "out of service." This temporary suspension of the will does not replace heroic willing's pathos of distance with a fatalistic, acquiescent passivity. Rather, it is the letting go of a conception of the will that believes it can wrest beauty from wildness through an oppositional struggle. The *Glück* that smells of the earth, then, is not a "kill [*Jagdbeute*]" gained in a hunt, not something one can hunt down and make one's own through a triumphant struggle. Instead, it arises, like the smell of the freshly tilled earth, from a temporary lightness after division. *Glück* arises during the calm following the completion of cultivating work: it emerges from the temporary cessation of work and, more generally, from the suspension of (heroic) willing. The unlearning of the heroic will would thus constitute the convalescence of the suffering, pained sublime one. It would make the earth a "site of convalescence" (*KSA* 4:101) in which *Glück* is possible.

As the "heaviest" thing for all those who hunt knowledge and heroically will themselves above earth and animality, the descent of spirit toward the earth remedies the heroic error of sublimity. Such a "descent," however, could easily be misunderstood as a triumph of the "spirit of gravity" against which many, maybe even all, of Zarathustra's efforts are directed. The ability to evade the spirit of gravity, which always pulls downward, therefore constitutes a key demand on any figure of Zarathustrean *Glück*. The smell of the earth, in fact, fulfills such a demand: the descent to the earth—if understood as a dividing cultivation leading to a subsequent calm—produces a countermovement in the *uprising* of smell. Gravity is thus not denied but nevertheless does not triumph. The core problem of the heroic will, in a Munchausenesque delusion, is that it believes it can lift *itself* up, that it can counteract the spirit of gravity through an oppositional struggle. True lifting up, by contrast, cannot be an active *erheben* of oneself, as the sublime one claims, but must entail letting oneself be lifted upward: "his heroic will, too, he must unlearn: he shall be a lifted one [*Gehobener*] for me and not just a sublime one [*Erhabener*]:—the ether itself shall lift him, the one without a will [*den Willenlosen*]!" (*KSA* 4:151). True height cannot be intended in an act of the will; the spirit of gravity cannot be opposed by heroic deeds but only through letting oneself be affected. This is the meaning of the curious formulation that Nietzsche's olfactory genius enables his *Widerspruch* (objection) without him therefore becoming a naysayer: the smell of the earth resists the double temptation of the spirit of gravity (giving in to gravity would mean not objecting at all) and sublimity (a misguided ascent would say no to gravity): instead, it lets itself be lifted. It is this feat of objecting without saying no that olfaction can accomplish.

The state of being "without a will," a highly unusual and thus deeply significant occurrence in the Nietzschean corpus, is articulated as a state of being *tired*, of being *depressed*. There is in fact, so "On the Sublime Ones" claims, a right way to be tired: a bit of depression is necessary to free oneself from the heroic will: "When he would tire of his sublimity, this sublime one: only then would his beauty rise up [*anheben*]" (*KSA* 4:151). This tiredness is the counter-term to the "tiredness of the earth" (*KSA* 4:259) that Zarathustra diagnoses as part of the "contempt" for the earth: if being tired means letting oneself be pulled down to earth, then *this* depression will in fact be uplifting. The conventional (and so often abused) image of Nietzsche's work as an unending, quasi-militaristic, and heroic struggle receives here a crucial modification: the "smell of the earth" constitutes a key moment of a cessation of heroic fighting, recalling his claim in *Ecce Homo* that "I am the opposite [*Gegensatz*] of a heroic nature" (*KSA* 6:294). "Inventing" a new smell articulates such a *Gegensatz*. In the smell of the earth, the will may rest without ceding victory to the spirit of gravity.

The downward pull toward the earth and the corresponding uprising of smell constitute the two poles of the question of weight that Zarathustra positions at the heart of what should be called his earthly aesthetics. Responding to the common pronouncement *De gustibus non est disputandum*, Zarathustra states, "But all life is a struggle over taste and tasting!" (*KSA* 4:150). Taste, in turn, is a question of weight: "Taste: that is simultaneously weight and scale and the one who weighs; and woe to everything living that would want to live without a struggle over weight and scale and the ones who weigh!" (*KSA* 4:150). Taste, or the question of aesthetic judgment, is a question of how weight establishes *valuation*: something valued matters; it weighs and thus pulls downward. With the weakening of horizons and perspectives, olfaction, however, threatens the possibility of any such valuation: no context for such a valuation, no reference point seems to be available. It is in this respect that the smell of the earth attains its centrality in Nietzsche's olfactory reflections: in the logic of scent, the earth produces a substitute for the horizon of vision. It delimits the sphere of olfaction—which is unbounded in the upward direction—and in fact establishes the possibility of "direction"—namely, the possibilities of being pulled down or rising up, of being depressed or *gehoben*. Zarathustra's earthly aesthetics in "On the Sublime Ones" centers on the demand that aesthetics be returned from reflections on the supersensible to the one reference point that is the *conditio sine qua non* for all orientation: the earth.[34] Yet the downward return effected here, as a return that simultaneously rises upward in the smell of the earth, precludes that aesthetics then becomes depressive in the sense of being governed by the spirit of gravity. In other words, the "smell of the earth" figures the possibility of a transvaluation of the value of sublimity into a new value—it expresses Nietzsche's attempt to smell otherwise and engage the threats to valuation inherent in smell by the invention of a new smell that draws on the threatening features of smell and turns them into the characteristics of a new type of valuation.

This is the major reordering of aesthetics and sense-making that Zarathustra's insistence on olfaction proposes: the smell of the earth discloses that the earth is the *orienting middle* of the chaos of becoming. Zarathustra, in other words, discerns "Erde" (earth) in all "*werden*" (becoming). The Nietzschean emphasis on the earth derives its force from the earth being the only possibility to orient valuations in the chaos of becoming. In the middle of becoming lies the earth: the relationship between becoming and earth is one of radical co-implication—Zarathustra's overturning of aesthetics, his revolution of the senses taking place in "new smells," discovers that the earth and becoming are folded into each other at the root.

Loyalty, Freedom

The uplifting smell that arises from the double movement of descending toward the earth and then rising up from it fulfills Zarathustra's main demand with respect to the earth: loyalty. (An echo of Hölderlin's "most loyal sense" that found articulation in the aerial-olfactory aesthetic regime of "Patmos" can be detected here.) Zarathustra tells his disciples, "I beseech you, my brothers, *stay loyal to the earth* and do not give credence to those who speak to you of otherworldly [*überirdisch*] hopes" (*KSA* 4:15). The only "über-irdisch," the only "above the earth" that is acceptable to Zarathustra is the rising upward of a smell. Consequently, the smell of the earth constitutes a kind of terrestrial transubstantiation: earth is transformed into something more than earth and less than earth; it is infused with lightness, *begeistert* as it were, in an earthly transformation that does not abandon but stays loyal to what it transforms. When it becomes a smell, the heavy earth rises up, overcoming its heaviness without losing its earthly character: this is Nietzsche's loyalty, a parting from without abandoning. The introduction of an "olfactory genius" into aesthetics enables a loyalty to the earth that, while staying loyal, also enacts transformation, overcoming, and the tendency toward chaos and change.

Just as the smell of the earth joins two separate elements—earth, air—the loyalty expressed in the lightness of the smell of the earth joins what might at first glance be seen as its antithesis: freedom. In the smell of the earth, loyalty and freedom, far from being opposed to each other, articulate themselves through the other. The import of this conclusion—and hence the centrality of the smell of the earth to both Nietzsche's earthly, olfactory aesthetics and his thinking more broadly—becomes clear when it is contrasted with a striking misunderstanding found in what is perhaps the only substantial investigation of Nietzsche's relationship to air and smell by a major twentieth-century thinker: Gaston Bachelard's book *Air and Dreams*, an investigation of the "material imagination" attached to air and its various modulations, which includes an entire chapter dedicated to Nietzsche. Bachelard's central claim consists in the argument that air, the element of olfaction, is the element of freedom par excellence for Nietzsche, for whom "air is in fact the very substance of our freedom, the substance of superhuman joy. Air is a kind of overcome matter."[35] In air, matter (to keep Bachelard's term, foreign to Nietzsche in this context) is overcome, transformed into lightness, and this transformation frees from all strictures, thus constituting the medium of freedom. Without the strictures of materiality, total becoming is possible, according to Bachelard: air "liberates us from our attachment to matter: it is thus the matter of our freedom. To Nietzsche, air brings *nothing*."[36] It is this nothingness that functions as the indispensable precondition of freedom for Nietzsche: only when freed from all attachment and thus given nothing can one rise into freedom. At bottom, this conception of aerial freedom is based on a notion of *purity*: mere air (*bloße Luft*, as one could perhaps say in German), untainted by anything other than itself and guarded against a contagious mixing, is required for us to be free.

Consequently, according to Bachelard, smells are detrimental to Nietzsche's conception of freedom: "In general, for material imaginations, what are the most strongly *substantial* qualities of air? Odors."[37] Bachelard goes on to argue that the nose, Nietzschean flair, merely serves to "give testimony" of the absence of all odors: "For a true Nietzschean, the nose must give the happy *certainty* of an unperfumed air; the nose must testify to the immense happiness, the blessed consciousness of not feeling anything. It is the guarantor of the nothingness of odors. The sense of *smell* [*le* flair], in which Nietzsche so often took pride, does not have the quality of *attraction*. It is given to the superhuman so that he *remove* himself at the most minor indication of an impurity."[38] For Bachelard, in a word, freedom is equivalent to *deodorization*. Anticipating many of the central questions investigated in the epilogue on Ponge's deodorizing soap poems, this removal of scents is supposed to guard against "impurity," and Nietzsche's olfactory method—his "flair"—would merely function as a warning system that produces a repellent reaction in case such an impurity is detected. Bachelard's misunderstanding is grave: it misrepresents Nietzsche as a thinker of purity (a danger that also applies to Ponge, as will be shown below) and thus plays into many of the most nefarious appropriations of Nietzsche's thought; his "such and such" quality would lie in the upholding of a pathos of distance that keeps all mingling, all chaos and confusion, at bay. Seen via the logic of olfaction, Bachelard stands in the position of the sublime one who insists on separating himself from the earth and consequently falls into the trap of "contempt." In a section titled "On Scholars," which is found two sections after "On the Sublime Ones," Zarathustra explicitly links freedom and the earth: "I love freedom and the air above fresh earth" (*KSA* 4:160). For Zarathustra, in contrast to the scholar Bachelard, the smell of the earth and freedom are far from incompatible; they stand, in fact, next to each other in his love. In the smell of the earth, the heavy element becomes light; the earth frees itself from itself, or put differently, opposes itself to itself in the sense of rising up from itself but without saying no to itself: it stays loyal and does not abandon. It is not deodorization and purity that make freedom possible but the peculiar free loyalty of a smell in which two elements, air and earth, mingle in impurity. We never have been and shall not seek to be deodorized. This impure, scented freedom in loyalty and loyalty in freedom thus distill into one figure two strands that constitute the fundamental and productive tension of much of *Thus Spoke Zarathustra* and indeed of Nietzsche's work more broadly: on the one hand, lightness, freedom, and the overcoming of strictures; on the other, an insistence on the indispensability of the earth and animality that demands a transformative loyalty to those alleged strictures. In olfaction, Nietzsche's work thus reaches an extreme point: two aspects of his thought that seemingly pull in opposing directions in fact join each other.

Qua extreme point, this freedom of loyal lightness and a novel aesthetics that allows for olfaction maintain a peculiar relationship to limits and boundaries. Zarathustra links the earth to the question of delimitation precisely via the question of lightness: "Whosoever will one day teach human beings to fly will have dislodged [*verrückt*] all boundary stones [*Grenzsteine*]; all boundary stones will fly into the air for him, he will baptize the earth anew—as 'the light one'" (*KSA* 4:242). Boundary stones are a product of the spirit of gravity; they pull down and arrest. But the boundary stones' horizontal delimitation—their crucial impediment to freedom of movement—is overcome by lightness, in the triumph of vertical lightness-loyalty over any horizontal limitation. The heaviness of a boundary stone is contrasted implicitly with the heaviness of the earth itself, where only the latter is capable of being rebaptized in the name of lightness. The futural promise ("one day") of an abolition of these stones promises that no point in space is defined with respect to a delimiting border. Consequently, all and any points can be understood to be found in the *middle*—a term of central importance to the next "new smell" invented by Zarathustra, the "smell of eternity." With the shift to air and scent, boundaries are devastated, and freedom and loyalty emerge in the middle.

Smell of Eternity

While the importance of the earth can hardly be overstated for *Thus Spoke Zarathustra*, the significant locales on this earth are highly varied: islands, a desert, mountains, a village, a marketplace, a swamp, forests, to name but a few. Of particular relevance here is Zarathustra's cave: his descent and ascent, his wandering about, his engagement with his animals and the so-called higher human beings all take place in, outside of, or in orientation toward this cave. The logic that governs this movement with respect to the cave concerns to a significant extent the element of air and its modification as odors; a logic that stands in relation to but differs from the logic of cultivation, loyalty, and calm that marked the "smell of the earth."

Zarathustra's cave, like much of the book, responds to the tradition of philosophy, here in particular the most famous philosophical cave: the cave of Plato's *Republic*. If the cave might even be considered the most Platonic of locales, then Zarathustra's cave will continue in intensified form the *Auseinandersetzung* (engagement, altercation) with Platonism so prominent in many of Nietzsche's other writings: the revolution of the senses that Nietzsche's "olfactory genius" effects will consist in an overturning of the Platonic paradigm of the cave. In a first step, it can be said that Zarathustra's cave differs from Plato's cave on the question of visuality—the ocularcentrism of the ἄνθρωπος θεωρητικός, the theoretical human being, as contrasted with the activation of the element of air and the attendant logic of smell. The logic that governs the exits and entries from the cave—the logic that governs *emergence* out of the cave—is an olfactory logic. Emergence should be heard here in the strong sense of *Ausgang*: an emergence out of certain conditions of immaturity, captivity, or incapacity—in other words, an *emancipation* that works on and through the senses. While the emergence of Plato's cave allegory in the *Republic*, as has been developed again and again in the scholarship, is governed by a powerful heliotropism, Zarathustra does not exit the cave to escape from shadows and to turn toward the central light (the sun) but rather because the cave's air has become stuffy, malodorous, and suffocating. As Hans Blumenberg has remarked, "What distinguishes Zarathustra's cave from the Platonic, shadowy one is the detectability of its state via the sense of smell instead of the eye. Zarathustra cannot stand the air that arises from the dubious nature of his guests. He must leave the cave, not to step out into real reality [*in die wirkliche Wirklichkeit*] but to breathe a different air."[39] Nietzsche's most cherished work functions not only through a rewriting of the solar and luminous vocabulary of philosophy but also via a radical shift of terrain: instead of attempting to "see" the "true" world, Zarathustra wants to be able to *breathe good air*; the value of beholding the truth is supplanted by the vital value of breathing well. Philosophy's forgetfulness of the nonvisual senses, with Plato as the high point of "theoretical man," replaces this vital activity of breathing with a vision-based model of seeing appearances and truth. This ocular- and heliocentric model is organized around the sun as a single source and origin, ignoring the always already present medium that engulfs and penetrates the human being—without fixed location but giving place to both the body and life.[40] Zarathustra's more than reversal of Platonism operates as a stepping out of, an *Ausgang* and emancipation from this vision-based model that functions otherwise than a simple inversion of Platonism. A simple inversion, if understood as, say, an uncovering of a "deeper," hidden truth of metaphysics that must be "unveiled," would operate within the parameters of shadows and heliotropism. Air, by contrast, dissolves this logic. In the fourth book of *Thus Spoke Zarathustra*, Nietzsche operates an *aerotropism* instead of a heliotropism: instead of turning toward the sun, a turning toward and within air, a sensory and elemental revolution of sorts.[41]

The replacement of the Platonic heliotropism as the governing principle of exits out of and entries into the cave is supplemented by an additional logic that governs the interior of the cave, structuring it as a *container*. As developed above, an essential feature of vision in Nietzsche's work is its being structured by perspective and horizon. Olfaction, by contrast, is marked by a lack, or at the very least attenuation, of both those features. Of particular interest here is the lack of horizon in smell: the limits of olfactory perception cannot be perceived in that perception itself, whereas the limits of the line of sight are visually perceptible. Not only are these limits not perceptible, whether they exist in a determinable and perceptible form seems doubtful: in perception, the reach of olfaction merely decreases indefinitely. Herein lies part of the importance of the cave for the olfactory poetics of *Thus Spoke Zarathustra*: the cave functions as a container; that is, it limits the aerial element in a way that substitutes for a horizon. While not making these limits perceptible to smell, the cave qua container nevertheless restores to smell part of the well-formed delimitation that it lacked in comparison to vision. If the radical threat emanating from the compromising nature of smell lies in its undermining the possibility of valuation—since all values are perspectival and derive from the limitation of a particular horizon—then the import of the delimiting function of the cave becomes apparent: qua container, *the cave establishes a valuation-enabling frame*, very much like the earth found at the heart of all becoming. This is the reason for its centrality as the point of orientation for the wandering of Zarathustra; it is also the reason for Zarathustra bringing the higher human beings to his cave: it is here that he can evaluate them, gauge their weight, establish their value. (Conversely, the interpretation proposed below of the attempt to exit definitively from the cave shows precisely that from such an emergence ensues the loss of the possibility of ascribing values.)

Yet the cave, if it is to be an actual cave, cannot be completely closed—it is not a sealed-off container. Rather, it permits one to enter and exit, which to a significant degree destroys its functioning as a *delimiting* container with respect to the element of air. In fact, the entirety of the fourth part is organized around various exits from and entries into Zarathustra's cave; Zarathustra sends the so-called higher human beings[42] (two kings, a leech, a magician, a soothsayer, a pope "out of service," the ugliest man, and a voluntary beggar) to his cave, and he himself exits and enters alone or with them a number of times—everything leading up to his final, solitary exit from the cave.

Both the question of the emergence from the cave and the question of the status of the higher human beings must be thought through the problem of distance and the compromising inflicted on distance by olfaction. The "higher human beings" are, in a first and rather obvious sense, supposed to be endowed with some sort of pathos of distance. They are "higher" than the "last human being"; their comparative highness enables them to move up into the realms of the mountains in which Zarathustra generally dwells alone (only accompanied by his animals). In his speech titled "On the Higher Human Beings," Zarathustra contrasts them with the rabble: "But the rabble squints 'we are all the same [*gleich*]'" (*KSA* 4:357). This *blinzeln*, a squinting or blinking of the eye, constitutes a distortion of the perspective in which there would be no differences of height or greatness: if you squint enough, so the suggestion goes, you distort your line of sight just enough to make all differences disappear and let "equality" emerge. The comparative "higher" of these higher human beings, then, according to Zarathustra, lies in their denial and indeed "despising" (*KSA* 4:357) of such an equalizing distortion;[43] in contrast to the last human beings, they know of distance and differentiation. The decisive question of distance, then, concerns the relationship of these higher human beings to Zarathustra. How far or close are they to Zarathustra—that is, to Nietzsche's most prized persona?[44] Do they and Zarathustra share something? Do they have something *in common*? The answer lies in this: these higher humans are Zarathustra's "temptation," a temptation to commit his "last sin." This last sin would precisely be the abolition of all distance: the temptation is pity or compassion (*Mitleid*) (*KSA* 4:301), which consists in making the pain and suffering of someone else one's own, thereby abandoning all distance and, in the end, abandoning all differentiation between oneself and the suffering other—the higher human beings, and this is Zarathustra's last and greatest temptation, claim a distance-abandoning "equality" very much like that of the rabble; they tempt with an attraction toward the common and the shared.

Guarding against this equality and protecting a certain pathos of distance would thus require a differentiation between Zarathustra and the higher human beings. In this context, sending the higher human beings to his cave is a significant gesture of *bringing close* and even of letting them share in what is Zarathustra's own: "what is mine in my cave also belongs to you, my guest and friend" (*KSA* 4:303). Much hinges therefore on Zarathustra's possibility to (re)establish distance between him and his guests: without such distance, everything will be "the same." This, in turn, is the meaning of the recurring play of entering into and emerging from the cave, governed by olfaction: these entries and exits are so many attempts to create distance between those who remain in the cave and the one who emerges from it. Aerotropism concerns the possibility of establishing and maintaining distance and differentiation in the face of a threatening sameness, commonality, and equality.

As emphasized above, Zarathustra smells the air in the pseudo-container of the cave to see whether he needs to exit—that is, to turn out of the cave—and step into "the open" or "the free [*das Freie*]." This olfactory logic of the fourth part of *Thus Spoke Zarathustra* reconfigures significantly Zarathustra's earlier pronouncements in part 3: in the section titled "The Homecoming," Zarathustra had proclaimed himself "redeemed from the smell of all humanity" (*KSA* 4:234), finding "pure smells"; here, the temptation lay in deodorization as separation. In part 4, by contrast, such deodorizing redemption will prove elusive: his "home," his solitary cave in the mountains is now shared with the higher human beings who bring with them, their comparative highness notwithstanding, some of the "smell of all humanity." The possibility of a deodorizing redemption is revoked. More precisely, the olfactory logic of emergence from the shared cave oscillates between the register of purity—and thus a break and difference in kind that resembles the smells of "The Homecoming"—and a comparative logic that corresponds directly to the comparative form "higher." A key passage from "The Song of Melancholy" from part 4 thus reads as follows:

> As Zarathustra made these speeches, he stood near the entrance to his cave; but with his last words he escaped from his guests and fled for a while into the open [*in's Freie*]. "Oh *pure* smells around me, he exclaimed, oh blessed calm around me! But where are my animals? Come near, come near, my eagle and my snake! Tell me, my animals: these higher human beings on the whole—do they perhaps smell bad? Oh, *pure* smells around me!" . . . Thus the three of them were quietly together and sniffed and slurped the *good* air with one another. For the air out here was *better* than near the higher human beings. (*KSA* 4:369; emphasis added)

Zarathustra himself, in his direct speech, claims that his stepping out of the cave, away from the higher human beings, has led him to *pure* smells, just like he claimed in "The Homecoming." Qua pure, these smells disavow any continuity with the stink of the cave: when Zarathustra has stepped into "the open [*in's Freie*]" or "the free" a difference in kind marks the change in air. In short, emergence, *Ausgang* into freedom appears to be possible. The narration of this scene, however, recasts this repeated language of purity in terms of a comparison: the air outside was *better*. At first, the difference of kind seems to be maintained ("the good air") but the goodness of the air is immediately and directly relativized ("better"): the qualification of the air outside has an ineluctable reference to the air inside, and only as a comparative modification of the latter is the former's difference understandable at all. Zarathustra's *Ausgang*, his emancipation (of the senses, from compromising nearness) cannot be understood as a radical break but is merely a relational comparison.

In the end, emergence as meant to reestablish true distance cannot be said to succeed. Zarathustra's emergence does not, in fact, step out into the freedom of "the open [*in's Freie*]" (*KSA* 4:369). Far from being free from his foul-smelling guests, Zarathustra is tied to them by the comparative form. The olfactory-aerial logic of the cave articulates this fact with precision: by virtue of having an exit, the air outside remains ineluctably connected to the air inside; mingling and mixing, contagion and impurity are inevitable. In a manner resembling to a degree the loyalty of the "smell of the earth" but in a much more troubling setting—for would Zarathustra really want to be loyal to the higher human beings if they are his last temptation and sin?—and in a manner resembling the binding freedom developed above, the air of emergence is bound to the air of the cave. The continuation of the text articulates this fact: after Zarathustra has left the cave, the "old sorcerer" (*KSA* 4:370) sings "The Song of Melancholy," which gives the title to this section. While temporarily away from such grave and heavy melancholy (*Schwermuth*), away from such a spirit of gravity, the response of the higher human beings quickly dissolves such distance: "Air! Let in good air! Let in Zarathustra!" (*KSA* 4:375) shouts "the conscientious one of the spirit," and Zarathustra obliges: he, the good air that turns out to only be better air, reenters the cave of bad—that is, worse—air.

After "The Song of Melancholy," the tension between Zarathustra's claim of pure smells and the narration's comparative description, or in other words, Zarathustra's continuously diminished distance from the higher human beings, is intensified and disrupted in "The Sleepwalker Song"—and it is here that one last "new smell" emerges as the extreme point of Nietzsche's compromising, promising olfactory poetics. Reconsidering his earlier remarks, Zarathustra here develops in great detail the implications of what emergence from the cave, which is to say emergence from a contained frame into the uncontained realm of olfaction, entails in all its radicality.[45] The setup of "The Sleepwalker Song" is this: it begins after the section titled "The Ass Festival," where the higher human beings, and eventually Zarathustra too, perform a carnivalesque worshipping of the I-A—that is, of an always yes-saying ass. Zarathustra instructs his guests to "cool off" (*KSA* 4:393) outside of the cave; they obey him and step out into the freedom of "the open" (*KSA* 4:395). When midnight strikes, Zarathustra proclaims, "You higher human beings, don't you smell it? A smell secretly swells up, a fragrance and smell of eternity [*ein Duft und Geruch der Ewigkeit*], a rose-blessed brown gold-wine smell of old happiness [*Glücke*]" (*KSA* 4:400). Outside of the cave, now for the first time as an outside that *both* Zarathustra and the higher human beings occupy, no pure or comparatively better smells are to be found. Instead, there is nothing but the smell of eternity—a sensory configuration adjacent but not equivalent to Nietzsche's famous/infamous "eternal return of the same." This smell announces a desire to die, as the lines right before the description quoted indicate: "the world itself became ripe, the grape turns brown—now it wants to die, die of happiness [*Glück*]." In this smell, the world announces its end, to be superseded by eternity and happiness.

In the fragrance and smell of eternity, opposites collapse into each other and all possibility of valuation dissolves. Zarathustra's song repeats the formula "fragrance and smell of eternity" (*KSA* 4:400) once more in slightly altered, corrupted form as his "Sleepwalker Song" continues: "a vapor and fragrance of eternity [*Ein Dunst und Duft der Ewigkeit*]? . . . Don't you smell it? Just now my world became perfected, midnight is also midday—pain is also a pleasure, a curse is also a blessing" (*KSA* 4:402). Pain and pleasure, curse and blessing are equivalent, "the same" as the squinting rabble had claimed. In the perfection or completion (*vollkommen*) of the smell of eternity, no differentiation—no opposition-enabling distance—is possible. Instead, what is shared and common to both appears: *mid*night and *mid*day share that they are the *middle* of night and day, respectively. Smell is the marker of the eternally recurring *medium*, freed from all "boundary stones": valences, qualities, and properties continually change, but the medium in which they change—actively forgotten by theoretical man—is eternal. The position of this smell is the "position" in which and from which specific valorizations such as pain or pleasure disappear. In other words, all valuation-enabling perspectives are dissolved into pure positionality; instead of points of view, lines of sight, or horizons, mere mediality emerges. From the non-perspective of eternity, as radically different from the perspective of life and death—and only from this non-perspective—air, as Luce Irigaray puts it, is "equivalent in all its directions, no place is privileged. Deprived of sense for man."[46] Once the human being is seen as positioned in the middle of a medium where all absolute positions collapse, any directionality such as the upward directionality that marked the smell of the earth disappears. Air is "deprived of sense," where "sense" must be read as both sense and direction, and it is deprived of sense *for man*. The earth as the central weight that orients chaotic becoming—*wERDEn*—has disappeared; all that is left is an eternal smell that is, in a most emphatic sense, the common scent of commonality itself.

In Zarathustra's speech, this loss of hierarchized, privileged loci explicitly affects the depth/surface schema that Nietzsche's characterization of smell had already destabilized through the notion of scent as explosion. His first invocation of "a fragrance and smell of eternity" continues like this: "the world is deep *and thought more deeply than day*" (*KSA* 4:400). The complex thought folded into this short sentence can be explicated as follows. Day stands for visual phenomenality, finding its source and origin in the sun and operating according to the depth/surface schema: phenomena appear out of a depth onto a visible surface. Diurnal phenomenality is structured as the appearance out of an obscure depth (night) onto a clear surface (day) and, potentially, the redescending into the night. In the thought of the fragrance and smell of eternity, by contrast, depth is further deepened. Eternity is deeper than day, deeper than that which gives rise to depth and surface: it encompasses the day, all days, and thus abolishes diurnal, oppositional phenomenality as the governing paradigm. The last words of this section read, "*deep, deep eternity*" (*KSA* 4:404). If Nietzsche's notion of smell arising from minuscule explosions put an end to the "lie" of a flat, smooth, and unified surface, then this doubling repetition of "deep," pronounced as the modifier of eternity, dissolves the concept of depth as the oppositional term of surface and substitutes for it a depth that only ever doubles itself.

Another name for the supersession of the surface/depth schema is *chaos*. Without diurnal phenomenality, no perspectival ordering into foreground and background, or into higher and lower, is possible. The smell of eternity draws out the implications of the analysis of the interplay between chaos, on the one hand, and perspective and horizon, on the other, as developed above with respect to Heidegger's Nietzsche lectures. Emergence leads out of the cave and thus leaves behind the ersatz horizon that was the pseudo-container of the cave. The *wandeln*, the turning of this song (*Nacht-wandler*) is the turning about in the gaping openness of an element in which no ordering or hierarchization can be established. As opening, the pure mediality of the smell of eternity—its chaotic nature—constitutes the extreme end point of the discovery of the *compromising* quality of smell. Not only is all distance or value establishing perspective abolished, the compromise is extreme in that, to rephrase "The Sleepwalker Song," "bad air is also good air, good air is also bad air." When Nietzsche speaks of a "*compromising* mediocrity [*Mittelmäßigkeit*]" (NF 1887, 10[67]), he designates with exactitude the link between a thinking of the middle and the compromising quality it entails: two terms come together and give up their respective claims to defend what is their own; they are expropriated, moved out of that which is proper to them toward that which they share in common. The attempt of a radical *Ausgang* from the cave—that is, the abandoning of the cave as either pseudo-container or relative point of orientation—produces a paradoxically *absolute compromise*, an absolute inability to distinguish between Zarathustra, the higher human beings, and anyone else. Some commentators have claimed that Zarathustra's "parodic" reprisal of his earlier celebration of eternity should be seen on the oppositional model of Zarathustra's "privately lived" experience that cannot be "express[ed]" to others and hence falls into a parody:[47] yet precisely any such differentiation between Zarathustra's own, "private" experience and his distinction from the "higher" men is what "The Sleepwalker Song" renders impossible; the distance required for parody has disappeared. Only compromise remains.

The smell and fragrance of eternity is thus the marker of an "eternity for any and all [*Jegliches*]," as Nietzsche terms it in a fragment from 1887, and hence an eternity for all beings alike, beyond any possibility of a pathos of distance. Eternity's qualifier would be *quodlibet*.[48] Scented air as the element that continually effaces localized forms just as much as equilibria is particularly suited to express such an eternity or a whatever being. From the "perspective" of eternity, which is precisely not a perspective but nevertheless becomes perceptible in smell, there is only chaos—no loyalty, no valuation, no weighing. This is the price of emergence: without context and perspective, there is no downward or upward, no orientation, but only a chaotic middle.

But the text of *Thus Spoke Zarathustra* does not let such an interpretation stand as definitive or conclusive. Whether the pure mediality of the "fragrance and smell of eternity" can actually emerge in the text and whether the extreme end point of its compromising nature is indeed an "end point" becomes more or less immediately doubtful as the text continues. Put differently, the text retreats and moves out of the extreme point of absolute compromise. *Thus Spoke Zarathustra* withdraws from the confrontation with the smell of eternity in the much discussed and sometimes ridiculed subsequent and last section "The Sign." In the latter, Zarathustra appears in front of his cave, seemingly freed from the dilemmas of his previous song, without the reader having been told how the return, a "homecoming" if there ever was one, to the cave has taken place. Zarathustra's leaving of his cave on his own in "The Sign" appears as a recognition that any engagement with the higher human beings, be it in the cave or outside of it, is bound to fail at producing a distance that resists the last, and greatest, temptation—equalizing, leveling pity—that Zarathustra faces. Yet how Zarathustra could be said to accomplish this last, solitary exit without falling into the traps of ressentiment or an illusory pathos of distance that he himself had just undone so forcefully remains unclear in "The Sign." Accordingly, the ultimate section completely abandons all vocabulary of air and smell, thus suggesting that there simply cannot be a "solution" to the temptation of a lack of distance in air—in other words, that there might not be a way to withstand this temptation within the compromising relationality of olfaction. Outside of the cave, at the extreme middle point of olfaction stands only absolute compromise. Only a return to the sun can (attempt to) guarantee Zarathustra's emergence, differentiation, and distinction. This would, in the last instance, mean that existing in air is incompatible with the avoidance of being compromised and being turned toward what is common and shared. This is what *Thus Spoke Zarathustra* leaves its readers with: Out of the element of olfaction, no emergence appears possible that would not require a dubious move toward an unexplained solar "sign." In smell, all emancipation (of the senses and otherwise) ends up being thrown into doubt. Attempting to overturn the heliotropism and ocularcentrism of (Socratic, Platonic) theoretical philosophy, Zarathustra's revolution of the senses that turns toward and within air—replacing the dominance of the revolving around and of the sun—is thoroughly compromised and compromising, undoing all imaginations of purity, center, orientation, and separation from the common.[49]

4

Brecht's Stench

Bertolt Brecht stank. The memorable photographs of the playwright with his closely cropped hair, the invariably present cigar, and the hypermasculine overalls must be imagined as suffused with a persistent, repulsive smell. Far from being an accidental quirk, this olfactory idiosyncrasy originates in the young Brecht's desire to inscribe himself into a specific lineage of poets. At some point in his teenage years, his biographer Stephen Parker reports, Brecht started to emulate his heroes, the French *poètes maudits*: like Rimbaud and Verlaine, "he did not change clothes, rarely washed and did not brush his teeth. After a childhood spent withdrawn because of shame at his fragile condition, this boy with the impeccable manners was going on the offensive, displaying a neglect of personal hygiene, which, as many people attest, remained a life-long habit."[1] The fragile, perpetually sick Brecht turned his bodily frailty into an aggressive rejection of the somatic norms of his bourgeois, upper-middle-class upbringing. In this he created a version of the olfactory "pathos of distance" that so occupied (and eventually troubled) Nietzsche, whose work (in particular *Thus Spoke Zarathustra*) the young Brecht knew well:[2] the son of a successful manager of a paper mill, Brecht would henceforth display his opposition to and differentiation from his milieu through his olfactory appearance and put all those around him at a marked distance maintained by this self-induced, repulsive odor.[3] Like the pustulous Marx before him, Brecht would become a dirty, stinking revolutionary.

That Brecht's physical appearance, commented on in passing by many of his contemporaries, might be more than a biographical quirk and might indeed have a decisive relationship to his work was incisively suggested by his friend and occasional collaborator Walter Benjamin. In one of his earliest writings on Brecht, the 1931 review essay titled "Bert Brecht," Benjamin begins by rejecting conventional, "impartial" approaches of literary criticism and instead emphasizes the importance of giving an account of the poet's theoretical convictions and, most interesting for the purposes here, "even his outer appearance" (*GS* 2:661). The last lines of Benjamin's essay offer a glimpse of what such a critical approach to a poet's "outer appearance" might be: here Benjamin claims that Brecht's main object, "poverty," "is displayed [*zur Schau getragen wird*] in his puny, tattered appearance" (*GS* 2:667). In an almost physiognomic approach, Benjamin's assertion establishes a mode of interpretation that reads the poet's physical appearance as a phenomenon that displays, that carries into the realm of perception, "the decisive aspect" of the work. What, then, can be read in Brecht's stench? How might one interpret the poet's insistent, aggressive reminder that we have never been deodorized?

Brecht himself establishes initial signposts of an interpretation of his appearance in two poems concerning a "child who did not want to wash himself," a figure that should be read not only as an alter ego of Brecht but also as a more general poetic analysis of the implications of such a refusal of hygienic norms. The first of these two poems, collected in the "Svendborg Poems" written in Scandinavian exile during the 1930s, opens like a fairy tale:[4] "Once upon a time there was a child / who did not want to wash himself."[5] The recourse to the genre marker "Once upon a time" positions the poem at the intersection of autobiography and the time immemorial of the fairy tale, at the crossroads of a particular body—the poet's own body—and the possibility that this might be *any* body whatsoever. The poem, in other words, poses the question of the "common scents" of Brecht's body and of all bodies; it poses the question of the scent common to all bodies, and how this scent does or does not become erased, transfigured, remarked upon, or celebrated. This body, then, not only refuses hygienic demands but actively undoes any cleaning it is subjected to: "And when he was washed, quickly / He smeared ashes all over himself" (*Und wenn es gewaschen wurde, geschwind / Beschmierte es sich mit Aschen*). The rhyme scheme turns *waschen* into *Aschen*, wash into ash in an act marked, to use Benjamin's formulation, by a "joy of dirt." This joy of chosen dirt, the next two stanzas reveal, constitutes not only a rejection of hygienic norms but, more decisively, entails the rejection of an entire politico-moral order of which these norms are but a small part. When "the emperor came to visit," the child's mother attempts but fails to clean the child. Consequently, "the emperor walked away / Before the child could see him / The child could not demand it" (*GW* 9:646). The visitation by the emperor ends without the child seeing the head of state: his dirtiness subtracts him from the sphere of the monarch's presence. Only that which is clean can approach the center of political power. Cleanliness and political power, as the epilogue on Francis Ponge's soap poems below will develop further, thus appear tightly linked: their hinge is found in the concept of *order*. Inversely, dirt, understood as "matter out of place" in the well-known definition by the sociologist Mary Douglas, precisely disrupts the order that the monarch stands for, puts in place, and upholds. Consequently, the child's (and Brecht's) "joy of dirt" must be seen "as a stumbling block [*Stein des Anstoßes*], as a dark warning that stands in the way of order (not unlike the hunchback that in the old song dislodges the properly kept household [*das wohlbestellte Hauswesen aus den Fugen bringt*])" (*GS* 2:565). The dirty child (and the dirty Brecht by extension) emerges here as a version of the hunchback figure: the fairy tale creature that induces carelessness and the disruption of domestic order. Brecht's poem, however, situates the dirty child's dislodging effect (Douglas's "out of place" rather exactly corresponds to Benjamin's "aus den Fugen") not just in the *Hauswesen* (household) but rather in the *Staatswesen* (state): the emperor's climb up the "seven flights of stairs" signifies the monarchic power's extensive reach even into the depths of the home of the dirty child; the latter's subtraction from the imperial reach functions as a "stumbling block"—a *scandal* in the etymological sense—for the former. Refusing the order inherent in cleanliness scandalizes: it scrambles the organization of political space because the out-of-place character of dirt disrupts the orderliness of political power.

Benjamin's analysis offers a second interpretative direction, unwittingly pointing to another Brecht poem written in 1950, ten years after Benjamin's suicide. Benjamin asks, "does he [the child] perhaps only dirty himself with ashes because society does not channel his passion for dirt into a useful and good utilization?" (*GS* 2:565). In other words, is the self-besmirching of the child a reaction to a society that has no *use* for a passion for dirt? And further, what would a different sociopolitical order look like that had a place for dirt—that is, that made place precisely for the out-of-place? Can a society be imagined that can put to use that which dislodges it, that can derive a "useful and good utilization" from precisely that element that is "out of joint"? Brecht's reprisal of the dirty child motif in the later poem figures such a changed society, and one might even speculate that Brecht, who knew Benjamin's writings on his work, remembered the question his deceased friend had posed. Departing again from the classic fairy tale opening under the title "Song of the Child Who Did Not Want to Wash Himself," the 1950 poem's opening stanza reads,

> There once was a child
> Who never washed his ear.
> And then grew out of the ear, oh horror,
> A little tree. (Brecht, *Große Berliner Ausgabe* [*GBA*] 12:292)

Out of the refusal to wash, a tree—one of the most persistent motifs of Brecht's poetry—comes forth. The scandal of dirtiness becomes *productive* (a key word for the later Brecht) by a minute change turning washing ("wusch") not into ash but into growing ("wuchs"). The crucial moment then lies in the reaction of the other children, who, in stark contrast to the emperor, do not reject the dirty child but rather turn him into something useful to them:

> It didn't seem odd to them
> They planted the child on the schoolyard
> There he stood one, two years.
> He became a plum tree.

The "horror" of the mutating *Schmutzkind* (dirty child) is accepted as nothing "odd [*sonderbar*]"—as nothing separate, uncommon, or out of the ordinary by the other children. Instead, they find a "useful and good utilization" for that which is "out of joint."

Yet, lest this use be understood as a utopian vision that would be a naive reconciliation of the abnormal individual and "the others," of dirt and order, perhaps even of nature and humanity, Brecht's poem closes—in a relentless reconfiguration that seems to break into even the most peaceful moments of all of Brecht's poetry—with a reprisal of the opening "horror": "They had to pay him, oh horror / x pennies for a pound."[6] The school yard realm where a different relationship to dirtiness becomes possible cannot escape from the ubiquitous law of economic exchange. The child's titular desire ("wollte") is displaced by the final word, *gemußt* (had to). The new mode of relationality hinted at in the world of children cannot subtract itself from the economic constraints that inevitably appear in the guise of a "must": here, the limit of the refusal of hygienic norms—both of the *Schmutzkind* and of Brecht—emerges clearly for the first time. Any "useful and good utilization" that this poem can envision flounders on its eventual collapse into a constraint-driven sociality governed by economic laws of exchange and monetary mediation. The import of these last lines is far-reaching: a genuine revolution of the senses—a revolutionary stench as Brecht displayed it—that would overturn prevailing (hygienic, corporeal) norms and would establish new uses for that which is out of joint would have to account for this threat of floundering on the economic.

The combination of a rejection of political order and its turning into something useful—shot through by the caveat of the inevitability of economic exchange that threatens to undo both—will be the guiding thread of this chapter's investigations into Brecht's stench. This through line can be condensed, preliminarily, into a description of Brecht's own odor found in Lion Feuchtwanger's 1930 novel *Success*, which charts the rise and fall of the Nazi Party. Feuchtwanger, the first literary heavyweight to support the young Brecht's writing, and his friend and occasional collaborator for decades, describes the young Brecht in thinly veiled form as the figure of "the young Pröckl," an engineer. In a decisive passage, Pröckl-Brecht's appearance is described as follows: "The fellow really smelled like marching soldiers. . . . There was a certain smell of revolution [*ein sicherer Geruch von Revolution*] about him."[7] These two sentences condense some of the most poignant moments in the history of twentieth-century Germany into a description of Brecht's stench: the smell of soldiers turns into the certain *smell of revolution*, tracking the return of German soldiers from the front lines of World War I to the (failed) German revolution of 1918–1919. The olfactory appearance of Brecht, according to Feuchtwanger's suggestion, has something to do with the end of war and the possibility of revolution. And it is precisely these two questions, war and revolution, that form the context of Brecht's first two plays—*Baal* and *Drums in the Night*—whose olfactory moments this chapter now turns to.

The Body of the Revolution

Brecht's first staged play, *Drums in the Night*, which eventually earned him the Kleist Prize, was initially titled *Spartacus*, after the revolutionary Communist groups that staged an uprising in the early months of 1919.[8] At stake in the play is the "certain smell of revolution" that Feuchtwanger ascribed to Brecht: will the returning soldiers stage a full-blown revolution bringing about socialist rule in an echo of the Russian Revolution of 1917? Or do they "merely" want an end to the war and are satisfied with the rule of the Social Democrats under their pragmatist leader Friedrich Ebert, thus forgoing a veritable revolution?[9] The five-act, formally rather conventional play is structured around two main choices, the second of which turns on this urgent political choice. The first is an ordinary love story: Anna Balicke needs to choose between her lover, the soldier Andreas Kragler, who returns from Africa as a "ghost" long thought dead, and Friedrich Murk, a draft-dodging capitalist on the up and up who, it is revealed as the play progresses, impregnated Anna while Kragler was gone. This choice, while it takes up most of the first three acts, is the less weighty, almost trivial one: Anna chooses Kragler. The second choice, however, will cause the late Brecht to almost suppress and revoke his play: it is the choice Kragler makes between choosing his fiancée, who is "damaged," and the revolutionary uprising in the "newspaper district." After Kragler seems to initially decide to join the revolutionary forces, the play closes with Kragler's decisive turn away from the revolution and toward the petit bourgeois life—a choice Brecht, in a 1953 text titled "While Examining My First Plays," calls "the shabbiest of all possible variations" (GW 17:945). The rejection of the revolution even leads Brecht to consider the option of "suppressing" (946) this "rebellion [Auflehnung]" (945), language that rather clearly echoes a counter-revolutionary rhetoric. Brecht resists this temptation, largely because he believes that the play's value lies in showcasing Andreas Kragler as the typical "Ebert-Mann" of the time whose nonrevolutionary Social Democratic convictions led to the failure of the revolution. A closer reading of Kragler's "rebellion," which plays out in acts 4 and 5 of *Drums in the Night*, shows the reasons guiding Kragler and his kind—reasons that are legible in their relationship to smell.

The fourth act begins with the singing of a text of great importance within the Brechtian oeuvre: the "Ballad of the Dead Soldier." This ballad (from 1918) gained notoriety in the Weimar Republic as one of its most potent antiwar songs. It caused Brecht to be sued, landed him high up on the National Socialists' blacklist of enemies, and was used in 1935 as a pretext to revoke his German citizenship, rendering Brecht stateless.[10] In the play, the ballad is sung by Glubb, a distillery owner of revolutionary sympathies. The ballad narrates the story of a soldier who dies a "hero's death" due to the lack of any "prospect for peace." His death is deemed unacceptable by the emperor since he wishes to continue the war. Consequently, the emperor has a "medical commission" dig up the corpse and declare him "k.v.," or "kriegsverwendungsfähig," which might be translated as "useable in war." The crucial olfactory moment then occurs in the eighth stanza:

> And since the soldier stinks of decay
> A priest limps ahead of him

And swings a censer above him
So that he cannot stink.

Und weil der Soldat nach Verwesung stinkt
Drum hinkt ein Pfaffe voran
Der über ihn ein Weihrauchfaß schwingt
Daß er nicht stinken kann. (Brecht, *Ausgewählte Werke* [AW] 1:138–139)

The soldier's corpse stinks, violently resurrected in a scene that echoes both Lazarus and Baudelaire's use of the Lazarus figure analyzed in chapter 2,[11] and this stench must be covered over for the sake of the emperor: like the "child who did not want to wash himself," this soldier's dirtiness stands in the way of a *proper* relationship to political power—that is, a relationship of (clean, orderly) obedience that keeps the subject in his place, even if that place is in the line of fire in a hopeless war. Here, however, the stench emerges not from an intentional choice but rather from the processes of decay. This stench of decay figures as an act of resistance, albeit a feeble one: the last line of the stanza qualifies "stink" as a capacity ("can"), one that necessitates the priest's olfactory counter-operation.[12] The stench of bodily decomposition presents itself as a last refuge of resistance against the grasp of imperial-military power that subsumes even the dead.[13]

While the main thrust of this stanza certainly lies in a critique of the church's active complicity in the war, lending its sacralizing rituals to this-worldly martial efforts (incense burning is turned from a rite that is supposed to establish a relationship to the divine into an act that returns even the dead into the clutches of imperial power), the corpse's stench contains a more complex dimension: its pungent exhalation constitutes both a moment of change and an interpenetration of life and death. Against the always unending war, the corpse's stench asserts the possibility of change, as an alteration away from the always deployable and pliable body of the soldier. Smell marks time even, or in particular, against an assertion that nothing is changing. Kragler himself offers such an interpretation of stink when he speaks of the non-passage of time while he was deployed in Africa: "We stared [*glotzten*] at time. It never moved . . . it never moved, we couldn't do anything but stink" (AW 1:122). While time stands still, emitting smell is the only thing that "can" be done. In other words, the eternal sameness of unending war, of everlasting oppression and exploitation, is disrupted only by the act of bodies excreting a stench. Staring at time ("glotzen" denotes a fixed, dumbfounded looking—a visual relation to time) reveals no movement whatsoever; smelling, by contrast, discerns the olfactory emission, a movement of sorts, of bodies (one might think here of Nietzsche's conception of smell as little explosions disrupting a smooth surface), and thus keeps time going against any kind of arresting or homogenizing operation.

This assertion of time and change via the smell of the corpse constitutes what Benjamin calls in one of his Brecht interpretations the "interpenetration [*Durch*-

dringung] of death and life" (*GS* 7:658). In the early Brecht, death signifies above all a terrifying subtraction from change: "The poet finds the no longer participating in change to be the dreadful thing about death" (*GS* 7:658). Turning this insight on its head, in the "Ballad of the Dead Soldier," the eponymous figure precisely seeks death in order to participate in change—namely, the change from a never-ending war to peace. It is this change that the emperor denies. When the stench of the resurrected corpse meets the priest's counter-smell of incense, two smells thus join the soldier's insistence on change (which stands for life, here embodied by the attempt to die) to the clerico-imperial power's insistence on constancy (which stands for death, here embodied in the attempt to maintain alive in the ever-same deadly war). Life and death "interpenetrate" in the olfactory battle concerning the soldier's body. The resulting smell embodies the ambiguity, the *Zweideutigkeit* of the corpse of the dead soldier: the smell signifies both life and death, a continuation of war as well the (attempted, feeble) break from it. In the ballad, no resolution of this ambiguity is reached.

In the larger context of *Drums in the Night*, the dead soldier of the ballad and the figure of Andreas Kragler are overlaid one onto the other: Kragler repeatedly says that the war has left him in an in-between state of phantomaticity (the phantom also being an interpenetration of life and death), and he is described as a walking "corpse" both by himself and the other characters of the play. The choice Kragler faces with respect to the revolution is articulated through this ambiguity of life and death, of continuing war or breaking from it. More precisely, Kragler's oscillating choice—in act 4 he seems to consent to joining the revolution, while act 5 closes with a decisive rejection of it—must be understood as his attempt to break through the ambiguity and come down on either side: life *or* death, war *or* peace beyond any "interpenetration."

Consequently, when in act 4 Kragler agrees to participate in the revolution, this decision is predicated on the fact that he sees himself as nothing but a corpse: "I am a corpse, you can have it" (*AW* 1:127). Kragler sees in the revolution nothing but the continuation of the violence of war. And since war appears unending, he hopes for a final release found in revolutionary violence: "Onto the barricades with the ghost! Finishing it off is better than schnaps. It's no fun. Disappearing is better than sleeping" (127). In these moments, "Kragler is looking for the ecstatic moment of death," Peter Demetz has argued, "which would free him from his tormented consciousness, even at the price of self-annihilation. He has decided for the revolution because of private reasons."[14] Revolution, seen from this specific angle that illuminates considerable parts of the appeal of revolutionary violence, would be the fulfillment of an individual death drive that, instead of attempting to form a new world, merely seeks to "disappear."

Conversely, Kragler's final rejection of the revolution presents itself as the breakthrough of the ambiguity of his phantom status toward a (seemingly) firm position in *life*. He chooses his body's survival, over and against the "ideas" that the revolution stands for: "My flesh is supposed to rot in the gutter so that your idea can get into heaven? Are you wasted?" Where Kragler previously saw his body as a walking corpse that he sought to kill off conclusively by participating in the violence of the revolution, he now rejects all decay. Along with his body, he chooses his fiancée, Anna, and the possibility of reproduction, both articulated through the promise of a tomorrow: "All the shouting is over tomorrow morning, but I will lie in bed tomorrow morning and multiply myself so that I do not die out" (AW 1:137). When the break of revolution threatens to break corporeal and generational reproduction, Kragler demonstrates, revolution runs the danger of being broken in turn. This line of thought continues in his final speech, which culminates in a euphoric celebration of the pleasures of *fresh laundry*: "I put on a fresh shirt. . . . Now comes the bed, the large, white, broad bed comes!" (137). The apologia of the life of the petite bourgeoisie that refuses revolutionary action reaches its climax in a celebration of clean clothes and clean bedding:[15] throughout the play, the reference to a fresh shirt serves to dismiss Kragler as ineligible to be a fiancé for Anna,[16] and Kragler, in fact, explicitly links having a fresh shirt to *not* being a phantom: "I am a piece of flesh and I am wearing a fresh shirt. I am not a ghost after all!" (106). The affirmation of fleshly corporeality goes hand in hand with a return to clean order, where nothing is "out of place." Expelling Kragler from the realm of orderly, bourgeois life links, conversely, stench, corpse, and a lacking "sense for cleanliness." Murk attacks Kragler: "Is that you? What do you even want? You are a corpse! You are stinking already! *Pinches his nose.* Don't you have a sense for cleanliness [*Reinlichkeitssinn*]?" (107). Having a sense for cleanliness, so crucial to Nietzsche as the previous chapter showed, is here seen as the price of admission into life, reproduction, and order. Kragler's rejection of revolution occurs for the sake of the body, the possibility of (sexual) reproduction, and a certain type of bourgeois orderliness.[17]

It is this seemingly unambiguous final alignment of life and a rejection of the revolution that made the late Brecht remark, "I did not manage to let the spectator see the revolution differently than the 'hero' Kragler, and he saw it as something romantic" (GW 17:946). Revolution only appears on the side of death. No link between revolution and life could be established. Yet the notion of a smell of the revolution reveals a minor moment—perhaps just one—during the closing pages of the play that does, in fact, point to a different way for the reader to see, or rather to smell, the revolution. In the final dialogue between Kragler and the spirits distiller Glubb, Kragler indicts Glubb's commitment to the revolution: "You are running against the wall, man." Running against a wall: not only as the running up against an obstacle that cannot be overcome but, more drastically, the execution that threatens Glubb. Glubb, who had sung the "Ballad of the Dead Soldier," responds, "Yes, the morning smells *a great deal* [*viel*], my boy. The night passes away like black smoke" (AW 1:136; emphasis added). Against the rejection of revolution, Glubb asserts a different smell: the smell of the morning (recalling Hölderlin's "Morgenluft" in "Patmos") that contains a *multiplicity* (*viel*), as opposed to the unambiguous, single sense that Kragler seeks. This smell—in contradistinction to the unambiguous, ordering smell of fresh laundry—gambles on the openness of the future and the proliferating ambiguity of new beginnings. Revolutionary action, according to Glubb's suggestion, is like such a smell: it begins a "morning," a new chain of actions that is unpredictable and uncontainable, where this unpredictability might very well be, as the Brecht admirer Hannah Arendt argued often, the hallmark of true political action. The ambiguity of a new beginning forgoes the phantasy of being able to break up the interpenetration of life and death. And it asserts the possibility of a sensory subtraction from the reach of ordering political power that disallows any change. Brecht realized the importance of this moment in his late revision of *Drums in the Night*. In the most heavily revised fourth act, he elevates a line from the closing stanza of "Ballad of the Dead Soldier" to the status of title of the act: "There comes a red dawn [*Morgenrot*]." The morning is the beginning of redness: socialist rising and multiplicity of morning smell correspond to each other. This morning, then, its dawn and its multiple smell, is the feeble, ephemeral antidote to the antirevolutionary thrust of *Drums in the Night*—it is here that revolution can be perceived differently, not in a "certain" or "secure" smell, as Feuchtwanger's description of Brecht had it, but in a "smell of revolution" nevertheless.

"Virtual Revolutionaries"

While the "viel" of the smell of the morning, its multiple and ambiguous potential, is nothing but a brief and ephemeral moment in *Drums in the Night*, a different figure of the early Brecht gives greater weight to the potential contained in such a revolutionary writing of odors: the notorious Baal. As the first major play written by the playwright,[18] and by far the most scented one in his entire oeuvre, *Baal* occupies a privileged place with respect to Brecht's stench since it opens up a different conception of the "smell of revolution" and the revolution of the senses that it articulates. At first glance, the figure of Baal would appear to be categorically different from Kragler. On the one hand, revolution goes, except for one brief moment,[19] unmentioned in *Baal*. On the other, Baal, presented as a young poet, is marked by a vehement and unrestrained rejection of all the trappings of bourgeois existence that Kragler desires. Instead, he appears as the height of an asocial figure unconcerned with the well-being of others, driven by an insatiable appetite for wine, the sky, the earth, and women as well as men. In short, Baal embodies a vitalist appetite for life that positions him in opposition to societal constraints.[20]

Yet Baal's egoism and his opposition to bourgeois society are far from a mere contrarian stance of juvenile self-assertion, as Benjamin first observed: "it is after all Brecht's perpetual striving to sketch the asocial one, the hooligan, as a *virtual revolutionary* [*virtuellen Revolutionär*]" (GS 2:665; emphasis added).[21] While Kragler refuses the revolution for the sake of his own bodily well-being and his bourgeois existence, Baal's refusal of those very payouts must be seen, conversely, as the stance of a *virtual revolutionary*. Benjamin elaborates on this claim by showing how Brecht's Baal negotiates a key Marxian concern: "When Marx, so to speak, has posed himself the problem of letting the revolution emerge out of its complete other, capitalism, without having recourse to ethos, then Brecht transposes this problem into the human sphere: he wants to let the revolutionary emerge [*hervorgehen lassen*] on his own from the bad, egoistic type without any ethos whatsoever" (*GS* 2:665). What capitalism is to Marx, the asocial type is to Brecht. In a curiously active-passive movement, capitalism and the asocial type will "let emerge" a revolution and a revolutionary, respectively. As was shown in the introduction, the young Marx's attempt to develop such a new type of human being hinged, in part, on an "emancipation of all the senses." A transformation of sensory existence is linked, albeit in complicated and uncertain, perhaps even undecidable ways, to the onset of revolution. The young Brecht, in turn, attempts a similar feat: "in a retort out of lowliness and meanness [*Gemeinheit*]" (*GS* 2:664), Brecht seeks to develop a new type of revolutionary, and it is his stench—as precisely what is "lowly" and "mean"—that provides the terminus a quo for this emergence. Benjamin's observation that it is out of "Gemeinheit" that the new type emerges is crucial since the German word means both that which is lowly, unrefined, or mean, and that which is ordinary, shared by many or all: it is, in other words, the *commonality* of these scents that marks the possibility of a "letting emerge" contained within them. In short, what Baal discovers and works on is the potential contained in emancipating odors from the strictures of capitalist servitude and bourgeois propriety, and it is out of asocial, common stench that a new type of human being comes forth.

In *Baal*, the common and lowly smells that articulate the protagonist's stance as a virtual revolutionary fall into two groups, which rather exactly correspond to the two crucial smells that Freud was concerned with in his account of the olfactory counterforces threatening civilization: the smell of bodies, in particular bodies qua animalistic or sexual, and the smell of wheat fields—that is, of the cultivated earth. The latter evidences the young Brecht's intense interest in *Thus Spoke Zarathustra* and positions this odor as a reprisal of Zarathustra's invention of "new smells." The smell of the cultivated earth first emerges, albeit only implicitly, in the opening scene of the second version of *Baal*.[22] The scene, titled "Soirée," sees Baal reading some of his poetry in the company of members of the (self-proclaimed) high society. Their indiscriminate praise for Baal's literary production, showing the vapidity of their interest in art, is interspersed with talk of business: "Wheat is at 49 1/8.—Fabulous. Baumann & Co already ceased all payments yesterday" (*AW* 1:22). Listening to and praising poetry is nothing more than background music for the thoroughly commercialized character of this soirée: above all, the guests are interested in the price of wheat—the grain having no sensory, olfactory existence for them, but merely being mentioned with respect to its monetary value—and how much money can be made from literary production. The choice of wheat is deeply significant in Brecht's oeuvre: it is precisely the desire and inability to understand and explain the machinations of the wheat exchange that will bring Brecht to Marxism a decade later. Yet, for now, it is the double commercialization of art and the products of the earth (wheat) that form the foil for Baal's "enmity" that the rest of the play unfolds.

This opposition—and with it the potential for the emergence of revolution—is contained in the *smell* of the wheat fields, in contradistinction to their price. Two scenes after "Soirée," Ekart, Baal's companion, tries to lure Baal away from the gregarious bar where they are drinking. This is how he articulates the "seduction" of Baal away from the crowd: "Come, brother Baal! We fly blessedly into the blue like two white doves . . . the smell of infinite fields [*Geruch der unendlichen Felder*] before they are chopped down!" (*AW* 1:32). The escape from the gregariousness of the bar is articulated as a flight toward the smell of "infinite fields," a smell that emerges precisely before they are fed into the circulation of economic goods: "before they are chopped down." The earth beckons before any commercial use or exploitation, before what Brecht calls *Verwertung*. Throughout the 1920s and 1930s, Brecht returns to *Baal* to rewrite and reconfigure the play, and one of the most insistent and clearest changes he carries out lies precisely in emphasizing Baal's opposition to the *Verwerter*, those who utilize and exploit: "the utilizers [*Verwerter*] try to ascertain through cautious questioning what might be usable in Baal. // Baal triumphs over the utilizers."[23] It is not that Baal is not a type of *Verwerter*, but he is of a different kind: "even though Baal himself is a utilizer, he cannot come to an agreement with these people because his kind [*seine art*] is too great."[24] What this different, "greater" type of a *Verwerter* might be is indicated by Brecht when he, while rereading his early plays toward the end of his life, offers a conceptualization of Baal's principal opposition to the world: what he opposes is that the world knows "not a usable [*ausnutzbare*] but only an exploitable [*ausbeutbare*] productivity." Brecht introduces in the word "Verwertung" a critical difference between use and exploitation, in certain ways echoing the question of the usability of the unhygienic child's being out of place: what *Baal* opposes is a relationship to productivity—in this case, the primordial instantiation of productivity; namely, the productivity of the earth—that knows only exploitation.[25] By contrast, the smell of infinite fields indexes a potential productivity that would be used but not exploited.

The smell of the wheat fields points to such a different productivity in Ekart's offer of expanse instead of narrow confinement: before the fields are harvested and sold, they are "unendlich"—infinite, uncontained, open. This is what this smell embodies: *a definitizing moment of escape from economy*. A moment of virtual revolution par excellence: the temptation of Ekart and Baal to turn against society, away from the gregariousness of the bar, contains a novel relation to the earth and its nourishing products as well as to individuation. While the egoism suffusing *Baal* might suggest a centering on the individual who seeks to assert himself, the play itself counteracts this naive concept of the asocial type at every turn: the escape that tempts is precisely a flight toward definitization that undoes the world as structured by containment and exploitability. Baal at first resists Ekart's temptation. Soon, however, he and Ekart roam the country roads and pass through those very fields whose smell beckoned them. Baal is submerged in and suffused by this odor, even approaching an atmospheric dissolution into the field. Walking through the fields, he exclaims, "I have the smell of fruit-bearing seas of wheat in my nose.... My hair shines like yellow wheat. And I can breathe! Breathe! My back arches hollowly when I lie on it. That's how strongly I notice that the earth is a sphere and is covered by me" (*AW* 1:63).[26] Baal's "asocial body," thoroughly suffused by the smell of wheat, appears in the position of the field (as that which "covers" the earth) and hence occupies the position of what emits the smell. Dissolving into the smell, Baal joins the definitizing moment of the "infinite" fields and thus the promise of escaping from economy.

In the rest of the play, Baal's olfactory body—the body of the virtual revolutionary—continues to excrete smells, most forcefully odors related to the twinned powers of animality and sexuality that characterize the "bad, egoistic type." What "use" could the animal and sexual character of this body have for the emergence of a revolutionary type out of asociality? The young Brecht's answer can be traced most clearly in two scenes that correspond to each other in a trajectory of intensification. In the first one, Baal seduces or rather assaults a young woman named Sophie Dechant. The figure could hardly be more overdetermined: she is introduced as wearing all white (signifying virginity and innocence) and her name, Sophie Dechant, is easily deciphered (wisdom of song). Baal, then, takes the innocent, virginal wisdom associated with song and introduces her to the ecstasies of sexuality. The crucial moment of overwhelming Sophie is accompanied by Baal's description that links his powers to his smell: "you can smell me. That's how it goes with animals. *Gets up*. And now you belong to the wind, white cloud!" (*AW* 1:45). It is his body odor that draws innocent Sophie under his spell, like an animal. Brecht, in a literary operation typical of his work, shows that wisdom, for all its supposed distance from the realm of bodily functions and pleasures, is eventually governed by olfactory signals and attractions in a way that does not rise above the animalistic. It is the smell of Baal's body, in short, that triumphs over the resistance of a purity that claims to keep itself apart from corporeality and sexuality.

This olfactory triumph of the body is intensified further in a later scene that sees Baal walk through the fields with both Ekart and Sophie Dechant. In a typical erotic triangle, Baal and Ekart begin to quarrel, ostensibly over the question of who is allowed to be with Sophie. The quarrel devolves into a physical brawl, which reaches its climax right when Sophie shouts, "They are beasts of prey!" Baal, whom the stage directions describe as "pressing Ekart against him," addresses his companion: "Do you see now that we will never again get away from each other? Can you smell me? Do you see that there is more than the closeness of women?" (*AW* 1:58). The approach of the brawl over a woman ends in a homoerotic bond "between men," as Eve Sedgwick would put it, that leads to the exclusion of the woman: Ekart and Baal abandon Sophie (who disappears from the play after this scene). While earlier, Baal's corporeal smell overwhelmed the claims to innocence and distance from sexuality embodied in Sophie/wisdom, here his smell mediates an even greater break from bourgeois convention: the homosexual relation presents itself throughout the play as the relationship of true outcasts, of transgressive amoralism. It is in this sense that the strong homoerotic tendencies that are present in almost all of Brecht's early plays must be understood: they present the "virtual revolutionary" of moral and interpersonal norms in the full sense of the word "virtual," as deriving from the Latin *virs*, thus joining—classically masculinist and misogynist—strength, power, and masculinity. *Drums in the Night* showed the temptation of heterosexual, bourgeois marriage as the main obstacle to Kragler becoming a revolutionary: *Baal*, the inverse of *Drums*, presents the flight out of bourgeois sexuality into homosexual relations as the virtual nucleus of a revolution of sexual relations. Unable to envision a sexuality that would not fall into the exploitation of sexual productivity under capitalism and imperialism (where sexuality serves only the reproduction of the labor force and the imperial army, respectively), Brecht diverts sexuality away from reproduction altogether toward a realm of waste, excess, and spoilage. The refusal of (sexual) productivity is thus simultaneously articulated as the hypersexual powers of Baal (who can seduce anyone whatsoever) and the impotence of homosexuality:[27] both too much and too little, a multiplied masculinity and a subtraction from proper masculinity that turn Baal's sexuality into the fulcrum of a *virtual* overturning. And this virtuality inheres in the bodily smell that forges an indissoluble bond ("we will never again get away from each other") between Baal and Ekart: the "lowliness and commonness" of the smell of homosexual relations contains precisely the *virs* that endows the figure of Baal with such force.

This flight into the asocial, however, is dangerous. In fact, it might be that the virtual revolutionary cannot be delineated without a certain exposure to radical destruction. Ekart repeatedly indicates as much in the scene when Baal merges with the smell of the wheat fields: Baal covering the earth with his body, like the field whose smell enters his nose, appears to no longer be Baal but rather a being who, through the smell, joins the earth. This extreme point of Baal's dissolution troubles even Ekart, who, after all, had been the one who first introduced this smell: he calls his companion a "fool," an "enthusiast [*Schwärmer*]," and "mad." Smell threatens with foolery, enthusiasm, and madness: the proliferation of these descriptors indicates Ekart's strained efforts to find a determinate designation for the threat of the boundless.

The threat of madness that inheres in this early concept of virtual revolutionaries emerges even more clearly when the family resemblance of *Baal* and *Thus Spoke Zarathustra* is considered once more: in a later, fragmentary poem titled "On Nietzsche's 'Zarathustra,'" Brecht describes Zarathustra's attempts to escape from the herd, the mediocre masses, and to rise like "white spray" out of "muddied waves!" The danger, as the poem puts it succinctly, is this: "Beyond the markets lies only madness [*die Irre*]" (*GW* 9:614). Baal's danger is that, in escaping from the wheat market that opened the "Soirée" scene toward the infinite, open fields, he will only end up in error and madness: an asocial position in the strong sense is self-destructive. The asocial, Brecht comes to realize almost two decades later, is merely "*the* gospel of the enemy of humankind." Just as the second poem about the child who did not want to wash himself ended with a turn to economic mediation, Brecht's literary trajectory moves toward a thought of the virtual revolutionary's relationship to the "markets," and the wheat markets in particular.

Poetological Excursus: Against Aromatic Words

(Poetic, theoretical) writing that forgoes any attempt to be "beyond" the market and does not blithely move past talk of the price of wheat requires a language of smell that differs from what *Baal* could offer, one that does not obscure its status as economically mediated and does not fall into madness. Brecht most directly develops criteria for such a writing in a text from 1935, titled "Five Difficulties in Writing the Truth." The text, addressed as advice to writers confronted with fascism, returns—a clear echo of *Baal*—to the question of fields of wheat, wheat's price, and how one might speak of its smell: "Thus whoever says soil [*Boden*] and describes the fields to the nose and the eye by speaking of their *smell of the earth* [*Erdgeruch*] and their color supports the lies of the rulers; because it is not the fertility of the soil that matters, nor the love the human being feels for it, nor hard work, but primarily the price of wheat and the price of labor" (*GW* 18:231; emphasis added). For Brecht, speaking of the "smell of the earth" (perhaps including the use Nietzsche's Zarathustra made of this expression) is nothing but an obfuscation that supports the lies of the capitalist class: it diverts attention from the fact that the sensory form of the earth, the love and diligence with which a human being might relate to it, are overwhelmed by a subsumption under economic structures, a subsumption that constitutes the dissolution of these other relationships to the earth. Since the "smell" of the earth, presumably just like the smell of "infinite" fields before harvest, is unknown to the market, it must be excised from the writer's lexicon and replaced by a juridico-economic term: "The ones who extract profit from the soil are not the ones who extract wheat from it, and the earthly smell of the soil is unknown to the stock markets. The latter smell of something else. Against this, land ownership [*Landbesitz*] is the right word" (*GW* 18:231–232). The task of the writer is to rid language of the "lazy mysticism [*faule Mystik*]" that inheres in expressions such as "smell of the earth": relying on a sensory, romanticized description allegedly beyond juridico-economic realities constitutes a writer's laziness that upholds a mysticism covering over reality.

In a text from 1927 on the state of contemporary lyric poetry, Brecht had already contrasted a materialist and economic assessment of poetry with what he calls the poetry of "aromatic words." Aromatic words, in Brecht's assessment often tied to the production of an "atmosphere," serve a specific function: the poetry of Rilke, George, and Werfel, when employing such lazy mysticism, functions as "manifestos of the class struggle" (*GW* 18:58). Class struggle is fought via a poetry that relies on words that emit an aroma—one might also say words that are surrounded by an aura—as it seeks to establish a "pure beauty value" (58) ignorant of the economic realities that both enable and subsume such poetry.[28] Brecht's own poetry seeks to rid itself of all such aroma in an act of "washing language [*Sprachwaschung*]." His refusal to wash his own body meets his attempt—resonating strongly with Ponge's soap poems investigated below—to *wash the body of language*. These two acts only seemingly pull in opposite directions: they meet in the shared opposition to the bourgeois paradigm of the pretty and the pleasing. While bourgeois bodies are supposed to be clean and unscented (subtracted from the sensual), bourgeois poetry is supposed to be aromatic (artificially restituted to an olfactory but contained sensuality). Brecht's two charges against bourgeois conventions, contained in his bodily stench and the washing of poetic language, operate on the same grounds: a *dirty body* and a *nonaromatic poetry* demystify and oppose what bourgeois conventions both require and present as naturalized.

Brecht is clear-eyed when it comes to the implications of such a washing of language. When he introduces this term in a journal entry from 1940 concerning his Finnish epigrams, he explicitly characterizes it as a deterioration: "what a descent!" More precisely, this descent—*in nuce* a theory of what the decline of theories of "decadence" (so important to Nietzsche and Baudelaire) could mean—must be explicitly articulated as a tendency toward linguistic poverty: "seen from the bourgeois standpoint, an astonishing impoverishment has occurred."[29] This impoverishment corresponds to the devastation of the poet's environment: "capitalism has forced us to fight; it has devastated [*verwüstet*] our surroundings; I no longer go about 'in the forest by myself' but among policemen." Devastation, more literally, desertification, is the condition of poetry under capitalism—"die Wüste wächst" (the desert grows), as Nietzsche famously wrote. Such a condition requires a cleaning of language that gets rid of all ornamental and atmospheric excess that could hide a *verwüstet*, deserted and devastated, reality.

The poverty of poetry is thus dictated to the poet by the economic conditions of devastation that he finds himself in. Poetic poverty, as Benjamin remarks, must consequently be conceived of as a "mimicry that allows to get closer to the real [*das Wirkliche*] than any rich person can achieve it" (*GS* 2:510). Cleansed of all obfuscating aroma, Brecht's poetry approaches the actual: the poverty of *life* under capitalism requires a poverty of *poetry* under capitalism. Yet this poverty of poetry has a double exhortatory and oppositional impetus, as Theodor W. Adorno argues in his *Aesthetic Theory*: "art indicts superfluous poverty by voluntarily undergoing its own; but it indicts asceticism as well and cannot establish it as its own norm."[30] Adorno thus calls this poverty the "deaestheticization of art [*Entkunstung der Kunst*]," and explicitly lauds Brecht's poetry: "one need only compare good poems by Brecht that are styled as protocol sentences with bad poems by authors whose rebellion against being poetic recoils into the pre-aesthetic. In Brecht's disenchanted poetry what is fundamentally distinct from what is simplistically stated constitutes the works' eminent rank."[31] The worth of Brecht's poetry lies in its demystification, which according to the poet himself is contained in his attempt to write smells, bodies, and the earth without recourse to obfuscating "aromatic words." Acknowledging the reality and force of economic mediation requires a poetics that can write sensuality and common scents at a remove from all mysticism, thus also rewriting the language of *Baal*. Brecht's poetry from the 1930s onward will attempt just this.

Hollywood *Non Olet*

Within the Brechtian oeuvre, the fine line between the simplistic, "preaesthetic" and the disenchanted poetry of great worth is not always easy to discern. A test case for such a distinction can be found—once more with insistent reference to the question of how one might write smells under a regime of thorough economic mediation—in his remarkable *Hollywoodelegien*, written in 1942, the second year of his exile in California. These poems constitute the extension of his poetic trajectory after the Finnish epigrams to which Brecht applied the "washing of language" claim and continue the impoverishment of poetic diction: he characterizes the language of the Hollywood poems as "basic German." Using the English term, Brecht elaborates: "This corresponds in no way to a theory, I feel the lack of expression and rhythm when I read through such a collection, but while writing (and correcting) every unusual word repels me."[32] The poems written in and about Hollywood are marked by a "lack"—but any poem that would be richer than these would betray the kind of writing this place requires. American exile seems to necessitate a particularly stripped down, impoverished language.

While Brecht's Scandinavian exile in the 1930s already posed numerous challenges to the writer and his family, his arrival in the US in 1941 increased his irritation significantly. Brecht struggled to find work; he found the sizeable community of German intellectual exiles suffocating; and the American way of life did not suit his German sensibilities. For the first time in exile, his literary production decreases significantly and he turns more and more to the semi-private *Arbeitsjournal* (*Work Journal*) to record his thoughts. One of these entries, from January 21, 1942, describes an odd feature of his Californian stay that interweaves this sense of irritation with a reflection on lack, loss, and smell: "How curious, I cannot breathe in this climate. The air is completely deodorized, the same in the morning and in the evening, in the house just as in the garden. And there are no seasons. Everywhere it was part of my morning rituals to lean out of the window and gasp for air; I have scrapped this ritual here. There is neither smoke nor smell of grass."[33] Whereas his fellow exiles, such as Thomas Mann, found themselves "enchanted by the light, by the special fragrance of the air" in these "paradisical scenes,"[34] Brecht was struck above all by the *deodorized* nature of Californian air. This lack of smell leads to a double homogenization: both time and space, in an uncanny echo of the latest Hölderlin poems, lose all differentiation; inside and outside blend together, as do morning and evening. If the "virtual" potential of smell was found in the "viel" of the smell of the morning that comes to end the night, as Glubb argues at the end of *Drums in the Night*, then such a loss of differentiation proves devastating for the olfactory sense Brecht labors to establish. Any kind of change resembling the "interpenetration of life and death" of the dead soldier, for instance, or of bodies stinking against nonmoving time seems to be immobilized by the ever-same air of California: nothing new can emerge, no intimation of an impending overturning is accessible to the senses in this alleged paradise.

This deodorization and its ramifications leave their mark on Brecht's poetry. In "On Thinking about Hell," a poem written shortly after his arrival in Los Angeles, Brecht evokes "my brother Shelley," who had compared hell to London in "Peter Bell the Third." Brecht, half playfully, half seriously, advances the counterclaim that hell "must be / Still more like Los Angeles" (*GW* 10:830).[35] The central lines of the poem then read,

> And fruit markets
> With entire heaps of fruit that indeed
> Have neither smell nor taste.

The heaps or bounty of this paradise-hell are the bounty of a market, a commercial accumulation that lacks everything besides quantity: neither taste nor smell can be ascribed to these fruits. While the abundance of fruit must have been a shock to the war-deprived refugee, Brecht's attention is immediately drawn to a different kind of lack, a different kind of poverty: things might look pretty and appealing, but their olfactory qualities are lost, overwhelmed by the quantity of their commercial availability. Abundance exists on the (visual) surface only. The sense of smell, by contrast, betrays this visual overflow for what it really is: a poverty in disguise.

This tension between the promises presented on the visual plane and their olfactory deflation comes to be a central theme of Brecht's poetry about his exilic surroundings. In particular, as Brecht, like many of his fellow writers in exile, seeks to make a living by writing for the big film studios of Hollywood, the dominance of the visual promise of happiness that is sold to the masses by the entertainment industry becomes ever clearer to him. Taking recourse to the Latin tradition that Brecht knew so well, the sensory situation of his US-American exile can thus be captured in the following dictum: *Hollywood non olet*. Not only does Hollywood not smell, it effects a deodorizing transformation of scented, smelly life into a circulation of images and money: "pecunia non olet" (money does not smell), the emperor Vespasian famously proclaimed when pressed by his son on a new tax levied on urine; the sphere of monetary circulation is deodorized and thus detached from the life processes that underlie and sustain it—to the extreme degree that one might not even be able to perceive the link between that which used to smell and the pure commodity or deodorized money it has become. In this context, Brecht's characteristic attention to smell then steps to the side of the dominant aesthetic and economic regime: it seeks to discern and elaborate the smell of both Hollywood and *pecunia*.

The fifth of the *Hollywood Elegies* does precisely that: it takes up the motif of the fruit market and its lack of odor and shows that *behind* such commercial deodorization a different smell can be found. The poem opens with the following verses: "The angels of Los Angeles / Are tired out from smiling [*Die Engel von Los Angeles / Sind müde vom Lächeln*]" (*GW* 10:850). The angels found in Los Angeles (whose identity will be addressed in the next section) are worn out from smiling: the smile, in the German tradition at least since Hölderlin strongly associated with the promise of reconciliation and the attainment of a calm state of harmony, has here become something that fatigues. A smile, in the "keep smiling" culture of the United States that so many German exiles found disconcerting, must be performed as an exhausting act of labor and thus perverts any promise of reconciliation that used to inhere in it. This perverted promise leads to despair: the angels are said to be "verzweifelt" (desperate). This despair, in turn, drives them, at the end of the day ("Am Abend" [in the evening]), to make a purchase "behind the fruit markets": they buy "small bottles / Filled with the smell of sex [*kleine Fläschchen / Mit Geschlechtsgeruch*]." While the deodorization of fruit might be tolerable, the lack of a different smell must be remedied—namely, the lack of the smell of "Geschlecht," a word oscillating among genitals, sex, and generation, thus recalling Freud's claim that one of the two main smells at odds with civilization is the smell of sexuality. The placid, angelic smile of the inhabitants of Los Angeles, meant to signal their happy and harmonious existence in paradise, lasts only through the day. In the evening, this smooth surface is disrupted by a desperate desire for the smell of sex, a desire that can, in turn, only be fulfilled by a commercial transaction. Indicating, in the word "verzweifelt," a scission not only of the smiling yet desperate hellish-paradisal existence but also of (twofold) sexual difference, the fifth elegy shows that the *Haufen* (heaps) of fragrance-free fruit covers up the *Kaufen* (buying) of little bottles that reasserts the power of fragrance. Poetry, in other words, shows that behind the tendency of deodorization lies the thorough commodification even of sexuality—and the ineluctable reemergence of smell, which cannot be done away with, even in the proclaimed visual purity of Hollywood.

Beyond the rather traditional Marxist claim that there is no such thing as (sensory) experience that is not economically mediated,[36] these small bottles thus delineate a more far-reaching and precise sketch of sensory existence in the deodorized world of commodification and of Hollywood. The diminutive form of the bottles (*Fläschchen*) points to the weakening of the power of sexual smell once it has been subsumed by the market, in particular in contrast to *Baal*: while in the early play, odor emerged as an overwhelming force that could not be resisted, the *Geschlechtsgeruch* of the market is not only small but also literally *contained*. A small bottle can be opened and closed at will; it suggests a fantasy of control in which the olfactory powers of sexuality are part of an on-demand system. A greater distance to *Baal* could hardly be imagined: not only can Baal's odors not be contained, but they are described as "infinite," as subtracting themselves from any and all finitizing moments such as a container. All of this is (allegedly) erased in Hollywood.[37]

Containment and smallness indicate the larger and indeed crucial problem of distance that pervades the *Hollywood Elegies* in general and the question of (de)odorization in these poems in particular. In a journal entry, Brecht reports the following exchange with his friend Hans (John) Winge concerning the elegies: "[Winge says] 'they resemble poems written from Mars.' We realize that this 'distance' isn't proper to the writer but is supplied by the city: its inhabitants almost all have it."[38] This distance of the Californian city and its inhabitants constitutes the obverse of the homogenization of its air: as soon as distance dominates a sensory constitution, olfactory differentiation tends toward erasure. Seeking out smell, as the bottle of *Geschlechtsgeruch* encapsulates it, thus amounts to the seeking out of *intimacy* in a city and life structured above all by distance. In this, too, smell stands as the counterpoint to the tiring smile of the angels of Los Angeles: a smile is, after all, a visual device that functions only via distance and keeps at a distance by signaling a friendly but not intimate relation. Distinctly echoing the Nietzschean problematic of smell, for Brecht in Hollywood smell also stands for the desire and danger to overcome distance, for the incapacity and promise to get up close.

From this perspective, it also becomes clearer why these short, "laconic" poems are presented as elegies, a generic designation that seems at first surprising. Brecht's collaborator Hanns Eisler, when he arrived in California in the spring of 1942, suggested the model of Goethe's classic *Roman Elegies* to Brecht: "I said to Brecht in this gloomy, eternal spring of Hollywood . . . : 'this is the classic place where one has to write elegies.' There are after all the *Roman Elegies* by Goethe, which are one of my favorite works and that Brecht also admired a lot" (*GBA* 12:400). In Goethe's masterpiece, the "place" where he writes his elegies is ineluctably tied to his theme via a palindromic inscription: *Roma/Amor*. Rome is the city of love, and it is love that provides "asylum," as Goethe writes: "my asylum / That Amor the Prince, royally protecting, bestowed on me."[39] Brecht's asylum, by contrast, contains nothing but the *negative image* of what love would be: no intimacy is possible; smiling tires; sexuality is contained in little, commodified bottles. In short, these elegies tell of the loss of a time when a poet could write about Roma/Amor—recall Brecht's exclamation "what a descent!" when he compares his poems to Goethe's—and write a topos that is intimately intertwined with love. In this, too, the *Hollywood Elegies* stand in direct correspondence to *Baal*: Baal's corporeal smell drew both Sophie Dechant and Ekart to him; in his body odor, the possibility and eventual failure of sexual and amorous relations was negotiated. Neither the elegies nor the early play could develop a viable mode of loving relationality—but both indicate, as a negative index, what a different love and a different place, no longer homogeneously deodorized, would be.

Smelly Angels of History

If for Goethe "Roma" spells "Amor," then Brecht equally discerns that the place name "Los Angeles" spells the theme of his elegies: *Engel* (angel). But who are these angels that populate the *Hollywood Elegies*? While the range of Brecht's Christian and biblical references is wide and their occurrences frequent, angels appear rather rarely in his work.[40] The rarity of their occurrence emphasizes the importance of the topical link between place and image and positions the elegies as occasional poetry in the strict sense: they arise out of the *Gelegenheit*, out of the opportunity of the poet's exilic circumstances, where Los Angeles constitutes his "asylum."[41]

Being in the City of Angels provides the poet Brecht with a most suitable opportunity to carry out the type of "washing of language" he had already envisioned a few years prior. More precisely, his treatment of angels will be a paradigmatic case of what washing language might mean: namely, a "cleansing" of the other great cycle of German elegies named after a place, Rainer Maria Rilke's *Duino Elegies*, which to a significant degree concern angels. The first of Rilke's elegies famously opens with a pathos-laden invocation of an angel ("Who, if I cried out, would hear me among the angelic / orders?"), and both the first and the second elegies characterize these angels primarily through the horror they inspire: "Every angel is terrifying [*schrecklich*]." This terror derives from an angel being "the creature in whom that transformation of the visible into the invisible we are performing is already complete," as Rilke writes in an often-quoted letter to his Polish translator. The angel is supposed to reside in spheres higher than our own; he attains a "higher degree of reality" than the human being. The poet's relationship to the angel, in turn, is structured as a plea for access to these higher regions. None of this applies even remotely to Brecht's angels. For the poet of a washing of language, Rilke's angels cannot but be the epitome of "lazy mysticism," of an obscurantist sprinkling of "aromatic words" employed in an undercover manifesto of class struggle. Beyond an intra-German poetic altercation, then, the stakes are clear: What kind of poetry can, and should, one write faced with the realities of a class society? What place can creatures such as angels find in poetry? The first lines of the second Hollywood elegy that mentions angels indicates the main thrust of Brecht's counterimage to Rilke's mystic, all-too-mystic angel:

> The city is named after the angels
> And one encounters angels everywhere. (*GW* 10:850)

If one (ever) encounters angels, then it is here in Los Angeles—because that is all an angel could be: an inhabitant of a city that bestows the name "angel" on its inhabitants. The mystic element is dissolved into an ordinary, vulgar, *com-*

mon name—that is, into a name of the people that might be shared by all. This is a prime example of the "vulgar thinking [*plumpes Denken*]" that Brecht was so often accused of and that he embraced fervently: a poet is having all these encounters with angels? Must be because he is in the City of Angels!

Brecht's poetry, however, does not stop there but rather develops a full description of these nonmystical angels, a description that one by one transforms angelic characteristics and washes off their mysticism in a paradigmatic transformation of poetic language. The elegy continues: "They smell of oil and wear golden diaphragms / And with blue rings under the eyes" (GW 10:849). The angel's halo is transformed into two different types of rings: those under the eyes (referring back to the "tired," exhausted nature of the smiling Angelenos) and those of the "Goldene Pessare," also known as "Mutterringe" in German, a diaphragm—that is, a device enabling non-procreative and hence primarily pleasure-oriented sex—marks this type of angelic intercourse. The theme of intercourse is then continued by a reference to the angels' messenger function (whence the word *angelos*, or messenger, derives): every morning, they bring words to the writers; they "feed" them in their "swimming pools [*Schwimmpfühlen*]." The higher, quasi-divine inspiration so dear to Rilke, supposedly derived from these intermediary beings, is dragged into the thoroughly earthly realm of food and, through Brecht's playful translation of "pool" as "Pfühl," swamps.

Most importantly, these angels "smell of oil." This is a key feature of Brecht's poetic strategy: the washing of language—the freeing from aromatic words—enables plain, basic words describing different scents to emerge and take the place of mystification. In this case, the smell of oil belongs to a larger account of the "petroculture" of Los Angeles that Brecht develops throughout the *Hollywood Elegies*, long before that word would be introduced into scholarly discourses. In particular, this petroculture dominates the atmospherics of this city: "The four cities / Are suffused by the smell of oil" (GW 10:849). That Brecht might have a certain affinity with the drilling of petroleum had already been sensed by Benjamin, years before Brecht explicitly wrote about the oil towers of California. Brecht's poetic activities, according to Benjamin, can be described as follows: "like an engineer begins with petroleum drillings in the desert, [Brecht] takes up his activities in the desert of the present at exactly calculated points" (GS 2:506). Brecht qua poet resembles a petrol engineer: he goes out into the "desert of the present [*Wüste der Gegenwart*]"—echoing the "verwüstet" character Brecht himself ascribes to his dark times, in turn echoing Nietzsche—and takes probes from which he deduces the proper place for his activity. In California, then, the poet-engineer Brecht took his probes and found in the smell of the city and the air of California a suitable point for his activities—namely, his language-washing operations, turning the lazy mysticism of a certain type of lyric poetry into his vulgar, common, "basic German."

The import of these desert drillings becomes clearer when the smell of oil is compared to the smells of *Baal*. The smell of oil is irresistible and triumphs over all other smells, as a later poem by Brecht (from 1950, the same year as the second poem about the dirty child was written) emphasizes: "but irresistibly / Smells after all only oil" (*GBA* 15:225). This recalls Baal, once more, whose body odor was above all characterized by a similar irresistibility. Yet here the triumph of the smell of oil is primarily a triumph over bodily pleasures: "And the smell of fresh white bread / Of peaches and pistachios / Is also good but nothing / Against the smell of oil." Baal's amoral vitalism and hedonistic desire have lost out to the Hollywood petro-capitalism of Los Angeles: despite (visual) appearance to the contrary, the "mausoleum of easy going," as Brecht called Los Angeles, is far from being a place where the body and its pleasures actually take center stage. Since it was precisely this feature of Baal that marked his egoism as something other than a mere free market competition, and that consequently bore the potential of the "virtual revolutionary," the danger of the smell of oil emerges clearly: it threatens, in its irresistibility, the "letting emerge" of the new, revolutionary type that was contained in the smell of Baal's asocial body.

This insight situates Brecht's smelly angel at a particular juncture of history: What revolutionary potential, if any, does the historical situation of Los Angeles contain? Where could virtual revolutionaries be located in Hollywood petro-capitalism? From this point of view, Brecht's poems can be read as a response to another angel, one who is much closer to him than the Rilkean one: the famed "angel of history" as he appears in Walter Benjamin's *On the Concept of History*. While Benjamin certainly enjoys a very different status in Brecht's estimation than Rilke, the two figures are temporarily aligned, at certain points, by Brecht's disdain for mysticism. In July 1938, for instance, Brecht writes the following in his journal, regarding Benjamin's work on his Baudelaire essay while he was staying with Brecht in Denmark: "everything mysticism, combined with a stance against mysticism."[42] Brecht's attitude to Benjamin can be schematized as follows: admiration combined with the demand that Benjamin's images and thought be rid of remnants of mysticism. More specifically, Brecht encounters Benjamin's angel of history at a moment of great poignancy. As he records in his journal, he received the *Theses* in August 1941, shortly after arriving in the United States, from Günther Anders, Benjamin's cousin, along with the news that Benjamin had killed himself in a Spanish border town while fleeing from the Gestapo a year prior. Reading the *Theses* is thus deeply intertwined with the painful loss and memory of the dear friend, a loss that Brecht, according to Hannah Arendt, characterized as "the first real loss that Hitler had caused German literature."[43] That Benjamin's text, in turn, is in conversation with Brecht is evidenced not only by the fact that he intended to send a copy to Brecht,[44] but also by the fact that Benjamin uses a quote from Brecht's *Threepenny Opera* as the motto for the seventh thesis, which contains the often-quoted claim that it is the "task" of the historian "to brush history against the grain" (*GS* 1:697). Benjamin's and Brecht's understandings of history in the late 1930s are formed in dialogue with each other.

It is against this background that Brecht's angels emerge as a rejoinder to the deceased friend's conception of history. While Gershom Scholem in *Walter Benjamin and His Angel* claims that it is "no wonder that Brecht, as we now know from his diary, did not know what to make of these *Theses*,"[45] a closer look at Brecht's journal entry evidences a clear albeit critical orientation with respect to the *Theses*: "Günther Stern [Anders] gives them to me with the remark that they are dark and confused, I believe the word 'already' was also mentioned. . . . In short, this small work is clear and clarifying (despite all metaphors . . .) and one thinks with dismay [*schrecken*] of how small the number is of those who are at least willing to misunderstand it."[46] Benjamin's *Theses* are clear and clarifying, in particular, so the rest of the entry argues, when it comes to the conception of history: Brecht joins Benjamin in opposing a facile understanding of history as inevitable progress toward a socialist or communist future; a progress that is supposed to be only briefly interrupted by fascism.

The critical impetus of Brecht's note is contained in the parenthetical remark "despite all metaphors," which recalls the earlier criticism "everything mysticism, combined with a stance against mysticism."[47] In this light, the last poem of the *Hollywood Elegies* cycle offers a final, deeply troubling transformation of the angelic image. While the two preceding images of angels encountered thus far do not describe them as being in motion—a crucial feature of Benjamin's angel—such movement, a movement of history of sorts, is offered in the last poem: above Los Angeles "circle the fighter jets [*kreisen die Jagdflieger*]." The winged creatures of history are fighter jets, and their high-up, circular movement is motivated by an attempt to escape from smell "So that the stench of greed and misery / Does not reach up to them" (*GW* 10:850). Pace Rilke, there are no rarefied, transcendent "higher regions," only the height of airplanes that "hunt": it is these beings that are "terrifying" and thus a "messenger of misfortune [*Bote des Unglücks*]," to quote Brecht's famous designation of the refugee. With this image, Brecht takes the theme of distance to an extreme point. If the little bottles of "the smell of sex" sought to overcome the distance of the sprawling city that lacked any intimacy, these fighter jets fly in "great heights" precisely to distance themselves from the smells of the city: the stench of "greed" and "misery" pervades the City of Angels, but the fighter jets—the military might of the United States—claims to be detached from both. The movement of history, as it appears to Brecht in exile, is contained in this image: the circling of militarized winged creatures that hover high above misery and greed. For Brecht in 1942, the angel of history is nothing but a fighter jet escaping from the stench of human life.[48]

The *Glücksgott* and His Students

At the same time as Brecht works out the figure of the angels populating a Los Angeles that simultaneously tends toward deodorization and reeks of oil, he also produces a series of poems that correspond directly to his poetic critique of American life. These poems sketch out a counterimage to the *Hollywood Elegies* by centering on the figure of a "Glücksgott" (a god of happiness, luck, or good fortune).[49] As Brecht explains in "While Examining My First Plays," this *Glücksgott* is modeled on a "Chinese figure" that shows a "little fat god of *Glück* who stretches luxuriously" (*GW* 17:947). The *Glück* of this god consists in "eating, drinking, dwelling, sleeping, loving, working, thinking, the great delights";[50] the poems about this figure are "a thoroughly materialistic work" (590). This *Glück*, then, constitutes the opposite of any claims to "higher regions" or a "great height":

> I am the god of lowliness
> Of palates and of testicles
> For happiness lies indeed, I'm sorry,
> Rather close to the ground.

> Ich bin der Gott der Niedrigkeit
> Der Gaumen und der Hoden
> Denn das Glück liegt nun einmal, tut mir leid
> Ziemlich niedrig am Boden. (*GW* 10:892)

The greatness of these pleasures lies precisely in their materialist, "lowly," and common character, in their closeness to the body and to the ground. In contrast to the fighter jets that circle high above smell, the *Glücksgott* is the one who stays low: *Glück* for Brecht, very much like Zarathustra's *Glück* that is figured by the smell of the earth, is attainable only to those who do not take flight into higher regions detached from odors.

This lowly and materialistic character of *Glück* constitutes the difference from the only time "Glück" is mentioned in the *Hollywood Elegies*: "Greater wealth [*Vermögen*] is brought by the dreams of happiness [*Glück*] / That are written here on celluloid" (*GW* 10:849). For the angels of Los Angeles, *Glück* only appears as a dream, understood as the visual mirage produced by the mass entertainment industry. "Great" applies not to pleasure but to wealth, not to a capacity (the other meaning of the German word *Vermögen*), but to stored riches. Against the Hollywood image of happiness, the *Glücksgott* poems produce an exact countertype that is legible, for instance, in the first stanza of the third song of the *Glücksgott* series, which presents a counterimage to the little bottles filled with the "smell of sex":

> When the bride had finished her beer
> We went outside. The yard lay in the night.
> Behind the outhouse it stank
> But there was a great deal of lust.

> Als die Braut ihr Bier getrunken
> Gingen wir hinaus. Der Hof lag nächtlich.

Hinterm Abtritt hat's gestunken
Doch die Wollust was beträchtlich. (*GW* 10:890)

Instead of a commercial transaction that hinges on a contained and attenuated smell of sex, the *Glücksgott* presents a scene of corporeal desire and intercourse: in an outdoor milieu of stink, voluptuousness is acted upon. The omnipresent tendency toward commodification retreats. The stench of excrements mingles with the procreative function of the body, perhaps an instance of "cacaphonies" as Annabel L. Kim has recently called it, without any hint of shame, attempted deodorization, or containment. Whereas the function of poetry in the *Hollywood Elegies* was to lay bare the sensory and corporeal poverty of Hollywood petro-capitalism, here the function of poetry is to invent and transmit a counterimage of a different sensory and corporeal world.

The free reign of desire, perhaps in violation of marital bonds (the poem leaves it indeterminate whether the lyric I is the rightful spouse of the "bride"), recalls the figure of Baal, the key olfactory figure of voluptuousness of the early Brecht. Brecht, in fact, conceived of the *Glücksgott* figure explicitly as transforming the "basic idea" or "grounding thought [*Grundgedanke*]" of *Baal* (*GW* 17, 947). The *Glücksgott* preserves but attenuates Baal's opposition to bourgeois norms (sexual and otherwise); the asocial, egoistic, and oppositional character is muted, and its force shifted to a "demand for *Glück* [*Glücksverlangen*]." This latter still conflicts, of course, with the social realities that stifle it, but that conflict is no longer, as it often seemed to be the case with the "hooligan" Baal, an end in and of itself.

The full force of this shift comes into view with a return to the insight that Brecht wants to "let emerge" as a "retort out of lowliness"—out of common scents; that is, out of scents shared by all—a new, revolutionary type coming out of the egoistical Baal and his asocial body. The *Glücksgott* explicitly presents himself as a god of "lowliness," taking up Benjamin's word—but the new type that the *Glücksgott* heralds already displays something that was present only as a negative index in *Baal*: the emergence of a *new sociality*. This can be traced in particular in the materials Brecht assembled in the mid-1940s as he tried to write an opera on the *Glücksgott* figure in cooperation with Paul Dessau. Among the unfinished fragments, a "prelude" seeks to motivate the return of the *Glücksgott* from his temporary place "high above the clouds," where, after all, a god of lowliness does not belong. The *Glücksgott*'s return to earth occurs in response to the message brought to him by a messenger, clearly legible as another angel: "You messenger, with the singed wings / Welcome to these hills of clouds / What fires have bitten you?" (*GBA* 10.2:933). The devastation of the earthly state that singed this angel is encapsulated in an exchange between the *angelos* and the *Glücksgott* that links the devastation on earth to a perversion of the latter's precepts: the angel claims, in a clearly legible reference to one of the most cherished founding principles of the country of Brecht's exile, that "out of the pursuit of happiness of the many / Only a few become happily fatter" (934). The *Glücksgott* responds, "But that has nothing to do with me!" It is this abuse of the pursuit of happiness that devastates the earth and necessitates the god's return.

It turns out, however, that the perversion of the *Glücksgott*'s instruction is made possible by the indeterminacy of the teaching itself. Not only can anyone follow his precepts, but the *Glücksgott* himself offers a teaching of only limited reach: "How they shall become happy, he doesn't know." This lowly god only teaches the *Verlangen*, the demand itself. Realizing the insufficiency of this teaching, Brecht adds a crucial twist to the *Glücksgott*'s story when he works on the opera. Now out of this demand a new type of being emerges—namely, a student: "But now he gains new students. They know new paths to *Glück*, organize a new kind of struggle for *Glück*. The peasant needs land but also the cooperation of all peasants. The worker [needs] the factory and the planning etc." (*GBA* 10.2:926). The *Glücksgott*, in contrast to the asocial Baal, now attracts "new students." In other words, his *Glücksverlangen* transcends the boundaries of egoistical hedonism and issues into a new type of sociality: a teacher-student relationship, where the teacher teaches the impetus (the demand for happiness), and the students know the way to fulfill this demand and organize in a struggle for it. The emergence of the happiness of the many requires the emergence of a new, organized collectivity—a collectivity that is brought into being by the desire for "lowly" *Glück*.

This new sociality goes hand in hand with a specification of the previously rather indeterminate *Glücksverlangen* that covered all kinds of "lowly" pleasures and activities. The note just quoted continues, "Productivity is named as the highest *Glück*" (*GBA* 10.2:926). This productivity, widely recognized in the secondary literature on Brecht as crucial to his later work,[51] is further specified in a note that echoes Marx's famous lines from the *Critique of the Gotha Program*: "The *Glücksgott* deems only those happy who can be productive in their manner [*in ihrer Weise*]" (927). This new emphasis on productivity is primarily thought of in opposition to *order*.[52] The further development of Baal that Brecht sought throughout the late 1930s must issue not into a differing set of ordering precepts that establish a rigid structure of the economic and social sphere of human society, but rather into a freeing from "constraints." In a journal entry from March 7, 1941, Brecht elaborates:

> The great error that prevented me from producing the little learning plays concerning the evil, asocial Baal lay in my definition of socialism as a great order; instead, it must be defined much more practically as a great production. Production, of course, must be understood in the widest sense, and the struggle concerns the liberation of the productivity of all human beings from all shackles. The products can be bread, lamps, hats, pieces of music, chess moves, irrigation, complexion, character, games, etc. etc.[53]

Brecht comes to realize, through his attempts to transform the "virtual revolutionary" Baal and further develop his "basic idea" in the figure of the *Glücksgott*, that his mistake had been to buy into the premise of the critiques of socialism prevalent at the time. The assumption that socialism was primarily an ordering system had to be rejected, and the *Glücksverlangen* was the perfect vehicle for reorienting his understanding of socialism, including his position within the intra-Marxist debates among the members of the Frankfurt school who were also in exile in Los Angeles at the time.[54] The emergence of the new revolutionary type that Brecht attempts to develop out of his sensory-aesthetic emphasis on the overturning potential of "lowliness" must consist in the emergence of an "unpredictable,"[55] unleashed, and ever-proliferating production.

The first instance of such a "liberation of productivity" that Brecht mentions—bread—positions the *Glücksgott* even more clearly with respect to the virtual revolutionaries of the early Brecht and his interest in smells. In a four-line poem that presents itself as a companion piece to "I Am the *Glücksgott*," Brecht develops a figure that is both an intensification and a certain pacification of the indomitable *Glücksverlangen*. Here, the god is described not only as "the patron god of ploughmen and sowers" but also, twice, as a "teacher" (*GW* 10:894). This teaching and protecting god, then, brings rather common goods: "The foaming milk, the fragrant bread [*das duftende Brot*] / Grape and pear, that's what I offered" (894). This poem, written in early 1945 for the opera project with Dessau, combines the desire for *Glück* with pedagogy, and what this god teaches harkens back to the frequent references to wheat, fields, seeding, and harvest that constitute not only a crucial topos of *Baal* but also, as was shown above, of Brecht's olfactory poetics of virtual revolutionaries. Ekart's temptation of Baal articulated itself as the temptation of the smell of wheat fields *before* the harvest: "smell of infinite fields, before they are chopped down!" This smell is now transfigured into the smell of bread: *after* the harvest, wheat has been rendered useful; it has found a *Verwertung*. Under the protection of this god, the transformation of the infinity of fields has been turned not into deodorized money or a pure commodity but into something that continues to carry a fragrance. The definitizing moment of *Baal*'s smells has not disappeared into the "49 1/8" of the wheat exchange but continues to open a sensory moment to the side of the market. In excess of the nutritious, sustaining usefulness of the "Verwerten" of the infinite field, the fragrance of bread lingers to the side of the (welcome) finitizing that occurs in the loaf of bread.

At this point, however, an urgent question arises: When referring to the "fragrance" of bread, is Brecht himself not speaking of the type of "smell of the earth" that he excoriated for obscuring materialist and economic realities? Is not the return of an imagery of gods, even if it is a god of "lowliness," a return of a mystical poetry of which his "washing of language" tried to purge his poetic production? Brecht might have sensed these difficulties and grown suspicious of the *Glücksgott*: for more than a decade, he tried but failed to complete the opera. The integration of the *Glücksgott*'s teaching of the demand for happiness, on the one hand, and the knowledge of his students, on the other, is never accomplished. In this sense, the reference to a god and to "fragrant bread" might have been misguided: it arrogated to itself an image to which it did not have a right in times of devastation.

Yet the poetic use of bread also points to a different reading. Bread is, of course, nearly synonymous with any number of revolutionary programs that demanded a solution of the "social question" for the populace. Seen through the lens of this short poem, bread triangulates three terms: the individual (whom it feeds); the collective (that produces it through cultivation); the earth (that produces it as it brings it forth). Such a triangulation was unavailable to Baal but now appears possible to the teacher-student constellation that the *Glücksgott* poems delineate. This is the main insight Brecht's "fragrant bread" proposes: it is only within a constellation of an organized collectivity, spurred on by a demand for lowly happiness, that a poetry of fragrance is permissible. Only in a context of "cooperation" and organized struggle can fragrance emerge without being obscurantist.[56]

In 1950, while continuing to attempt the completion of the opera, Brecht made a remark that explicates this link between organized, cooperative struggle and *Glück*. Paul Dessau records that Brecht told him, "I believe that I have now found the ending for our *Glücksgott*: *Glück* cannot be killed (in the last image, the *Glücksgott* was supposed to be executed). *Glück* is: communism" (*GBA* 10.2:1258). This should be juxtaposed with Marx and Engels' dictum on communism found in the *German Ideology*: "Communism is for us not a *state of affairs* still to be established, not an *ideal* to which reality [will] have to adjust. We call communism the *real* movement which abolishes the present state of things."[57] If communism is the real movement that abolishes the present state of things, and if happiness, for Brecht, is communism, then happiness—or rather the demand for happiness that the *Glücksgott* teaches—is this real abolishing movement. And, under the right conditions, this movement becomes perceptible in the fragrance of bread, a most common scent.

Epilogue

CLEANUP

It is the spring of 1942, and something is in the air. In Los Angeles, Bertolt Brecht begins writing his *Hollywood Elegies*: a cycle of poems juxtaposing an analysis of the political economy of his Californian exile with reflections on smell and the lack thereof. Back in Europe, more precisely in Roanne, France, another communist poet begins to write a strange dossier-book of prose poems eventually titled *Le Savon* (*Soap*): Francis Ponge here juxtaposes an implicit, somewhat hidden analysis of the political economy of the continent Brecht had fled from with, once more, reflections on smell and the lack thereof. In fact, these two works by Brecht and Ponge, two poets born a mere year apart, correspond to each other exactly: on the one hand, the poet of stench; on the other, the poet of cleaning, of washing up, of getting rid of all dirt. In Los Angeles, the poet as a "child who did not want to wash himself" and who lamented the loss of smell that accompanied his flight from fascism; in Roanne, the poet as a man who wants to wash himself, ceaselessly, and who washes himself under the conditions of resistance to fascism. Responding to fascism and the losses it produces seems to entail, for these two communist poets,[1] a writing of poems about cleanliness—about cleaning and, perhaps, its devastating derailment in clean*sing*; about the difference, so to speak, between ethnic cleansing and ethical cleaning.

Cleaning, among other things, deodorizes: what Nietzsche called his *Reinlichkeits-Instinkt*, his instinct for cleanliness, above all seeks to erase unwanted smells and extricate him from bad air. This question of deodorization runs like a bass note through the olfactory idioms of all four thinkers of this book: Hölderlin's latest poetry tends toward an "olfactory degree zero" that seeks to take back or reverse the potential and danger of smell. For Baudelaire, the erasure of smells and atmosphere figures an inconsolable loss that his poetry unremittingly attempts to overcome by establishing a climate of scented, adorable inclination that would constitute a revolutionary lull. Nietzsche's "olfactory genius" strives for, yet fails to attain, the crisp, clear air of detachment from mediocre commonality. And for Brecht, of course, Los Angeles's fruit markets with their pretty but odorless fruit as well as Hollywood's hiding of the smell of sex indicate a generalized loss of *aisthesis*, vitality, and, above all, revolutionary potential. Yet in all these writers, deodorization remains somewhat in the background as a receding point of reference, a fleeting threat, or unattained ideal. All this changes with Ponge: *Soap* takes the question of deodorization and turns it from being a vanishing point of olfactory poetics into its explicit theme.

The removal of dirt and the erasure of smells are posited in front of the reader while the question of smell, inversely, becomes subordinated to the deodorizing movement of cleaning. Ponge, often known as the "poet of things," thus places the slippery thing of hygiene front and center, raising once more questions that were already latently present throughout the works of Hölderlin, Baudelaire, Nietzsche, and Brecht: What happens to the element or medium of air when (certain) smells are subtracted from it?[2] How do subjectivation, aesthetics, and the (re)distribution of the senses operate via the removal of scents? And what kind of (revolutionary) politics emerges from a taste for cleaning, especially under the threat of fascism? For Ponge, these questions are ineluctably intertwined with the question of *purity*: Does cleaning purify? And if so, how does this purity of hygiene and sanitation relate to the fascist demands for purity that wrought such havoc in the 1930s and 1940s? These questions, too, were latent in all previous chapters since, throughout this book, smell emerged as a *privileged sense of impurity*. Smells mingle and mix: for Hölderlin, olfaction makes the mutual, "durchgängig" interpenetration of subject and air perceptible; Baudelaire figures the possibility of an intermixing across the gap of sexual difference via the fragrance of perfumes; Nietzsche's olfactory genius is constantly sniffing out impurities of air and "innards" while becoming thoroughly compromised in the process; and Brecht emphasizes smelling as counteracting the imagined (that is, imaged) purity of the commodity and the Hollywood movie. What then happens to (im)purity when it is investigated from the vantage point of the deodorizing, re-scenting, and cleaning operation of washing with soap? What kind of politics and what kind of literature emerge out of these questions? The ordinary, common activity of using soap and the common scents that accompany it, Ponge suggests, point the way to a response.

Poetry's Common Place

Ponge's *Soap* is framed by a strange proposition: it introduces the theme of deodorization and cleaning via an attempt to escape earthbound air. In both its first section, titled "Beginning of the Book," and the last one, "End of the Book," the image of a rocket's liftoff into an "orbit," away from the atmosphere toward the stratosphere, stands for the movement of the poem. This leaving of the earthly atmosphere, in which both breathing and smelling occur for human beings, articulates the fantasy of an ultimate movement of deodorization, of an ultimate escape route found by a cleanliness instinct that seeks to establish and maintain a distance from the aerial contamination of others. Ponge thus inscribes his reflections on soap into the question of a "pathos of distance" that was so dear to both Nietzsche and Brecht:[3] both writers grappled with the fact that being-in-the-air affords possibilities of differentiation and distance but, in the end, resists any attempt at a definitive emergence—out of a cave, for instance, or a bourgeois economic market society—into an air that would be radically separate. Smell's sensory logic is one of nearness, compromise, and ephemeral contamination—yet what about, the odd framing of *Soap* asks, an emergence not out of a cave, not out of one air or milieu into another, but out of air altogether? What about *emergence out of air*? *Soap*'s cleanup presents itself to the reader within the frame of such an escape, moving away from the atmosphere and hence also away from the potential atmospheres harbored, in the other writers read in this book, for a (terrestrial) revolution of the senses.

For Ponge, the function of this liftoff into the orbit and the attendant escape from atmosphere is intimately tied to the difference between writing and speech. In an interview with Serge Gavronsky, he explains: "one arrives at a kind of orbital flight, leaving the atmosphere, the atmosphere being the place of breath, and of the *logos*, the oral expression . . . one can go in the direction of the stratosphere and . . . one finds oneself in orbit at the moment of writing."[4] Oral expression is tied to breath, and breath to the atmosphere. Writing, by contrast, leaves behind the atmosphere, the possibility of breathing, and with it the various modulations of spoken language: writing is *epi-logic* in this sense; it comes after and supersedes the spoken logos. Writing extracts itself, according to Ponge, from the atmosphere via the "intention of writing"—that is, via its directedness beyond the sphere of breath and speech: "And in a way, the desire that makes me write, the intention of writing, these are like the successive chapters that lead to the orbiting. They are comparable to the stages of a rocket that allow successive stages to orbit, but once the thing is in orbit, in its written form, at that moment, it no longer depends on the atmosphere. It is in a state of weightlessness."[5] The written text, launched outward, orbits around the sphere of breathing in a higher, "upper" layer that would overcome the weighty pull of gravity. Ponge's claim that "it no longer depends on the atmosphere," however, must be modified by the implications of his own image: the orbit is precisely the path of circulation that, by going around the atmosphere of breath and speech, always remains oriented toward it; here, as in Nietzsche's earthly aesthetics, the earth remains inscribed at the heart of all oriented movement, and the "intention" of writing, like all directedness, ineluctably carries with it its point of origin.

Soap itself articulates this insight precisely when in appendix 5, at the very end of the book, the word "orbit" returns one last time: "So here this book is linked up [*bouclé*]; our top set spinning; our *Soap* in orbit. (And all the *stages* or successive chapters fired for its launching may well, already, have re-entered the *atmosphere*, the platitude [*lieu commun*] of oblivion, as it was that of the project.)" (*S*, 97; *LS*, 128; emphasis in the original). The closing ("bouclé") of the book occurs when the soap is used up, when the reading ends—then and only then does the buckle, the loop link up and close. In other words, poetry reaches the orbiting stage and leaves the atmosphere of breath and logos only after the reading ends: the different "chapters" of launching the book into orbit—that is, the text itself that composes the book—do not reach the stratospheric orbit but fall back to earth. They remain in the atmosphere, in the "lieu commun," which the English translator renders correctly as "platitude," but which designates also, and more forcefully, the *common* place in which the buckle is not yet closed upon itself: the mode of existence of the text is determined by a sharing of that which is common to all and hence does not close onto itself but keeps itself open to all. The language of *Soap* exists in shared ordinariness, and the ensuant platitude character of this language is precisely its chance and potential. Consequently, the *lieu commun* of poetry is also the place in which mingling and mixing is possible: it is only here that the chapters of *Soap* can exist for any reader who wants to mingle with it—that is, read it.[6] Any attempt to shoot writing into stratospheric heights ultimately gets pulled back into the sphere of commonality.

After takeoff and before orbiting, the text thus ineluctably exists not in the upper stratosphere but in the shared sphere of breath and common speech. Deodorization as reaching a closed orbit beyond any earthly atmosphere is merely the limit case of a writing of cleaning, an extremity that is never actually attained in the text. Writing *Soap* consequently allows for a variety of aerial-olfactory modulations: "Finally, that one always senses it [soap] as being in hand, i.e. that its perfume, say, more or less vulgar, persist until the end of the discourse, and not leave these hands while they are writing, so that it continually reach as far as you, dear Reader" (*S*, 64; *LS*, 88; translation modified). As long as the writing occurs and its soapy object is sensed, the scent of soap/*Soap* "continually" moves from writer to reader. An olfactory encounter thus takes place in the *lieu commun* relating writer and reader; the atmospheric space of logos and breath is modulated by the smell of soap and through this modulation establishes a social relation in and around *Soap*. Poetry, in the end, cannot do without the common places of atmosphere and smell—and that is, as the rest of the epilogue will show, a good fortune and even a cause for joy.

From Pebble to Soap: The Character of Resistance

The perfumed hands of writing indicate a central insight of *Soap*, of crucial significance for a thought of deodorization, olfaction, and purity: the cleaning process that subtracts malodorous improprieties is itself scented. Cleaning, washing with soap, produces a *smell of deodorization*—an "olfactory degree zero" is never, in contrast to the latest Hölderlin's poetry, reached when it comes to Ponge's poetics. As with all modifications and modulations of smell, this smell of deodorization, too, corresponds to a specific notion of the subject that addresses the questions of distance, differentiation, distribution, and demarcation. In the case of *Soap*, the specificity of this fragrant, "soapy subject" emerges not only out of the historical context in which *Soap* is first written—more on this later—but also from its specific position in Ponge's oeuvre: the poetry of soap presents itself as a transformation of a related but in the end rather different thing—namely, the pebble.

Still one of the best-known poems of Ponge's work, "The Pebble" constitutes a paradigmatic instance of the Pongian thing poem. In particular, Jean-Paul Sartre's 1944 lengthy review essay "Man and Things [*L'Homme et les choses*]," which launched Ponge's literary renown,[7] sees in the pebble *the* central instance of the *parti pris des choses*, the side taken of things, as the title of one of Ponge's collections of poetry puts it. Ponge, according to Sartre, "has the passion, the vice of the inanimate, material *thing*. Of the solid. For him, everything is solid: from his phrase to the profound layers of his universe. If he endows minerals with human behaviors, then he does so in order to mineralize human beings."[8] This passion for petrification issues into the "great dream" of rendering everything solid through writing: "It is perhaps permitted to glimpse behind his revolutionary endeavor a great necrological dream: one of entombing everything that lives, the human being above all, in the shroud of matter."[9] For Sartre, Ponge's revolutionary undertaking turns out to be a dangerous dream of interment. It is no accident that these terms echo rather exactly Sartre's critique of Baudelaire: with respect to Ponge, too, the danger of the dream—its "catastrophe" as Sartre puts it—lies in a fascination with total rest as the abdication of the task of being a subject: "What fascinates him in the thing is its mode of existence, its total adherence to itself, its rest. . . . This effort to see oneself through the eyes of a foreign species, to finally rest from the painful duty of being a subject."[10] At stake in the nature of the Pongian thing are the possibilities of subjectivity and, indeed, the very necessity of subjecthood. The thing poems ask: Must subjectivity reign, and if so, how?

Sartre opposes to Ponge's alleged passion for mineralization and petrification his existentialist thought of the "viscous." Ponge himself, by contrast, takes a different, perhaps more sophisticated and more difficult path. He explicitly presents soap as a transformation of the pebble and its relationship to subjectivity, thus responding to Sartre's narrowing of the Pongian thing to the mineral realm. In an entry dated June 3, 1943, Ponge thus writes, "Here is a sort of mediocre pebble, flatly reposing in the plainest saucer. . . . Soap has its particular dignity. It is a stone, but one which does not allow itself to be unilaterally rolled about by the forces of nature. It slips between their fingers" (*S*, 20; *LS*, 26). In fact, soap leads a *double life*, wet and dry, where its dry existence resembles that of the pebble: "At first a reserve, a bearing, a patience in its saucer as perfect as those of the pebble." Yet even in its dry, pebble-like state, soap differs from the pebble, with one of the differences being found in its scent: "But, at the same time, less roughness, less dryness. It is, certainly, obstinate, compact, holding itself in check, but also amenable, attractive, polished, soft, agreeable in the hands. And scented (although not *sui generis*)" (*S*, 41; *LS*, 53). While resembling the pebble in its dry form, soap can also enter a relation with both the liquid element (water) and the gaseous element (air):[11] soap's doubleness does not so much oppose the pebble as much as add the possibility of transformation via a mingling and mixing with that which is other than itself. Soap's peculiarity, its difference from the pebble, is found in its capacity to link up disparate elements and bring about their transformation.

It is out of this constellation of soap's triple relation with the mineral, the liquid, and the gaseous, its partial resemblance to the pebble and its decisive divergence from it, that its singular ability to figure a novel type of subjectivity arises. This "soapy subject" as it emerges from *Soap* is situated in the context of Ponge's participation in the French Resistance against the German occupation and the collaborationist Vichy regime. While Ponge's work, *Soap* included, is often read apolitically, some scholars have drawn attention to both the easily legible and the more hidden traces the occupation has left on the text.[12] The first obvious trace of the peculiar circumstances of the text's genesis can be found in the opening pages.[13] Ponge wrote the various parts of *Soap*, dating the entries and noting the place of writing for most of them, over a period stretching more than two decades, from 1942 to 1965.[14] Most of the entries were written in the 1940s, before and after the end of World War II, but Ponge reprised his "dossier" in the 1960s when he was asked to give a radio lecture in Stuttgart, Germany. This occasion was part of the reason why, at the "Beginning of the Book," Ponge thus asks the reader who faces the French text to lend himself "German ears": "The reader, right off, is kindly asked (he will very soon understand why)—I mean to say: for taking off—to give himself, in his imagination, *German ears*" (*S*, 3; *LS*, 7; emphasis in the original). In the Franco-German interplay of *Soap*, the reader finds himself not only "on a path of Babel" (*S*, 3; *LS*, 7) but also on the path of history: reading a French text written partly during the height of German violence and destruction as well as French resistance and collaboration, where the radio (and clandestine listening) played a central role in social and political life. *Soap*, then, can only be understood via "German ears."[15] This is particularly evident when, in the first entry from 1942, Ponge uses a lonesome German word in his French text: "There we were, then, in the midst of war, that is to say of *restrictions* of all kinds, and soap, real soap, was particularly missed. We had only the worst *ersätze*—which did not *froth* at all" (*S*, 11; *LS*, 15; emphasis in the original). With a German ear one hears that the bad *ersätze*—the German word once more drawing attention to the Franco-German relation, replacing (*ersetzen*) what could have been a French word—do not foam at all; that is, they do not produce cleaning and the mingling of water, air, and thing that attracts to soap in the first place. Among its many devastating effects, the German fascist occupation restricts the possibility of proper cleaning, of a foaming and transforming that holds the key for understanding *Soap*.

The failure of the poor substitutes for soap attains increased urgency once the double life of soap is seen in its political valence: soap figures Ponge's own double life during the occupation.[16] As part of the Communist resistance, Ponge was asked to maintain his ordinary day-to-day life as an insurance agent and journalist to maintain a cover that would allow him to host meetings of high-ranking members of the Resistance at his apartment and, later, function as a messenger. It is in this context of resisting fascism that soap's contrast to the pebble achieves greatest clarity: "It is a stone, but one which does not allow itself to be unilaterally rolled about by the forces of nature. It slips between their fingers" (*S*, 20; *LS*, 26). Soap's ability to transform upon contact with the overwhelming force of water—it should be remembered that the name of the collaborationist regime of Vichy refers, among other things, to the spa town known for its waters—enables it to slip away and to avoid becoming a passive object of unilateral action. In other words, instead of obstinately insisting on its unchangeable form, soap puts up a fight against an overwhelming attack through asymmetrical warfare: sliding into the opposing element, it gives a little, dissolves a little, thus changing the enemy in enormous ways. The soap-water struggle is not a gigantomachy but rather a struggle where one side, soap, uses its ability to give in as its prime and, in fact, only weapon. Soap, Ponge writes,

> finally prefers to dissolve itself, give up the ghost, to give up the body rather than let itself be groped, unilaterally rolled about by water.
> Shall we say that it leads a dissipated life there? No doubt . . . But this may just as well be understood as a particular kind of dignity.
> Besides, the water is very disturbed and troubled by it, very seriously punished. It does not easily rid itself of the traces of its crime. . . .
> At this point, let's take the soap out of the water and consider each of the two adversaries. One, very much diminished, attenuated, but not in its quality. The other, an enormous amount troubled, having lost face. Which one is the victor? (*S*, 42; *LS*, 54–55; translation modified)

Soap redefines what it means to show "character": no longer a firm, petrified imprint that persists by being unchangeable, but the ability to become "diminished" in its quantity and its spatial outline without giving up its quality. Water, by contrast, does not retain its character and "loses face": all its quantity cannot make up for its qualitatively changed appearance (with the limit case of overwhelming "reinforcements" being able to overcome this obstacle after all). Soap, as a figure of clandestine resistance, manages to perform the delicate operation of *maintaining its distinct character in and through dissolution*.

Through its peculiar character, soap thus articulates what might be the minute but all-decisive difference on which *Soap* stakes its main claim: cleaning resists cleansing. The latter would be the core of fascism: fascism, as an overwhelming movement, cleanses by sweeping away everything in its path; all difference must be overcome and homogenized. Nothing that was previously fixed and stable can survive its all-consuming onslaught. Ponge's response, by contrast, places its bet on soap: the resistance to fascism must take the form not of a frontal opposition but rather of a slipping into its movement, via a double life, that intervenes decisively by seemingly yielding to the movement's force. Such yielding eventually triumphs or, at the very least, holds open the question of who the "victor" in this battle will be. Soap's yielding, in turn, fulfills a further function: it cleans. While guarding its "dignity," it cleans up, as it were, the devastation fascism wreaks. Cleaning, correctly understood, would be a mode of resistance to forceful overwhelming. Its operation safeguards the possibility of character against fascist destruction via its own gradual dissolution—and it is this resistance that contains the possibility, to be explored further below, of thinking cleanliness beyond fascism's taint.[17]

Ponge's description of the soapy subject, however, does not exhaust itself in this wager on slippery resistance but instead opens onto further considerations of the possibilities afforded by a thinking of subjectivity via this particular thing. The passage cited above introducing soap's character thus continues, "No bark, or even skin: since it makes no claim to be autonomous" (S, 41; LS, 54). The absence of a protective bark that would close soap in on itself can be understood as an instance of a certain *frankness* (recalling Hölderlin's great interest in the shared but ultimately divergent constellation Frankfurt/France): being frank, soap opens itself to its surrounding element.[18] The diffusion of soap's perfume into the air,[19] alongside soap's dissolution into water, thus indexes a mode of being that is subtracted from the attempt to shut itself into self-containment. More precisely, "the law of the thing" that Derrida sees at the center of Ponge's poetics is in this case precisely that soap does not pretend to be *autonomous*: the obverse of soap's slippery escape from the fingers that grasp it lies in its lack of a pretense to be self-governing; it yields.[20] Ponge's explicit references to hands grasping the soap and losing grip underline, especially in a context of "German ears," that this is a question of *Be-griff* (concept) and *begreifen* (understanding). The conceptual grasp of soap is faced with a double movement: soap does not put up any protective bark against being seized, but by virtue of this very lack it produces a slipperiness that can, at times, elude a firm grasp even more effectively. Since its yielding to heteronomy thus simultaneously constitutes its resistance to this other law, soap's mode of being must be said to be located between two equally dissolved poles: soap exists in the interstices of a closed, indivisible, and autonomous "individual," on the one hand, and a fatalistic surrender to an all-dominating and sovereign grasp that comes from elsewhere, on the other.

This slippery movement of giving up any pretense of autonomy while also eluding a firm grasp leads to one of the main principles governing soap and *Soap* being the principle of an "exhaustion of the subject" (S, 13; LS, 17), as Ponge calls it already in the very first entry of his book. *Soap* writes a subject that is subject only in its being exhausted: its only ability to resist water being its dissolution as well as its lack of autonomy and protective outer layers make soap into a subject that is continuously being exhausted—that is, worn out and worn away. The form of the dossier-poem with its repetitions and "variations" on a "theme" equally displays this structure: *Soap* writes about its subject again and again until it (and the reader) become exhausted. Exhausting and exhaustive, soap's existence lies only in its *use*: "it has only to remain adequate to its use—and there, certainly, is a lesson" (S, 65; LS, 90). Soap's remaining adequate to its utility is its only law: a law dictated to it from elsewhere, from the point of its use, and that it fulfills until it is completely exhausted (or forgotten about).

Vulgar Scent: Of Pilate

The use of soap and of *Soap* lies in its functioning as a product of an "intellectual washing-up [*toilette intellectuelle*]" (*S*, 25; *LS*, 32; translation modified). More precisely, *Soap* has an intra-hygienic function, so to speak, in that it replaces one type of cleaning with another. This replacement emerges from the fact that, in this book, there is nothing extraordinary or extramundane: "Yes! Living under the pump is good for nothing. Or even remaining in the waters of the Jordan. (The simplest washbowl would be much better . . .)" (*S*, 25–26; *LS*, 32–33). *Soap* repeatedly draws on religious, and more specifically Christian, images of cleaning such as baptism (here the river Jordan stands for the baptism of Jesus), but only in order to displace them from their set-apart position in the realm of the sacred toward a "simplest," everyday process.[21] Ponge, put differently, replaces the Christian notion of baptism and of Christ as the "Exalted One" with an ordinary, most common cleaning and the exalting exuberance of soap's upward-directed, airy foaming. Christianity has become exhausted, as it were, and the poet consequently imagines, in one of the appendixes to *Soap*, the writing of "a new *Scripture*": "and this is the wherefore of *things* (and, for example, soap) in my book, ma bible (in *mon* bible, I would like to write" (*S*, 86; *LS*, 118; emphasis in the original). The envisioned replacement of the feminine definite article (correct in French when referring to the Bible) by the masculine definite article—that is, by a perverted nomination—embodies the core of Ponge's operation with respect to Christianity: it profanes "the Book" and turns it into a book; it turns writing away from sacred scripture—always set apart and removed from ordinary life—toward a writing of the quotidian.[22] This profanation of *Soap*, then, is a question of a repeated, ongoing process of washing off the pretense of the sacred, not a historical, one-time event as theorists of the beginning of a "secular age" might have it. Soap's profaning washing underlines that any *Reinlichkeit*, to refer back to Nietzsche's "instinct for cleanliness," must be located in the realm of mundane and quotidian caretaking via a repeated, common operation—and only there.[23]

In this sense, soap, and not baptism, belongs to the people, and the cleaning maneuver appropriate to the people is found in soap only. Soap is gregarious and vulgar; that is, as the etymology of "vulgar" indicates, it belongs to the common people: "And scented (although not *sui generis*). More vulgar, perhaps, but in compensation more sociable" (*S*, 41; *LS*, 53). Its scent resists an ascription of a "sui generis" status, a being that is one of a kind and that would be incomparable to all others and thus refusing all commonality. The paradigmatic instance of such a one-of-a-kind smell, set apart from all others, would be, in the distribution of the sensible of Ponge's work, the smell of the Anointed One, of Christ: only Christ smells like Christ. It is precisely against Christ—although this "against" should not be misunderstood as an oppositional posture—that Ponge affirms his descendance from Pontius Pilate: "No, it is only a matter of soap and washing one's hands, like my ancestor Pontius Pilate—of whom I am

Epilogue | 161

so proud that having said: 'What is truth?'—he should wash his hands of the death of the Just One (or the exalted one) and thus be the sole person in the story to enter history with clean hands [*mains pures*], having done his duty without big gestures, big symbols, wailing and fatuity" (*S*, 77; *LS*, 106; translation modified). Faced with a decision concerning the status of the Exalted One, Ponge's ancestor[24] Pontius Pilate—to whom Ponge is linked through the resemblance of their names ("Ponce Pilate" in French)—refused to decide either way and instead washed his hands. Ponge here hints only briefly and enigmatically at an extremely complex politico-theological constellation (involving questions of Jewishness, the law, etc.).[25] The crucial point of Ponge's affiliation with Pilate, however, emerges clearly: it positions *Soap* and soap to the side of the question of the truth of the Exalted One. It positions this poetic work as disengaging or deactivating the question of the truth of Christ and the aromatic apparatus that accompanies Christian practices and instead turns toward vulgarity. Soap bypasses claims to a sui generis status by turning toward that which is shared by and common to all.

Similarly, *Soap* opposes, to the exaltation of Christ, the launching upward—recall the liftoff toward the orbit—of soap's interaction with air: "Saturated with soap, the water froths at the least movement. Wants to join the air, climbs in the assault of the sky. . . . Displays even a sort of aerostatic pretention. Displays a sort of exaltation" (*S*, 75; *LS*, 103). These soapy bubbles rise up, open up the vertical dimension—but only as an everyday, playful, vulgar climbing toward the sky via a frothing and bubbling up.[26] If Hölderlin's Christ turns out to be airy, *wie Morgenluft*, then the related but divergent provocation of Ponge's poetics is a turn away from Christ and toward the quotidian by severing air from anything that might suggest a transcending of the realm of ordinary smells: any movement of trans*cent*ing is only found in common scents.

Purity Otherwise

The notion of cleaning as a mundane, repetitive process paves the way for a reconceptualization of the concept of purity, a concept that is always latently in play when it comes to the intermingling of olfaction. Purity is inscribed into the text of *Soap* not only through the historical context of "German ears" listening to a text written during the National Socialist occupation that centered on a political project of racial purity, but also through an explicit positioning of soap as the object best suited to displaying a (different kind of) purity:

> (Idea of The Intellectual Toilet)
> If I wished to prove that purity is not obtained by silence, but by any
>   exercise of language whatsoever (in certain conditions, a certain ridiculous little object held in the hands), followed by a sudden catastrophe of pure water,
> Would anything be better than soap? (*S*, 23; *LS*, 29; translation modified)

Instead of abandoning or disavowing the term "purity" altogether, Ponge reconfigures its meaning: purity is not found in abstaining from speech (silence, "inner emigration") or in racial cleansings but in the double life of resistance modeled by soap, in its "volubility" and repetitive process of mundane cleaning.

The further development of this thought issues into a central and productive paradox: purity must be understood as thoroughly heterogenous—that is, as *impure*. In the third appendix to *Soap*, Ponge approaches this thought by drawing attention to the material transformations underlying the cleaning process of soap: "this sort of compound of fatty matters (consequently not soluble in water) and caustic alkaline salts (καυστικός, καίειν, to burn) which possesses detergent qualities and which is used to wash" (S, 88; LS, 120). Fatty matter and caustic alkaline salts would, in isolation, appear to be the very opposite of what soap seeks to achieve: they are dirty and abrasive. Yet, this very heterogeneity underlies the metamorphosis of cleaning and constitutes its profane transubstantiation: only through the combination of such disparate elements can cleaning occur; conversely, all cleaning indelibly displays the mark of difference. Being "propre"—that is, being both proper and clean—derives from being improper: there is no properness without impropriety; in the common product of soap, the proper is continually expropriated. Any attempt to establish purity or properness that would erase the impropriety at its heart would fall into the fascist temptation that soap is precisely meant to counteract and undo.[27] Soap cleans by being dirty; cleaning resists cleansing by safeguarding heterogeneity—this, in the end, is the core of the "revolutionary undertaking" that Sartre diagnosed at the heart of Ponge's poetry. A revolution of the senses, to be sure: what is proper and how that properness is distributed within the sensible is overturned and redistributed; more incisively, it is subtracted from any alleged property, propriety, and properness in a movement of expropriation that points toward the commonality of common scents.

The third appendix continues by tracing this transformation of a fatty and caustic matter to its extreme point—namely, the airy bubbles that emerge from soap's triangulation with water and air. A soapy bubble has a double character: it cleans but "also renders, in a way, this operation joyous" (S, 89; LS, 121). Soapy bubbles not only contribute to the cleaning process but also—perhaps precisely enabled by the paradox of dirty cleanliness, by the expropriation of the proper— make this cleaning process *joyful*. Airy exaltation produces what Ponge on the very last page of *Soap* calls "objoy [*objoie*]" (S, 96; LS, 128). In the 1940s, at the same time as Ponge begins writing his dossier-poem, Brecht's *Glücksgott* poems had posed a question: What does happiness smell like? Brecht's answer (like "fragrant bread") is now supplemented, at the close of this book, by Ponge's reference to the "paradise" (S, 96; LS, 128) of reading and the scent of objoy that emerges from *Soap*. The "closing up" of the text approaching, the object of reading becomes suffused with the scent of joy: with the final "exhaustion" of the subject arrives a certain kind of jubilation that releases the written text from the hands of the writer to the hands of you, "dear reader."

Epilogue | 163

Notes

Introduction

1. Irigaray, *Forgetting of Air*, 8.
2. Irigaray, 8.
3. Canetti, "Broch," 13; translation modified. Correspondingly, Susan Sontag claims in an essay about Canetti's thought that "breathing may be the most radical of occupations." Sontag, "Elias Canetti," 89.
4. This "being-in-the-air" syntagma can be found in Sloterdijk, *Terror from the Air*, 93, where he discusses Irigaray in the context of his consideration of modernity's concern with "air conditioning," which will be addressed below.
5. For a recent investigation of just this dynamic, see Tremblay, *Breathing Aesthetics*, which opens with the claim that "breathing makes life out of an orientation toward death. To be a breather is to be vulnerable; this is an existential condition. As long as we breathe, and as long as we're porous, we cannot fully shield ourselves from airborne toxins and toxicants as well as other ambient threats" (1).
6. Irigaray, *Forgetting of Air*, 14.
7. To be sure, smell is far from the only way of sensing air, as the first chapter, on Hölderlin, demonstrates with respect to sensing wind and warmth as modulations of the air. More broadly, what Dora Zhang writes concerning the related question of atmospheres also holds for the sense of smell and its relationship to air: "sensing an atmosphere cannot be reduced to the perception of any discrete elements or limited to any one sensory mode. Instead, such perception responds to the relation between all the elements in a setting as they interact with each other in the environment created by their co-presence." Zhang, *Strange Likeness*, 79.
8. Aristotle, *De Anima*, 419b; translation modified.
9. Condillac, *Condillac's Treatise*, xxxi. From here one could develop a larger account of eighteenth-century philosophy's interest in the relationship between the senses and the formation of ideas in cognition and in the mind, as well as smell's specific position in this discourse.
10. Kant, *Anthropologie*, 453. Chapter 1 below will further develop Kant's theory of smell in his *Anthropology from a Pragmatic Point of View*. Regarding Kant and Hegel on smell, see Le Guérer, *Les Pouvoirs*, chap. 12.
11. Kant, *Kritik der Urteilskraft*, 211.
12. Kant, *Anthropologie*, 452.
13. This phrase comes from Caroline A. Jones and her work on smell in the context of the "bureaucratization" of the senses. See Jones, "Sensorium."

The work of Constance Classen, Jim Drobnick, and other anthropologists and sociologists over the past two decades has shown the variegated modes of smell's relegation to an allegedly primal state and its continuous reemergence. See Classen, *Aroma*; Drobnick, *The Smell Culture Reader*. For a gathering of olfactory tropes in literature, see Rindisbacher, *The Smell of Books*. For a more recent sketch of scholarship on olfaction in literary criticism, see Krause, *Glaube und Geruch*, vii–ix, 13–17. Krause produces an account of smell's role in (Germanophone) literature that goes beyond the modernity-focused approach pursued here. Regarding philosophy and smell, see Le Guérer, *Les Pouvoirs de l'odeur*, chaps. 7–14. For a historical investigation, see Reinarz, *Past Scents*. Recent research in neuroscience has shown the divergent ways in which olfactory stimuli, as opposed to visual stimuli, are processed in the brain and how this upends beliefs about the brain's functioning. See Barwich, *Smellosophy*.

14. W. H. Auden, "Precious Five," in *Collected Poems*, 587.

15. For an incisive account of Auden's understanding of odors and deodorization, an account that anticipates some of the reflections regarding fascism and smell proposed in the epilogue below, see Gottlieb, *Regions of Sorrow*, chap. 2, especially the section "Order and Odors."

16. Hegel, *Ästhetik*, 1:199. The syntagma "world of prose" and its variants have been taken up by a number of authors, most prominently and at the same time as Auden wrote "Precious Five," by Maurice Merleau-Ponty in his unfinished and only posthumously published book *The Prose of the World* (drafted in 1950–1951). The name of Merleau-Ponty marks what this book will *not* do, at least not primarily—that is, develop a phenomenology of the sense of smell. Fragments of such a phenomenological account can be found in Tellenbach, *Geschmack und Atmosphäre*.

17. Hegel, *Ästhetik*, 3:244.

18. For a different methodological orientation concerning the question of smell and genre, see Hsuan L. Hsu's recent book *The Smell of Risk*, which argues that "the most prominent olfactory literary forms [are] detective fiction and naturalism" (23). A significant amount of scholarship on literature and smell addresses the question of the allegedly unique difficulty to express smells in language due to the poverty of our olfactory vocabulary. See Krueger, *Perfume on the Page*, for references and critical discussion, in particular chapter 2, which includes a discussion of non-European languages' olfactory capaciousness that exceeds that of English or French (78).

19. Proust, *Swann's Way*, 48. As the madeleine scene emphasizes, smell is hard to separate from taste to the point that some phenomenologists have even proposed a single "oral sense" that would encompass both taste and smell. The larger issue at stake here is the question of *synesthesia*, how the senses exist "with" (*syn*) each other: this question of the unity and plurality of the senses, their "distribution" and division—in short, what is "common" to them all—

will make itself felt throughout the book. Susan Bernstein has recently proposed the notion of an "other synesthesia" that resonates with this project's orientation in that it articulates a synesthesia "that does not fuse the senses and transcend their differences but rather disarticulates final unity and opens up differences." Bernstein, "The Other Synesthesia," 131.

20. Proust, *Swann's Way*, 47.
21. Rancière, *Politics of Aesthetics*, 7.
22. Nancy and Rancière, "Rancière and Metaphysics (Continued)," 196.
23. Rancière, *Aux bords du politique*, 229.
24. Freud, *Unbehagen*, 65. Auden's elegy for Freud indicates how we might read this "theoretical speculation": "if often he was wrong and, at times, absurd, / to us he is no more a person / now but a whole climate of opinion / under whom we conduct our different lives." Auden, *Collected Poems*, 275. The Freudian speculations on smell might well appear wrong or even absurd (they will be modified below), but they are of great interest precisely because they constitute a whole climate of thinking about smell.
25. For a recent sociological investigation of smell's relationship to civilization, see Raab, *Soziologie des Geruchs*. Raab argues that the history of smell is marked by a "specific trajectory of civilization: it is primarily marked by an increasing *distancing, disciplining* and *rationalizing* in the handling of and attitude toward smell." Raab, *Soziologie*, 272; emphasis in the original.
26. Following Freud, psychoanalysis has been much more attentive to the powers of smell than most other disciplines. The tension between smell and civilization, as well as a focus on smell's relationship to coprophilia and anal eroticism, can be found in the work of Sandor Ferenczi, Karl Abraham, and Iwan Bloch, among others. See Le Guérer, *Les Pouvoirs de l'odeur*, chaps. 15–16, for an overview of the psychoanalytic literature on smell.
27. Freud, *Unbehagen*, 65n1.
28. See Cavarero, *Inclinations*.
29. Freud, *Unbehagen*, 64n1.
30. In literary studies, Fredric Jameson has recently hinted at the possibility of reading a similar olfactory break in literary history: opposing Balzac to Flaubert and Baudelaire, Jameson writes, "in Balzac everything that looks like a physical sensation—a musty smell, a rancid taste, a greasy fabric—always means something, it is a sign or allegory of the moral or social status of a given character." By contrast, Flaubert and Baudelaire display "the irreconcilable divorce between lived experience and the intelligible which characterizes modernity, between the existential and the meaningful. Experience—and sensory experience in particular—is in modern times contingent: if such experience seems to have a meaning, we are at once suspicious of its authenticity." Jameson, *Antinomies*, 33–34. In contrast to the analysis pursued

here, Jameson then ties this different mode of writing odors beyond allegorical-moral meanings to *affect*: "Odor . . . seems everywhere, from Baudelaire to Proust, to be a privileged vehicle for isolating affect and identifying it for a variety of dynamics" (35). I thank Erica Weitzman for bringing this passage to my attention. The connection between "affect" and smell was first argued for within the field of affect studies by Teresa Brennan in *The Transmission of Affect*, especially 9–10.

31. Corbin, *The Foul and the Fragrant*, 56. Corbin mostly studies the case of France, with some attention paid to England. Jürgen Raab has argued for a delay in the olfactory development of Germany in comparison to France and England, largely because Germany did not have a city comparable to Paris or London around 1800. Raab, *Soziologie*, 85–86.

32. Corbin, *The Foul and the Fragrant*, 55.

33. Samalin, *The Masses*, 58.

34. Samalin, 44. Samalin writes specifically about the case of Britain and the Great Stink of London in 1858, a turning point in European olfactory history.

35. As Anne McClintock has shown in *Imperial Leather*, hygiene and deodorizing regimes were central to colonial projects: soap, in particular, became the dividing line between metropole and colony, between civilized and allegedly uncivilized. This line of inquiry has been pursued by Hsu's investigations into "atmo-orientalism" and "olfactory racialization." See especially his introduction and chapters 4 and 5 in *The Smell of Risk* for further references. See also Kettler, *The Smell of Slavery*. The question of soap will be taken up in the epilogue below.

36. Benjamin, *Gesammelte Schriften*, 5:274. All further quotations from Benjamin's work will be from *Gesammelte Schriften* and will be cited parenthetically in the body of the chapter as *GS*, followed by the volume number.

37. See, for instance, Jay, *Downcast Eyes*; Blumenberg, "Licht als Metapher der Wahrheit."

38. Jones, *Eyesight Alone*, 397. Jones further describes the relegation of smell to the margins of humanity via a "bureaucratization" of the senses, an attempt to categorize and control any and all sensory experiences.

39. Lefebvre, *The Production of Space*, xx.

40. Jenner, "Smell, Smelling, and Their Histories," 341; emphasis in the original.

41. Sloterdijk, *Schäume*, 313.

42. Latour, *We Have Never Been Modern*. For a recent related claim, see Annabel L. Kim's *Cacaphonies*: "The literature produced under modernity recognizes, in ways that society more broadly does not, that we have never been modern, by expressing how we have always been fecal, and will continue to be fecal" (2).

43. For an overview of the literature on Marx and the senses, see Adams, "Aesthetics." In *Sensual Relations*, David Howes has attempted to mobilize Fourier against the fact that "Marx was evidently not ready for a sensory revolution" (230). Instead of Howes's psychologizing claim that Marx's own ailments (including "appalling odors" from his boils producing illness) led him to efface all sensuousness, the attempt here is to locate a critical potentiality in Marx's writings and mobilize it as a conceptual framework for the studies proposed in this book.

44. Marx, *Marx-Engels-Werke*, 40:546; emphasis in the original. Further references to Marx will be cited parenthetically as *MEW*.

45. Benjamin's remark continues: "as innervations of the collective." A detailed investigation of the functioning of the Freudian term "innervation" and its close link to the senses can be found in Hansen, "Benjamin and Cinema." For a historian's account of the relationship between revolution and the senses, informed by a recent "sensory turn" in historical studies, see Plamper, "Sounds of February, Smells of October." I thank Helmut Puff for bringing this article to my attention.

46. Rancière himself employs the term "aesthetic revolution" (and very rarely, but at least once, the term "revolution of the senses"; see *Politik und Ästhetik*, 37). Rancière locates this aesthetic revolution in Schiller's seminal *Letters on the Aesthetic Education of Man* and his attempt to think aesthetics (and the crucial "play drive" that Schiller, developing Kant, sees at the heart of aesthetics) as producing the "formation of a new sensorium" (Rancière, "The Aesthetic Revolution," 137) that holds the "promise of both a new world of Art and a new life for individuals and the community" (133). From here, Rancière traces a through line to the *Systemfragment* written by Hegel, Schelling, and Hölderlin, and from there to Marx's concept of revolution. The account pursued here shifts emphasis away from Rancière's reading of this aesthetic revolution as an "aestheticization" that seeks the establishment of a new collective "ethos" as a replacement for genuine politics in favor of a "non-polemical, consensual framing of the common world" (137), and instead recovers precisely the *dissensual* moments of the interplay of revolution and aesthetics.

47. Regarding the question of Benjamin's relationship to smell, see Geller, "Walter Benjamin Reproducing the Scent of the Messianic."

48. In her reading of Benjamin's artwork essay, Susan Buck-Morss has indirectly argued that Benjamin also falls into this category: he "is demanding of art a task far more difficult—that is, to undo the alienation of the corporeal sensorium, to restore the instinctual power of the human bodily senses for the sake of humanity's self-preservation." Buck-Morss, "Aesthetics and Anaesthetics," 5. Pace Buck-Morss, it could be shown that Benjamin's concept of "innervation," under which he treats the question of revolution and the senses,

does not amount to a restoration of instincts and, relatedly, exceeds the term "humanity"—hence distinguishing Benjamin from Marcuse.

49. Schmidt, *Emanzipatorische Sinnlichkeit*, 54–55; emphasis added.
50. Marcuse, *Counterrevolution and Revolt*, 63.
51. Marcuse, 62–63.
52. Benhabib, *Critique, Norm, and Utopia*, 178.
53. Adorno and Horkheimer, *Dialektik der Aufklärung*, 193.
54. Adorno and Horkheimer, 193; emphasis added. See also Condillac's incisive remarks on his statue's inability to develop a notion of itself as distinguished from the smells it perceives: "If we give the statue a rose to smell, to us it is a statue smelling a rose, to itself it is smell of rose. The statue therefore will be rose smell, pink smell, jasmine smell, violet smell, according to the flower which stimulates its sense organ. In a word, in regard to itself smells are its modifications or modes. It cannot suppose itself to be anything else." Condillac, *Treatise*, 3.
55. One could productively compare this expropriating sensory mode with the "appropriation" at the heart of the senses that Daniel Heller-Roazen's magisterial study *The Inner Touch* recovers from the ancients: this appropriation concerns, "at the heart of every living being, a difference without which it could not come to be itself: the difference between the self and its constitution, that 'most proper thing' to which the animal, in relating itself to the world about it, comes by nature to be appropriated." Heller-Roazen, *The Inner Touch*, 114.
56. Olfaction played an important and complicated role for the ancient Greeks, for whom it was generally located in the middle of the hierarchy of the five senses. For a useful overview, see Bradley, *Smell and the Ancient Senses*. Aristotle's main remarks on smell can be found in *De Anima* and *Problems*; Plato addresses smells in, among other texts, the *Timaeus*, the *Philebus*, and the *Symposium*. Sophocles evidences sustained interest in scents in particular in the *Philoctetes*. Regarding the crucial role of aromatic spices in ancient Greek myth, religion, and the history of sexuality, see Detienne, *The Gardens of Adonis*.
57. Aristotle, *De Anima*, 424b18.
58. Canetti, "Broch," 13.
59. See Kelly, "Where the Water Meets the Sky," for a recent example. Kelly argues that atmospheres should be understood to fall under the "public trust doctrine." From the perspective of Roman law, one would here want to distinguish between "public" and "common" things. For a helpful overview of the various distinctions of those things that fall outside of "our patrimony," see Heller-Roazen, *The Enemy of All*, 59–62.

60. Quoted in Heller-Roazen, *The Enemy of All*, 62. See also the formulation in Justinian's *Institutes*: "The things which are naturally everybody's are: air, flowing water, the sea, and the sea-shore" (55).
61. Tremblay, *Breathing Aesthetics*, 158.
62. Hsu, *The Smell of Risk*, 10. For Hsu, olfaction, then, becomes a tool of "citizen science." If Hsu's project, as indicated by the title of his book, is to think *The Smell of Risk*, the intent here, conversely but perhaps complementarily, is to think the "risk of smell," both its (imagined, real) danger and its potential.
63. It is in this direction that Lauren Berlant has recently sought to develop the concept of the commons: as "a tool, and often a weapon, for unlearning the world." Berlant, *On the Inconvenience of Other People*, 80. Note that Berlant repeatedly draws attention to how this unlearning must include an unlearning of the sensorium. From here, one could further reflect on the various connections to other discourses of the "commons" found in, inter alia, Hardt and Negri, Federici, or Harney and Moten.
64. Heller-Roazen, *The Enemy of All*, 62. The following paragraphs suggest that an alternative title for *Common Scents* would be *No One's Scents*.
65. For an extensive reading of the late Kant's remarks, see Fenves, *Late Kant*. Fenves's reading culminates in the claim that Kant intimates or runs up against the thought—an inconsistent "one"—that human beings must concede the earth to another species or race that is still to come, a claim that resonates with the link between futurity and smell proposed in the Hölderlin chapter below.
66. Kant, *Practical Philosophy*, 404–405; Kant, *Die Metaphysik der Sitten*, 354; emphasis in the original. The following argument is indebted to Peter Fenves's reading of Kant in *Niemands Sache*, in particular the insight that the postulate's goal is "to produce a divisible space of things [*einen teilbaren Raum aus Dingen*]" (139), which is precisely what air disallows. For an argument concerning the limits and "excesses" of property (mostly with respect to the earth) in Kant, see also Oliver, "The Excesses of Earth in Kant's Philosophy of Property."
67. There are, of course, "air-tight containers," but these disallow living. The closest thing to such a division can be found in the "atmotopes" of air conditioning mentioned above: but their absolute status as fully determined and closed (an "apathetic sphere," as Auden would put it) is merely *imagined*—containers always leak. See the chapter on Nietzsche below for more reflections on air, containers, and smell.
68. In this sense, the air is like language. Cf. Benjamin; Fenves, *Niemands Sache*, 159.
69. Kant, *Die Metaphysik der Sitten*, 359; Kant, *Practical Philosophy*, 404.
70. See Heller-Roazen, *The Enemy of All*. Heller-Roazen investigates not only the high sea but also airspace as (always at least potentially) extraterritorial,

where distinctions of the criminal and the political collapse and a shift to a (proclaimed) relationship to "all of human kind" occurs.

71. Kant, *Die Metaphysik der Sitten*, 360. For Kant, and various thinkers before and after him, interest, then, turns to dividing up the sea into *mare clausum* and *mare liberum* (381). Auden indicates a potential—playful, perhaps even satirical—analog when it comes to the body and air: "Some thirty inches from my nose / The frontier of my Person goes / And all the untilled air between / Is private *pagus* or demesne." Auden, *Collected Poems*, 688. Here it is not a question of how far a cannon can reach into the sea in defense of the *mare clausum*, but rather of spit reaching through the air.

72. Kant, *Die Metaphysik der Sitten*, 362; Kant, *Practical Philosophy*, 407.

73. Kant, *Anthropologie*, 451. More on this in chapter 1 below.

74. Canetti, "Broch," 13.

75. For a recent argument regarding smell's potential to effect just such a "return," see Han, *Duft der Zeit*. Han diagnoses our time as one of information as opposed to history, where "information does not smell. That is what distinguishes it from history" (23). Referencing Proust, the late Heidegger, and the *hsiang yin* (an ancient Chinese incense burning clock), Han advocates for a "return-to-oneself [*Rückkehr-zu-sich*]" (50) that can be found in a contemplative lingering with, for instance, the smell of incense or the "smell of oakwood" (78). Pace Han, the authors studied here show precisely that any "return-to-oneself" in the realm of olfaction is impossible.

76. What Alfred Schmidt has labeled the "abstract and romanticizing anthropology of the Paris Manuscripts" (Schmidt, *Der Begriff der Natur*, 148) is revoked, at least partially, once Marx reaches the phase of the *Communist Manifesto* and *German Ideology*. Schmidt explains that Marx changes course "as soon as he notices that these terms are becoming ideological chatter from the lips of petty-bourgeois authors, and not the point of leverage for empirical study of the world and its change" (149).

77. As Derrida points out in the recently published seminar *Theory and Practice*, the "labor of transformation is regularly defined as human; no practice that is not human. Humanity forms an indisputable part of this definition of practice" (59). The "implication of the human within the definition of praxis in general" is also Heidegger's question with respect to Marx, in particular, as Derrida shows, in the *Letter on Humanism*. Here Marx is lauded for having recognized the historicity of being in a way that escapes existentialism and, in the ultimate consequence for Heidegger, requires an abandoning of humanism.

78. Hamacher, *Two Studies*, 109. In a footnote to this passage, Hamacher hints at the possibility that it might be sensibility, or more broadly materiality, that opens Marx's thought beyond the strictures of Hegelian idealism: "Even Marx's definition of the proletarian revolution as the negation of negation

belongs in formal terms to the context of Idealism, whereas the material expositions within the critique of political economy evince implications of the Hegelian formula diverging from metaphysical ones" (195n89).

79. Hamacher, 108.
80. Dante, *De vulgari eloqentia*, 39.
81. Dante, 39.
82. Agamben, *The Fire and the Tale*, 81.
83. Horn, "Air as Medium," 8; emphasis in the original. For some related reflections on "language as medium" and the question of "impartability" ("Mitteilbarkeit") in Benjamin, see Weber, *Benjamin's -Abilities*, 34–48. For an extended inquiry into the question of the middle, including with respect to Hölderlin and Benjamin's reading of Hölderlin that will be important in chapter 1 below, see Sng, *Middling Romanticism*, introd. and chap. 5.
84. Hamilton, *Security*, 224.
85. Nietzsche to Ernst Schmeitzner, February 13, 1883, letter 375, in *Digitale Kritische Gesamtausgabe*.

Chapter 1

1. All translations are mine, although I have consulted existing translations with great benefit, in particular Michael Hamburger's and those contained in the edition *Essays and Letters*, translated by Jeremy Adler and Charlie Louth. This chapter quotes from three main Hölderlin editions: Friedrich Beißner's *Große Stuttgarter Ausgabe*, D. E. Sattler's *Frankfurter Hölderlin Ausgabe*, and Jochen Schmidt's *Deutsche Klassiker-Ausgabe*. Citations will be given parenthetically, using the *Hölderlin-Jahrbuch*'s abbreviations *StA*, *FHA*, and *KA*. Sattler's edition will be used most frequently for the poems, due to the superior comprehensiveness of its editorial material; differing editorial choices on the part of the author of this chapter will be justified throughout, often with reference to Beißner's or Schmidt's editions.
2. Ebel's letter is lost but an extant letter from Susette Gontard, Hölderlin's great love and at the time employer, records the core of it: "Doctor Ebel has written Hölderlin a letter full of complaints from Paris. . . . He is extremely dissatisfied and has been deceived in all his expectations" (*KA* 3:851). For a recent intervention into the discourse surrounding revolution and disillusionment, especially with respect to Hölderlin's writings in the 1790s, see Adler, *Politics and Truth in Hölderlin*, especially 13–16.
3. Both the question of shame and the color red, later so ubiquitously associated with revolution, would deserve a closer reading. Immanuel Kant, too, speaks of "a revolution in the orientation [*Gesinnung*] of the human being." Kant,

Akademie-Ausgabe 6:47. For a reading of Kant's relation to revolution in the context of Hölderlin's poetry, see McLaughlin, *Poetic Force*, 38ff. The theme of a "revolution in the air" is prominent in stunning fashion in the late Kant, who was concerned about changes in the electrical charge of the atmosphere making him ill and preventing him from completing his critical philosophy. For a detailed reading of the relevant passages, see Fenves, *Late Kant*, 136–161.

4. Heidegger, *Aus der Erfahrung des Denkens*, 111.

5. For a detailed analysis of these anagrams, see in particular Roman Jakobson and Grete Lübbe-Grothues, "Ein Blick auf *Die Aussicht* von Hölderlin," 31ff.

6. Sattler speculates that this might be a misreporting of "prachatig" (as in "prächtig"), which is attested in Gustav Schlesier's *Unterredung mit Schwab* (*FHA* 9:438). "Asia" and its "Pracht," however, recur throughout Hölderlin's work, in particular the later *Gesänge*; consequently, the possibility of Hölderlin associating his gift with the splendor of Asia should not be dismissed too easily. The smell of Asia and its flowers will, in fact, be crucial to the "geopoetics of smell" developed below.

7. John T. Hamilton draws attention to a different but deeply related image of the latest Hölderlin: "The image of Hölderlin at the piano, speechlessly looking out at the frozen waters of the Neckar, suggests that language had run its course. As if words no longer worked. As if writing had become impossible." Hamilton, *Music, Madness, and the Unworking of Language*, xiv. Both of these images could be linked to the "madness" of the author to whom chapter 3 will turn: Friedrich Nietzsche.

8. In his well-known text titled "Parataxis: On Hölderlin's Late Poetry," Theodor W. Adorno develops a similar thought: "That identity, like in Hegel's logic, can only be conceived of as an identity of the non-identical, as 'interpenetration [*Durchdringung*]'" (201). The necessity to think nonidentity will emerge toward the end of this chapter and will not be immediately derived from the *Durchdringung* character of relation. ("Durchdringung" is also a key term in Walter Benjamin's reflections on the late Hölderlin, which will be interpreted below.)

9. Close to the term "air" is Hölderlin's use of "ether." Determining the relationship of air and ether is exceedingly difficult: while they cannot be identified with each other, they do stand in an important relationship. Further investigation would have to consider Hölderlin's thought of the elements and how his knowledge of contemporaneous natural science—for instance, his reception of the work of the leading European anatomist, Samuel Sömmerring—reconfigured it. For some indications, see Link, "Aether und Erde"; for some general remarks on ether, air, and questions of mediality, see Christian, *Objects in Air*, 13–14.

10. Aristotle, *De Anima*, 424b18.

11. A fourth one, air's combination with water in the form of condensation, what Hölderlin refers to as "Morgenthau," will be left aside here. As often in his early poetry, Hölderlin closely models himself on his early master, Friedrich Klopstock. Klopstock's ode "To Cidli" from 1752 constitutes an important precursor to "Hymn to Love," including almost all elements of the lines quote from "Hymn to Love":

> Lüfte, wie die, welche die Himlischen
> Sanft umathmen, umathmen dich!
> Rosen knospen dir auf, daß sie mit süßem Duft
> Dich umströmen! dort schlummerst du!
> Wach, ich werfe sie dir leis' in die Locken hin,
> Wach vom Thaue der Rosen auf. (Klopstock, *Werke 1: Oden*, 130)

12. Kant, *Anthropologie*, 451.
13. Kant, *Anthropologie*, 452. This is also the source of smell's exclusion from aesthetics proper in Kant since it makes smell antisocial and unsuitable to the universal communicability that grounds his aesthetics. On some of these questions, see Diaconu, *Tasten—Riechen—Schmecken*.
14. Henrich, *The Course of Remembrance*, 154. On the literary and cultural tradition of ascribing conciliatory powers to gardens, see Trotha, "Der Landschaftsgarten."
15. Plato, *Philebus*, 51b.
16. Plato, 51b.
17. Plato, 51e.
18. The relationship between Hölderlin and German Idealism is exceedingly complex and has received a large amount of scholarly attention. The dispute concerning Hölderlin's role in the drafting of the *Ältestes Systemfragment*, written by him, Schelling, and Hegel, is only the most tangible form of the intellectual (and personal) conflicts that shaped the trajectory of German philosophy. Concerning these questions, see in particular Dieter Henrich's by now classic "Konstellationsforschungen," especially *Der Grund im Bewusstsein*, that argue for attributing to Hölderlin a crucial position in the early development of German Idealism, which other accounts of the work of Fichte, Schelling, and Hegel often tend to erase (as does Eckart Förster's major work, *25 Jahre der Philosophie*, which will be used below). Cf. also Waibel, "Kant, Fichte, Schelling"; Kreuzer, "Hölderlin im Gespräch"; Pöggeler, "Philosophie im Schatten Hölderlins"; and Binder, "Hölderlins Dichtung im Zeitalter des Idealismus."
19. Kant, *Kritik der reinen Vernunft*, B72.
20. Förster, *Twenty-Five Years*, 145.

21. Eckart Förster has shown that intellectual intuition in Kant needs to be carefully distinguished from an *"intuitive understanding* which goes from the intuition of the whole to its parts and thus perceives no contingency in the way the parts are assembled into a whole." Förster, *Twenty-Five Years*, 145. Förster then links intuitive understanding to Goethe's largely Spinozistic *scientia intuitiva*. The contrast between Goethe and Hölderlin will be developed below, not so much through their differing responses to Kant (although this is always at stake), but through the difference in their poetic practice and their treatment of smell.

22. For an incisive reading of intellectual intuition in this text along the lines proposed here, see Hamacher, *Two Studies*, 129–130.

23. Hölderlin's tonal conception of poetics is highly complex and rather difficult to unfold beyond its basic structure; for helpful secondary literature, see Schmid, "Wechsel der Töne"; Gaier, *Der gesetzliche Kalkül*; Ryan, *Hölderlin's Wechsel der Töne*. One can find a distant but related precedent for linking the three tones to Hölderlin's elemental concerns in Gaier, *Kalkül*, 290.

24. See Adorno, "Late Style in Beethoven," and Said, *On Late Style*. For a broader account of lateness, see Hutchinson, *Lateness and Modern European Literature*.

25. A notable exception can be found in Böckmann, "Das 'Späte' in Hölderlins Spätlyrik."

26. At the forefront of these explicitly "political" interpretations of Hölderlin's trajectory stands the work of Pierre Bertaux, who, to use terminology from Hölderlin's own work, emphasizes a certain (contested) convergence of *vox populi* and *vox dei* that can be read to produce a type of Jacobin sympathy. More broadly, Bertaux points out that Hölderlin's period of poetic activity (not counting the "latest" poems) is rather exactly coextensive with the main political events in France: "before Hölderlin the *ancient régime*, after him Napoleon's empire, the Restauration, Metternich and everything that comes with it. Accordingly, the active phase of Hölderlin's life coincides precisely with the great events in France that ended the medieval Holy Roman Empire and founded the modern world." Bertaux, *Hölderlin*, 11. Bertaux's work elicited a flurry of responses, cf., among others, Günther Mieth (for instance, Mieth, *Friedrich Hölderlin*), Jürgen Link, as well as the various (brief) writings on revolution and politics in Hölderlin by D. E. Sattler. For a different, but not unrelated, approach to the question of revolution in the late Hölderlin, see Fenves, "Afterword: Toward a 'Non-Metaphysical "Concept" of Revolution.'" See also Adler, *Politics and Truth in Hölderlin*, for incisive reflections on "the unceasing weather of revolution" and, in particular, its relationship to time. The effect of Bertaux's thesis can also be traced in some literary works of the twentieth century, most prominently Peter Weiss's *Hölderlin*.

27. Hölderlin scholarship has addressed this question most prominently via the difficult relationship between the late Hölderlin and the early/middle Hegel

(or sometimes more broadly, as shown above, to German Idealism). Some scholars (most insistently, Werner Hamacher) emphasize Hölderlin's divergence from Hegel to the point of making this divergence the very defining feature of Hölderlin's lateness. Others (such as Paul de Man, in his quest to wrest Hölderlin from what he sees as Heideggerian abuse, where Hegel must be located on the side of Western metaphysics while Hölderlin is already beyond such metaphysics) see a certain convergence between the late Hölderlin and Hegel. Often these questions hinge on the status of synthesis, reconciliation, and separation, which will be addressed below. Discussions in Hölderlin scholarship about the distance between Hölderlin and Hegel might, at least sometimes, be not so much a question of a disagreement with respect to Hölderlin but rather with respect to Hegel.

28. See, for instance, Böschenstein-Schäfer, "Die Sprache des Zeichens," especially 26.

29. In a comparison between smell and synesthesia, this disarticulating function of smell can be thought alongside the "other synaesthesia" articulated in Bernstein, *The Other Synaesthesia*.

30. Adorno, "Parataxis," 186.

31. Such an insight into fragrance's importance for Hölderlin's concept of the earth is absent from the otherwise significant body of scholarly work concerning his complex poetics of the earth, his geographical knowledge, and his spatial imagination. Several scholars have shown that Hölderlin was familiar with some of the major travel reports of his time, such as Georg Forster's account of James Cook's travels or Richard Chandler's travels through "Klein Asien." A number of useful articles on the question of geopoetics, some of them quoted below, can be found in issue 35 of the *Hölderlin-Jahrbuch*; see, similarly, issue 38, dedicated to the theme "Hölderlins Räume." As Jürgen Osterhammel has shown, part of the history of "Realia" that constitutes the context for Hölderlin's thinking of geography can be found in the newly invigorated discipline of cartography. Osterhammel, "Stratosphärische Phantasie," 20.

32. Reitani, "Ortserkundungen," 24; emphasis in the original.

33. Heidegger, *Unterwegs zur Sprache*, 37.

34. For some indications regarding this question of Hölderlin and colonialism, see Kreutzer, "Kolonie und Vaterland."

35. Herder, *Werke 6*, 290.

36. In "The Eagle," the strong but invariably pleasant fragrance of the origin finds its olfactory counterpoint in the "caves of Lemnos" (*KA* 1:399): these caves were known in mythology to have been the dwelling place of the exiled Philoctetes, whose banishment derived in part from his insufferable smell.

37. On the Spice Islands and the type of cultural exchange as well as "culinary imperialism" they stood for, see Nabhan, *Cumin, Camels, and Caravans*.

38. The "Indians [*Indier*]" of "Remembrance [*Andenken*]" are more ambiguous than the "fragrant island" in "The Titans": while "Indier" could refer to the West Indies (what today is called the Caribbean), the Indies (India, Sri Lanka), or the East Indies (Southeast Asia), only the latter two are associated with fragrance through the rather common designation of the "fragrant islands."

39. Many other olfactory moments from the late Hölderlin could be added, where each one would reconfigure the argument made here. To name just a few: the fragrant sacrifices of "The Archipelago"; the caves of Lemnos; the "fragrance" of the "holy flames of the hearth" ("heiligen Flammen des Herdes") (*KA* 1:380) in "German Song"; "the holy forests and the flame, fragrant-blossoming [*blühendduftend*] / Of Growth" (*KA* 1:406) in "Whatever Is Next [*Das Nächste Beste*]"; and another island, "Tinian," where the following encounter—peculiar and difficult to interpret and translate—is described: "And among willow trees / Fragrant / Bees encounter / Butterflies" ["Und an Palmtagsstauden / Wohlduftend / Mit Sommervögeln / Zusammenkommen die Bienen"] (*KA* 1:407).

40. Hölderlin himself uses this term prominently, albeit with a slightly different meaning, in *Hyperion*—for example, in the prologue to what Schmidt calls the "penultimate version": "We all travel along an eccentric trajectory [*exzentrische Bahn*], and no other path is possible from childhood to completion [*Vollendung*]" (*KA* 2:256).

41. Michael Hamburger translates this verse as "For from the abyss," thus opting for the meaning of "nemlich" as "for" or "indeed" but obscuring the legible and decisive roots of "Grund" and "Name." Hölderlin, *Poems and Fragments*, 679.

42. In addition to the differences between France and Frankfurt developed here, the political valences of these two places must continuously be kept in mind: on the one hand, Frankfurt as the center of the German or rather Holy Roman emperorship; on the other, France as the place of revolution—that is, perhaps, of an ecstatic *turning*. Cf. also the remarks on Bertaux and Hölderlin's relationship to the Jacobins above.

43. For a shorthand summary of the Frankfurt/Frankreich opposition in a slightly different terminology, see Hornbacher, "Wie ein Hund," 240. For a different reading of the "Frank" relation of these two places, see Eldridge, *Lyric Orientations*, 104–106.

44. Walter Benjamin, in his reflections on the late Hölderlin quoted above, names the counter-principle to "Gestalt" the *Oriental* principle at work in Hölderlin: "This is the oriental, mystical principle that overcomes borders [*das orientalische, mystische, die Grenzen überwindende Prinzip*], which in this poem so evidently sublates [*aufhebt*] time and again the Greek, forming [*gestaltende*] principle" (*GS* 2:124). The Oriental elements in the poem are those that "rise up as unlimited [*unbegrenzte*] against the formed, limited appearance that rests in itself" (*GS* 2:126). Benjamin himself acknowledges that he does

not justify the use of the term "Oriental"; while the heat of southern France might be seen to entertain certain similarities with it, the term will not be used here. Instead of an "unlimited" oppositional principle, the rest of this section will develop a different movement of an ephemeral, disseminated undoing of gestalt.

45. With respect to the constitution of these lines in particular, editors disagree heavily. For a meticulous reconstruction of the manuscript and the editorial decisions by Beißner, Sattler, and others, see Burdorf, *Hölderlins späte Gedichtsfragmente*, especially chap. 2.

46. See Grimm, *Deutsches Wörterbuch*, s.v. "gestehen."

47. Kant, *Anthropologie*, 550. Note also that in the tradition of antiquity, the smell of lemons is associated with the fact that some people enjoy it, while others detest it, as Theophrastus and Pliny the Elder attest, without there being a determinable reason for this discrepancy. This, of course, is a major challenge to a Kantian aesthetics founded on universal communicability. On the larger context of Hölderlin's poetic transformation of Kant, see Nägele, *Hölderlins Kritik der poetischen Vernunft*.

48. A hapax legomenon poses numerous methodological problems that derive from the commentator's inability to establish a context of usage for the term and thus glean insights into its meaning. The many pitfalls of such a "Parallelstellenmethode," in turn, have been analyzed incisively in Peter Szondi's *Hölderlin-Studien*, in "Über philologische Erkenntnis." See Szondi, *Schriften*.

49. Goethe, *Hamburger Ausgabe Band 7*, 145. The poem is already included in Goethe's *Theatralische Sendung*, on which he worked in 1782–1783. Lemons are commonly associated with Italy by Goethe, for instance in *Tasso*. See Goethe, *Band 7*, 734.

50. Regarding the contrast between Goethe and Hölderlin, Binder writes incisively, "Hölderlin's human being is conceived of as an intersection [*Schnittstelle*] of metaphysical processes, not as a naturally given and personal unity as Goethe knows it." Binder, "Hölderlins Dichtung," 59. The opposition between Hölderlin and Goethe is first articulated in all its (polemical) force by Hellingrath, who begins his lecture "Hölderlin and the Germans" by opposing "Goethe's people [*das Volk Goethes*]" to "Hölderlin's people." Hellingrath, *Zwei Vorträge*, 16. One of the key aspects of this opposition is articulated through the question of richness and poverty, which will become crucial in the section on "Patmos" below. See Hellingrath, 17.

51. The references to lemons in Hölderlin's earlier work appear to be much more in line with the Goethean imagery; *Hyperion*, for instance, also uses a calm and non-olfactory but visual reference to lemons: "where the golden fruit of the lemon tree gleams in dark foliage" (*KA* 2:98). The move from passages such as these to "Namely from the un-ground" should thus be seen as part and parcel of Hölderlin's increasingly singular poetic path that distances him more and more from his contemporaries.

52. Heidegger, *Hölderlins Hymne "Der Ister,"* 190. Heidegger had already explicated the centrality of pain as "Unterschiedensein" ("being differentiated") for his reading of Hölderlin in his earlier (1934–1935) lectures on "Germania." See Heidegger, *Hölderlins Hymnen,* 82.
53. Heidegger, *Hölderlins Hymne "Der Ister,"* 190.
54. On this question, see, among others, Nägele, "Fragmentation und fester Buchstabe."
55. Bart Philipsen thus writes, "The predominantly visual presentation of the landscape of Asia Minor is replaced by a distinctively auditory conjuring up of the otherwise desolate, 'poorer' island." Philipsen, "Gesänge," 372. See also Binder, "Patmos-Hymne," 105.
56. On the relationship between home and secret, see Derrida, *Donner la mort*: "Herein lies perhaps the secret of the secret, namely that there is no knowing of its subject and that it does not exist for anyone. A secret does not belong, is never attached to a 'home' ['*chez soi*']" (127).
57. Cf. Fenves, "Toward Another Teichology."
58. Etymologically, "cedar" might even lead back to the smell of lemons, Hölderlin's paradigmatic instance of inaccessible *Sinnlichkeit* that splits into pains and resists song: the Greek word κέδρος gives both the word "Ceder" (cedar) and "Citrone" (lemon). The smell of lemons and the inaccessible cedar palaces thus both "stand" in the (non-)position of inaccessibility that nevertheless relates to song. For an extensive discussion of the convoluted etymology of "Citrone," see *Der neue Pauly: Enzyklopädie der Antike*, 3:2, s.v. "citrone."
59. Note that the cedar tree also carries strong biblical connotations: as the tree mentioned most often in the Old Testament/Hebrew Bible (Musselman, *A Dictionary of Bible Plants*, 37), it symbolizes power, strength, majesty, and wealth, and is associated with the Davidic dynasty: "In biblical literature, Lebanon's cedars symbolized (royal) majesty. . . . Jerusalem was on a mountain, and one of the royal buildings was 'The house of the forest of Lebanon' (I Kings 7:2; named after the cedar used in its construction)." Greenberg, *The Anchor Bible Ezekiel 1–20,* 310.
60. On the centrality of the desert in the late Hölderlin, see Hamacher, *Version*. Cf. also Derrida's formulation of a "messianism of the desert [*messianisme désertique*] without content and without identifiable messiah" (*Spectres de Marx*, 56) that partly guides the considerations proposed here. The possible difference in messianic thought between the formulation of a "to come" (used by Derrida) and a "coming" (used, for instance, by Giorgio Agamben) is left aside here since Hölderlin's own word, "künftige," allows for both of these translations.
61. To use the words of "Patmos" itself, which recur in a number of the late *Gesänge*, "Vieles wäre / Zu sagen davon" (Much could / Be said of this). A close reading of these dense stanzas would far exceed the purposes of the

interpretation attempted here. For useful scholarship on these stanzas, see the article on "Patmos" by Binder cited above, as well as Stierle, "Dichtung und Auftrag," and Böschenstein, "Patmos."

62. The rejection of remembrance as image within "Patmos" is exceedingly complex as the following stanza, stanza 12, juxtaposes a number of figures and tropes; for the purposes of the analysis here, the opposition between the riches of visuality and the poverty of Patmos suffices.

63. Much has been written about this "firm letter" and the way in which it can be said to respond to or even overcome the danger mentioned in the opening verses of "Patmos." Some of the most pertinent positions include the following: "The saving [*Das Rettende*] is a form of indirectness [*Mittelbarkeit*] that overcomes the dangerous nearness by building bridges." Böschenstein, "Patmos," 141. "In the mediated presence of writing [*der Schrift*], nearness and farness are sublated for the experience of the 'calm gaze' [*des 'stillen Blicks'*] in which that memory can occur anew again and again." Stierle, "Dichtung und Auftrag," 58. "'Patmos' cannot and does not want to offer what the Landgraf had hoped for from Klopstock, namely a pietistic apologia of Scripture against historical-critical exegesis; instead, it offers insight into the necessity of the becoming writing, of the compacting of the holy [*die Notwendigkeit der Verschriftung, der Verdichtung des Heiligen*]. For that does occur in it." Timm, "Dichter am dürftigen Ort," 217.

64. Timm, "Dichter," 213. Despite the allure of the faux etymological affinity between "dicht" (dense) and "dichten" (poetizing, making poetry), one should distinguish, pace Timm, between density and hardness: the wide expanse of certain Hölderlinian images appears compatible with the latter.

65. "Morgenluft" might also be read to stand in relation to "Morgenland," to the East and the so-called Orient. The air of Patmos, as an intermediary island, transforms Asia: this new morning stands in between the *Morgenland* and the *Abendland*, between Orient and Occident. It is from this in-between position that futurity can emerge. This would oppose, in certain respects, Heidegger's insistence on the possibility of renewal being grounded in the *Abendland* (with all the latent and not-so-latent nationalistic and racializing overtones that Derrida and others have shown to lie in that conception) that he sees in the poetry, heavily influenced by Hölderlin, of Georg Trakl. See Heidegger, "Die Sprache im Gedicht," especially his closing claims.

66. A more extensive interpretation of these lines would take into account the difficult development of Hölderlin's thought concerning names from the important passage dedicated to this question in *Hyperion* onward. Wolfgang Binder has written extensively on this question. Cf. in particular Binder, "Namenssymbolik."

67. Instead of naming the "unspoken [*Ungesprochene*]," the following verses demand that we "Circumscribe it thrice [*Dreifach umschreibe du es*]" (*KA* 1:337).

68. Binder, "Namenssymbolik," 121.

69. Duvillard, "Das hymnische Fragment 'Die Titanen'—von der Mythologie zur Meteorologie," 150.

70. Peter Szondi has identified a similar tendency in the late Hölderlin: "The reason for the late Hölderlin avoiding the proper names of the gods can be found in his attempt to bring home the gods from the systems of religions into the concretion of their existence in nature." Szondi, *Schriften*, 331. See also Ulrich Gaier's writings on the role of "climate" in Hölderlin, in particular Gaier, "Klimaerscheinungen."

71. "Christ" could be considered a *title* instead of a *name*, where presumably the logic of a title differs from that of a (proper) name. Within the context of "Patmos," it seems justified, however, to consider "Christ" as a name. The most important biblical link between names and scent is found in the opening lines of the Song of Songs, which read in Luther's translation, "Es riechen deine Salben köstlich; dein Name ist eine ausgeschüttete Salbe, darum lieben dich die Jungfrauen," and in the King James Version, "Because of the savour of thy good ointments thy name is as ointment poured forth, therefore do the virgins love thee" (Song of Songs, 1:3).

72. This is the limitation of Wolfgang Binder's "Patmos" interpretation when he writes, "In 'Patmos,' Christ's Word, the spoken revelation, completely disappears behind his *historical appearance*, that is, behind the fact that he was here and that he will return." Binder, *Hölderlin-Aufsätze*, 365. The word of Christ and the word "Christ" are central precisely to the question of his (dis)appearance.

73. Hamacher, *Two Studies*, 74; Hamacher, *Version*, 64.

74. Biblical scholars generally distinguish two types of anointing in the Hebrew Bible/Old Testament: On the one hand, the anointing of priests, kings, and prophets (most crucially of King David, who is said to have been anointed twice), which functions as a marker of the special relationship the anointed person entertains with God. On the other hand, the Messiah, whose arrival is still outstanding and who is endowed with the full force of Jewish messianism, is also referred to as the Anointed One. In the New Testament, Christ is usually thought to have been anointed twice: at incarnation and at the baptism through the Holy Spirit; neither involves a material anointing oil, and he is thus considered to be *anointed in spirit*. On these questions, see De la Potterie, "L'onction du Christ," and the sources mentioned there.

75. For a discussion of some of the key biblical passages supporting this claim, see Houtman, "Holy Incense and Sacred Anointing Oil." See also Harvey, *Scenting Salvation: Ancient Christianity and the Olfactory Imagination*, for a broader account of the smell/Christianity constellation. The wider literary-historical context of the argument concerning the link between Christ and smell can be found in the extensive literary history of what Frank Krause has called "religious smelling." For Krause, the emancipation of olfaction is

not just a transgression against the rationalization or bureaucratization of the senses in modernity but also needs to be traced in the religious realm. See Krause, *Geruch und Glaube*.

76. The necessary correlation of opening and the possibility of futurity has also been emphasized by Binder in his "Patmos" interpretation. See especially Binder, "Patmos-Hymne," 94.
77. Hamacher, *Two Studies*, 82; Hamacher, *Version*, 74–75.
78. Binder, "Patmos-Hymne," 95.
79. Hellingrath, *Zwei Vorträge*, 69.
80. Echoing certain thoughts that Walter Benjamin would come to develop in *Origin of the German Tragic Drama* (which he claimed to have "drafted" at exactly the same time, in 1916), Hellingrath points to the inevitable link between the Baroque (and hence by implication the late Hölderlin) and death: "The Baroque is an end point; there is no onward out of the Baroque. There is only complete reversal [*es gibt nur gänzlichen Umschwung*] and most of the time this reversal is death or madness." Hellingrath, *Zwei Vorträge*, 69. "Umschwung," of course, will be one of the key words of the final pages of Benjamin's study.
81. Much of the Romantic reception along these lines can be found in the circle around Bettina von Arnim, Achim von Arnim, and Clemens Brentano. Bettine, in particular, played a crucial role in this respect, as the passages collected in *FHA* 9, especially from *Die Günderode*, show: Hölderlin is here presented as "the priest of God in madness." For a thorough overview of the Romantic reception, see Kudszus, *Sprachverlust und Sinnwandel: Zur späten und spätesten Lyrik Hölderlins*. A variant of the thought that madness is an index of truth can be found in Sattler, who would surely object strenuously to being associated with the authors just named, but nevertheless maintains a certain affinity with them on this point when he writes, "The decline of his life constitutes testimony to and proof of the truth of his thought." Sattler, "Al rovescio," 22.
82. Cf. for a related thought Sattler, "Protokoll der Diskussion": "It is unbearable when it is said that this man was as reasonable as us because that would mean that Hölderlin's existence could not be the counter-conception [*Gegenentwurf*] to a madness that, as Michael Hamburger has said, kills the earth" (65). The French tradition in particular knows a further, rather complex engagement with Hölderlin's "madness" through the tradition of psychoanalysis. A milestone in this regard was Jean Laplanche's study *Hölderlin and the Question of the Father*. Laplanche closes his book with the following provocation: "A poet because he opens schizophrenia as a question, . . . [Hölderlin] opens this question because he is a poet" (118). The debate that resulted from Laplanche's work, not only in the direct engagement by Foucault and Blanchot, but also, more indirectly, in Derrida's writing on Artaud from roughly the same time, must be left aside here.

83. Sattler, "Al rovescio," 19.
84. Sattler, 25.
85. Sattler, 25–26.
86. The vocabulary of air persists while often being tied to visual (or auditory) descriptions such as "hellere Lüfte" (clearer or brighter airs) (*FHA* 9:72). In the Scardanelli phase, air frequently articulates the splendor of the opening vista of an "outlook": "And splendid is the air in open spaces" ("Und herrlich ist die Luft in offnen Räumen") (*FHA* 9:150). On the connection between air and splendor, see Böschenstein, "Hölderlins späteste Gedichte," 40.
87. The other poem is "When down from the sky . . . " ("Wenn aus dem Himmel . . . ") (*FHA* 9:67), similarly written in the early years of Hölderlin's "madness." The crucial line, verse 23, reads, "And fragrance lingers among wild bushes" ("Und Duft an wilden Heken weilet"). This line, too, is deeply inscribed in the olfactory poetics developed above: on the one hand, the wildness of the "Heken" positions it in opposition to the image of the fragrant garden as unification of nature and culture presented by "Heidelberg"; on the other, the modification of "lingers" points to the analysis of the transience of smells found in "Patmos," which constituted, at least partly, a reconfiguration of the Kantian notion of the "lingering" of beauty.
88. Jakobson and Lübbe-Grothues similarly point out the tight connection between these two poems; see Jakobson and Lübbe-Grothues, "Ein Blick auf Die Aussicht von Hölderlin," 51.
89. See, for instance, Pöggeler, "Vollkommenheit ohne Klage."
90. It is instructive to compare these "simple" poems to the poetry of Eduard Mörike, who knew Hölderlin, obtained some of his papers, and wrote simple-seeming poetry, some of it also dedicated to the seasons, around the same time. One of his best-known poems, "Er ists," in fact, also speaks of the seasons, but, in stark contrast to the latest Hölderlin, it maintains the link between fragrance, spring, and an intimation of something new and to come: "Sweet, well-known fragrances / Filled with anticipation waft through the land" ("Süße, wohlbekannte Düfte / Streifen ahnungsvoll das Land." Mörike, *Gesammelte Werke 1*, 38.
91. Cf. also Böschenstein's analysis: "The gaze of the poet never clings to any fixed state. Through each season he sees the whole of the march of time so that everything that shows itself to him also shows him his own being no-longer or not-yet." Böschenstein, "Hölderlins späteste Gedichte," 44.
92. Reitani, "Ortserkundungen," 29.

Chapter 2

1. See Bernstein, "The Other Synesthesia," 131.
2. Bataille, "The Language of Flowers," 12. See Marder, "Inhuman Beauty," for the claim that "it is almost certain that Georges Bataille had Baudelaire in mind when he wrote these lines" (1).
3. Perfumes are almost entirely absent from Hölderlin's poetry. In part, this difference can be attributed to the different sociohistorical contexts of the two poets; among other things, this chapter thus traces the ramifications of the perfume industry's rise for poetics in the mid-nineteenth century.
4. Sartre, *Baudelaire*, 19. Translations are the author's, in consultation with the translation produced by Martin Turnell.
5. See, for instance, Rosemary Lloyd's statement that Baudelaire is the "great olfactory poet" of the French tradition. Lloyd, *Baudelaire's World*, 181. Jean Prévost, whose book *Baudelaire* was written in 1943–1944, shortly before Sartre's study and in the shadow of his own activities for the French Resistance, begins his investigation with this statement: "Aucun poète n'a eu un odorat plus illustre que Baudelaire" (No poet has had a sense of smell as illustrious as Baudelaire). Prévost, *Baudelaire*, 217. A detailed reading of the centrality of odors can be found in Benveniste, who claims that "à la naissance de sa création, comme à la source vive et inépuisable de tout, il y a chez Baudelaire un vécu primordial, l'expérience et l'appel d'une sensation, la plus riche et la plus féconde étant celle d'une *odeur*" (at the birth of his creation, like at the lively and inexhaustible source of everything, there exists in Baudelaire a primary lived experience, the experience and the call of a sensation, the richest and most fertile one being that of an *odor*). Benveniste, *Baudelaire*, 674. The depth of the olfactory engagement of Baudelaire's poetry is indicated by the fact that the poem generally considered to be the oldest in *The Flowers of Evil*, "À une Dame créole," already includes smell references. By contrast, some scholars have argued for a centrality of vision in Baudelaire (e.g., Ulrich Baer, who speaks of "the sustained emphasis on vision and the passion of the gaze, which characterize a large number of poems in *The Flowers of Evil*. Most of Baudelaire's poetry is staked on visual perception." Baer, *Remnants of Song*, 109). Many others have stressed the synesthetic character of sense perception in Baudelaire (see most recently, for instance, Bernstein, *The Other Synaesthesia*, chaps. 3 and 6; the argument proposed here entertains multiple affinities with Bernstein's account.)
6. Sartre, *Baudelaire*, 160.
7. In addition to the politico-poetico-existential implications traced here, the interplay of Baudelaire's insistent attention to smells and his *revolting* character—"revolting" heard here in the two senses of the word—can also be traced in the "dangerous cluster of aesthetic decadence, sexual deviance, and hypersensitivity to odors": as Cheryl Krueger has shown in detail, "Charles Baude-

laire's status as writer of smells owes as much to neurologists, psychologists, criminologists, and sexologists, as to literary critics." Krueger, *Perfume*, 96.

8. Sartre, *Baudelaire*, 50. This is reminiscent of Max Stirner's distinction between revolt and revolution that Marx addresses in *The German Ideology*. Giorgio Agamben has suggested a third position: "the absolute indiscernibility between revolt and revolution." Agamben, *The Time that Remains*, 33.

9. For a useful overview, see Burton, *Baudelaire and the Second Republic*. Burton emphasizes that "for most critical opinion, Baudelaire's undisputed participation in the street-fighting that brought down the Bourgeois Monarchy in February 1848 and again in the predominantly working-class uprising of June that year was to be attributed to 'personal' rather than to 'political' considerations" (v). These "personal" reasons would lie in the fact that in 1848 Baudelaire presumably acted against his stepfather, General Aupick; they would then easily issue into a "depoliticization" that occurs at the latest around December 1851 with Napoleon III's unconstitutional seizure of power. A contrasting, radical leftist revolutionary reading can be found in Dolf Oehler, whereas Claude Pichois emphasizes Baudelaire's anarchist tendencies: "la seule caractéristique politique de Baudelaire est une pensée résolument anarchiste. Il a été anarchiste de gauche. Il va devenir anarchiste de droite" (Baudelaire's only political character trait is a resolutely anarchist thought. He was an anarchist of the left. He would become an anarchist of the right). Quoted in Burton, ix.

10. For an extensive engagement with Sartre's book along these lines, see Bataille, *La littérature et le mal*. Bataille stresses that "Charles Baudelaire's refusal is the most profound refusal because it constitutes in no way the affirmation of an opposing principle" (Le refus de Charles Baudelaire est le refus le plus profonde, puisqu'il n'est en rien l'affirmation d'un principe opposé). Bataille, *La littérature*, 45. Bataille's introduction of the term "fascination" as "the ruin of the will [*la ruine de la volonté*]" (45) should be considered alongside the suggestion below that for Baudelaire it is "vaporization" that constitutes the ruin of the will.

11. The penultimate line specifically rewrites an episode narrated in Matthew 26:51–52. After Judas—who will become important below—has betrayed Jesus and the latter is arrested, "one of those who were with Jesus stretched out his hand and drew his sword, and struck the slave of the high priest, and cut off his ear. Then Jesus said to him, 'Put your sword back into its place; for all who take the sword will perish by the sword.'" Baudelaire's apparent siding with Judas is significant in light of the rewriting of a further passage from the gospel involving Judas (Mary Magdalene's use of a precious perfume) discussed below.

12. See, for instance, Richard Burton's argument: "using the Gospel narratives, Baudelaire has provided nothing less than a history and interpretation in code

of the evolution and fate of the Second Republic." Burton, *Baudelaire and the Second Republic*, 180.

13. Burton, 181.
14. "Baudelaire's probably brief membership of Blanqui's *Société Républicaine Centrale* in February–March 1848 together with the likelihood that he remained in contact with the Blanquist milieu until the very end of the June uprising." Burton, 29. See also Burton, 105–109.
15. Sartre, *Baudelaire*, 50.
16. Sartre, 52.
17. Sedgwick, *Epistemology*, 149.
18. Sedgwick, 149.
19. For an analysis of the implications of this shift in industry, see Stamelman, *Perfume*, and, with specific attention paid to literature's intertwinement with perfume making, Krueger, *Perfume on the Page*.
20. Stamelman, *Perfume*, 103.
21. This transformation of, say, flowers into perfumes, when it is effected by a burgeoning perfume industry, renders perfumes *reproducible*: smell becomes a commodity that can circulate as a "Massenartikel," a mass commodity, to use a term Benjamin repeatedly employs in his Baudelaire studies. (More on smell and the commodity form below.) Yet the reproducible character of perfumes becomes transformed by the contact between the olfactory essence and a body's skin: upon contact, the perfume takes on what one might call a *singular* instantiation. Perfumes smell different each time depending on the skin from which they evaporate. In other words, the nature/artifice pair is supplemented by the conceptual couple reproducibility/singularity as the structuring of perfumes.
22. These questions of dissipation and loss of self always touch on the crucial question of *hygiene*, prominent in some of these journals. For an overview of some of the questions involved, see Cohen, "Mud into Gold." The epilogue on Ponge below explicitly takes up these hygienic questions.
23. Regarding this image, see also "The Pipe" (*OC* 1:68).
24. Poe, *The Portable Edgar Allan Poe*, 903; emphasis added. Regarding the relationship between Poe and Baudelaire, see Valéry, *Situation de Baudelaire*.
25. Julia Kristeva takes up the thought of dissipation under the term of "pulverization" and ties it directly to the possibility or impossibility of writing: perfume, for her, is "above all the allegory of the pulverization of sense and of language, of the pulverization of proper identity." Kristeva, *Histoires d'amour*, 407. This leads her to the claim that perfume is "a metaphor of metaphor as such [*métaphore de* la *métaphore*]" (414; emphasis in the original).
26. Derrida, *Spectres*, 165.

27. Derrida, 25.
28. For an account of the olfactory overlaps and divergences between Baudelaire and Christianity, in particular with respect to Baudelaire's notion of love and the medieval mystics, see Albert, "Parfums et mysticisme."
29. The eerie counterpart to this olfactory resurrection of a rancid, spectral cadaver can be found in "Danse Macabre." Here, death insinuates itself into humanity's company by scenting itself with myrrh; the final stanza, a masterful combination of gut punch and irony, reads, "En tout climat, sous tout soleil, la Mort t'admire / En tes contorsions, risible Humanité, / Et souvent, comme toi, se parfumant de myrrhe, / Mêle son ironie à ton insanité" (*OC* 1:98).
30. This thought could be extended to include the question of reading. Jean-Luc Nancy provides a concise gloss of resurrection's relationship to reading, or more precisely, sense: "the resurrection designates access to that which is beyond sense." Nancy, *Dis-enclosure*, 93. In *The Space of Literature*, the text Nancy here comments on, Maurice Blanchot delineates two different interpretations of the relationship between reading and the figure of Lazarus. The first sees reading as the command to move the stone and to bring forth what was hidden, dead, out of sight: "The mission of this reading seems to be making this stone fall: to make it transparent, to dissolve it by the penetration of a gaze that, with momentum, goes beyond [*va au delà*]." Blanchot, *L'espace*, 257. By contrast, the second mode of reading would subtract itself from such an imperative of transparency: "what responds to the call of a literary reading is not a door that swings open or that would become transparent or even that would thin out a bit; it is rather a tougher stone, better sealed, crushing, an excessive deluge of stone that shakes the earth and the sky." Blanchot, 257–258.
31. Carson links her title to one of the perennial questions in Baudelaire scholarship—namely, the difference between his lyric poems and prose poems: "If I were marketing the poetry/prose distinction as a perfume, I would call it *Economy*. . . . As I am someone who cannot define or effectively describe the distinction between poetry and prose, I will speak instead about its fragrance. For I do believe I can smell the distinction." Carson, "Economy," 14. Latent in this description is the question of the commodification of smell.
32. This might be, among other things, an explanation for the conspicuous absence, for the most part, of smell in the lesbian poems of *The Flowers of Evil*: Baudelaire imagines homosexual relations to escape from sexual difference, and hence no function for fragrance remains.
33. Sartre, *Baudelaire*, 23.
34. For some of the most incisive approaches to reading and rereading Baudelaire's misogyny, see Kamuf, "Baudelaire's Modern Woman"; Wolff, "The Invisible *Flâneuse*"; Johnson, *The Feminist Difference*, especially chap. 6; and the work by Elissa Marder quoted below.

35. Marder, "Inhuman Beauty," 8.
36. Krueger, *Perfume on the Page*, 5.
37. Benveniste, *Baudelaire*, 402.
38. Sartre, *Baudelaire*, 161.
39. Brombert, "The Will to Ecstasy," 55.
40. Marder, *Dead Time*, 47.
41. The term "hemisphere" should be applied to both the male I and the woman's hair as a syntactical ambiguity contained in the title's construction indicates: the "in" of "A Hemisphere in a Head of Hair" could signal either that the hemisphere consists of the "chevelure" or that, within the hair, there is, separately, a hemisphere. It is easy to see that this account directly recalls Aristophanes's famous spherical creatures from Plato's *Symposium*: all individuals are actually half spheres perpetually seeking their other half, from which they have been split.
42. "Parfum exotique," among other poems, includes a similar verse, underscoring the importance of the link between charm, climate, smell, and transport: "Guidé par ton odeur vers de charmants climats" (Guided by your smell toward charming climates) (*OC* 1:25).
43. The word "chevelure," too, carries a semantic ambiguity that reconfigures the fragrant hair's relationship to the hemisphere as celestial half sphere. The *Littré* defines its secondary meaning thus: "La chevelure d'une comète, traînée de matière lumineuse et diffuse qu'elle emporte avec elle." The "chevelure" is what *crosses through* the half sphere. Stars might no longer exist—but a line crossing through the otherwise dark night sky, a momentary shooting star providing fleeting illumination, can nevertheless be found in this "chevelure."
44. Marder, *Dead Time*, 29–30.
45. Marder, 31.
46. Cf. Christian, *Objects in Air*, 18–23.
47. The following paragraphs quote, with minor modifications, Keith Waldrop's translation in Baudelaire, *Paris Spleen*, 9–11.
48. Nancy, *L'Adoration*, 18.
49. Nancy, 32.
50. Nancy, 32.
51. Nancy, 22.
52. Of the Christian notion of an "eternal life," Nancy thus writes correspondingly: "Christian life lives, within time, the outside of time. This characteristic evidently maintains an intimate relationship with what I call here adoration, which I could characterize as a relationship to the outside of time (to the

pure instant, to the ceasing of duration, to truth as the interruption of sense)." Nancy, *L'Adoration*, 37.

53. In *My Heart Laid Bare*, Baudelaire records the following apropos the coup d'état of Napoleon III: "My fury over the coup d'état. How many shots I've had to endure. Another Bonaparte! What a disgrace!" (*OC* 1:679). One should think here, of course, of Marx's *Eighteenth Brumaire* and the various spirits, specters, and ghostly revenants that mark revolutions and counterrevolutions.

54. For a lengthy account of Baudelaire's relationship to money, including Baudelaire's "personal" inability to grasp (or rather adjust to) the functioning of money, see Meltzer, *Seeing Double*: "Money and writing are part of the same system of exchange; texts are an available resource that money rewards" (161).

55. See also Klein, *Cigarettes Are Sublime*: "The taste of infinity in a cigarette resides precisely in the 'bad' taste the smoker quickly learns to love" (2).

56. Cf. also Hegel's claim that, in modernity, the daily reading of the newspaper becomes the new prayer ritual. Toward the end of his life, Théodore de Banville, of the Parnassian school and much admired by Baudelaire, reflected on the fate of cigarette smoking in the age of Napoleon III (who was "one of the greatest, one of the most obstinate smokers of cigarettes" [quoted in Klein, *Cigarettes*, 47]), dandyism, and their frivolity. For an extensive reading of Banville, see Klein, 40–49.

57. Richard Klein writes of cigarette smoking's ability to bring about a "little revolution": "but the cigarette interrupts and reverses the decline, accomplishes a little revolution in time, by seeming to install, however briefly, a time outside itself. . . . Smoking cigarettes . . . is permanently linked to the idea of suspending the passage of ordinary time and instituting some other, more penetrating one, in conditions of luxuriating indifference and resignation." Klein, *Cigarettes*, 8. Also recall these sentences from "Hémisphère": "At the blazing hearth of your hair I breathe the odor of tobacco mixed with opium and sugar; in the night of your hair, I see glittering the infinite tropical azure." Baudelaire, *Paris Spleen*, 32. Here, Baudelaire seems to articulate a positive effect of tobacco and, in fact, links it to infinity.

58. Derrida, *Donner le temps*, 134.

59. Derrida, 143.

60. For an extensive reading of this passage, see Françoise Meltzer, who argues that "this economy of a lost past on the one hand, and of its unlikely but nonetheless anticipated return in the future, is not limited to the notion that chronological time has taken back its power. It is also the economy of the advent of Christ and the promised Second Coming, to which the poem briefly but emphatically alludes with its emphasis (twice, the second time in italics) on 'good news' (*bonne nouvelle*)." Meltzer, *Seeing Double*, 174. Within this

framework, one could then claim that "Jesus is the unacknowledged specter that comes knocking at the poet's room of bliss" (175).

61. On the question of news and announcements, in particular in Nietzsche, Blanqui, Marx, and Benjamin, see Mendicino, *Announcements*. For instance: "Despite and because of the frequent changes in fashion, however, the character of new commodities, insofar as they are 'new,' seemed determined to be ever the same within the sphere of the everyday" (xix). These reflections on the commodity form and its links to both newness and an "eternal return" could also be linked to the question of the newly booming perfume industry in Baudelaire's time, which commodified scent and subjected it to the whims of fashion. See also Stamelman, *Perfume*.

62. Marder, *Dead Time*, 21.

63. In addition to scented air, water and in particular the sea can often function as the preferred medium for a lulling into sleep. Benjamin thus relates Baudelaire's desire to the rocking back and forth of ships (a quasi-paradisal state already found in Rousseau's *Reveries of the Solitary Walker*): "Baudelaire longed to be rocked back and forth between the extremes, as it is the prerogative of ships" (*GS* 1:598–599).

64. Note that this is not a question of comfort or shallow pleasure, as Brecht rightly argued in a remark recorded by Benjamin: "the eminent sensual refinement [*sinnliche Verfeinerung*] of a Baudelaire keeps itself completely free from coziness [*Gemütlichkeit*]. This fundamental incompatibility of sensual enjoyment and coziness is the decisive characteristic of a true culture of the senses [*wirklicher Sinneskultur*]" (*GS* 1:675).

65. In this respect Benjamin once again emphasizes the affinity between Baudelaire and Blanqui, for he describes the latter as characterized above all by an interruptive desire: "This determination [*Entschlossenheit*] to tear humanity, in the last hour, out of each catastrophe that threatens it, was for Blanqui in particular the ultimate measure [*das Maßgebende*], more than for any other revolutionary politician of his time" (*GS* 1:687).

66. For an incisive reading of the relationship between Baudelaire and Marx, see Bajorek, *Counterfeit Capital*. In particular, Bajorek's question of "revolutionary irony" could be read alongside the reflections on the prose poem proposed here.

Notes to Chapter 3

1. All quotations from Nietzsche's work are taken from the *Kritische Gesamtausgabe Werke und Briefe*, which is based on the critical text edited by Giorgio Colli and Mazzino Montinari (*Sämtliche Werke: Kritische Studien-Ausgabe in 15 Bänden* [Berlin: de Gruyter, 1967–1977]); citations will be given parenthetically as "*KSA*" followed by the volume and page numbers,

except for citations from his unpublished fragments, which will follow the citation method of the digital version of the critical edition, cited as "NF" (for "Nietzsche Fragmente," followed by the year of the fragment, its group within the digital critical edition, and the fragment's number). Since the vast majority of passages cited in this chapter include typographical emphasis in the original, only added emphases will be indicated. All translations are mine.

2. Nietzsche had access to Baudelaire's *Oeuvres posthumes et Correspondance inédites, précédées d'une étude biographique par E. Crépet*, published in 1887. In a letter to Heinrich Köselitz from February 26, 1888, he speaks of his delight in discovering a letter from Wagner to Baudelaire that confirmed his earlier hypothesis that the two are closely linked.

3. Among the many attempts to understand the status of *Ecce Homo*, see in particular Kofman, *Explosion I*, for an account that resonates with the investigation proposed here, in particular the question of "explosion."

4. While some scholars have noticed the prevalence of olfactory moments in Nietzsche's work, almost none have attempted to develop an account of it. A notable exception can be found in Eric Blondel's work, for instance, *Nietzsche le corps et la culture*. Blondel here develops the notion of a "otorhinological" genealogy in Nietzsche that displays some affinities with the account proposed in this chapter but differs on multiple decisive points, such as Blondel's joining of hearing and smelling, the question of depth, and, most importantly, the treatment of the "compromising" nature of smell and the corresponding development of new smells. Cf. Blondel, *Nietzsche*, 166–189.

5. It is no accident that Nietzsche portrays his olfactory genius through recourse to an animalistic vocabulary ("Nüstern" is commonly used to refer only to an animal's nose): when smelling, the human being lowers the barriers erected between humanity and animality; something Nietzsche was acutely aware of. One of the few thinkers who recognized this was Jacques Derrida, who, in his book *The Animal that Therefore I Am*, states, "one would have to ask oneself *first of all* what there is about scent [*flair*] and smell in man's relation to the *animot*—and why this zone of sensibility is so neglected or reduced to a secondary position in philosophy and in the arts" (55). For an analysis of this constellation, see Naas, "Derrida's Flair (For the Animals to Follow . . .)."

6. Within the voluminous scholarship concerning the relationship between Nietzsche and Socrates, see, for instance, Alexander Nehamas's influential *Nietzsche: Life as Literature* for the claim that Socrates is Nietzsche's "real antipode" (26–27).

7. Xenophon, *Symposium*, 5.6.

8. Several commentators have argued for the pair Hegel/Nietzsche to be important to Nietzsche interpretations. Cf., for instance, Gary Shapiro's *Nietzsche's Earth: Great Events, Great Politics*, which seeks to show how Nietzsche's emphasis on the earth contrasts with Hegel's concept of "world"; Robert Gooding-Williams's claim in *Zarathustra's Dionysian Modernism* regarding

the "philosophy of the future" found in Hegel's *Phenomenology of Spirit*, that "the plot of *Zarathustra* is structured as if to show the kind of text the *Phenomenology* would be . . . were it written as a preface not to logic, but to Nietzsche's modernist philosophy of the future. *Zarathustra* can be interpreted as a re-creation of the *Phenomenology* that expresses a modernist rejection of traditional philosophy" (27).

9. Into this constellation one should additionally inscribe the question of Christianity: a further text from 1888, *Der Antichrist*, explicitly mentions the smells of Christianity that come up repeatedly in Nietzsche's work. Against the generalized stink that rises up from Christians, Nietzsche seems to position, at least in some of his notes, "Jesus—like a sweet smell" (NF 1883, 10[6]).

10. To a certain degree, this is true of other senses too: I might not see or hear something I am used to, such as the subway's noise outside my apartment. The difference, however, lies in the fact that I can overcome this failure of perception by redirecting my attention, if someone points it out to me, for example. This is generally not true of a habitual smell such as a body odor.

11. To name just two recent, representative studies on this topic published in *Nietzsche-Studien*: Loeb, "The Priestly Slave Revolt in Morality"; Piazzesi, "*Pathos der Distanz* et transformation de l'expérience de soi chez le dernier Nietzsche." For an exception to this ethico-political focus, see Rampley, *Nietzsche, Aesthetics and Modernity*.

12. As Jean-Luc Nancy has emphasized in many of his writings (and in personal correspondence with the author), all sense perception, in a certain sense, leads to some type of contact: light hitting the retina, odorous particles touching the olfactory receptors in the nose, etc. Nevertheless, phenomenologically and in the imagination attached to each sense, there is a unique logic of sense-making that differs for each sense, and it is this logic that Nietzsche is interested in above all.

13. Zöllner, *Über die Natur*, 343.

14. The link between nearness and the possibility of contagion is evident in many passages from Nietzsche's work; consider, for instance, this passage from "On the Teachers of Virtue," from the first part of *Thus spoke Zarathustra*: "Happy is already who lives in the vicinity [*Nähe*] of this wise one! Such a sleep is contagious" (*KSA* 4:34).

15. Nietzsche uses the term "innards" (*Eingeweide*) rather frequently: one can detect here, besides the connotation of the "innermost" that interests in this context, his concern with digestion but also the use of innards in the prophetic activity of ancient Greek oracles. It is from the "innards" that the most important "insights" are drawn.

16. As Derrida has argued, the opposition of inside and outside is in fact a condition of possibility for oppositionality as such: "In order for these contrary values (good/evil, true/false, essence/appearance, inside/outside, etc.) to be

in opposition, each of the terms must be simply *external* to the other, which means that one of these oppositions (the opposition between inside and outside) must already be accredited as the matrix of all possible opposition." Derrida, "Plato's Pharmacy," 106.

17. This is generally taken to be the core of Nietzsche's thinking on perspectives, a belief that this chapter seeks to problematize. Cf. Abel, *Nietzsche*: "It is impossible to look 'around one's own corner,' behind the perspective that one does not choose in the first place but already always *is*" (151). Of course, for Nietzsche, "one" is also always already multiple perspectives at once as the introductory reading of *Ecce Homo* above pointed out, which complicates claims such as Abel's.

18. See "stereoscopic vision" in *Cambridge Dictionary of Human Biology and Evolution*. For a more detailed description of depth perception, especially the difference between "absolute" and "relative" distance derived from "binocular depth cues," as well as certain "monocular depth cues" that do provide a limited amount of depth perception, see Braunstein, "Depth Perception."

19. Heidegger, *Nietzsche*, 517.

20. Heidegger, 506.

21. Heidegger, 506. Heidegger goes on to link Nietzsche's chaos to life itself and, crucially, the body: chaos would be "the name for embodied life [*das leibende Leben*]" (509). In his formulation "the body is a letting through and going through at once [*der Leib ist Durchlaß und Durchgang zugleich*]" (509), one can discern a variant, unintended to be sure, of the description of the "durchgängig" relation of the subject to its aerial element that was developed in the Hölderlin chapter and resurfaces in Nietzsche. For an incisive reading of Heidegger and the question of air, see Irigaray, *Forgetting of Air*.

22. This passage distinctly echoes Roger Joseph Boscovich's *A Theory of Natural Philosophy*, which Nietzsche read repeatedly in the years 1870 to 1874. See Mittasch, *Friedrich Nietzsche als Naturphilosoph*, 35. He valued this work highly for its rejection of atoms in favor of "points of force [*Kraftpunkte*]."

23. Derrida, *Marges*, 109.

24. Sedgwick, *Epistemology of the Closet*, 149.

25. For an incisive reading of the question of novelty in Nietzsche (and some of the other authors analyzed here), see Mendicino, *Announcements*.

26. For an analysis of how Nietzsche's thinking of the earth fits into contemporary concerns in ecology, see Graham Parkes, "Staying Loyal to the Earth: Nietzsche as an Ecological Thinker," where he argues that Nietzsche should be considered "one of the most powerful ecological thinkers of the modern period," as well as Adrian Del Caro, *Grounding the Nietzsche Rhetoric of Earth*. The challenge for much of the scholarship that tries to enlist Nietzsche in environmentalist causes is double: first, the egalitarian impetus of many of these causes is hard to square with Nietzsche's praise for rank ordering

and hierarchies; cf., for instance, Ralph R. Acampora, "Using and Abusing Nietzsche for Environmental Ethics," which disputes claims made by Max Hallman and others that Nietzsche is a "biospheric egalitarian." Note, however, that the analysis of smell and the smell of the earth proposed here precisely complicates the assumption of Acampora's rebuttal, which he bases on Nietzsche's alleged "endors[ing] [of] exploitation in the quest of nobility." The second problematic aspect is the emphasis on *conservation* in environmentalism, where "loyalty," for instance, is understood as preserving the status quo; see here Del Caro's claim in *Grounding*: "I submit that the most serious use to which Nietzsche can be put, and the one that least violates his own preference to remain free of causes, is the reclamation and *preservation* of the earth" (49; emphasis added). That this "use" of Nietzsche is "the most serious" one in a way already indicates the danger of such an approach becoming un-Nietzschean. This section will develop an interpretation of Nietzsche's "loyalty" that shows how close his loyalty is to disloyalty or, more precisely, to transformative—non-preserving—alteration. These concerns could be tied together in the question of whether Nietzsche's thought is useful in the context of the admittedly *grave* environmental concerns of our time: the tentative answer implied here is that while Nietzsche does not "ground" environmentalism (to take up a gesture from Del Caro), his criticism of a misguided pathos of distance that positions itself in a "contempt" that rises above both the earth and animality can indeed be a part, if not of advocating for a preservation of the environment, then of arguing *against* a haughty disregard for it that underpins the environmental destruction seen today.

27. See Gooding-Williams, *Zarathustra's Dionysian Modernism*, 176–178; and Lampert, *Nietzsche's Teaching*, which claims that this sublime one directly figures "the heroic labors of these highest men of science, Kant and Hegel" (121).

28. In the Kantian typology of the sublime, this would correspond to the "dynamically sublime"; one might wonder whether its counterpart, the mathematically sublime, could also be found in *Thus Spoke Zarathustra* or elsewhere in Nietzsche's writings.

29. Gooding-Williams, *Zarathustra's Dionysian Modernism*, 176; emphasis in the original.

30. Gooding-Williams instead sees in this passage a more generic "will to truth," emphasizing the sublime one's return from the "forest of insights" and the fact that he is "decorated with ugly truths." While the "heroic will" of the sublime one certainly entertains a relationship with the will to truth, it is crucial for the development of the logic of this section that his "insights" are supposed to set him above the earth and above animality specifically; much of the impetus of Zarathustra's criticism is contained in this concretion.

31. The consistent designation of the bull as being white could be read in relationship to the paleness of the sublime one, but more importantly it points

to the mythological background of this entire section: when Zeus abducted Europa, he disguised himself as a white bull (and, in some of the tradition's accounts at least, carried her over the sea, which finds resonances in the reference to the sea in the opening sentence of "On the Sublime Ones.") The white bull, then, turns out to be a god in disguise—which could also be said of the "Über-Held" at the very end of "On the Sublime Ones," which refers, in disguise, to Dionysus and Ariadne. For the latter claim, including a reading of a preparatory note by Nietzsche that explicitly mentions Ariadne and Dionysus but then adds "Dionysos ganz zu verschweigen," see Gooding-Williams, *Zarathustra's Dionysian Modernism*, 180–182.

32. In this splitting open of the earth, Nietzsche develops a specific version of what Jean-Luc Nancy has posed as the task of his two-part *Deconstruction of Christianity*: "It is also not a question of repainting the skies, or of reconfiguring them: it is a question of opening up the earth—dark, hard, and lost in space." Nancy, *Dis-enclosure*, 1. The plough and the activity of tilling have a long and distinguished history of being associated with writing, as is still legible in the term "verse" deriving from *versus*, the turn of the plough on the field. See Assmann, "Pflug, Schwert, Feder. Kulturwerkzeuge als Herrschaftszeichen." For a direct link between the white bull and writing, see Braun, "'Ein weißer Stier will ich sein,'" 174.

33. In the context of the description of odorous particles as resulting from an *explosion* that was developed above, the smell of the earth could be understood as a series of constant explosions. In fact, the fragment quoted above, in addition to referring to volcanoes (a rather literal explosion of the earth), continues like this: "In this way, the earth is always enveloped by thick clouds of the most fine materials: without this, the steam could not ball up into clouds" (NF 1881, 11[277]). The earth is here imagined in a state of constant explosions that cloud its atmosphere and surround it with accumulations that constitute an enveloping cover.

34. In *Nietzsche's Earth*, Shapiro makes a similar claim: "The earth is the ultimate focus of all orientation" (8). The usage of "focus," however, as an optical term should be questioned. For an analysis of the relationship between orientation on earth and the deeply confounding implications of outer space for the possibility of orientation, see Jörg Kreienbrock's *Sich im Weltall orientieren: Philosophieren im Kosmos 1950–1970*, which speaks of "Nietzsche's Copernican fall."

35. Bachelard, *L'Air et les Songes*, 175.

36. Bachelard, 175; emphasis in the original.

37. Bachelard, 176.

38. Bachelard, 176.

39. Blumenberg, *Höhlenausgänge*, 620.

40. For an incisive analysis of the relationship between philosophy, air, and the dominance of the sun, see Irigaray, *Forgetting of Air*.

41. For a detailed analysis of Nietzsche's heliotropism and the importance of solar metaphors, especially in *Thus Spoke Zarathustra*, see Pautrat, *Versions du soleil*: "without a doubt, the most obsessive reference of this text, its major scene [is] *the solar scene*" (17). Pautrat's main starting point is Derrida's essay "White Mythology."

42. Nietzsche uses the term "höhere *Menschen*" (higher human beings), but only includes men in this group; indeed, the question of women (for instance, Ariadne) and femininity as a counterpoint to these men—but also to Zarathustra—is a complicated and important one. Cf. Krell, *Postponements*, for some useful indications. The translation "higher human beings," instead of the often-used "higher men," is thus invoked reluctantly here: while it might be more accurate in some literal sense, it also obscures the gendered aspect of the conception of these "higher human beings."

43. Reading the higher human beings through the pathos of distance provides a more precise and contextualized interpretation than the more general claim advanced by Robert Pippin and others that "it could be said that the basic dilemma in the book is 'political,' one that calls to mind again the classic Platonic political dilemma—how to establish a relation between the philosopher and the city, how to reconcile the wise and not wise." Pippin, "Irony and Affirmation," 51.

44. That Zarathustra's encounters with these higher human beings in some sense constitute encounters with beings that reflect, parody, or distort who he is has been remarked upon often in the secondary literature. Cf., for instance, Shapiro, *Nietzschean Narratives*: "In his long episodic series of meetings with the higher men Zarathustra sees nothing but parodies, misunderstandings, and fragments of himself" (102). See also Bennholdt-Thomsen, *Nietzsches* Also sprach Zarathustra *als literarisches Phänomen*, 133. For a contrasting view, see Lampert, *Nietzsche's Teaching*, 289. Against all these approaches, following the text's description of a "temptation," as attempted here, appears both sounder and more unsettling.

45. Gooding-Williams also points out that "The Sleepwalker Song" must be understood as Zarathustra reprising his earlier positions as he "transforms a lyric he initially sang to his soul (see 'The Other Dancing Song') into a sleepwalker's song (see 'The Sleepwalker Song'), his performance of which is a *degenerate rendition of the second act of recurrence*, a farcical satire of the sublime celebration of eternity that, in the closing sections of Part 3, brought his tragedy to an end. . . . Parodying himself, Zarathustra completes the task of vindicating himself, by establishing conclusively that he has triumphed over the spirit of resignation." Gooding-Williams, *Zarathustra's Dionysian Modernism*, 280. "The Other Dancing Song" does not employ olfactory terms; it appears that the introduction of these terms enables Zarathustra to reconfigure

the (on Gooding-Williams's reading) seemingly unambiguous celebration of eternity—whether and how such reprising can be seen as parody that "vindicates" will be analyzed below.

46. Irigaray, *L'oubli de l'air*, 145.
47. See, for instance, Gooding-Williams, *Zarathustra's Dionysian Modernism*, 289.
48. Nietzsche explicitly seeks out this eternity as a response to the ephemerality of things, pointing to smell's particular suitability to articulate this thought: "That emperor constantly thought of the transience of all things so that he would not consider them *too important* and could remain calm among them. For me, by contrast, everything seems to be much too valuable to be allowed to be so fleeting: I seek an eternity for any and all [*Jegliches*] . . . my consolation is that everything that was is eternal" (NF 1887, 11[94]). The term "quodlibet" is used prominently in Giorgio Agamben's *The Coming Community*, describing "whatever being."
49. One might compare this compromised overturning with Alain Badiou's remarks concerning Nietzsche's disdain for all previous "revolutions" (as opposed to, perhaps, a "coming revolution"): "the Nietzschean critique of the Revolution . . . consists in saying that, essentially, the Revolution did not take place. What we should understand by this is that it has not happened as revolution. . . . It has not taken place, because it has not truly broken the history of the world in two, thus leaving the Christian apparatus of the old values intact." Badiou, "Who Is Nietzsche?," 5. See also Mendicino, *Announcements*, 21.

Chapter 4

1. Parker, *Brecht*, 55.
2. As Stephen Parker remarks, the young Brecht "and his friends had been discussing Nietzsche's Zarathustra. . . . Zarathustra resonated deeply with Eugen [Bertolt] Brecht, fueling his imaginative projections of radical transformation and the sarcastic, scornful mode of theological disputation." Parker, *Brecht*, 66. For a summary of the secondary literature's consensus that Nietzsche had great influence on the young Brecht, see Knopf, *Brecht-Handbuch*, 1:76–77, including a discussion of the claim that Nietzsche was Brecht's "first and most lasting, but from the beginning intentionally and carefully hidden teacher." For a collection of Brechtian passages that echo Nietzsche (and some analysis of their relation), see Grimm, *Brecht and Nietzsche*.
3. His olfactory appearance at times even interfered with his professional success. When the New York Theatre Union in 1935 took interest in staging Brecht's *The Mother*, Albert Maltz, a member of the Theatre Union's executive board, "openly admits that he came to loathe him as a person, in part

because the stench of his unwashed body (Brecht disliked bathing) made it an ordeal to sit next to him." Lyon, *Bertolt Brecht in America*, 11.

4. Brecht's recourse to popular literary forms is frequent and significant, as Hannah Arendt, among others, has shown. See Arendt, "Beyond Personal Frustration." On the topic of a child who does not wash himself, there also exists a fairy tale collected by Ludwig Bechstein that Brecht might have known.

5. Brecht, *Gesammelte Werke* 9:646. This edition will be cited parenthetically as *GW* in the rest of the chapter. All translations of Brecht's poems are the author's, in consultation with existing translations, primarily those in Brecht, *Poems*, ed. John Willet and Ralph Manheim. Existing translations often strenuously try to efface the plain character of Brecht's "basic German," as he himself will come to call it, and add in supposedly "lyrical" nuances and diction choices, hence necessitating "plainer" translations for the analysis proposed here.

6. Regarding the "x," Brecht specified the following: "the correct price is to be inserted while singing" (*GBA* 12:441). The "x" thus marks the poem's ability to be spoken in various economic contexts, with the core message—that a monetary exchange *must* take place—staying unchanged.

7. Feuchtwanger, *Erfolg*, 145.

8. Scholars have often pointed to Brecht's involvement with the workers' and soldiers' councils in Augsburg after the war as the backdrop of this play, but Brecht's own assessment was that this involvement was not driven by deeply held convictions or political commitments but was, rather, a result of the circumstances. See in particular Parker, *Brecht*, 107–129.

9. The scholarly consensus among historians largely sides with the second option. See, for instance, Haffner, *Die deutsche Revolution 1918/19*. Regarding the situation in Bavaria, which directly implicated Brecht, see Mitchell, *Revolution in Bavaria, 1918–1919*. See further Broué, *The German Revolution 1917–1923* for a comprehensive account of the events in those years.

10. See Knopf, *Gelegentlich*, 17–18.

11. The appearance of the priest emphasizes the closeness to the figure of Lazarus: as was shown in the chapter on Baudelaire, the main objection to the possibility of (Lazarus's) resurrection is articulated in olfactory terms: "he stinks already." Christianity emerges once more as a triumph over the stench of death, but this triumph is one in the service of death-inducing war. This implicit transformation of a Christian figure is part and parcel of Brecht's insistent practice of drawing on biblical and theological tropes; recent scholarship has thus designated Brecht a "hyper-Christian." See Pornschlegel, *Hyperchristen*.

12. For a similar claim, see Pnevmonidou, "Brecht, Kafka und der Körper": "The only hint of a resistance on his part is that he decays" (71). A different ballad, titled "Larrys B," includes the following refrain, similarly positioning the

stench of a corpse as its only capacity: "When one is dead, all one can do is stink [*Wenn man tot ist, kann man nur mehr stinken*]" (*GW* 8:40–41).

13. This violation of the dead prefigures Walter Benjamin's warning in "On the Concept of History" that "*even the dead* will not be safe from the enemy if he is victorious." If for Benjamin, "the only historian capable of fanning the spark of hope" is the one "firmly convinced" (*GS* 1:695) of the possibility of this violation of the dead, then Brecht can be seen here to create a poetic image of this conviction. More on Brecht's relationship to "On the Concept of History" below.

14. Demetz, *Art and Revolution*, 9. Contemporary scholars have used such a reading to attribute a materialistically motivated counter-revolutionary impetus to Brecht. See, for instance, Neumann-Rieser, "Materialismus und Revolution," 240. An opening for a different reading of the Kragler figure will be proposed below. See also Oesmann, *Staging History*, on Kragler's resistance to easy typification.

15. In alternating fashion, Brecht juxtaposes, opposes, or intertwines death and fresh laundry in several of his works, most notably perhaps in the poem "Apfelböck." Brecht imagines the true story of the teenage boy Joseph Apfelböck murdering his parents through the lens of the deed's aftermath: the boy hides the corpses in the laundry closet, where the slowly onsetting decay starts to diffuse through more and more of the apartment, eventually betraying the boy's attempt to hide the murder.

16. The failure to have clean laundry returns as a reproach throughout the play, occasionally even used as a shorthand description for the solider: "The one who has no fresh shirt on his body" (*AW* 1:116). Kragler himself emphasizes how devastating the lack of proper shirts was, see (*AW* 1:106).

17. This is emphasized by Peter Demetz: "Kragler's 'Yes' to the revolution (Act 4) has to do with the unchanging world as well as with his longing for the expressionist ecstasies of death that do away with all consciousness. His 'No' to the revolution (Act 5) has to do with the defense of his corporeality (*Leibhaftigkeit*) against everyone and everything." Demetz, *Art and Revolution*, 9. In contrast to the line of interpretation pursued here, Demetz's reading seems motivated to foreclose a more generative, ambiguous reading of *Drums in the Night* that would keep open the possibility of revolution.

18. The importance of *Baal* for the rest of Brecht's development as a playwright has been emphasized repeatedly in the secondary literature. For an overview, see Knopf, *Brecht-Handbuch*, 1:69–84. The occasion that triggered Brecht's writing of this play is his opposition to the expressionist playwriting (in particular Hanns Johst's play *Der Einsame*) that dominated the theater stages and cultural criticism of the immediate postwar years.

19. The only time the word "revolution" is mentioned in *Baal* occurs in a scene of Baal transgressing an employment contract. He has been hired to perform in a cabaret; in other words, he is tired of letting his talents be exploited

for the entertainment of the paying customers who, in the end, enrich Baal's employer. At some point, Baal rebels against the entertainment imperative and descends into obscenities. It is this breaking of the entertainment contract that an audience member labels, certainly at least half in jest, a revolution: "The devil! he bolts! Revolution!" (*AW* 1:51).

20. The term "appetite" is used here in a preliminary fashion only, following Fredric Jameson's discussion of Baal as a figure of appetite: "it cannot evolve, it knows no interesting history but ultimate exhaustion and death. It is not even tragic-pathetic like the Id or Desire, which can be thwarted and pine away like unrequited love." Jameson, *Brecht and Method*, 8. That Baal does undergo a kind of history, not just in the play itself but through Brecht's reworking of that figure over the span of multiple decades, will be shown in the rest of the chapter.

21. An extensive reading of *Baal* in conjunction with Benjamin's dictum, as well as contextualizing information concerning Baal's name, can be found in Schnell, *Baal*.

22. This section refers to the widely used, second version of *Baal*, from the summer of 1919, before the revisions that Brecht would later criticize as too "smooth" and academic. Only from the fourth version onward would Brecht claim a historical model for the Baal figure; for a discussion of this claim, see *Handbuch*, 72. For a brief discussion of Brecht's last revisions in the 1950s, see below.

23. Brecht, *Baal: Drei Fassungen*, 84.

24. Brecht, 89.

25. A similar constellation can be found in the lumberjack scene. The lumberjacks exploit the forest, which takes revenge by killing one of them, a man named Teddy. Teddy's corpse, however, does not start to smell, as Baal points out: "He still does not stink" (*AW* 1:40). Even in death, the exploiter's return to nature via putrefaction is foreclosed.

26. It is in these passages of *Baal* that some of the clearest echoes of a Hölderlinian poetic vocabulary can be discerned, transformed through the idiosyncratic material-sensual imagination of the young Brecht; for instance: "Weißstaubige Straßen ziehen mich wie Seile von Engeln in den unermeßlich blauen Himmel" (Streets of white dust pull me like ropes of angels into the immeasurably blue sky) (*AW* 1:63). More on Brecht's transformation of "angels" below. While discussing Brecht's lack of an "audience" that stems from the people (*das Volk*) not recognizing itself despite Brecht's poetry being that of a "Volksdichter," Ingeborg Bachmann draws precisely here the comparison to Hölderlin: "I think he has no audience. He is as foreign [*fremd*] as Hölderlin." Bachmann, *Werke 4*, 366.

27. One of the two main theater critics of the Weimar Republic, Herbert Ihering, discerned this already on the occasion of a production of *Baal* by the

Junge Bühne des Deutschen Theaters in Berlin in 1926: "the devouring force that does not become creative, overflowing but nevertheless infertile, Baal, dumbfounded [*entgeistert*] and disgusted by the pregnant woman." Quoted in Brecht, *Baal: der böse Baal der asoziale*, 186.

28. This criticism of the mysticism of "aromatic words" accords with the larger critique of "culinary" theater and literature that Brecht advanced throughout his life. "Culinary" literature or theater is a cultural production aimed at a merely *tasteful* consumption. Regarding Rilke, who will be important below, Brecht thus writes, "Rilke or the development of taste to the detriment of appetite." Brecht, *Arbeitsjournal*, 1:310. Louis Althusser has claimed that Brecht's critique of culinary theater is isomorphic with the critique of "speculation-interpretation" found in Marx; see Althusser, "On Brecht and Marx." Some of the most incisive analyses of Brecht's use of language and its relationship to ideology and politics can be found in French structuralist writers. See especially Roland Barthes's work, for instance, "Brecht, Marx, et l'histoire" and "Diderot, Brecht, Eisenstein."

29. Brecht, *Arbeitsjournal* 1:28.

30. Adorno, *Aesthetic Theory*, 54; Adorno, *Ästhetische Theorie*, 66.

31. Adorno, *Aesthetic Theory*, 110; Adorno, *Ästhetische Theorie*, 123. The relationship between Adorno and Brecht in those years was an odd one, presumably in part due to the circumstances of exile. On the one hand, Adorno and Brecht saw each other regularly and were on the politest terms: "By September of 1942 Adorno tells his parents that Brecht is one of a '"select" circle of people' who he sees regularly." Cronan, "Class into Race," 75. On the other hand, Adorno was highly critical of Brecht's plays (although much less so of his poetry), and Brecht saw in Adorno one of the archetypes of his "Tui" figure that he lampooned and lambasted in his *Tui-Roman*.

32. Brecht, *Arbeitsjournal* 2:715.

33. Brecht, *Arbeitsjournal* 1:362. These (factually certainly inaccurate but hence even more interesting) claims regarding an allegedly scentless and homogenized Californian air continue to resonate in the remarks of other great Germanophone writers coming to Los Angeles. See, for instance, Christa Wolf's remarks in *City of Angels*: "Aber ob sie noch gar nicht bemerkt habe, daß das Wasser hier geruchslos sei? Dieser herrliche Pazifische Ozean unter uns, dieses unvergeßliche durchsichtige Grün mit dem weißen Schaumrand, schöner könnte kein Naturschauspiel sein, aber riecht es denn auch nach Meer?" (But hadn't she noticed yet that the water here was without smell? This magnificent Pacific Ocean below us, this unforgettable, transparent green with the white edge of foam—no natural spectacle could be more beautiful—but did it also smell of the sea?). Wolf, *Stadt der Engel*, 411–412.

34. Quoted in Nash, *The American West Transformed*, 188. A fair amount of scholarship on German intellectuals in Californian exile exists. For an overview, see Bahr, *Weimar on the Pacific*, and Jenemann, *Adorno in America*.

35. Brecht had worked on translating Shelley, including parts of "Peter Bell the Third," with Margarete Steffin in 1938, seeking to demonstrate the realist possibilities of lyric form and seeking to produce a kind of left German Shelleyanism. See Plass, "Die Entfremdung umfunktionieren," and the work of Robert Kaufman cited by Plass. Brecht's translation also surfaces in Benjamin's *Arcades Project*, in convolute M concerned with the figure of the flaneur (*GS* 5:563–564). The third section of "Peter Bell," titled "Hell," is, in fact, framed by two considerations of *air conditioning* and the aerial quality of hellish London. The section opens with the verses "Hell is a city much like London— / A populous and a smoky city" (vv. 147–148) and closes with a stanza that begins, "All are damned—they breathe an air, / Thick, infected, joy-dispelling" (vv. 256–257).

36. Alfred Schmidt, in his much-quoted book on Marx and nature, singles out Brecht for his piercing understanding of the far-reaching effects of economic mediation: "Like almost no other contemporary writer, Bertolt Brecht has perceived the atrophied relation between human beings and nature in the commodity society." Schmidt, *Der Begriff der Natur*, 176. More generally, Schmidt's work, in particular on the influence of Feuerbach's sensualism, forms an important backdrop to these investigations of an "emancipation of the senses"; see the introduction above. Cf. also Oesmannn, *Staging History*, 10ff., for an account of the relations among Lukacs, Benjamin, Adorno, and Brecht on the question of mediation.

37. At this point, a question, formulated insistently by Mike Davis in his reflections on LA and political economy in his book *City of Quartz*, should be raised: To what extent was Brecht familiar with and sufficiently attentive to the existing labor struggles or, more generally, the specific and localized instantiations of historical materialism to be found in the Los Angeles of the 1940s? Davis rightly criticizes Brecht on this point (and perhaps even more rightly the members of the Frankfurt school also present in those years), but the rest of this chapter will seek to demonstrate the value of Brecht's insights into LA nevertheless. See in particular the chapter "Sunshine or *Noir*?" in Davis, *City of Quartz*.

38. Brecht, *Arbeitsjournal* 2:523.

39. Goethe, *Werke: Hamburger Ausgabe*, 1:158.

40. These exceptions are found in the very early poems, a passage from *Baal* quoted above in note 26, and the raunchy 1948 poem "On the Seduction of Angels," which echoes both *Baal* and some of the *Glücksgott* poems discussed below. Cf. also the angel in the play *Simone Machard*.

41. On the general importance of the genre of *Gelegenheitsdichtung* in Brecht's vast poetic oeuvre, see Knopf, *Gelegentlich: Poesie*. Brecht writes the *Hollywood Elegies* in the summer of 1942, right after he and his family moved into a new house in Santa Monica, where Brecht felt at ease for the first time in his American exile. As a measure of the serenity of his new surroundings, he

records in his diary that he can finally reread Lucretius's *De Rerum Natura*, perhaps the work of ancient philosophy most interested in scents. Brecht, *Arbeitsjournal* 2:513.

42. Brecht, *Arbeitsjournal*, 1:16.
43. Wizisla, *Benjamin and Brecht*, 181.
44. Wizisla, 172.
45. Scholem, *Walter Benjamin und sein Engel*, 67.
46. Brecht, *Arbeitsjournal*, 1:294.
47. Brecht, 16.
48. A different transformation of the (American) angelic image can be found in Tony Kushner's *Angels in America*, a work deeply influenced by both Brecht and, to a lesser degree, Benjamin. Kushner also studied at NYU with Carl Weber, who was the American translator of Heiner Müller, to whom this chapter will briefly turn below.
49. The German words "Glück" and "Glücksgott" will be kept in the original throughout to emphasize the polyvalence of these terms: "Glück" oscillates among happiness, luck, and good fortune.
50. Brecht, *Arbeitsjournal*, 2:590.
51. Fredric Jameson, in his book on Brecht, suggests "that productivity is the deeper meaning for progress in Brecht, and that it has to do with activity as such." Jameson, *Brecht and Method*, 177. This must be seen in opposition to a thought of *Bestand* or "dead labor." Brecht would then be "the Goethe reader and admirer of the unmentionable and still scandalous Spinoza himself, who proclaimed: 'I hate everything that does not heighten and increase my intellectual activity.' 'Intellectual' will now gradually become 'collective,' and activity will come to take on a historical dimension: this is the point at which Brechtian productivity takes its place as an exemplary and still actual form of praxis itself" (178). Jacques Rancière, in "The Gay Science of Bertolt Brecht," points in a similar direction: "the key word in the Brechtian orthodoxy is 'production'" (103).
52. In the "Buch der Wendungen," a collection that Brecht worked on throughout the 1930s, this becomes articulated as an explicit ethics, and in fact the only ethical precept of general validity: "Me-ti and ethics: Me-ti said: I have found few 'you should' sentences that I would enjoy speaking. I mean sentences of a general nature, sentences that can be directed to the general public. But one such sentence is: 'you should produce'" (*GW* 12:498–499).
53. Brecht, *Arbeitsjournal*, 1:247.
54. One of the major liberal critiques of socialist programs lay in the claim that Marxism issued in the imposition of an abstract order that stifles production, spontaneity, and freedom. This stifling was then thought, in particular in the so-called socialist calculation debate, partially ignited by the Austrian school

around Ludwig von Mises and Friedrich Hayek in the 1920s, to lower overall productivity. Brecht's emphasis on an unleashing of productivity further constitutes an intervention into intra-Marxist debates, in particular those of the Frankfurt school. In Los Angeles, Brecht regularly attended discussion groups with the members of the Frankfurt school, the most important of which for this context was a four-part series on need. In these discussions, Brecht's emphasis on productivity is also a response to Friedrich Pollock's much discussed thesis of "state capitalism." Brecht continuously insisted that capitalism of all kinds rests on artificial scarcity, and that an unleashing of productivity would thus counteract the perceived problem of a satiation of needs as the foreclosure of revolutionary potential. This conviction is important to keep in mind to distinguish Brecht's celebration of productivity from capitalism's obsession with a different (namely, in the end, restrictive, limiting) productivity.

55. Unpredictability is one of the key features of (socialist) productivity for Brecht. In a conversation with Benjamin that the latter recorded, Brecht states this in all clarity: "'One simply cannot form a state with these people,' I said, referring to Lukacs, (Andor) Gabor, Kurella. Brecht: 'Or just a state but no community [*Gemeinwesen*]. They are enemies of production. Production seems suspicious to them; one cannot trust it. It is the unpredictable. One never knows what will result from it. And they themselves do not want to produce. They want to play the apparatchik and control others'" (*GS* 6:537).

56. The great problems that arise when the *Glücksgott* figure is supposed to be integrated into "real existing socialism" can be seen in the attempts by Heiner Müller and his wife Inge Müller to take up and "complete" the fragmentary *Glücksgott* text after Brecht's death. See Müller, *Die Stücke 1*. Note also that the Müllers produce an intense transformation of the angel figure that, after all, appears only briefly in Brecht's text. In the end, the Müllers' work, too, remained incomplete.

57. Marx, *Selected Writings*, 120; emphasis in the original.

Epilogue

1. Ponge belonged to the Communist Party of France from 1937 to 1947. His break with the party after the war occurred for a number of reasons, which can be partly summarized by saying that Ponge found organized party communism to be a suitable vehicle for resistance but would not toe the party line (or any dogma for that matter) outside of the circumscribed function of resisting fascism. For a useful overview of Ponge's changing politics, see Auclerc and Gorrillot, eds., "Politiques de Ponge," especially Gleize, "L'être quelconque," in the same issue.

2. While Ponge's poetic vocabulary is, more generally speaking, often visual or auditory, his work nevertheless evidences a sustained and nuanced interest in olfaction beyond *Soap*. See, for instance, "The Orange."
3. Ponge read and engaged Nietzsche's work at various points in his life, in particular *The Birth of Tragedy*. See Cuillé, "Fautrier," who emphasizes that Ponge's engagement with Nietzsche was always shaped by the historical context of Franco-German relations, in particular due to the National Socialist appropriation of Nietzsche. Cf. also Gavronsky, "Nietzsche ou l'arrière-texte pongien." All quotations from Ponge, *Le Savon*, will be cited in-text by page number, referring to both the English translation (*S*) and the French original (*LS*).
4. Gavronsky, "From an Interview," 687. For an interpretation of this passage in the broader context of space travel and cosmo-philosophies, see Kreienbrock, *Sich im Weltall orientieren*, 13–15. Thomas Schestag offers an interpretation of these passages in the context of Ponge's *La Fabrique du Pré* and explicitly links the question of the atmosphere to those of respiration, oxidation, the breathing of plants, etc. See, in particular, Schestag, *Para*, 477–478.
5. Gavronsky, "From an Interview," 687.
6. For some reflections on how this medial space and the element of air are linked to forgetting, the "l'oubli" of the "lieu commun" that Ponge mentions, see the introduction above and Luce Irigaray, *L'oubli de l'air*.
7. Since Sartre's review (and Camus's active support for a few years), Ponge's work has received scholarly attention in a variety of discourses: besides existentialism, he now occupies a canonical position in the French tradition of poetry and poetics, as well as in reflections on (the tail end of) modernism (cf., for instance, the work of Hannah Freed-Thall quoted below), and was of great interest to figures associated with the *Tel Quel* group. Scholars associated with deconstruction have taken up Ponge's challenge (Derrida, Barbara Johnson, Thomas Schestag, Elissa Marder, and others), as well as, more recently, those interested in thing theory or object-oriented ontologies. See, for instance, Bruns, "Francis Ponge." Cf. also the interest of scholars working to revive formalist methodologies in literary studies, for instance, Eyers, *Speculative Formalism*, esp. 62.
8. Sartre, "L'Homme et les choses," 264.
9. Sartre, 265.
10. Sartre, 265–266.
11. Scholars have shown that Ponge's work continuously fights a "threat of the elemental": the elements in their pure, amorphous, unbound form almost never enter into a Pongian poem but only ever as, for instance, the "bords de mer" or the delimitation of water in a glass. Similarly, *Soap* is also "about" the qualities of water—but only in relationship to something non-elemental; namely, soap. See, for instance, Higgins, *Ponge*, 14.

12. Ponge's writing should thus be regarded as being political without being "engagé" in the vein of Sartre and Ponge's (sometime) close friend Albert Camus. Of much greater import than explicit calls to action is, for Ponge, the work on language that transforms both language and object, both speaker and reader. In fact, his break with the Communist Party, to which he belonged throughout his work for the Resistance, came about to a significant degree due to a disagreement regarding the question of language. One of the political contexts of soap that *Soap* effectively disregards consists in the hygienic projects that have historically constituted (and still constitute) certain colonial, racist, and imperialist politics; traces of this can be found in *Soap*'s occasional reference to the ability to "whiten." Some incisive analyses of these questions can be found in Anne McClintock, *Imperial Leather: Race, Gender and Sexuality in the Colonial Contest*. A possible Pongian response will be outlined below as the thinking of a "purity otherwise."

13. One particularly provocative and disturbing reference has been developed by Nathalie Rachlin, with respect to the repeated uses of a "pump" in *Le Soap*: "But the pump might also be an oblique reference to the rue de la Pompe, which, during the Occupation, was the location of the headquarters of the French Gestapo, the collaborationist organization to which the Germans had entrusted, among other missions, the task of dismantling Resistance networks. One of the instruments favored by the Gestapo in its efforts to 'loosen the dry tongue' of anyone suspected of subversive activities was the infamous torture known as 'la baignoire.' This terror tactic consisted of submerging the prisoner's head in a tub of ice water." Rachlin, "Occupation," 93.

14. *Soap* thus occupies a pivotal position in the trajectory of Ponge's work: "*Le Savon* appeared at precisely the moment Ponge's writing shifted focus away from the objectal poetry of the early years toward the metapoetic concerns that preoccupied him from *Pour un Malherbe* onward." Rachlin, "Occupation," 85.

15. The outer limit of the invocation of Germanness in the context of a reflection on soap lies in the persistent rumors during and after Hitler's reign that the corpses of Jews were processed into soap in some extermination camps. See Heiner Müller's poem "Seife in Bayreuth" for a painful unfolding of the manifold links among the soap-corpse nexus, anti-Semitism, and a German striving for cleanliness.

16. Cf. also Rachlin, "Occupation," 91.

17. The logic of cleaning and cleansing continued to be audible, for "German ears," after the end of fascism in 1945: in fact, the effort at denazification in Germany was colloquially known as handing out "Persilscheine," slips of "Persil," still to this day the best-known German detergent: to what degree any actual washing or cleaning of fascistic remainders occurred is, of course, a fraught and still live question.

18. As Derrida has shown in great detail in *Signéponge*, both Francis Ponge's first name and his family name can be read in and through his poetry in an ever-proliferating way, the question of *francité* and frankness being clearly related to the name Francis.

19. Scent as it diffuses from the thing—*per-fume* in the etymological sense—thus constitutes one instance of Ponge's recurring reflections on *excretions*, in particular on language as the paradigmatic excretion (aerial, to be sure, when it is spoken) of the human being. See in particular Marder, "Snail Conversions: Derrida's Turns with Ponge," which reads the snail's trail in the context of "Ponge's aneconomic poematics": "When snails leave a 'sillage argenté' as they move throughout the world, there is no discernible difference between their secretions, their expressions, their affections, and their excretions . . . the sillage argenté makes it impossible to discern any palpable difference between speaking, writing, emoting, and defecating" (190).

20. In the context of the aftermath of fascism, *Soap*'s giving up on (or exhausting) autonomy receives special poignancy when compared to Theodor W. Adorno's well-known exhortation in "Education after Auschwitz" that the primary way of preventing a repetition of Auschwitz is the development of "autonomy."

21. A lengthier and more patient development of Ponge's relationship to Christianity would have to unfold in detail what he takes Christianity to be and stand for: a tradition spanning two millennia and numerous cultural, political, and literary contexts displays a rich variety of concepts, dogmas, beliefs, and practices.

22. In *Spoiled Distinctions*, Hannah Freed-Thall has recently read Ponge's work through the optics of profanation, drawing on Giorgio Agamben: "To profane, as Agamben puts it, is to 'open the possibility of a special kind of negligence' that ignores the separation between spheres or registers. Ponge cultivates such playful negligence, such disregard for hierarchies and lines of demarcation" (94). And "How such enigmatically profane 'difference' is felt and made perceptible but not sacralized and set apart: this is the difficulty at the heart of Ponge's work" (95). Through this focus on profanation Freed-Thall inscribes Ponge's work into the context of modernism's interest in the ordinary and the common more generally: "throughout his oeuvre, Ponge explores conjunctions of the singular and the common, inventing a new literary language in order to convey the formal variation and variability of the modernist ordinary" (93).

23. Ponge's affinity with Brecht emerges clearly here: the latter's *Sprachwaschung* (washing of language) was similarly directed toward vulgarity (see chapter 4 above). A different and perhaps more surprising connection to a Germanophone poet can be found in Jean Daive's *Under the Dome: Walks with Paul Celan*, who draws attention to the centrality of washing in Ponge— and in this context links him to Paul Celan. See Daive, *Under the Dome*, 48.

24. The genealogical language points to the paternal-filial setup of *Soap* more broadly. Ponge recalls that his love for soap is to a significant degree his father's: "J'aimais (tant) voir mon père se laver les mains . . . c'est l'un des souvenirs les plus précis que je retrouve incessament de lui (dans ma mémoire). J'observais avec admiration (et amour) cette façon à lui de savonner et de rincer ses mains." Quoted in Schestag, *Para*, 294. Here, once more, the Father is replaced by the father.

25. A starting point for larger reflections on these questions can be found in Agamben, *Pilate and Jesus*, which analyzes Pilate's actions as a response to the "non liquet" faced by the attempt to judge.

26. This soapy, exuberant, playful exaltation that comes to replace transcendence as the outside of this world resonates with Jean-Luc Nancy's remarks on "adoration" in the second volume of his "deconstruction of Christianity" that were analyzed in chapter 2 above: "L'adoration consiste à se tenir au rien—ni raison, ni origine—de l'ouverture. Elle est cette tenue même" (Nancy, *L'Adoration*, 25). See chapter 2 above for a longer engagement with Nancy's concept of adoration and smell.

27. Similarly, a different concept of deodorization presents itself from this perspective: deodorization is not a homogenizing purification but a heterogeneous, never-final process that consists in a back-and-forth movement of difference. The statement "we have never been deodorized" can thus be supplemented by the statement "we have always been deodorizing," where this continuous process marks the differential movement of subtracting and producing smells.

Bibliography

Abel, Günter. *Nietzsche: Die Dynamik der Willen zur Macht und die ewige Wiederkehr.* Berlin: de Gruyter, 1984.

Acampora, Ralph R. "Using and Abusing Nietzsche for Environmental Ethics." *Environmental Ethics* 16, no. 2 (1994): 187–194.

Adams, William. "Aesthetics: Liberating the Senses." In *The Cambridge Companion to Marx*, edited by Terrell Carver, 246–274. Cambridge: Cambridge University Press, 1991.

Adler, Anthony. *Politics and Truth in Hölderlin.* Rochester, NY: Boydell & Brewer, 2021.

Adorno, Theodor W. *Aesthetic Theory.* Translated and edited by Robert Hullot-Kentor. New York: Bloomsbury, 2013.

———. *Ästhetische Theorie.* Frankfurt am Main: Suhrkamp, 1970.

———. "Late Style in Beethoven." In *Essays on Music*, 564–568. Edited by Richard Leppert. Translated by Susan H. Gillespie. Berkeley: University of California Press, 2002.

———. "Parataxis." In *Noten zur Literatur*, vol. 3, 156–209. Frankfurt am Main: Suhrkamp, 1965.

Adorno, Theodor W., and Max Horkheimer. *Dialektik der Aufklärung: Philosophische Fragmente.* Frankfurt am Main: Fischer, 1969.

Agamben, Giorgio. *The Coming Community.* Translated by Michael Hardt. Minneapolis: University of Minnesota Press, 1993.

———. *The Fire and the Tale.* Translated by Lorenzo Chiesa. Stanford, CA: Stanford University Press, 2017.

———. *Pilate and Jesus.* Translated by Adam Kotsko. Stanford, CA: Stanford University Press, 2015.

———. *The Time that Remains: A Commentary on the Letter to the Romans.* Translated by Patricia Dailey. Stanford, CA: Stanford University Press, 2005.

Albert, Jean-Pierre. "Parfums et mysticisme." *VOIR barré*, nos. 28–29 (November 2004): 42–56.

Althusser, Louis. "On Brecht and Marx." In Warren Montag, *Louis Althusser*, 136–149. London: Palgrave Macmillan, 2017.

Arendt, Hannah. "Beyond Personal Frustration: The Poetry of Bertolt Brecht." In *Reflections on Literature and Culture*, edited by Susannah Young-ah Gottlieb, 133–142. Stanford, CA: Stanford University Press, 2007.

Aristotle. *On the Soul, Parva Naturalia, On Breath.* Translated by W. S. Hett. Cambridge, MA: Harvard University Press, 1957.

———. *Problems.* Vol. 1, *Books 1–19.* Edited and translated by Robert Mayhew. Cambridge, MA: Harvard University Press, 2011.

Assmann, Aleida. "Pflug, Schwert, Feder. Kulturwerkzeuge als Herrschaftszeichen." In *Schrift*, edited by Hans Ulrich Gumbrecht and Ludwig K. Pfeiffer, 219–232. Munich: Fink, 1993.

Auclerc, Benoît, and Bénédicte Gorrillot, eds. "Politiques de Ponge." *Revue des Sciences Humaines* 316 (October–December 2014).

Auden, W. H. *Collected Poems.* Edited by Edward Mendelsohn. New York: Vintage, 1991.

Bachelard, Gaston. *L'air et les songes: Essai sur l'imagination du mouvement.* Paris: Librairie José Corti, 1943.

Bachmann, Ingeborg. *Werke 4.* Munich: Piper, 1982.

Badiou, Alain. "Who Is Nietzsche?" Translated by Alberto Toscano. *Pli* 11 (2001): 1–11.

Baer, Ulrich. *Remnants of Song: Trauma and the Experience of Modernity in Charles Baudelaire and Paul Celan.* Stanford, CA: Stanford University Press, 2000.

Bahr, Ehrhard. *Weimar on the Pacific: German Exile Culture in Los Angeles and the Crisis of Modernism.* Berkeley: University of California Press, 2007.

Bajorek, Jennifer. *Counterfeit Capital: Poetic Labor and Revolutionary Irony.* Stanford, CA: Stanford University Press, 2008.

Barthes, Roland. "Brecht, Marx, et l'histoire." *Cahiers Renaud-Barrault*, no. 21 (December 1957): 21–25.

———. "Diderot, Brecht, Eisenstein." *Revue d'Esthétique* 26 (1973): 185–191.

Barwich, A. S. *Smellosophy: What the Nose Tells the Mind.* Cambridge, MA: Harvard University Press, 2020.

Bataille, George. *La littérature et le mal.* Paris: Gallimard, 1957.

———. "The Language of Flowers." In *Visions of Excess: Selected Writings, 1927–1939.* Edited and translated by Allan Stoekl. Minneapolis: University of Minnesota Press, 1985.

Baudelaire, Charles. *Œuvres complètes*. Edited by Claude Pichois. 2 vols. Paris: Gallimard, 1975.

———. *Paris Spleen: Little Poems in Prose*. Translated by Keith Waldrop. Middletown, CT: Wesleyan University Press, 2009.

Benhabib, Seyla. *Critique, Norm, and Utopia: A Study of the Foundations of Critical Theory*. New York: Columbia University Press, 1986.

Benjamin, Walter. *Gesammelte Schriften*. Edited by Rolf Tiedemann and Hermann Schweppenhäuser. 7 vols. Frankfurt am Main: Suhrkamp, 1991.

Bennholdt-Thomsen, Anke. *Nietzsches* Also sprach Zarathustra *als literarisches Phänomen. Eine Revision*. Frankfurt am Main: Athenäum, 1974.

Benveniste, Émile. *Baudelaire*. Limoges: Lambert-Lucas, 2011.

Berlant, Lauren. *On the Inconvenience of Other People*. Durham, NC: Duke University Press, 2022.

Bernstein, Susan. *The Other Synaesthesia*. Albany: State University of New York Press, 2023.

———. "The Other Synesthesia." In *Points of Departure: Samuel Weber between Spectrality and Reading*, edited by Peter Fenves, Kevin McLaughlin, and Mark Redfield, 131–148. Evanston, IL: Northwestern University Press, 2016.

Bertaux, Pierre. *Hölderlin und die französische Revolution*. Frankfurt am Main: Suhrkamp, 1969.

Binder, Wolfgang. *Hölderlin-Aufsätze*. Frankfurt am Main: Insel Verlag, 1970.

———. "Hölderlins Dichtung im Zeitalter des Idealismus." *Hölderlin-Jahrbuch* 14 (1965–1966): 57–72.

———. "Hölderlins Namensymbolik." *Hölderlin-Jahrbuch* 12 (1961–1962): 95–204.

———. "Hölderlins Patmos-Hymne." *Hölderlin-Jahrbuch* 15 (1967–1968): 92–127.

Blanchot, Maurice. *L'espace littéraire*. Paris: Gallimard, 1955.

Blondel, Eric. *Nietzsche le corps et la culture*. Paris: PUF, 1986.

Blumenberg, Hans. *Höhlenausgänge*. Frankfurt am Main: Suhrkamp, 1989.

———. "Licht als Metapher der Wahrheit: Im Vorfeld der philosophischen Begriffsbildung." In *Ästhetische und metaphorologische Schriften*, 139–171. Frankfurt am Main: Suhrkamp, 2001.

Böckmann, Paul. "Das 'Späte' in Hölderlins Spätlyrik." *Hölderlin-Jahrbuch* 12 (1961–1962): 205–221.

Böschenstein, Bernhard. "Hölderlins späteste Gedichte." *Hölderlin-Jahrbuch* 14 (1965–1966): 57–72.

———. "'Patmos' im Überblick." *Hölderlin-Jahrbuch* 38 (2012–2013): 141–145.

Böschenstein-Schäfer, Renate. "Die Sprache des Zeichens in Hölderlins hymnischen Fragmenten." *Hölderlin-Jahrbuch* 19–20 (1975–1977): 267–284.

Boscovich, Roger Joseph. *A Theory of Natural Philosophy.* Chicago: Open Court, 1922.

Bradley, Mark, ed. *Smell and the Ancient Senses.* London: Routledge, 2015.

Braun, Stefan. "'Ein weißer Stier will ich sein'—über die Kultur der Zukunft bei Nietzsche." In *Nietzsche—Philosoph der Kultur(en)?*, edited by Andreas Urs Sommer, 173–182. Berlin: de Gruyter, 2008.

Braunstein, Myron L. "Depth Perception." In *Encyclopedia of Cognitive Science*, edited by L. Nadel, 943–947. Hoboken, NJ: Wiley, 2005.

Brecht, Bertolt. *Arbeitsjournal.* Frankfurt am Main: Suhrkamp, 1973.

———. *Ausgewählte Werke.* Frankfurt am Main: Suhrkamp, 2005.

———. *Baal: Drei Fassungen.* Edited by Dieter Schmidt. Frankfurt am Main: Suhrkamp, 1966.

———. *Baal: Der böse Baal der asoziale.* Edited by Dieter Schmidt. Frankfurt am Main: Suhrkamp, 1968.

———. *Gesammelte Werke in 20 Bänden.* Frankfurt am Main: Suhrkamp, 1967.

———. *Poems.* Edited by John Willet and Ralph Manheim. London: Methuen, 1976.

———. *Werke. Große kommentierte Berliner und Frankfurter Ausgabe.* 30 vols. Frankfurt am Main: Suhrkamp, 1988–2000.

Brennan, Teresa. *The Transmission of Affect.* Ithaca, NY: Cornell University Press, 2004.

Brombert, Victor. "The Will to Ecstasy: The Example of Baudelaire's 'La Chevelure.'" *Yale French Studies* 50 (1974): 54–63.

Broué, Pierre. *The German Revolution, 1917–1923.* Edited by Ian Birchall and Brian Pearce. Translated by John Archer. Boston: Brill, 2005.

Bruns, Gerald L. "Francis Ponge on the Rue de la Chaussée d'Antin." *Comparative Literature* 53, no. 3 (2001): 193–213.

Buck-Morss, Susan. "Aesthetics and Anaesthetics: Walter Benjamin's Artwork Essay Reconsidered." *October* 62 (1992): 3–41.

Burdorf, Dieter. *Hölderlins späte Gedichtfragmente: "Unendlicher Deutung voll."* Stuttgart: Metzler, 1993.

Burton, Richard D. *Baudelaire and the Second Republic: Writing and Revolution.* Oxford: Oxford University Press, 1991.

Canetti, Elias. "Hermann Broch: Speech for His Fiftieth Birthday. Vienna, November 1936." In *The Conscience of Words*, 1–13. New York: Seabury Press, 1979.

Carson, Anne. "Economy, Its Fragrance." *The Threepenny Review* 69 (1997): 14–16.

Cavarero, Adriana. *Inclinations: A Critique of Rectitude.* Stanford, CA: Stanford University Press, 2016.

Christian, Margareta Ingrid. *Objects in Air: Artworks and Their Outside around 1900.* Chicago: University of Chicago Press, 2021.

Classen, Constance, David Howes, and Anthony Synnott. *Aroma: The Cultural History of Smell.* New York: Routledge, 2002.

Cohen, Emily Jane. "Mud into Gold: Baudelaire and the Alchemy of Public Hygiene." *Romanic Review* 87, no. 2 (1996): 239–255.

Condillac, Étienne Bonnot de. *Condillac's Treatise on the Sensations*. Translated by Geraldine Carr. London: Favil Press, 1930.

Corbin, Alain. *The Foul and the Fragrant.* Cambridge, MA: Harvard University Press, 1986.

Cronan, Todd. "Class into Race: Brecht and the Problem of State Capitalism." *Critical Inquiry* 44, no. 1 (2017): 54–79.

Cuillé, Lionel. "Fautrier ou le Palladium anti-nietzschéen." In *Ponge, résolument*, edited by Jean-Marie Gleize, 179–191. Lyon: ENS Editions, 2004.

Daive, Jean. *Under the Dome: Walks with Paul Celan.* Translated by Rosmarie Waldrop. San Francisco: City Lights, 2020.

Dante. *De Vulgari Eloquentia.* Translated and edited by Steven Botterill. Cambridge: Cambridge University Press, 1996.

Davis, Mike. *City of Quartz: Excavating the Future in Los Angeles.* London: Verso, 1990.

De la Potterie, Ignace. "L'onction du Christ: Étude de théologie biblique." *Nouvelle Revue Théologique* 80, no. 3 (1958): 225–252.

Del Caro, Adrian. *Grounding the Nietzsche Rhetoric of Earth.* Berlin: de Gruyter, 2004.

Demetz, Peter. *Art and Revolution: Brecht and Spartacus*. New Brunswick, NJ: Department of Germanic, Russian, and East European Languages and Literatures, Rutgers University, 2009.

Der neue Pauly: Enzyklopädie der Antike. Stuttgart: Metzler, 1996.

Derrida, Jacques. *The Animal That Therefore I Am*. Translated by David Wills. New York: Fordham University Press, 2008.

———. *Donner la mort*. Paris: Galilée, 1999.

———. *Donner le temps*. Paris: Galilée, 1991.

———. *Marges de la Philosophie*. Paris: Les Éditions de Minuit, 1972.

———. "Plato's Pharmacy." In *Dissemination*, 61–171. Translated by Barbara Johnson. Chicago: University of Chicago Press, 1981.

———. *Signéponge/Signsponge*. Translated by Richard Rand. New York: Columbia University Press, 1984.

———. *Spectres de Marx*. Paris: Galilée, 1993.

———. *Theory and Practice*. Edited by Geoffrey Bennington and Peggy Kamuf. Translated by David Wills. Chicago: University of Chicago Press, 2019.

Detienne, Marcel. *The Garden of Adonis: Spices in Greek Mythology*. Translated by Janet Lloyd. Princeton, NJ: Princeton University Press, 1994.

Diaconu, Madalina. *Tasten—Riechen—Schmecken: Eine Ästhetik der anästhesierten Sinne*. Würzburg: Königshausen and Neumann, 2005.

Drobnick, Jim, ed. *The Smell Culture Reader*. Oxford: Berg, 2006.

Duvillard, Brigitte. "Das hymnische Fragment 'Die Titanen'—von der Mythologie zur Meteorologie." In *"Es bleibet aber eine Spur/Doch eines Wortes": Zur späten Hymnik und Tragödientheorie Friedrich Hölderlins*, edited by Christoph Jamme and Anja Lemke, 135–152. Munich: Wilhelm Fink, 2004.

Eldridge, Hannah Vandegrift. *Lyric Orientations: Hölderlin, Rilke, and the Poetics of Community*. Ithaca, NY: Cornell University Press, 2015.

Eyers, Tom. *Speculative Formalism: Literature, Theory, and the Critical Present*. Evanston, IL: Northwestern University Press, 2017.

Fenves, Peter. "Afterword: Toward a 'Non-metaphysical "Concept" of Revolution.'" In Werner Hamacher, *Two Studies of Friedrich Hölderlin*, 165–179. Stanford, CA: Stanford University Press, 2020.

———. *Late Kant: Towards Another Law of the Earth*. New York: Routledge, 2003.

———. "Niemands Sache: Die Idee der 'Res Nullius' und die Suche nach einer Kritik der Gewalt." In *Philo: Xenia*, 123–205. Basel: Engler, 2009.

———. "Toward Another Teichology." In *Babel: Festschrift für Werner Hamacher*, edited by Aris Fioretos, 142–150. Basel: Urs Engeler, 2008.

Feuchtwanger, Lion. *Erfolg: Drei Jahre Geschichte einer Provinz*. Frankfurt am Main: Fischer Verlag, 1975.

Förster, Eckart. *Die 25 Jahre der Philosophie. Eine systematische Rekonstruktion*. Frankfurt am Main: Vittorio Klostermann, 2012.

———. *The Twenty-Five Years of Philosophy: A Systematic Reconstruction*. Translated by Brady Bowman. Cambridge, MA: Harvard University Press, 2012.

Freed-Thall, Hannah. *Spoiled Distinctions: Aesthetics and the Ordinary in French Modernism*. Oxford: Oxford University Press, 2015.

Freud, Sigmund. *Das Unbehagen in der Kultur*. Frankfurt am Main: Fischer, 1994.

Gaier, Ulrich. *Der gesetzliche Kalkül. Hölderlins Dichtungslehre*. Tübingen: Niemeyer, 1962.

———. "'Unter Gottes Gewittern': Klimaerscheinungen als Erfahrung und Mythos." *Hölderlin-Jahrbuch* 35 (2006–2007): 169–1996.

Gavronsky, Serge. "From an Interview with Francis Ponge." *Books Abroad* 48, no. 4 (1974): 680–688.

———. "Nietzsche ou l'arrière-texte pongien." In *Ponge, inventeur et classique*, edited by Philippe Bonnefis and Pierre Oster, 305–330. Paris: UGE, 1977.

Geller, Jay. "Walter Benjamin Reproducing the Scent of the Messianic." In *The Other Jewish Question: Identifying the Jew and Making Sense of Modernity*, 256–302. New York: Fordham University Press, 2011.

Gleize, Jean-Marie. "L'être quelconque." In "Politiques de Ponge," edited by Benoît Auclerc and Bénédicte Gorrillot. *Revue des Sciences Humaines* 316 (October–December 2014): 175–184.

Goethe, Johann Wolfgang von. *Werke. Hamburger Ausgabe*. Edited by Erich Trunz. Munich: Deutscher Taschenbuch Verlag, 2000.

Gooding-Williams, Robert. *Zarathustra's Dionysian Modernism*. Stanford, CA: Stanford University Press, 2001.

Gottlieb, Susannah Young-ah. *Regions of Sorrow: Anxiety and Messianism in Hannah Arendt and W. H. Auden.* Stanford, CA: Stanford University Press, 2003.

Greenberg, Moshe. *The Anchor Bible: Ezekiel 1–20.* Garden City, NY: Doubleday and Company, 1983.

Grimm, Jacob, and Wilhelm Grimm. *Deutsches Wörterbuch.* 16 vols. Leipzig: S. Hirzel, 1854–1954.

Grimm, Reinhold. *Brecht und Nietzsche: Oder Geständnisse eines Dichters.* Frankfurt am Main: Suhrkamp, 1979.

Haffner, Sebastian. *Die deutsche Revolution 1918/19.* Hamburg: Rowohlt, 2018.

Hamacher, Werner. *Two Studies of Friedrich Hölderlin.* Edited by Peter Fenves and Julia Ng. Translated by Anthony Curtis Adler and Julia Ng. Stanford, CA: Stanford University Press, 2020.

———. "Version der Bedeutung: Studie zur späten Lyrik Hölderlins." Unpublished manuscript, 1971.

Hamilton, John T. *Music, Madness, and the Unworking of Language.* New York: Columbia University Press, 2008.

———. *Security: Politics, Humanity, and the Philology of Care.* Princeton, NJ: Princeton University Press, 2013.

Han, Byung-Chul. *Duft der Zeit: Ein philosophischer Essay zur Kunst des Verweilens.* Bielefeld: Transcript, 2009.

Hansen, Miriam. "Benjamin and Cinema: Not a One-Way Street." In *Benjamin's Ghosts*, edited by Gerhard Richter, 41–73. Stanford, CA: Stanford University Press, 2002.

Harvey, Susan Ashbrook. *Scenting Salvation: Ancient Christianity and the Olfactory Imagination.* Berkeley: University of California Press, 2006.

Hegel, G. W. F. *Vorlesungen über die Ästhetik: Werke 13.* Edited by Eva Moldenhauer und Karl Markus Michel. Frankfurt am Main: Suhrkamp, 1970.

Heidegger, Martin. *Aus der Erfahrung des Denkens. Gesamtausgabe*, vol. 13. Frankfurt am Main: Vittorio Klostermann, 2002.

———. *Hölderlins Hymnen "Germanien" und "Der Rhein." Gesamtausgabe*, vol. 39. Frankfurt am Main: Vittorio Klostermann, 1989.

———. *Hölderlins Hymne "Der Ister." Gesamtausgabe*, vol. 53. Frankfurt am Main: Vittorio Klostermann, 1993.

———. *Nietzsche.* 2 vols. Stuttgart: Klett-Cotta, 1961.

———. *Unterwegs zur Sprache.* Stuttgart: Klett-Cotta, 2007.

Heller-Roazen, Daniel. *The Enemy of All: Piracy and the Law of Nations.* New York: Zone Books, 2009.

———. *The Inner Touch: Archaeology of a Sensation.* New York: Zone Books, 2007.

Hellingrath, Norbert von. *Zwei Vorträge.* Munich: Hugo Bruckmann Verlag, 1922.

Henrich, Dieter. *The Course of Remembrance and Other Essays on Hölderlin.* Edited by Eckart Förster. Stanford, CA: Stanford University Press, 1997.

———. *Der Grund im Bewusstsein: Untersuchungen zu Hölderlins Denken (1794/95).* Stuttgart: Klett-Cotta, 1992.

Herder, Johann Gottfried. *Werke.* Vol. 6, *Ideen zur Philosophie der Geschichte der Menschheit.* Frankfurt am Main: Deutscher Klassiker Verlag, 1989.

Higgins, Ian. *Francis Ponge.* London: Athlone Press, 1979.

Hölderlin, Friedrich. *Die Briefe. Briefe an Hölderlin. Dokumente.* Edited by Jochen Schmidt. Frankfurt am Main: Deutscher Klassiker Verlag, 1992.

———. *Essays and Letters.* Edited and translated by Jeremy Adler and Charlie Louth. New York: Penguin, 2009.

———. *Hyperion Empedokles.* Edited by Jochen Schmidt. Frankfurt am Main: Deutscher Klassiker Verlag, 2008.

———. *Poems and Fragments.* Translated by Michael Hamburger. London: Anvil Press, 2004.

———. *Sämtliche Gedichte.* Edited by Jochen Schmidt. Frankfurt am Main: Deutscher Klassiker Verlag, 2005.

———. *Sämtliche Werke, Frankfurter Ausgabe.* Edited by D. E. Sattler. 20 vols. Frankfurt am Main: Roter Stern, 1975–2008.

———. *Sämtliche Werke, Große Stuttgarter Ausgabe.* Edited by Friedrich Beißner. 15 vols. Stuttgart: Cotta, 1943–1985.

Horn, Eva. "Air as Medium." *Grey Room* 73 (2018): 6–25.

Hornbacher, Annette. "Wie ein Hund: Zum 'mythischen Vortrag' in Hölderlins Entwurf 'Das Nächste Beste.'" *Hölderlin-Jahrbuch* 31 (1998–1999): 222–246.

Houtman, Cornelis. "On the Function of the Holy Incense (Exodus XXX 34–8) and the Sacred Anointing Oil (Exodus XXX 22–33)." *Vetus Testamentum* 42, no. 4 (1992): 458–465.

Howes, David. *Sensual Relations: Engaging the Senses in Culture and Social Theory.* Ann Arbor: University of Michigan Press, 2003.

Hsu, Hsuan L. *The Smell of Risk: Environmental Disparities and Olfactory Aesthetics.* New York: New York University Press, 2020.

Hutchinson, Ben. *Lateness and Modern European Literature.* Oxford: Oxford University Press, 2016.

Irigaray, Luce. *The Forgetting of Air in Martin Heidegger.* Translated by Mary Beth Mader. Austin: University of Texas Press, 1999.

———. *L'oubli de l'air chez Martin Heidegger.* Paris: Éditions de Minuit, 1983.

Jakobson, Roman, and Grete Lübbe-Grothues. "Ein Blick auf *Die Aussicht* von Hölderlin." In Roman Jabokson, *Hölderlin, Klee, Brecht*, 27–97. Frankfurt am Main: Suhrkamp, 1976.

Jameson, Fredric. *The Antinomies of Realism.* London: Verso, 2013.

———. *Brecht and Method.* London: Verso, 1998.

Jay, Martin. *Downcast Eyes: The Denigration of Vision in Twentieth-Century French Thought.* Berkeley: University of California Press, 1993.

Jenemann, David. *Adorno in America.* Minneapolis: University of Minnesota Press, 2007.

Jenner, Mark. "Follow Your Nose? Smell, Smelling, and Their Histories." *American Historical Review* 116, no. 2 (2011): 335–351.

Johnson, Barbara. *The Feminist Difference: Literature, Psychoanalysis, Race, and Gender.* Cambridge, MA: Harvard University Press, 2000.

Jones, Caroline A. *Eyesight Alone: Clement Greenberg's Modernism and the Bureaucratization of the Senses.* Chicago: University of Chicago Press, 2006.

———. "Sensorium: New Media Complexities for Embodied Experience." *Parachute: Contemporary Art Magazine* 121 (2006): 80–97.

Justinian's Institutes. Translated by Peter Birks and Grant McLeod. Ithaca, NY: Cornell University Press, 1987.

Kamuf, Peggy. "Baudelaire's Modern Woman." *Qui Parle* 4, no. 2 (1991): 1–7.

Kant, Immanuel. *Gesammelte Schriften.* Edited by Königlich-Preußische [later, Deutsche] Akademie der Wissenschaften. 29 vols. to date. Berlin: Reimer; later, de Gruyter, 1900–.

———. *Kritik der reinen Vernunft.* Edited by Wilhelm Weischedel. Frankfurt am Main: Suhrkamp, 1956.

———. *Practical Philosophy*. Translated and edited by Mary J. Gregor. Cambridge: Cambridge University Press, 1996.

———. *Werkausgabe*. Vol. 8, *Die Metaphysik der Sitten*. Edited by Wilhelm Weischedel. Frankfurt am Main: Suhrkamp, 2009.

———. *Werkausgabe*. Vol. 10, *Kritik der Urteilskraft*. Edited by Wilhelm Weischedel. Frankfurt am Main: Suhrkamp, 1974.

———. *Werkausgabe*. Vol. 12, *Schriften zur Anthropologie, Geschichtsphilosophie, Politik und Pädagogik 2*. Edited by Wilhelm Weischedel. Frankfurt am Main: Suhrkamp, 1977.

Kelly, Carolyn. "Where the Water Meets the Sky: How an Unbroken Line of Precedent from Justinian to *Juliana* Supports the Possibility of a Federal Atmospheric Public Trust Doctrine." *NYU Environmental Law Journal* 27, no. 2 (2019): 183–239.

Kettler, Andrew. *The Smell of Slavery: Olfactory Racism and the Atlantic World*. Cambridge: Cambridge University Press, 2022.

Kim, Annabel L. *Cacaphonies: The Excremental Canon of French Literature*. Minneapolis: University of Minnesota Press, 2022.

Klein, Richard. *Cigarettes Are Sublime*. Durham, NC: Duke University Press, 1993.

Klopstock, Friedrich Gottlieb. *Werke 1: Oden*. Edited by Horst Gronemeyer and Klaus Hurlebusch. Berlin: de Gruyter, 2010.

Knopf, Jan. *Brecht-Handbuch*. Berlin: Springer Verlag, 1984.

———. *Gelegentlich: Poesie. Ein Essay über die Lyrik Bertolt Brechts*. Frankfurt am Main: Suhrkamp, 1996.

Kofman, Sarah. *Explosion I: De l'*Ecce Homo *de Nietzsche*. Paris: Galilée, 1992.

Krause, Frank. *Geruch und Glaube in der Literatur: Selbst und Natur in deutschsprachigen Texten von Brockes bis Handke*. Düsseldorf: Düsseldorf University Press, 2023.

Kreienbrock, Jörg. *Sich im Weltall orientieren: Philosophieren im Kosmos 1950–1970*. Vienna: Turia and Kant, 2020.

Krell, David Farrell. *Postponements: Woman, Sensuality, and Death in Nietzsche*. Bloomington: Indiana University Press, 1986.

Kreutzer, Hans Joachim. "Kolonie und Vaterland in Hölderlins später Lyrik." *Hölderlin-Jahrbuch* 22 (1980–1981): 18–46.

Kreuzer, Johann. "Hölderlin im Gespräch mit Hegel und Schelling." *Hölderlin-Jahrbuch* 31 (1998–1999): 51–72.

Kristeva, Julia. *Histoires d'amour.* Paris: Editions Denoël, 1983.

Krueger, Cheryl. *Perfume on the Page in Nineteenth-Century France.* Toronto: University of Toronto Press, 2023.

Kudszus, Winfried. *Sprachverlust und Sinnwandel: Zur späten und spätesten Lyrik Hölderlins.* Stuttgart: Metzler, 1969.

Lampert, Laurence. *Nietzsche's Teaching.* New Haven, CT: Yale University Press, 1986.

Laplanche, Jean. *Hölderlin and the Question of the Father.* Edited and translated by Luke Carson. Victoria: ELS Editions, University of Victoria, 2007.

Latour, Bruno. *We Have Never Been Modern.* Translated by Catherine Porter. Cambridge, MA: Harvard University Press, 1993.

Le Guérer, Annick. *Les Pouvoirs de l'odeur.* Paris: Odile Jacob, 2002.

Lefebvre, Henri. *The Production of Space.* Translated by Donald Nicholson-Smith. Oxford: Blackwell, 1991.

Link, Jürgen. "Aether und Erde: Naturgeschichtliche Voraussetzungen von Hölderlins Geo-logie." *Hölderlin-Jahrbuch* 35 (2006–2007): 120–151.

Lloyd, Rosemary. *Baudelaire's World.* Ithaca, NY: Cornell University Press, 2002.

Loeb, Paul S. "The Priestly Slave Revolt in Morality." *Nietzsche-Studien: Internationales Jahrbuch für die Nietzsche-Forschung* 47, no. 1 (2018): 100–139.

Lucretius. *De Rerum Natura/On the Nature of Things.* Translated by W. H. D. Rouse. Revised by Martin F. Smith. Cambridge, MA: Harvard University Press, 1924.

Lyon, James K. *Bertolt Brecht in America.* Princeton, NJ: Princeton University Press, 1980.

Marcuse, Herbert. *Counterrevolution and Revolt.* Princeton, NJ: Princeton University Press, 2014.

Marder, Elissa. *Dead Time: Temporal Disorders in the Wake of Modernity (Baudelaire and Flaubert).* Stanford, CA: Stanford University Press, 2002.

———. "Inhuman Beauty: Baudelaire's Bad Sex." *Differences* 27, no. 1 (2016): 1–24.

———. "Snail Conversions: Derrida's Turns with Ponge." *Oxford Literary Review* 37, no. 2 (2015): 181–196.

Marx, Karl. *Marx-Engels-Werke*, vol. 40. Berlin: Dietz Verlag, 1968.

---. *Selected Writings*. Edited by Lawrence H. Simon. Indianapolis, IN: Hackett, 1994.

McClintock, Anne. *Imperial Leather: Race, Gender and Sexuality in the Colonial Contest*. Ann Arbor: University of Michigan Press, 1995.

McLaughlin, Kevin. *Poetic Force: Poetry after Kant*. Stanford, CA: Stanford University Press, 2014.

Meltzer, Françoise. *Seeing Double: Baudelaire's Modernity*. Chicago: University of Chicago Press, 2011.

Mendicino, Kristina. *Announcements: On Novelty*. Albany: State University of New York Press, 2020.

Merleau-Ponty, Maurice. *The Prose of the World*. Edited by Claude Lefort. Translated by John O'Neill. Evanston, IL: Northwestern University Press, 1973.

Mieth, Günther. *Friedrich Hölderlin: Dichter der bürgerlich-demokratischen Revolution*. Würzburg: Königshausen and Neumann, 2001.

Mitchell, Allan. *Revolution in Bavaria, 1918–1919: The Eisner Regime and the Soviet Republic*. Princeton, NJ: Princeton University Press, 1965.

Mittasch, Alwin. *Friedrich Nietzsche als Naturphilosoph*. Stuttgart: Kröner, 1952.

Mörike, Eduard. *Gesammelte Werke in zwei Bänden*. Edited by Hans Jürgen Meinerts. Gütersloh: Bertelsmann, 1957.

Müller, Heiner. *Werke 3: Die Stücke 1*. Frankfurt am Main: Suhrkamp, 2000.

Musselman, Lytton John. *A Dictionary of Bible Plants*. Cambridge: Cambridge University Press, 2012.

Naas, Michael. "Derrida's Flair (For the Animals to Follow . . .)." In *The End of the World and Other Teachable Moments: Jacques Derrida's Final Seminar*, 17–40. New York: Fordham University Press, 2014.

Nabhan, Gary. *Cumin, Camels, and Caravans: A Spice Odyssey*. Berkeley: University of California Press, 2014.

Nägele, Rainer. "Fragmentation und fester Buchstabe: Zu Hölderlins 'Patmos'-Überarbeitungen." *Modern Language Notes* 97, no. 3 (1982): 556–572.

---. *Hölderlins Kritik der poetischen Vernunft*. Basel: Urs Engeler, 2005.

Nancy, Jean-Luc. *Dis-enclosure: Deconstruction of Christianity*. Translated by Bettina Bergo, Gabriel Malenfant, and Michael B. Smith. New York: Fordham University Press, 2008.

---. *L'Adoration: Déconstruction du christianisme II*. Paris: Galilée, 2010.

Nancy, Jean-Luc, and Jacques Rancière. "Rancière and Metaphysics (Continued)." In *Rancière Now: Current Perspective on Jacques Rancière*, edited by Oliver Davis, 187–201. Cambridge: Polity, 2013.

Nash, Gerald D. *The American West Transformed: The Impact of the Second World War*. Lincoln: University of Nebraska Press, 1990.

Nehamas, Alexander. *Nietzsche: Life as Literature*. Cambridge, MA: Harvard University Press, 1985.

Neumann-Rieser, Doris. "'Denn alle Kreatur braucht Hilf von allen.' Materialismus und Revolution bei Brecht und Büchner." In *The Brecht Yearbook / Das Brecht-Jahrbuch* 39 (2014): 236–256.

Nietzsche, Friedrich. *Digitale Kritische Gesamtausgabe Werke und Briefe*. Edited by Paolo D'Iorio. Nietzsche Source. Accessed April 16, 2024. http://www.nietzschesource.org/#eKGWB.

---. *Sämtliche Werke: Kritische Studien-Ausgabe in 15 Bänden*. Edited by Giorgio Colli and Mazzino Montinari. Berlin: de Gruyter, 1967–1977.

Oesmannn, Astrid. *Staging History: Brecht's Social Concepts of History*. Albany: State University of New York Press, 2005.

Oliver, Kelly. "The Excesses of Earth in Kant's Philosophy of Property." *The Comparatist* 38 (2014): 23–40.

Osterhammel, Jürgen. "Stratosphärische Phantasie: Räume, Karten und Sehepunkte zu Hölderlins Zeit." In *Hölderlin-Jahrbuch* 38 (2012–2013): 9–34.

Parker, Stephen. *Bertolt Brecht: A Literary Life*. London: Bloomsbury, 2014.

Parkes, Graham. "Staying Loyal to the Earth: Nietzsche as an Ecological Thinker." In *Nietzsche's Futures*, edited by John Lippitt, 167–188. London: Palgrave Macmillan, 1999.

Pautrat, Bernard. *Versions du soleil: Figures et système de Nietzsche*. Paris: Éditions du Seuil, 1971.

Philipsen, Bart. "Gesänge." In *Hölderlin-Handbuch: Leben, Werk, Wirkung*, edited by Johann Kreuzer, 347–378. Stuttgart: Metzler, 2002.

Piazzesi, Chiara. "*Pathos der Distanz* et transformation de l'expérience de soi chez le dernier Nietzsche." *Nietzsche-Studien: Internationales Jahrbuch für die Nietzsche-Forschung* 36, no. 1 (2007): 258–295.

Pippin, Robert. "Irony and Affirmation in Nietzsche's *Thus Spoke Zarathustra*." In *Nietzsche's New Seas: Explorations in Philosophy, Aesthetics, and Politics*, edited by Michael Allen Gillespie and Tracy B. Strong, 45–72. Chicago: University of Chicago Press, 1988.

Plamper, Jan. "Sounds of February, Smells of October: The Russian Revolution as Sensory Experience." *American Historical Review* 126, no. 1 (2021): 140–165.

Plass, Ulrich. "Die Entfremdung umfunktionieren: Brecht und Adorno in Los Angeles." In *The Brecht Yearbook / Das Brecht-Jahrbuch* 38 (2013): 60–94.

Plato. *Complete Works*. Edited by John M. Cooper. Indianapolis, IN: Hackett, 1997.

Pnevmonidou, Elena. "'Schreiend zu beten, um angeschaut zu werden und Körper zu bekommen': Brecht, Kafka, and the Body." In *The Brecht Yearbook / Das Brecht-Jahrbuch* 35 (2010): 60–87.

Poe, Edgar Allan. *The Portable Edgar Allan Poe*. New York: Penguin Classics, 2006.

Pöggeler, Otto. "Philosophie im Schatten Hölderlins." In *Der Idealismus und seine Gegenwart*, edited by Ute Guzzoni, Bernhard Rang, and Ludwig Siep, 361–377. Hamburg: Felix Meiner, 1976.

———. "Vollkommenheit ohne Klage?—Der Nachklang von Hölderlins Hymnen und Elegien." In *"Es bleibet aber eine Spur/Doch eines Wortes" Zur späten Hymnik und Tragödientheorie Friedrich Hölderlins*, 281–293. Edited by Christoph Jamme and Anja Lemke. Munich: Wilhelm Fink, 2004.

Ponge, Francis. *Le Savon*. Paris: Gallimard, 1967.

———. *Soap*. Translated by Lane Dunlop. Stanford, CA: Stanford University Press, 1998.

Pornschlegel, Clemens. *Hyperchristen: Brecht, Malraux, Mallarmé, Brinkmann, Deleuze*. Vienna: Turia and Kant, 2011.

Prévost, Jean. *Baudelaire: Essai sur l'inspiration et la création poétiques*. Paris: Mercure de France, 1953.

"Protokoll der Diskussion." In *Le pauvre Holterling*, vol. 7. Frankfurt am Main: Roter Stern, 1984.

Proust, Marcel. *Swann's Way*. Translated by Lydia Davis. New York: Penguin, 2002.

Raab, Jürgen. *Soziologie des Geruchs: Die soziale Konstruktion olfaktorischer Wahrnehmung.* Konstanz: UVK, 2001.

Rachlin, Nathalie. "Francis Ponge, *Le Savon*, and the Occupation." *SubStance* 87, no. 3 (1998): 85–106.

Rampley, Matthew. *Nietzsche, Aesthetics and Modernity.* Cambridge: Cambridge University Press, 2000.

Rancière, Jacques. "The Aesthetic Revolution and Its Outcomes: Emplotments of Autonomy and Heteronomy." *New Left Review* 14 (2002): 133–152.

———. *Aux bords du politique.* Paris: Folio essais, 2004.

———. "The Gay Science of Bertolt Brecht." In *The Politics of Literature*, translated by Julie Rose, 99–127. Cambridge: Polity, 2011.

———. *Politics of Aesthetics: The Distribution of the Sensible.* Edited and translated by Gabriel Rockhill. New York: Bloomsbury, 2004.

———. *Politik und Ästhetik: Im Gespräch mit Peter Engelmann.* Translated by Gwendolin Engels. Vienna: Passagen Verlag, 2016.

Reinarz, Jonathan. *Past Scents: Historical Perspectives on Smell.* Champaign: University of Illinois Press, 2014.

Reitani, Luigi. "Ortserkundungen, Raumverwandlungen. Zur poetischen Topographie Hölderlins." *Hölderlin-Jahrbuch* 35 (2006–2007): 9–29.

Rindisbacher, Hans. *The Smell of Books: A Cultural-Historical Study of Olfactory Perception in Literature.* Ann Arbor: University of Michigan Press, 1992.

Ryan, Lawrence. *Hölderlin's Wechsel der Töne.* Stuttgart: Kohlhammer, 1960.

Said, Edward. *On Late Style: Music and Literature Against the Grain.* London: Bloomsbury, 2007.

Samalin, Zachary. *The Masses Are Revolting: Victorian Culture and the Political Aesthetics of Disgust.* Ithaca, NY: Cornell University Press, 2021.

Sartre, Jean-Paul. *Baudelaire.* Paris: Gallimard, 1947.

———. "L'Homme et les choses." In *Situations*, vol. 1. Paris: Gallimard, 1947.

Sattler, D. E. "Al rovescio: Hölderlin nach 1806." In *Le pauvre Holterling*, vol. 7. Frankfurt am Main: Roter Stern, 1984.

Schestag, Thomas. *Para—Titus Lucretius Carus, Johann Peter Hebel, Francis Ponge—zur literarischen Hermeneutik.* Munich: Boer, 1991.

Schmid, Holger. "Wechsel der Töne." In *Hölderlin-Handbuch: Leben, Werk, Wirkung*, edited by Johann Kreuzer, 118–127. Stuttgart: Metzler, 2002.

Schmidt, Alfred. *Der Begriff der Natur in der Lehre von Marx*. Hamburg: Europäische Verlagsanstalt, 2016.

———. *Emanzipatorische Sinnlichkeit: Ludwig Feuerbachs anthropologischer Materialismus*. Frankfurt am Main: Ullstein, 1977.

Schnell, Axel. *"Virtuelle Revolutionäre" und "Verkommene Götter": Brechts "Baal" und die Menschwerdung des Widersachers*. Bielefeld: Aisthesis Verlag, 1993.

Scholem, Gershom. *Walter Benjamin und sein Engel*. Frankfurt am Main: Suhrkamp, 1983.

Sedgwick, Eve. *Epistemology of the Closet*. Berkeley: University of California Press, 2008.

Shapiro, Gary. *Nietzschean Narratives*. Bloomington: Indiana University Press, 1989.

———. *Nietzsche's Earth: Great Events, Great Politics*. Chicago: University of Chicago Press, 2016.

Shelley, Percy Bysshe. *The Complete Poetical Works of Percy Bysshe Shelley*. Cambridge: Riverside Press, 1901.

Sloterdijk, Peter. *Sphären III: Schäume*. Frankfurt am Main: Suhrkamp, 2004.

———. *Terror from the Air*. Translated by Steve Corcoran and Amy Patton. Los Angeles: Semiotext(e), 2009.

Sng, Zachary. *Middling Romanticism: Reading in the Gaps, from Kant to Ashbery*. New York: Fordham University Press, 2020.

Sontag, Susan. "Elias Canetti." *Granta*, no. 5 (March 1982): 73–89.

Stamelman, Richard. *Perfume: Joy, Scandal, Sin: A Cultural History of Fragrance from 1750 to the Present*. New York: Rizzoli, 2006.

"Stereoscopic Vision." In *Cambridge Dictionary of Human Biology and Evolution*, edited by Larry L. Mai, Marcus Young Owl, and M. Patricia Kersting, 504. Cambridge: Cambridge University Press, 2005.

Stierle, Karlheinz. "Dichtung und Auftrag: Hölderlins 'Patmos'-Hymne." *Hölderlin-Jahrbuch* 22 (1980–1981): 47–68.

Szondi, Peter. *Schriften*, vol. 1. Frankfurt am Main: Suhrkamp, 2011.

Tellenbach, Hubert. *Geschmack und Atmosphäre. Medien menschlichen Elementarkontaktes*. Salzburg: O. Müller, 1968.

Timm, Hermann. "Dichter am dürftigen Ort. Johanneische Christopoetik in Hölderlins 'Patmos.'" *Hölderlin-Jahrbuch* 31 (1998–1999): 207–221.

Tremblay, Jean-Thomas. *Breathing Aesthetics*. Durham, NC: Duke University Press, 2022.

Trotha, Hans von. "Der Landschaftsgarten des 18. Jahrhunderts als literarisches Phänomen." *Hölderlin-Jahrbuch* 33 (2002–2003): 13–34.

Valéry, Paul. *Situation de Baudelaire*. Monaco: Imprimerie de Monaco, 1924.

Waibel, Violetta L. "Kant, Fichte, Schelling." In *Hölderlin Handbuch: Leben, Werk, Wirkung*, edited by Johann Kreuzer, 90–106. Stuttgart: Metzler, 2002.

Waiblinger, Wilhelm. *Phaëton: Roman über Hölderlin*. Tübingen: Schwäbische Verlagsgesellschaft, 1979.

Weber, Samuel. *Benjamin's -Abilities*. Cambridge, MA: Harvard University Press, 2010.

Weiss, Peter. *Hölderlin*. Frankfurt am Main: Suhrkamp, 2016.

Wizisla, Erdmut. *Benjamin and Brecht: The Story of a Friendship*. Translated by Christine Shuttleworth. London: Verso, 2016.

Wolf, Christa. *Stadt der Engel: Oder The Overcoat of Dr. Freud*. Berlin: Suhrkamp, 2010.

Wolff, Janet. "The Invisible *Flâneuse*: Women and the Literature of Modernity." In *Feminine Sentences: Essays on Women and Culture*, 34–50. Cambridge: Polity Press, 1990.

Xenophon. *Xenophon in Seven Volumes*. Vol. 4, *Symposium*. Cambridge, MA: Harvard University Press, 1979.

Zhang, Dora. *Strange Likeness: Description and the Modernist Novel*. Chicago: University of Chicago Press, 2020.

Zöllner, Karl Friedrich. *Über die Natur der Cometen: Beiträge zur Geschichte und Theorie der Erkenntnis*. Leipzig: Engelmann, 1872.

Index

absence, 1, 18, 82–86, 105–8. *See also* presence
abyss, 33–34, 44–47, 51–58, 76–78
action, 71–73; revolutionary, 85–86, 131–33
addiction, 88–92
adoration, 88–92, 209n26
Adorno, Theodor W., 15, 38–40, 52, 139–40, 174n8, 202n31, 208n20
aesthetics, 2–3, 13–14, 109, 169n46; deodorization and, 153–54; earth and, 113–15; pain and, 47–48; of smell, 52–53, 110–11, 175n13, 179n47
agency, 13–14, 32–33, 76–77
agriculture, 111. *See also* wheat
air, 1, 31–32, 52, 197n40; chaos and, 107; as common, 15–20, 52, 155–56, 162; deodorization and, 153–55; distance and, 154–55; freedom and, 115–16, 120–21; language and, 155; as medium, 9–10, 15–19, 21, 29–39, 57–64, 115–24, 153–54; sensing, 1–2, 18, 29–32, 60–61, 165n7. *See also* atmosphere; smell
aisthesis, 1–2, 18, 24, 29–30, 33–34, 60–61, 86–87, 153–54. *See also* aesthetics
alcohol, 92
alienation, 11, 18–19
alterity, 11, 18–19, 81–83
ambiguity, 12–13, 53, 57–58, 60–61, 77–78, 87, 131–33
anachronism, 3–5
Anders, Günther, 146
anesthesia, 13–14, 92–94
angels, 142–50; "angel of history," 146–47
animals, animality, 97, 101–2, 110–13, 115–17, 120, 134–36, 192n5
anointing, 60–61, 79–80, 161–62, 182n74
Anschauung, 34–37, 40, 63–64. *See also* intuition

anthology, 26–28, 46–47, 61–62, 64, 69–70. *See also* gathering
appropriation (*Aneignung*), 10–11, 15–20, 25–26, 170n55
Arendt, Hannah, 132–33, 146, 199n4
Aristotle, 1–2, 15–16, 29–30, 170n56
artifice, 74–76, 187n21. *See also* nature; perfumes
atmosphere, 9–10, 15–18, 41, 83–92, 154–56
atmospheric turn, 29
Auden, W. H., 3–5, 166n15, 172n71
audibility, 5–6, 40
autonomy, 160–61, 208n20

Bachelard, Gaston, 115–16
baptism, 116, 161, 182n74
Barthes, Roland, 64
Bataille, Georges, 69–70, 186n10
Baudelaire, Charles, 16, 21–22, 95, 153–54, 157, 186n9; *Artificial Paradises*, 75, 92–93; "Correspondences," 75–76; "The Denial of Saint Peter," 71; "Double Bedroom," 87–93; "Evening Harmony," 76–77; *The Flowers of Evil*, 69–74, 77–78, 85–87, 92–93; *Fusées*, 81; "Head of Hair," 81–84; "A Hemisphere in a Head of Hair," 81–83; "Lethe," 92–93; *My Heart Laid Bare*, 74–75; "The Perfume Flask," 75–79, 89–90; "A Phantom," 77–78; sexual difference and, 80–85, 92–93; "The Taste for Nothingness," 86–90
beauty, 2–3, 47–48, 53–54, 59–60, 65–66, 110, 112. *See also* aesthetics; sublime
becoming, 105–7, 114–15, 118, 121–22
Begeisterung (poetic enthusiasm, inspiration), 30–31

Index | 229

being: identity and, 34–37; nonbeing, 77–78, 86–87; revolution and, 70–71; smell and, 70, 73, 82–83
Benhabib, Seyla, 13–14
Benjamin, Walter, 8–9, 10–12, 39, 72–73, 85–87, 93–94, 125–26, 130–34, 139–40, 145–47, 178n44, 200n13
Benveniste, Émile, 81–85
Bertaux, Pierre, 62, 176n26
Bible, 50–51, 60–61, 79–80, 180n59, 182nn74–75, 186n11, 188n30. *See also* Christ, Christianity
Bildung, Bildungsroman, 46–49
Binder, Wolfgang, 59
Blanqui, Auguste, 72–73, 85–86
Blumenberg, Hans, 8–9, 117–18
body: gender and, 80–85; hair and, 80–85; integrity of, 83; nose, 1–5, 50, 115–16; pleasure, 91, 145–46; revolution and, 131–32; smell and, 81–83, 88–89, 126–27, 134–39, 145–49
boundary, boundary stones, 5–6, 18, 21–22, 59, 116, 121–22
breath, breathing, 1–2, 60–61, 117–18, 165n5; language and, 155–56; necessity and, 29–30; sensation and, 31–32; smoking and, 91
Brecht, Bertolt, 21–22, 153–54; *Arbeitsjournal* (Work Journal), 140–41; *Baal*, 133–38, 142–46, 149–51, 200nn18–19; "Ballad of the Dead Soldier," 129–33; *Drums in the Night*, 128–33, 136–37; "Five Difficulties in Writing the Truth," 138; *Glücksgott* poems, 147–52, 163; *Hollywoodelegien* (Hollywood Elegies), 140–49, 153; "On Nietzsche's 'Zarathustra,'" 137–38; "On Thinking about Hell," 141; physical appearance of, 125–27, 198n3; "Song of the Child Who Did Not Want to Wash Himself," 127–28; "Svendborg Poems," 126–27; *Threepenny Opera*, 146; "While Examining My First Plays," 128–29, 147–48
bridges, 32–34, 51–52
bulls, 111–12, 195n31. *See also* animals, animality
Burton, Richard D., 72

Canetti, Elias, 1, 15–18, 165n3
capitalism, 13–14, 21–22, 133–40, 145–46, 204n54
Carson, Anne, 80
caves, 117–24, 154–55, 177n36
Celan, Paul, 49–50
chaos, 105–9, 114, 123, 194n21
Christ, Christianity, 55–61, 71–72, 78–84, 91–92, 144, 161–62, 182nn71–72, 182nn74–75, 188n28, 193n9, 199n11, 208n21
cigarettes, 89–91, 190nn55–57
civilization, 6–8, 41–42, 44, 52–53, 167nn25–26, 168n35; nature and, 45–47; poetry and, 46–50
class, 138–39, 144–45; smell and, 8
cleaning, cleanliness, 131–32, 153–63; cleansing and, 153, 159–60, 162–63, 207n17
climate, 83–84. *See also* air; atmosphere
cognition, 8–9, 101–2, 104, 169n9
collectivity, 150, 152
colonialism, 8, 41–42, 168n35, 177n34, 207n12
commerce, commercialization, 42–43, 134–35
commodity, commodification, 91, 141–43, 148–49, 151
commons, the common, 5–6, 15–22, 40–41, 84, 95–96, 98, 102, 119–27, 134–35, 144–45, 149–50, 154–56, 161–63, 171n63
communism, 22, 152–53, 158–59, 205n1, 207n12
comprehension, 56–57
compromise, 102, 107–9, 118–19, 123–24, 154–55
Condillac, Étienne Bonnot de, 2–3
Corbin, Alain, 8, 168n31
corporeality. *See* body
Crary, Jonathan, 8–9
Critobulus, 96–97
cultivation, 6–7, 35–36, 48–49, 111–12, 134–35
culture, 6–7, 43–44, 111–12

Dante (Alighieri), 20–21
death, 78–80, 85–86, 89–91, 96–98, 129–33, 188n29, 200n15. *See also* decay; life
debt, 89–91
decadence, 85–86, 89–90, 95, 97, 99–100, 104–5, 108–9, 139
decay, 23–24, 61–62, 69–70, 85–86, 89–91, 96–97, 99–100, 108, 129–32, 200n15
degree zero, 64, 105, 153–54, 156
delimitation, 5–6, 74, 83, 105–8, 116, 118–19. *See also* horizon
Demetz, Peter, 131, 200n17
deodorization, 6–10, 19–22, 63–64, 67, 86–89, 108, 115–16, 120, 140–43, 153–56, 168n35, 209n26
depression, 113–14
depth, 104–7, 122–23, 194n18. *See also* perspective; surface
deracination, 25–26
Derrida, Jacques, 19, 77–78, 91–92, 160n172n77, 192n5, 208n18
descent, 112–13, 117, 139
deserts, desertification, 18–19, 44–46, 54–55, 139, 145–46, 180n60
desire, 83–84, 86, 92–93, 142–43, 145–46, 148–49; distance and, 111–12
Dessau, Paul, 149–52
difference, differentiation, 49–50, 80, 101–2, 109, 111–12, 119–24, 140–43, 154–56
dirt, dirtiness, 125–30, 138–39, 153–54, 163
disappearance, 55–56, 59–61, 65–67, 86–89, 121–22, 131
dissipation, 26, 40–42, 74–76, 187n22, 187n25
dissolution, 15, 24–33, 38, 46–50, 103–8, 120–23, 135–38, 158–60
dissonance, 24–33, 38, 46–50
distance, 101–9, 115–16, 120–24, 143, 147; desire and, 111–12; differentiation and, 102, 109, 119–22, 143, 154–56; pathos of, 101–12, 115–16, 119–20, 123–24, 154–55, 194n26
disunion, division, 15–18, 30–32, 34–38, 40–41, 62, 87–90, 166n19, 171n67
domestication, 45–47, 111
Douglas, Mary, 126–27
drugs, 92

Durchdringung (interpenetration), 39, 174n8
durchgängig (going through), 17–18, 29–30, 36–37, 39, 153–54
Duvillard, Brigitte, 59

earth, 7, 17–18, 41–42, 109–16, 121–22, 134–38, 149–50, 154–55, 177n31, 194n26, 196n33. *See also under* smell
Ebel, Johann Gottfried, 23
Ebert, Friedrich, 128–29
ecocriticism, 9–10, 29, 41, 194n26
ecology, 109, 194n26
economy, 80, 127–28, 134–44, 151–52; of debt, 89–91
egoism, 11–12, 15–16
Eisler, Hanns, 143–44
emancipation, 11–15, 18–19, 117–18, 120, 123–24, 133–34, 182n75, 203n36
emergence (*Ausgang*), 41–44, 117–24, 133–36, 154–55
Emerson, Ralph Waldo, 74
Engels, Friedrich, 152
environmental humanities, 9–10, 29
equality, 104–5, 119–20, 123–24
Erörterung, 41
escape, 90–91, 117–18, 135–38, 147, 154–55
ethics, 13–14, 80, 204n52
Eugen, Carl, 23
Euripides, 99–100
exchange, 42–44, 95–96, 127–28, 134–35
exhaustion, 92–94, 113, 142, 145, 160
exile, 54–55, 140–45, 147, 202n34, 203n41
exploitation, 135–37
explosion, 95–96, 106–7, 111–12, 122–23, 192n3, 196n33
expropriation, 15, 26–27, 103, 123, 163
externalization (*Entäußerung*), 10–11

failure, 8, 25–27, 43–44, 55–57, 72
fascism, 153–54, 158–63, 207n17
feminism, 81
Feuchtwanger, Lion, 128–29, 132–33
Fichte, J. G., 25–26, 34–35
figura etymologica, 55–58
flowers, 2–3, 23–28, 46–48, 61–62, 69–70, 74. *See also* perfumes

Index | 231

forgetting, 1–2, 85–86, 100
form, formation, 4–6, 10–12, 18–19, 29–30, 45–53, 61, 77–79, 90–91, 99–100, 105–8
Frankfurt, 45–47
Frankfurt school, 150–51, 204n54
freedom, 13, 70, 115–16, 120–21
French Revolution, 21–23, 38, 70–71
Freud, Sigmund, 6–10, 134–35, 142, 167n24
future, 5, 41–44, 50–51, 57–61, 63–64, 67, 70–71, 108, 110, 132–33, 147. *See also* time

Gang (movement), 7–8, 29, 44–45, 51–54. *See also* emergence (*Ausgang*)
gardens, 32–38, 45–47, 54–55, 175n14
gathering, 24–28, 46–47, 49–50, 55–56, 69–70. *See also* anthology
Gavronsky, Serge, 155
Gegenstand (object), 16–18, 34–37
gender, 197n42; body and, 80–85; sexual difference and, 80–85, 92–93; sexuality and, 136–37; smell and, 7–8, 79–85, 92–93; space and, 83–84
genre, 3–4
geopoetics, 20, 41–46, 50–55, 61–62, 67, 109, 177n31
German Idealism, 34–35, 175n18, 176n27
Gesang (song), 41–42, 44
Gesinnungen (orientations, dispositions, attitudes), 23–24
gestalt, 45–49. *See also* civilization
Glück (happiness), 111–13, 121, 147–52, 204n49
Goethe, Johann Wolfgang von, 48–49, 143–44, 176n21
Gontard, Susette, 38
Gooding-Williams, Robert, 110–11
ground, grounding, 16–18, 44–47, 51, 105–6

habit, habituation, 12, 98–99
Hamacher, Werner, 19–20
hardness, 55–57
hearing, 2–3, 6, 52. *See also* senses, sensation
Hegel, G. W. F., 3–4, 12–13, 34–35, 45–46, 97, 169n46, 176n27

Heidegger, Martin, 1, 25, 41, 49–50, 105–6, 172n77
heliotropism, 117–18, 123–24
Heller-Roazen, Daniel, 16–17, 170n55, 171n70
Hellingrath, Norbert von, 61–63, 69–70
hemisphere, 83–87, 189n41
Henrich, Dieter, 32–33, 175n18
Herder, Johann Gottfried, 41–42, 52–53
hero, heroism, 35–36, 42–43, 73, 75, 84; "heroic will," 110–14, 195n30
history, 3–7; atmosphere and, 85–86; Christ and, 59–60; philosophy of, 41–42; poetry and, 85–86; revolution and, 146–47; senses and, 10–14
Hölderlin, Friedrich, 11, 21–24, 38, 69–70, 153–54, 169n46, 175n18, 176nn26–27; "Bread and Wine," 37–39, 57; difficulty of, 24–27; "The Eagle," 41–42; *Fragment of Philosophical Letters*, 28–34; "Germania," 58–60; "Heidelberg," 32–40; *Homburger Folioheft*, 42–45; "Hymn to Love," 30–31; *Hyperion*, 24–28, 64; "The Ister," 49–50; "Judgment and Being" ("Being Judgment Possibility"), 34–37; lateness of, 38–41, 59, 61–67; "The lyric, in appearance ideal poem," 35–36; madness of, 61–63; "Namely from the un-ground," 44–50, 57–58; "The Outlook," 64–67; "Patmos," 41–42, 48, 50–62; "Remembrance," 42–43; as Scardanelli, 26–28, 66–67; "Seven Maxims" ("Reflections"), 30–31; "The Titans," 42–44, 54–55; on *Wechsel der Töne* (variation or alternation of tones), 35–36; "Whatever Is Next," 60. *See also Morgenluft*
holding, 16–18
Homburg, Landgrave von, 50–51
home, homecoming, 18–21, 52–55, 103, 120, 123–24, 180n56. *See also* return
homoeroticism, homosexuality, 136–37
hope, 4–5, 23. *See also* future
horizon, 105–7, 109, 113–14, 118, 123. *See also* perspective
Horkheimer, Max, 15

232 | Index

Hsu, Hsuan L., 9–10, 16, 166n18, 168n35, 171n62
human, humanity, 11–13, 18–19, 208n19; difference and, 41–42; intuition and, 34–37; nature and, 45–46; nonhuman, 19, 95–98; as supersensible, 110–11
humanism, 18–19
hunting, 110–11
hygiene, 8, 126–28, 153–54, 161, 168n35, 187n22, 207n12

identity, 34–37. *See also* being
imperialism, 41–42, 136–37, 207n12
individuation, 83, 107, 135–36, 160
infinite, infinity, 90, 151
intimacy, 31–32, 34–35, 143–44
intoxication, 77–78, 82–83
intuition, 34–37, 39–40, 176nn21–22
Irigaray, Luce, 1–2, 16, 121–22, 165n4
islands, 42–44, 51–52, 54–57, 117, 177n37, 178n38

Jakobson, Roman, 26–27, 63–64
Jay, Martin, 8–9
Jones, Caroline A., 8–9, 165n13
joy (objoy), 22, 163
Justinian, 15–16

Kant, Immanuel, 2–3, 16–18, 28–29, 31–32, 34–35, 47–48, 53–54, 59–60, 110–11, 171nn65–66, 172n71, 173n3, 175n13, 176n21, 179n47
Kim, Annabel L., 148–49
Klopstock, Friedrich Gottlieb, 30–31, 50–51, 175n11
knowledge, 49–50, 99, 110–13. *See also* cognition

labor, 19, 138, 142, 203n37, 204n51
language: firmness of, 55–60; human and, 208n19; politics and, 202n28, 207n12; self-reflexivity and, 52; smell and, 40, 69–70, 84–85; as undetermined, 57–61; writing and, 155
lateness, 37–39, 61–67
Latour, Bruno, 10
laundry, 131–33, 200nn15–16

Lazarus, 77–80, 92, 129–30, 188n30, 199n11
lemons, 47–50, 53–54, 56–58, 61, 179n47, 179n51, 180n58
life: air and, 1–2; atmosphere and, 85–86; death and, 1, 89–91, 130–33; dwelling in, 1; mediality of, 21. *See also* death
lingering, 59–61, 66–67, 184n87
loss, 2–5, 15, 18–19, 81–83, 122–23, 146, 153–54; of smell, 66–67, 86–87, 140–41
love, 77–78, 81–83, 92–93, 138, 143–44
loyalty, 114–16

madness, 27–28, 61–63, 137–38
Mann, Thomas, 140–41
Marcianus, 17–18
Marcuse, Herbert, 12–14
Marder, Elissa, 82–83
Marx, Karl, 10–15, 18–19, 28–29, 77–78, 152, 169n43, 169n46, 172nn76–78, 186n8
Marxism, 12–13, 18–20, 22–23, 133–35, 142–43, 150–51, 204n54
matter, materialism, 10–11, 75–76, 115–16, 138–39, 147–48, 151–52, 157–58, 163
meaning: property and, 14–15, 18; senses and, 24, 27–28
medium, 18, 21, 121–24; of air, 19, 21, 29–37, 39, 57–58, 60–61, 63–64, 115–24, 153–54; economic, 137–40, 142–43; as middle, 39; as space of relation, 29–30; of smell, 9–10, 15–18. *See also* air; middle
mediocrity, 107
Meltzer, Francoise, 87
memory, memorialization, 4–5, 55–56, 76–79
miasma, 8. *See also* air
middle, 3, 13–14, 20–21, 24–25, 29, 39, 101–2, 105–7, 114, 116, 121–24. *See also* medium
misogyny, 81, 188n34
modernism, 8–9
modernity, 8–10, 12, 69–70, 75, 84–86, 90–91, 105–6, 165n4
Morgenluft (air of the morning), 57–67, 70–71, 181n65
movement, 147; pain and, 47–50; poetic, 44–55, 61–62; of smell, 113–15
multiplicity, 132–33

Index | 233

mysticism, 138–40, 144–47, 151–52, 202n28
mythology, 59

names, naming, 45, 57–61, 144–45, 182n71
Nancy, Jean-Luc, 88–89, 188n30, 193n12, 209n26
nature, 110–11; artifice and, 74–76; civilization and, 45–47; humanity and, 45–46; time of, 66–67
needs, necessity, 11–13, 28–34
Niendorf, Emma, 27–28
Nietzsche, Friedrich, 17–18, 21–22, 153–54; *Beyond Good and Evil*, 101; *The Birth of Tragedy*, 99–100, 104–5; *Ecce Homo*, 95–99, 101–3, 107–9, 113; *The Gay Science*, 105–7; *On the Use and Disadvantage of History for Life*, 85–86; *Thus Spoke Zarathustra*, 101–2, 108–24, 134–35, 137–38; *Toward the Genealogy of Morals*, 100–101, 104; *Twilight of the Idols*, 96, 109
nightingale, 65
norms, normativity, 62, 125–28, 136–37, 149
novelty, 109–10, 113, 121, 194n25

objoy. *See* joy
ocularcentrism, 8–10, 12, 98–100, 106–7, 117–18, 123–24. *See also* vision
odor. *See* smell
olfaction. *See* smell
order, 101–7, 150–51; hygiene and, 126–28; politics and, 129–33
ordinary, ordinariness, 1, 20–21, 95–96, 107, 133–34, 144–45, 155–56, 161–62, 208n22. *See also* commons, the common
orientation, 1–3, 14–15, 18, 24, 70–72, 82, 84–86, 104, 113–14, 123–24
origins, 20–21, 33–34, 41–46, 52–56, 110, 117–18, 122–23

pain, 47–50
palaces, 53–55
parallax, 104–5. *See also* perspective
Parker, Stephen, 125
patience, 13–14, 19–20
pedagogy. *See* teaching

perception, 1–3, 5, 16, 18; of air, 29–30; of depth, 104–5; limits of, 118; nearness and, 103; non-perception, 98; property and, 14–15; revolution of, 8. *See also* senses
perfumes, 74–79, 83–84, 86–87, 92–94, 185n3, 187n21
perspective, 67, 101–9, 118–23, 194n17
petroculture, 145–46
Philipsen, Bart, 67
philosophy: air and, 197n40; poetry and, 34–38, 95–100; smell and, 95–99, 165n9, 165n13; truth and, 95–98, 107, 117–18
pity, 119
Plato, 33–34, 69–70, 117–18, 170n56
pleasure, 24–25, 33–34, 91, 145–46
Poe, Edgar Allan, 75
poetry, 3–4; appearance and, 125–26; civilization and, 46–50; class and, 144–45; commonality and, 155–56; desire and, 148–49; economics and, 138–40; enthusiasm and, 30–31; experience (*Erfahrung*) and, 41; history and, 85–86; intuition and, 35–37; language and, 55–61, 69–70, 138–40, 144–45, 151–52; madness and, 61–63; memory and, 78–79; modernity and, 69–70, 75, 84–86; philosophy and, 34–38, 95–100; reading, 24–25; revolution and, 38, 72–73, 75; senses and, 22, 32–33; sexual difference and, 80–84; smell and, 3–5, 28, 30–32, 39–40, 47–50, 52–55, 57–58, 61–67, 69–70, 74–75, 78–79, 84–88, 95–96, 145–46, 151; space of, 67; tones and, 35–36; unity and, 39–40; voice and, 44–47; writing and, 155–56
police, policing, 5–6, 8, 11–12
politics, 169n46; cleanliness and, 158–60, 162–63; as distribution of sensible, 6, 13–14; hygiene and, 126–27; language and, 202n28, 207n12; of revolution, 24, 38, 72–73; of smell, 9–10; order and, 129–33
Ponge, Francis, 9–10, 22, 205n1, 206n7; "The Pebble," 156–58; *Le Savon* (Soap), 153–63
position, positionality, 121–22

234 | Index

possession, 14–19, 26
praxis, 12–14, 19
presence, 1, 79–80, 82–83. *See also* absence
productivity, 135–37, 150–51, 204n54, 205n55
proper, property, 6, 14–17, 103, 130, 163; alterity and, 18–19; common, 16–20
prose, 83; world of, 3–6, 8, 13–14, 19–20
Proust, Marcel, 4–5
proximity. *See* distance
purity, 101–2, 115–16, 120, 153–54, 162–63
putrefaction, 8, 69–70, 89–90, 96–97, 109, 201n25

race, racism, 1, 207n12; difference and, 41–42; purity and, 162–63; smell and, 8
Rancière, Jacques, 5–7, 169n46
raven, 97–98
reading, 163; modes of, 24–28; time and, 91–92
reflection, reflexivity, 8–9, 40
Reitani, Luigi, 41
relation: to air, 31–32; division and, 40–41; of *durchgängiger*, 29, 36–37; economy and, 127–28, 143–44; emancipation and, 120; improper, 18; inward, 31–35; monarchy of, 39–41; necessity and, 28–34; to origins, 41–44; reading and, 25; of smell, 81–84, 123–24, 156; space of, 29; unity and, 40–41
repetition, 5, 90–91
representation, 50
reproduction, 130–31, 136–37
res nullius, 16–18
ressentiment, 73, 78, 109
return, 18–20, 51–59, 123–24. *See also* home, homecoming
revolution, 16–17, 21–22, 169n46, 173n3; action and, 72–73, 132–33; being and, 70–71; body and, 131–32; as coming, 23–24; counter-revolution, 128–29; deodorization and, 153–54; disappointment with, 23, 38; future and, 70–71; history and, 146–47; poetry and, 72–73, 75; politics and, 72–73; praxis and, 12–14; property and, 14–15, 19–20; rejection of, 131–33; of senses, 8, 11–14, 18–20, 24, 133–34; smell and, 44, 50–51, 70–73, 93–94, 128–30, 132–37, 145–46, 152; virtual, 133–38, 145–46, 150–51
rights, 16–17
Rilke, Rainer Maria, 144–46
Romanticism, 62
ruins, 32–33
Russian Revolution, 21–22

sacred, 161–62
Said, Edward, 38
Samalin, Zachary, 8, 168n34
sanitation, 8, 153–54. *See also* deodorization; hygiene
Sappho, 69–70
Sartre, Jean-Paul, 70, 72–73, 75, 81–82, 84, 157–58
Sattler, D. E., 28–29, 63–64, 176n26
scent, scented modulations, 1–2; as common, 16, 19–20, 26, 126–27, 133–34, 163; deodorization and, 6–7, 115–16, 153–54, 156; modernity and, 8–10; poetry and, 3–5, 70, 73; space of, 20–21, 36–37; time and, 60–61, 87–89. *See also* smell
Schelling, Friedrich Wilhelm Joseph, 34–35, 169n46
Schiller, Friedrich, 28–29, 110–11, 169n46
Schmidt, Jochen, 63
Scholem, Gershom, 147
sea, 17–18
secrets, secrecy, 70
Sedgwick, Eve, 73, 89–90, 136–37
senses, sensation, 1–2, 5; air and, 165n7; cognition and, 98–102, 104, 165n9; commons and, 15–18; deodorization and, 153–54; emancipation of, 11–12, 18–19; forming, 10–11; habit and, 98–99; hierarchy of, 2–12, 170n56; history and, 10–14; intimacy and, 31–32; intuition and, 34, 36–37, 39–40; modernity and, 8–10; movement and, 51–52; perspective and, 104–6; in philosophy, 98–100; poetry and, 22, 32–33; property and, 14–20; redistribution of, 5–7, 11–12; revolution of, 11–15, 19–20, 24, 133–34; sense-making, 22, 40, 86–89, 108, 193n12; subjectivity and, 50;

Index | 235

supersensible, 110–11; temporality of, 37–39; unity of, 38–40. *See also* perception; smell
sexuality, 7–8, 136–37, 142–44, 188n32
ships, 17–18. *See also* sea
Sieyès, Emmanuel-Joseph, 23
Sinclair, Isaac von, 50–51, 64
Sinnlichkeit (sensuality), 12–13, 37–42, 47–50, 54–55, 59–61, 63–64, 67, 180n58
sleep, 92–93
Sloterdijk, Peter, 9–10, 165n4
smell, 1–10, 167n30; aesthetics and, 52–53, 60–61, 175n13, 179n47; air and, 29–39, 52, 57–64, 115–18, 120–24, 153–54; anesthetic qualities of, 92–94; being and, 70, 73, 82–83, 86–87; body and, 50, 81–83, 88–89, 126–27, 134–39, 145–49; chaos and, 105–7, 109, 114, 123; civilization and, 44, 47–50, 52–53, 167nn25–26, 168n35; commodification of, 16, 91, 187n21; as common, 16–17, 19–20, 121–22, 126–27, 133–35, 149–50, 161–62; death and, 78–80, 89–93, 96–98, 129–31, 188n29; deodorization and, 9–10, 153–54, 156; desire and, 92–93; difference and, 20, 140–41; distance and, 101–9, 115–16, 119–24, 143, 147, 154–55; of earth, 7, 111–16, 134–38, 151–52, 196n33; economy and, 135–36, 138–39, 141–44, 151–52; of eternity, 121–24; freedom and, 115–16, 120–21; gender and, 79–85, 92–93; horizon and, 105–7, 109, 118; language and, 40, 166n18, 208n19; lateness of, 37–38, 40, 63–64; loss of, 86–89, 140–41, 153; madness and, 138; materiality of, 75–76, 147–48; medium of, 9–10, 15–18, 21; memory and, 76–79; modernity and, 90; movement of, 113–15; necessity and, 33–34; novelty and, 109–10, 113, 121; object of, 22; ordering and, 106–7; otherwise, 109, 113–14; perspective and, 103–7, 109, 118; philosophy and, 95–99; pleasure and, 33–34; poetry and, 3–5, 28, 30–32, 35–37, 39–40, 47–50, 52–55, 57–58, 61–67, 69–70, 74–75, 78–79, 84–88, 95–96, 145–46, 151; politics and, 6, 9–10; purity and, 120, 162–63; reading and, 20–21, 26–28; relations and, 18, 40–41, 81–84, 123–24, 156; revolution and, 13–14, 19–22, 44, 50–51, 70–73, 93–94, 128–30, 132–37, 145–46, 152; sense-making of, 18–19; sexuality and, 142–44, 188n32; space of, 41–44, 50–55, 61–65, 67, 83–85, 87, 101–22; subjectivity and, 15, 49–50; time and, 41–42, 50–51, 60–62, 66–67, 77–80, 87–89, 98, 110, 130–31; truth and, 95–98, 101–2, 107; unity and, 38–41, 47–50; valuation and, 113–14, 118, 121–23, 134–35. *See also* air; poetry; revolution
smoking, 90–92
social, 11–13, 149–50; asocial type, 133–38, 148–50
socialism, 132–33, 150–51, 204n54
Socrates, Socratism, 96–97, 99–100, 104–5, 109
space: distance and, 64–65, 67, 101–5, 108; hemispheres, 83–85; place and, 41–44, 87; poetry and, 67; of relation, 29–30; of shelter, 87; of smell, 20–21, 41–44, 50–55, 61–67, 83–87, 101–22; sexual difference and, 83–84; time and, 41–42
specters, spectrality, 77–78, 83, 89–90
spirit, spirituality, 75–76, 81–82, 112–13
Stamelman, Richard, 74
stars, 84–86
stasis, 47–49
stratosphere, 154–56
subject, subjectivity, 10–11; deodorization and, 153–54, 156–60; intuition and, 34–37; lateness and, 40; perception and, 103; property and, 14–15, 17–18; relations of, 28–29, 31–32; smell and, 15, 49–50; as supersensible, 110–11; unity of, 50; vision and, 67
sublime, 110–13, 115–16, 195n28
sun, 117–18, 123–24, 197nn40–41. *See also* heliotropism
surface, 17–18, 106–7, 111–12, 122–23. *See also* depth
synesthesia, 38–40, 166n19, 177n29

taste, 2–3, 113–14

236 | Index

teaching, 150–52
theory, theorization, 9, 20–21, 98–100, 108, 117
thought, 1–2; reading and, 24–26; senses and, 28, 36–37, 98–102, 104
time: coming, 23–24; difference and, 80; eternity, 88–90; future, 50–51, 57–61, 67, 70–71, 81–82, 110, 132–33; of geopoetics, 41–42; of lateness, 37–39; memory and, 77–79; of nature, 66–67; origins and, 41–42; past, 77–79; present, 66–67; reading and, 91–92; reign of, 87–92; of smell, 7–8, 87–89, 98, 110, 130–31; smoking and, 90–91; space and, 41–42; suspension of, 65; untimely, 98
tiredness. *See* exhaustion
touch, 12, 39
truth, 8–9, 95–98, 101–2, 106–7, 111–12, 117–18

uncanny, 103, 108
unity, 34–40, 106–7; disarticulation of, 40–42, 47–48, 50, 58–59, 63–64
unlearning, 16, 112–13, 171n63
utility, 11–12, 160

value, valuation, 107–8, 113–14, 118, 121–23, 134–35

vapor, vaporization, 74–76, 81–82
visibility, 5–6, 98–99, 122–23, 144–45
vision, visuality, 2–3, 6–8, 36–37, 52, 55–56, 113–14; binocular, 104–5, 194n18; depth and, 122–23; failure of, 58–59; hegemony of, 8–10, 12, 63–64, 66–67, 98–100, 108, 117–18; perspective and, 119; thought and, 104; truth and, 106–7, 111–12, 117–18
vulgarity, 104–5, 144–45, 161–62, 208n23

Wagner, Richard, 95, 192n2
Waiblinger, Wilhelm, 27–28
war, 128–31
weight, 113–14
Wendezeit (historic turning), 12
wheat, 134–38, 151
Widerspruch (objection), 97–98, 109, 112–13
wild, wildness, 45–49, 110–12
will, heroic, 110–13
Winge, Hans (John), 143
work. *See* labor
writing, 155–57

Xenophon, 96–97

Zöllner, Johann Karl Friedrich, 101–2